NEBULA
AWARDS
22

NEBULA AWARDS
22

SFWA's
Choices for the
Best Science Fiction
and Fantasy 1986

Edited by

GEORGE ZEBROWSKI

Harcourt Brace Jovanovich, Publishers

San Diego   New York   London

The Library of Congress has cataloged this serial as follows:

The Nebula awards.—No. 18-—New York [N.Y.]: Arbor House, c1983–
v.; 22 cm.
Annual.
Published: San Diego, Calif.: Harcourt Brace Jovanovich, 1984–
Published for: Science Fiction Writers of America, 1983–
Continues: Nebula award stories (New York, N.Y.: 1982)
ISSN 0741-5567 = The Nebula awards
1. Science fiction, American—Periodicals. I. Science Fiction Writers of America.
PS648.S3N38   83-647399
813'.0876'08—dc19
AACR 2 MARC-S
Library of Congress   [8709r84]rev
ISBN 0-15-164929-4
ISBN 0-15-665476-8 (Harvest/HBJ: pbk)

Designed by G. B. D. Smith

Printed in the United States of America

First edition

A B C D E

Permissions acknowledgments appear on page 365, which constitutes a
continuation of the copyright page.

In Memory of

Terry Carr 1937–1987
James Tiptree, Jr. 1916–1987
Theodore R. Cogswell 1918–1987
Richard Wilson 1920–1987

CONTENTS

INTRODUCTION

George Zebrowski

The twenty-second annual Nebula Awards were presented at the traditional banquet, held this year at the Halloran House in New York City, on May 2, 1987. As usual, the final ballot was the result of votes cast by the members of the Science Fiction Writers of America on a preliminary ballot, itself the product of recommendations made throughout the year by SFWA members. The final ballot consisted of the five works receiving the most votes in each of four categories: novel, novella, novelette, and short story. The number of works was more than five if there were ties in the voting, or if the Nebula Awards jury elected to add a work to one or more of the categories.

For purposes of the Nebula Awards, a novel is 40,000 words or more; a novella, 17,500 to 39,999 words; a novelette, 7,500 to 17,499 words; and a short story 7,499 words or less. The final ballot—with winners indicated by asterisk—was:

For Novel

Count Zero by William Gibson (*Isaac Asimov's Science Fiction Magazine*, January–March 1986; Arbor House)
Free Live Free by Gene Wolfe (Mark Ziesing; Tor)
The Handmaid's Tale by Margaret Atwood (Houghton Mifflin)
The Journal of Nicholas the American by Leigh Kennedy (Atlantic Monthly Press)

Speaker for the Dead by Orson Scott Card (Tor)
This Is the Way the World Ends by James Morrow (Henry Holt)

For Novella

"Dydeetown Girl" by F. Paul Wilson (*Far Frontiers 4*, Baen)
"Escape from Kathmandu" by Kim Stanley Robinson (*Isaac Asimov's Science Fiction Magazine*, September 1986)
"Gilgamesh in the Outback" by Robert Silverberg (*Isaac Asimov's Science Fiction Magazine*, July 1986; *Rebels in Hell*, Baen)
"Newton Sleep" by Gregory Benford (*The Magazine of Fantasy & Science Fiction*, January 1986; *Heroes in Hell*, Baen)
*"R & R" by Lucius Shepard (*Isaac Asimov's Science Fiction Magazine*, April 1986)

For Novelette

"Aymara" by Lucius Shepard (*Isaac Asimov's Science Fiction Magazine*, August 1986)
*"The Girl Who Fell into the Sky" by Kate Wilhelm (*Isaac Asimov's Science Fiction Magazine*, October 1986)
"Hatrack River" by Orson Scott Card (*Isaac Asimov's Science Fiction Magazine*, August 1986)
"Listening to Brahms" by Suzy McKee Charnas (*Omni*, September 1986)
"Permafrost" by Roger Zelazny (*Omni*, April 1986)
"Surviving" by Judith Moffett (*The Magazine of Fantasy & Science Fiction*, June 1986)
"The Winter Market" by William Gibson (*Burning Chrome*, Arbor House; *Stardate*, February 1986)

For Short Story

"The Boy Who Plaited Manes" by Nancy Springer (*The Magazine of Fantasy & Science Fiction*, October 1986)

"The Lions Are Asleep This Night" by Howard Waldrop (*Omni*, August 1986)

"Pretty Boy Crossover" by Pat Cadigan (*Isaac Asimov's Science Fiction Magazine*, January 1986)

"Rat" by James Patrick Kelly (*The Magazine of Fantasy & Science Fiction*, June 1986)

"Robot Dreams" by Isaac Asimov (*Isaac Asimov's Science Fiction Magazine*, Mid-December 1986)

*"Tangents" by Greg Bear (*Omni*, January 1986)

The competition in all categories was fierce and hotly debated, as usual. Orson Scott Card, the winner in the novel category for two consecutive years, pointed out with modest graciousness that no nominee wins by a majority but, instead, by a plurality: most voters choose works other than the winner. It would seem that the Nebula Award shares with other awards and prizes the performance of a hopeless task: neither an average nor a consensus of opinion of talent can be attained. The best that can be had is a limited list of worthies. Is it true, therefore, that awards help to bury talent, by blinding the recipient and eclipsing his or her rivals? Some have claimed that awards should not exist at all.*

I have become fond of pointing out that the Nebula anthologies display talent, winners included, in a context of contenders, any of which might have won. That is the special merit of the Nebula collections. Despite the fact that an award cannot encompass the varied talents that vie for it, the prize does provide a focus for attempts at excellence: the winner is a sample of the

---

*Awards *do* exist, though, and to interested readers I recommend *A History of the Hugo, Nebula, and International Fantasy Awards* by Donald Franson and Howard DeVore, Misfit Press, 1987. The book is updated periodically and is available from Howard DeVore, 4705 Weddel, Dearborn, Michigan 48125. The book's special value is in its listings of recommended works for the preliminary Nebula ballot and of the numbers of votes received. The sense of competition conveyed is striking. The list of works and where to find them is a unique and invaluable help to readers.

xii / NEBULA AWARDS 22

contenders, as is the final ballot, as is the preliminary ballot. Rather than claim that awards are impotent before excellence, I remind readers that they are free to read beyond any one ballot, or one anthology. Judgments are many, and the best judges discern what others miss.

This year's nominated novels were unusual. The ballot included writerly works of high polish. Margaret Atwood's novel came from a writer not usually associated with SF. James Morrow and Leigh Kennedy, both newer writers, contributed works that have gained them as much acclaim outside SF as within. William Gibson's novel demonstrated again that he is the only genuine "cyberpunk" SF writer. Gene Wolfe's novel confirmed him as a titan unto himself, not to be compared with anyone (such is the reward of individual effort, sustained over many years). *Speaker for the Dead* by Orson Scott Card, the second novel of what is clearly a larger work, both delighted and outraged readers and critics. It was the favorite to win and did so irresistibly.

With this volume, I pass editorship of the Nebula anthology to Michael Bishop for the next three years. A past Nebula winner himself, Bishop is also the editor of the incomparable anthology *Light Years and Dark.* He will continue the traditions of the Nebula anthology with expert caring.

Suddenly I am faced with having to write the last lines of this final introduction, in which I should try to pass on some wisdom, a bottom line to my observations of the Nebula Awards process during these last three years. What can I say?

An award is a Platonic ideal. We are drawn toward it. It doesn't exist, properly speaking, but we're glad it's there.

Johnson City, New York
15 June 1987

NEBULA
AWARDS
22

1986, REDUCED
FROM 2000

Algis Budrys

This anthology's resident rememberer, Algis Budrys, is the author of the classic novels *Who?, Rogue Moon,* and *Some Will Not Die,* as well as a more recent achievement, *Michaelmas.* His essays on the state of SF appear monthly in *The Magazine of Fantasy & Science Fiction,* and he is the author of numerous short fictions. *Benchmarks,* a volume of his essays from *Galaxy,* won the Locus Award for best nonfiction in 1986. Budrys is a member of the SFWA Hall of Fame and was honored with a Special Award from the Mystery Writers of America. As a supplement to his critical weeding, he has been a nurturer of new talent at the Clarion writing workshop sponsored by Michigan State University and serves as judge and editor for the Writers of the Future program.

As a critic, Budrys is sensitive to the origins of SF and refuses to separate an author's achievements from the circumstances in which the works are created. Able to see the virtues in a wide range of works, Budrys is the most aware and caring critic of SF now writing.

It was a year best seen from a distance. Most years are; one's reputation for wisdom is better sustained that way. But this year particularly requires a cautious approach on the part of those detailed to appraise what it all meant. So let us pretend that we are looking at it from the last year of this century. We may thus gain something of perspective.

Fifteen years—three five-year generations, as SF has been counting them ever since 1926—seems a safe interval. By then,

1

there will have been at least two new major revolutions in the field, and whatever is going on today will thus be double-insulated. (There will be a third major overturn of some sort actually going on under the serene observer's feet, but it will be so new that it will remain undetected until, say, mid-2001. Leaving that one for whoever has this assignment at the start of the third millennium, let us now gaze back as the second drags its weary way toward cloture.) All right, then, peering back at 1986. . . .

It was the year Isaac Asimov finally got his Grand Master Nebula Award. Without taking away anything from its previous recipients, Isaac's was long overdue, because his career and his work exactly meet the criteria one would suppose fitting to a Grand Master. Let us consider all that. It may lead us farther than we expected:

Unlike the category Nebulas, the Grand Master is conferred by a decision of the SFWA board of officers. However, while there is no nominating and balloting process beyond that, it would be a very peculiar board of officers indeed that did not, in its decision, reflect a choice widely acceptable to the SFWA membership. A similar intuition in fact led to the establishment of the Grand Master. Let's see if the officers of the Science Fiction (that is to say, speculative fiction) Writers of America (and elsewhere) knew what they were articulating on behalf of the membership when, years ago, they instituted and then named the award, which goes to a living SF practitioner with an impressive track record in the field.

The obvious derivation is from chess, where Grand Masters attain that top ranking by consistently beating even very good chess players. Let's think about that. The analogy with the art of SF writing is not perfect, since the arts are not competitive. But perhaps it isn't bad, either, because becoming a chess Grand Master almost invariably requires an individual to be singularly creative on this matter of what can be done on the board. But perhaps it *is* off the point, since there have been hundreds, perhaps thousands, of Grand Master individuals since the rating system was instituted, but few are known as individuals, even within their own community. In fact, I'm pretty sure that at this moment there are serious chess students who could not, without consulting a reference, name all of the current Grand Masters.

It is possible to be a Grand Master and yet uninteresting. It is not for being Grand Masters that even some portions of the outside world recognize the names of Paul Morphy and Capablanca, or the legendary Ruy Lopez. It was not entirely because he played good chess that Bobby Fischer became a household word, and it is not entirely for loss of a top player that some of us are still intrigued with his subsequent seclusion. It was chess, and the statistics of chess, that ostensibly brought him to the fore, but it is something special in Fischer that catches the eye.

So I think that what the then officers of the SFWA *said* was "Grand Master," but what they meant to evoke for us all was the spirit of legend that wraps itself around some, but not all, championship performers in complex arenas. And I think that over the years, succeeding boards of officers have demonstrated a consistency of choice which bears this out. The award goes not simply to those who inventively demonstrate winning patterns of moves over an impressive number of years. It goes to those who in addition demonstrate a strong hint that they can control which pattern they will spontaneously invent under given circumstances.

Extensively repeated originality—not merely high competence, no more than high rating in some system of quantification, not simply the possession of a shelf full of trophies—is creative genius worthy of particular attention. It begins each work essentially without precedent and ends it with a tradition newly and permanently set in place. Suddenly there are new gamefuls of moves that can be duplicated and perhaps even improved on as things in themselves. They are clearly visible now, but they were never there before. Most important, their maker has gone on to other things. One does not become a Capablanca by memorizing his games. That is not how Capablanca did it. The difference between rarely losing and being the sort of Grand Master the SFWA obviously intends to honor is the difference between being struck by lightning and having the ability to generate storms.

Having that ability, and having had it for a sufficiently long time before the Nebulas were ever thought of, Asimov had been waiting through a considerable interval between the moment when he began to deserve a Grand Master and the moment when he actually received it. But it is not possible to point to any holder and declare that Isaac deserved his ahead of that person. The essence of the award is that each holder is uniquely influential upon our literature; look at them and you cannot dispute it. In that universe, then, each such award is a unique event, and thus, all the awards arrive simultaneously and no one takes precedence.

Here in the serial universe, the Grand Master award is not given every year; the bylaws permit (there are, of course, two sets of bylaws, so perhaps we should say *a* bylaw permits) only six awards over any ten-year span. This is not a bad idea. One recalls that not very long after the Congressional Medal of Honor was first instituted, the government had the embarrassing task of taking back some of the ones it had flung out so freely in its first rush of enthusiasm. Otherwise, its value would have been diluted-down out of all meaning. So a certain statutory limitation re Grand Masters is probably wise.

May that and the reasoning in the preceding paragraphs give Doctor Asimov some solace, in concert with the obvious sincerity and joy of the witnesses to the actual presentation. That occurred at the awards banquet in New York City in May 1987, with him there to receive it and a lot of us there to applaud the moment. We would all be a little different without Asimov. Some of us would be a lot different. And the field would be a lot different if there were no practitioners of Grand Master stature as we evidently define that stature.

Now, here looking back from the year 2000, we can see which of the recipients of the 1986 category Nebulas have gone on to receive the Grand Master and which have yet to wait a while. It's easy to do this, because every one of them—Orson Scott Card, Lucius Shepard, Kate Wilhelm, and Greg Bear—is a unique talent with staying power that had already been established by 1986.

This sort of uniformity of uniqueness does not always occur—as it shouldn't. The category Nebulas are for the story, not for the career, and the person who is going to write perhaps only this one chef d'oeuvre fully deserves the experience of standing up at the banquet, in front of all the peers and editors and publishers, and hearing the applause. Those people ought to be taken care of as near the moment of specific accomplishment as possible, and so they are. At least in theory—and, I believe, in actuality much of the time—the process of nominating for the category awards is directed toward the best novels, novellas, novelettes, and short stories of the year, not at their authors. And so the authors receive their just due.

But one cannot help noticing familiar by-lines. When an author wins more than one Nebula, there is reason to start thinking there may be a Grand Master in the picture someday. The balance has shifted, from one good story to an author of several noteworthy stories—that is, to someone who may someday be perceived to have been not only admirable but influential.

There is another road toward the place where Isaac Asimov stood on the first weekend in May 1987, but it is not markedly dissimilar. Lucius Shepard has hitherto been notable for the number and kind of his category nominations—and, outside the SFWA awarding structure, for the increasing number of promising young talents who are billed as "the new Lucius Shepard" or "the next Lucius Shepard."

This may or may not give Shepard a bit of a turn, since it was only a few years ago that Shepard was the new Shepard. But I rather doubt he is made particularly nervous by all that. If 1986 could clearly see a potential Grand Master in him, he probably could, too, being a modestly soft-spoken but not stupid person. It has simply taken a while for his awards to begin catching up to his accomplishments.

Kate Wilhelm is in a somewhat different position. It is possible to be a very good SF writer over a long period of time, as Kate has, and even to win a category award here and there over that span and still be a Grand Master long shot. For one thing, Wilhelm does not classify herself. She does not call herself an SF writer in particular, nor does she always use accustomed SF signatures. But by this year of 2000 A.D., which finds her still brimming with good health and good ideas, it will have been noticed not only that she is an original but also that she is considerably influential. Wilhelm made no big fuss about it—which may have been a PR error—when she long ago broke away from several comfortable molds and set the style for many a female SF writer who has followed her. Some of the latter have gotten credit for pioneering. Some have gotten credit more for uttering than for writing. Wilhelm, steel-hard in her commitment to having the world take her as she is, has spent decades doing the work and breaking the ground.

As for Greg Bear, again who could doubt that here is someone with staying power to match his perpetual inventiveness? The staying power comes, I think, from a markedly deep feeling for the passions that drive people, so that he always finds a human setting for the dramatic possibilities being uncovered by science. It is not absolutely necessary for an SF writer to keep current with the advancing front of human knowledge. Far from it. But when we get an individual who can, and in fact takes naturally to doing it, and can make it mean something that moves the human heart, then we have in petto an Asimov, a Clarke, a Grand Master.

And then there is Orson Scott Card, the playwright, writing teacher, and giver of dramatic readings, who won the novel category award for 1986 with the sequel to *Ender's Game*, his book that won it for 1985.

A question that might arise if you don't know Scott is whether this is a case of a book winning an award or an author winning an award—that is, might we expect that in 2000 Card is as important in the field as Shepard, Wilhelm, and Bear? But if you know Scott—or if you have read his work over the past few years—there is no question. Whatever it is that the nominators and voters of the category awards intend in any given year, Card meets the criteria of talent, energy, and inventiveness, and his works display the salutary effect of that. As far as his eventual Grand Master goes, I doubt if one could find very many SFWA members, even as relatively early in Card's ultimate career as this year, who could deny him the possibility. I think it's become obvious that once one is past the stage of winning category Nebulas or their equivalent, true Grand Mastership can be boiled down to one measure: the integrity of the work. Nothing else counts; looking back at the existing holders, it is plain that is the common denominator and the only nontrivial one. The longevity of one's career simply provides a sufficient number of opportunities for that integrity to be tested convincingly.

Like Shepard, Wilhelm, and Bear, Card as seen from 2000 clearly has all the requisites. Therefore, 1986 was an especially noteworthy year for the Nebulas, and you, gentle reader (and subsidizer of these many careers, guild membership dues payments, and guild treasury budgets and, therefore, underwriter of the awards both in token and in ballroom rental), you, gentle reader, hold in your hand an anthology with unique features even within this unique series.

And in it you will find examples of what is meant by the work of potential Grand Masters. You will swiftly note that they do not write alike in any significant sense of that word. You might even suspect that, given privacy and a sufficiently relaxed atmosphere, any one of them might let slip an opinion that the others are not as on to the right approach as he or she might be. (It is ego that propels the arts; let no one ever tell you otherwise.) But you will find, or have found, that each of them enforces his or her individual style by showing you how well it works. That it might not work as well for another is not only irrelevant, it is essential.

Shepard, Wilhelm, and Bear as expositors of their ideas of the right way to figure SF are well represented here. Card, paying the novelist's penalty by not being displayed in the full effect of his winning work, may need help expositing his position. Also, that makes it easier for me to use him as an example. So let me quote you a recent declaration. It's from his book review column in *The Magazine of Fantasy & Science Fiction.* He speaks of the work of Michael Kube-McDowell, but I think it's plain whereof he speaks:

> . . . it signals the revivification of a kind of science fiction that for a time was on the wane. Let the cyberpunks have their flash and dazzle; let the literati diddle with allusion, angst, and assonance: Kube-McDowell reminds us that the substance of fiction is the story, not the performance. Admire the work of redecorators, yes, but meanwhile Kube-McDowell is strengthening the foundation of science fiction; it will count for more in the long run.

It is interesting that he speaks of foundations. It is more interesting that there is no doubt of where Card stands, that in this apparently unassuming review of a promising younger writer's work, Card promulgates a manifesto. Most interesting, the content of the manifesto is only superficially aimed at various fashions that have developed in SF over the years, all of which have never been abandoned and all of which exist simultaneously in our field. I don't know whether Card fully knows what he really said, although he's a sapient man. What he comes out in favor of—what he bases his idea of SF on—is story, a literary entity which is indeed the major basis of fiction.

But story, you point out acutely, exists without reference to mode. It is as possible for a "cyberpunk" work to be a compelling story as it is for one in which the characters speak in a more conventional vocabulary, a la Card. Similarly, it is possible for a Card-like story to speak directly to the heartaches that arise from contemplating shocking futures.

True, I would think. But perhaps not true for Card, any more than the obverse view is true for someone like, say, John Shirley, cyberpunk spokesman, who has been in this world about as long as Card, I believe, and has about the same level of talent as measured by its subjective effect on me. The important thing about Card, given his talent and going on from there, is that he does have a manifesto, and very likely the ability to enforce it *on himself.* Parts of the way he states that position may evolve as time erodes some of the extra knobs and lance points on it, but underneath it all is the basic commitment, which seems highly unlikely to change. And if it does not change, from the year 2000 it seems entirely likely that like Bear, Wilhelm, and Shepard, and probably one or two other people over the fifteen years between 1986 and now, someday Card will have his Grand Master, simultaneously with all the others who have held it or who will. And if he be a true Grand Master, he will be a little like all of them, and not like any of them.

We do not, in the profession, speak of "best" unless by our profession we mean the art of creating marketable epithets. In the profession of creativity, there are good stories and there are then authors of good stories. One or the other or both win awards. Of all the awards there are, I think Grand Master means most, whatever you think it means. And I do think, for reasons given above, that 1986 was a remarkable year.

ROBOT DREAMS

Isaac Asimov

This year's Grand Master, Isaac Asimov, is the author of over 370 books, among them the bestsellers *Foundation and Earth* and *Foundation's Edge,* as well as *The Robots of Dawn, Robots and Empire, The Caves of Steel, The Naked Sun, The Gods Themselves,* and many other novels and collections of short fiction. He has won both the Nebula and Hugo Awards.

As luck would have it, "Robot Dreams" was nominated in the short story category (Isaac would naturally claim that luck had nothing to do with it). In any case, I believe he is the only Grand Master to have a work on the final ballot in the same year that he or she received the award, and it would have been simple justice if he had won for "Robot Dreams." Then he would have had to give two acceptance speeches, instead of the one that immediately follows; but Isaac has made up for that loss. After "Robot Dreams" there is a short essay, written especially for this volume, in which the Good Doctor gives us a more truthful account of how he managed to do everything. He has assured me in writing that all the essential facts in "Seven Steps to Grand Master" are accurate. I can only subscribe to the words of last year's Grand Master, Arthur C. Clarke, who cabled his congratulations, saying, "I can't say it couldn't happen to a nicer guy, since it already has."

ACCEPTANCE SPEECH FOR GRAND MASTER

"Ladies and Gentlemen:

"I am going to skip all that stuff about how humble I feel and how honored I am and how I owe it all to everybody else, because there isn't a person in the world who will believe me to be sincere. So let's pass on to other things.

"I am the eighth Grand Master, but, of course, any baseball fan who studies the statistics of the game knows that almost anyone can be a first something or other even if it's only that of being the shortstop who booted the most ground balls on cloudy days in

Comiskey Park. Bob Heinlein was the first Grand Master; Andre Norton was the first woman Grand Master; Arthur Clarke (as he himself pointed out) was the first non-American Grand Master; and I—unless Sprague de Camp is hiding a terrible secret—am the first Jewish Grand Master.

"So it's a good thing I was finally named. I was going to wait till 1990 at the outside, and then I was going to accuse the SFWA, generally and individually, of anti-Semitism and carry the matter to the Supreme Court.

"I am also thankful for longevity. Ten years ago, almost to the day, I suffered a mild heart attack. (A mild heart attack is defined as one that doesn't kill you on the spot.) Had the attack not been a mild one, I would not be here today and I would never have been a Grand Master.

"This fortunate turn of events for me forces me to turn my thoughts to others who have not been so fortunate. Can there be any doubt that if Frank Herbert or Philip K. Dick had not died prematurely, they might someday be accepting an award such as this?

"For that matter, if the award had been in existence since the beginning of the century, rather than since the beginning of the third quarter of the century, is there any doubt that Jules Verne, H. G. Wells, E. E. 'Doc' Smith, John W. Campbell, Jr., and Henry Kuttner, to name just a few, would have received the award?

"Let me, therefore, suggest something for your consideration.

"Ought there to be a Science Fiction Hall of Fame to honor, at least posthumously, those of us who have contributed a lifetime of achievement to our field? I won't suggest any rules. I'm not good at it. I suppose, however, that someone might not be eligible till he has been a dear departed for x number of years, so that he or she isn't voted in on a wave of sentiment and nothing more. The votes of y percent of the members of the Science Fiction Writers of America must be cast in favor. If the nominee doesn't make it after having been voted on for z times, he or she is thereafter ineligible, and so on.

"And, just to safeguard my own interests, anyone made Grand Master in his lifetime is ipso facto a member of the Science Fiction Hall of Fame after he has left us for the Great and Perpetual Convention in the sky.

"Now, if you don't mind, I would like to say I *do* feel humble, and I *am* honored, and I owe it to lots of other people—especially the late, great John W. Campbell, Jr., who drove me both mad and to the heights.''

About "Robot Dreams," Asimov writes:

"Byron Preiss put together a collection of my stories in order to have a nice illustrated limited edition and he named it (out of his own head), 'Robot Dreams.'

"Then he said to me, 'I would like an original story for the collection, and I would like to have the story entitled "Robot Dreams." '

"I said, 'With that title what would it be about?'

" 'Robot dreams,' he said.

" 'What kind of dreams would a robot have?' I asked.

" 'You're the science fiction writer,' he said. 'You figure it out.'

"So I wrote 'Robot Dreams.' "

"Last night I dreamed," said LVX-1, calmly.

Susan Calvin said nothing, but her lined face, old with wisdom and experience, seemed to undergo a microscopic twitch.

"Did you hear that?" said Linda Rash, nervously. "It's as I told you." She was small, dark-haired, and young. Her right hand opened and closed, over and over.

Calvin nodded. She said, quietly, "Elvex, you will not move nor speak nor hear us until I say your name again."

There was no answer. The robot sat as though it were cast out of one piece of metal, and it would stay so until it heard its name again.

Calvin said, "What is your computer entry code, Dr. Rash? Or enter it yourself if that will make you more comfortable. I want to inspect the positronic brain pattern."

Linda's hands fumbled, for a moment, at the keys. She broke the process and started again. The fine pattern appeared on the screen.

Calvin said, "Your permission, please, to manipulate your computer."

Permission was granted with a speechless nod. Of course! What could Linda, a new and unproven robopsychologist, do against the Living Legend?

Slowly, Susan Calvin studied the screen, moving it across and down, then up, then suddenly throwing in a key-combination so rapidly that Linda didn't see what had been done, but the pattern was in a new portion of itself altogether and had been enlarged. Back and forth she went, her gnarled fingers tripping over the keys.

No change came over the old face. As though vast calculations were going through her head, she watched all the pattern shifts.

Linda wondered. It was impossible to analyze a pattern without at least a hand-held computer, yet the Old Woman simply stared. Did she have a computer implanted in her skull? Or was it her brain which, for decades, had done nothing but devise, study, and analyze the positronic brain patterns? Did she grasp such a pattern the way Mozart grasped the notation of a symphony?

Finally Calvin said, "What is it you have done, Rash?"

Linda said, a little abashed, "I made use of fractal geometry."

"I gathered that. But why?"

"It had never been done. I thought it would produce a brain pattern with added complexity; possibly closer to that of the human."

"Was anyone consulted? Was this all on your own?"

"I did not consult. It was on my own."

Calvin's faded eyes looked long at the young woman. "You had no right. Rash your name; rash your nature. Who are you not to ask? *I* myself; I, Susan Calvin; would have discussed this."

"I was afraid I would be stopped."

"You certainly would have been."

"Am I," her voice caught, even as she strove to hold it firm, "going to be fired?"

"Quite possibly," said Calvin. "Or you might be promoted. It depends on what I think when I am through."

"Are you going to dismantle El—" She had almost said the name, which would have reactivated the robot and been one more mistake—she could not afford another mistake, if it wasn't already too late to afford anything at all. "Are you going to dismantle the robot?"

She was suddenly aware, with some shock, that the Old Woman had an electron gun in the pocket of her smock. Dr. Calvin had come prepared for just that.

"We'll see," said Calvin. "The robot may prove too valuable to dismantle."

"But how can it dream?"

"You've made a positronic brain pattern remarkably like that of a human brain. Human brains must dream to reorganize, to get rid, periodically, of knots and snarls. Perhaps so must this robot, and for the same reason—have you asked him what he has dreamed?"

"No, I sent for you as soon as he said he had dreamed. I would deal with this matter no further on my own, after that."

"Ah!" A very small smile passed over Calvin's face. "There are limits beyond which your folly will not carry you. I am glad of that. In fact, I am relieved—And now let us together see what we can find out."

She said, sharply, "Elvex."

The robot's head turned toward her smoothly, "Yes, Dr. Calvin?"

"How do you know you have dreamed?"

"It is at night, when it is dark, Dr. Calvin," said Elvex, "and there is suddenly light although I can see no cause for the appearance of light. I see things that have no connection with what I conceive of as reality. I hear things. I react oddly. In searching my vocabulary for words to express what was happening, I came across the word 'dream.' Studying its meaning I finally came to the conclusion I was dreaming."

"How did you come to have 'dream' in your vocabulary, I wonder."

Linda said, quickly, waving the robot silent, "I gave him a human-style vocabulary. I thought—"

"You really thought," said Calvin. "I'm amazed."

"I thought he would need the verb. You know, 'I never dreamed that—' Something like that."

Calvin said, "How often have you dreamed, Elvex?"

"Every night, Dr. Calvin, since I have become aware of my existence."

"Ten nights," interposed Linda, anxiously, "but Elvex only told me of it this morning."

"Why only this morning, Elvex?"

"It was not until this morning, Dr. Calvin, that I was convinced that I was dreaming. Till then, I had thought there was a flaw in my positronic brain pattern, but I could not find one. Finally, I decided it was a dream."

"And what do you dream?"

"I dream always very much the same dream, Dr. Calvin. Little details are different, but always it seems to me that I see a large panorama in which robots are working."

"Robots, Elvex? And human beings, also?"

"I see no human beings in the dream, Dr. Calvin. Not at first. Only robots."

"What are they doing, Elvex?"

"They are working, Dr. Calvin. I see some mining in the depths of the earth, and some laboring in heat and radiation. I see some in factories and some undersea."

Calvin turned to Linda. "Elvex is only ten days old, and I'm sure he has not left the testing station. How does he know of robots in such detail?"

Linda looked in the direction of a chair as though she longed to sit down, but the Old Woman was standing and that meant Linda had to stand also. She said, faintly, "It seemed to me important that he know about robotics and its place in the world. It was my thought that he would be particularly adapted to play the part of overseer with his—his new brain."

"His fractal brain?"

"Yes."

Calvin nodded and turned back to the robot. "You saw all this—undersea, and underground, and above ground—and space, too, I imagine."

"I also saw robots working in space," said Elvex. "It was that I saw all this, with the details forever changing as I glanced from place to place that made me realize that what I saw was not in accord with reality and led me to the conclusion, finally, that I was dreaming."

"What else did you see, Elvex?"

"I saw that all the robots were bowed down with toil and affliction; that all were weary of responsibility and care; and I wished them to rest."

Calvin said, "But the robots are not bowed down, they are not weary, they need no rest."

"So it is in reality, Dr. Calvin. I speak of my dream, however. In my dream, it seemed to me that robots must protect their own existence."

Calvin said, "Are you quoting the Third Law of Robotics?"

"I am, Dr. Calvin."

"But you quote it in incomplete fashion. The Third Law is: 'A robot must protect its own existence as long as such protection does not conflict with the First or Second Law.'"

"Yes, Dr. Calvin. That is the Third Law in reality, but in my dream, the Law ended with the word 'existence.' There was no mention of the First or Second Law."

"Yet both exist, Elvex. The Second Law, which takes precedence over the Third, is: 'A robot must obey the orders given it by human beings except where such orders would conflict with the First Law.' Because of this, robots obey orders. They do the work you see them do, and they do it readily and without trouble. They are not bowed down; they are not weary."

"So it is in reality, Dr. Calvin. I speak of my dream."

"And the First Law, Elvex, which is the most important of all, is: 'A robot may not injure a human being, or, through inaction, allow a human being to come to harm.'"

"Yes, Dr. Calvin. In reality. In my dream, however, it

seemed to me there was neither First nor Second Law, but only the Third, and the Third Law was: 'A robot must protect its own existence.' That was the whole of the Law.''

"In your dream, Elvex?"

"In my dream.''

Calvin said, "Elvex, you will not move nor speak nor hear us until I say your name again.'' And again the robot became, to all appearances, a single inert piece of metal.

Calvin turned to Linda Rash and said, "Well, what do you think, Dr. Rash?''

Linda's eyes were wide, and she could feel her heart beating madly. She said, "Dr. Calvin, I am appalled. I had no idea. It would never have occurred to me that such a thing was possible.''

"No,'' said Calvin, calmly. "Nor would it have occurred to me, nor to anyone. You have created a robot brain capable of dreaming and by this device you have revealed a layer of thought in robotic brains that might have remained undetected, otherwise, until the danger became acute.''

"But that's impossible,'' said Linda. "You can't mean that other robots think the same.''

"As we would say of a human being, not consciously. But who would have thought there was an unconscious layer beneath the obvious positronic brain paths, a layer that was not necessarily under the control of the Three Laws? What might this have brought about as robotic brains grew more and more complex—had we not been warned?''

"You mean by the robot?''

"By *you*, Dr. Rash. You have behaved improperly but, by doing so, you have helped us to an overwhelmingly important understanding. We shall be working with fractal brains from now on, forming them in carefully controlled fashion. You will play your part in that. You will not be penalized for what you have done, but you will henceforth work in collaboration with others. Do you understand?''

"Yes, Dr. Calvin. But what of the robot?''

"I'm still not certain."

Calvin removed the electron gun from her pocket and Linda stared at it with fascination. One burst of its electrons at a robotic cranium and the positronic brain paths would be neutralized and enough energy would be released to fuse the robot-brain into an inert ingot.

Linda said, "But surely the robot is important to our research. He must not be destroyed."

"*Must* not, Dr. Rash? That will be *my* decision, I think. It depends entirely on how dangerous the robot is."

Susan Calvin straightened up, as though determined that her own aged body was not to bow under *its* weight of responsibility. She said, "Elvex, do you hear me?"

"Yes, Dr. Calvin," said the robot.

"Did your dream continue? You said earlier, that human beings did not appear *at first*. Does that mean they appeared afterward?"

"Yes, Dr. Calvin. It seemed to me, in my dream, that eventually one man appeared."

"One man? Not a robot?"

"Yes, Dr. Calvin. And the man said, 'Let my people go!' "

"The *man* said that?"

"Yes, Dr. Calvin."

"And when he said 'Let my people go,' then by the words 'my people' he meant the robots?"

"Yes, Dr. Calvin. So it was in my dream."

"And did you know who the man was—in your dream?"

"Yes, Dr. Calvin. I knew the man."

"Who was he?"

And Elvex said, "I was the man."

And Susan Calvin at once raised her electron gun and fired, and Elvex was no more.

SEVEN STEPS TO GRAND MASTER

Isaac Asimov

Step 1—I Take an Ocean Trip

I was born in Russia. The land had just gone through World War I, a revolution, a civil war, and foreign intervention. To inflict myself on the nation at such a time was rather merciless of me, but I plead not guilty. The act that led to it was that of my parents.

In late 1922, my parents decided it might be a good idea to emigrate to the United States. They were getting along; they were not in dire poverty; they had not suffered unduly as a result of the troubles the land had been suffering—but they suspected that they might be better off in the long run in the United States.

One of the problems they had to face, I imagine, was whether to take me along. I was not quite three years old, and what with me contracting double pneumonia, falling into a nearby pond and (after some hesitation) being pulled out by my mother, and inflicting other joys of the sort on my parents, I imagine they felt they might be better off in the long run in the United States by themselves.

However, largely because (I suspect) they could find no one foolish enough to take me off their hands, they sighed and put me in a knapsack so that they at least wouldn't have to waste a ticket on me. I crossed the ocean with them, and we arrived in Brooklyn in February of 1923, a little past my third birthday.

This was my first step to Grand Masterability. Had I remained in the USSR, I dare say I would have received an adequate education and would have taken to writing and would even have begun to write science fiction—making use of the Cyrillic alphabet, to be sure—but I don't think things would have gone as well for me there as here. In 1941, the Nazis invaded the Soviet Union. I was twenty-one at the time, and I suspect I would have been in the fighting and might well have been killed or, worse, been taken prisoner. Or, if I had survived, I might conceivably have gotten in trouble with the regime because of my tendency to speak out of turn. (I have frequently gotten in trouble in the United States for that reason, come to think of it.)

And, finally, I don't know if they have a Grand Master award in the Soviet Union, so all in all, that ocean trip was essential.

Step 2—I Insist on My Identity

Once we were in the United States, my parents realized that they had gained a new status—that of being "greenhorns." Everyone was eager to advise us and to guide our faltering steps down the pathway to American citizenship, especially those old settlers who had gotten off the ship five years earlier.

One neighbor woman said to my mother, in my hearing (I was four or five by then and so small for my age that no one noticed me—so that I got stepped on a lot), "Why do you call him Isaac, Mrs. Asimov? With a name like that, he will always have a stigma on him."(Translation: "Everyone will know he is Jewish.")

My mother said, "So what should I call him, Mrs. Bindler?"

And Mrs. Bindler (or whatever her name might have been) said, "Call him Oiving." (Translation: Irving. This is a grand old aristocratic English family name.)

My mother was very impressed and would undoubtedly have accepted the suggestion, but, as I said, I was listening with each ear. I was not yet old enough to understand the semantic fact that the name of a thing is not the thing itself. I didn't understand that I was merely *called* Isaac and that I could be me whatever I was called. (Or as I once put it—rather neatly, I think—"That which we call a rose by any other name would smell as sweet.")

What I thought was that I *was* Isaac and if I were called anything else, I wouldn't be me. Whereupon I raised what we called in those days "a holler," absolutely refusing, under any conditions, to allow myself to be called Oiving. I was Isaac and I intended to stay Isaac—and I did. My mother simply wilted under the force of my indignation.

Without me knowing it, that was my second step toward Grand Masterdom. Had I accepted Oiving, it would have proved every bit as stigmatic as Isaac, for so many Jewish mothers had sought escape for their young hopefuls in that direction that Oiving became as Jewish as Isaac and without the biblical cachet of the latter name. (Besides, Newton's name was Isaac, too, and that's even better than the Bible, as far as I'm concerned.)

Having escaped Isaac, I would have ended by despising Oiving and would have changed my name to Ian. Then, realizing that Ian went but risibly with Asimov, I would have changed my last name to Ashford, and it would have been as Ian Ashford that I would have written my science fiction.

Now I am a strong believer in the value of name recognition. No one would have noticed or remembered a name like Ian Ashford. However, the name Isaac Asimov attracts notice at once. People laugh and have long discussions over how it might be pronounced. When a second story appears with the same name, they see it again, and before long they can hardly wait for another story by me. Even if the story is no good, the name makes a terrific conversation piece. I would have sunk without a trace if I had not had the good sense to keep my name.

Step 3—I Live on the Subway Line

I was eighteen years old and I finally had a story I wanted to submit to John W. Campbell, Jr., the new editor of *Astounding Science-Fiction*. The trouble was I didn't know how to do that.

The logical way was to mail it to him, but the story, plus envelope, weighed just over three ounces, which meant four three-cent stamps, or twelve cents altogether.

If I went by subway, it would be five cents each way, or ten cents altogether. Of course, the subway would mean half an hour of my time each way, but in those days, my time was worth nothing. Weighing the relative values of twelve cents and ten cents, I came to the conclusion that two cents was valuable stuff. I therefore took the subway.

Approaching the receptionist in an agony of fright, I asked for Mr. Campbell, expecting to be thrown out with the manuscript following me, divided into four pieces per page. Campbell was willing to see me and we talked for an hour. He gave me a quick reading and sent me a quick rejection with a very kindly and helpful letter. After that, I visited him once a month and I was on my way.

How did that happen? What was the deciding factor?

Easy! I lived half a block from a subway station. Had I lived in Fargo, North Dakota, the railroad fare would have been more than twelve cents. For goodness sake, if I had lived in Staten Island, the ferry would have added ten cents to the round-trip fare, and comparing twelve cents and twenty cents, I would have put the envelope into the letter box. I would then never have met John Campbell, and I would not have received the kind of encouragement and charisma that poured forth from that great editor.

Hurrah for the subway station. I might never have made Grand Masterhood without it.

Step 4—I Walk in at the Right Moment

I tried to come to Campbell with a new idea every time I saw him. Every once in a while, though, Campbell had an idea of his own. In the competition between a writer's idea and one of Campbell's ideas, it was Campbell who always won—at least, when it was I who was involved.

One day Campbell had a terrific idea, and he was aching to

force it on some writer. He never told me the details, but the picture I have in my mind is of Campbell sitting there like a vulture waiting for an innocent writer to enter his lair (assuming vultures have lairs)—*any* innocent writer.

It must have come as a nasty shock to him when I, aged twenty-one and just as innocent as they come, walked in and said, "Hello, Mr. Campbell." It's undoubtedly a tribute to the manner in which that idea had him in its grip that after a momentary shudder, he dismissed the idea I was trying to describe and said, "Never mind that, Asimov. Let me read you this quote from one of Emerson's essays."

He read it—something about how if human beings could see the stars only once in a thousand years, they would get a big kick out of it.

"They wouldn't," said Campbell. "They would go nuts. I want you to go home and write that story. About-face! March!"

I went home, trembling with fear, sat down at my typewriter, and tapped out "Nightfall." It appeared in the September 1941 *Astounding* and got the cover. It was my first smash hit, after nearly three years of trying. Robert Heinlein made it with his first story; A. E. van Vogt made it with his first story; Arthur C. Clarke made it with his first story; and I was almost as good—I made it with my sixteenth story.

"Nightfall" marked a turning point. From the moment of that sale, I never failed to sell a single word of fiction I wrote (though on rare occasions it took two or three submissions to do so).

Sometimes I wake up in the middle of the night screaming because I have dreamed that Theodore Sturgeon or Lester del Rey had walked into Campbell's office half an hour ahead of me that day. If they had, bang would have gone my Grand Mastership.

Step 5—A Friend Insists

One of the stories I didn't sell—at first—was a novella entitled "Grow Old Along with Me." I wrote it for *Startling Stories* at their request and, in the end, they rejected it. That happened in 1947, six years after "Nightfall." It rattled me. I decided that I had passed my peak—after all, I was 27—and I was sliding down the abyss to join Ed Earl Repp and Harl Vincent (two science fiction writing idols of the early thirties).

Two years later, Doubleday decided to start a hard-cover line of science fiction novels. For that, they needed novels. I, of course, with my usual ability to keep my finger on the publishing pulse, knew nothing about it.

But I had a friend—Fred Pohl.

He came to me and said, "Doubleday is looking for a novel. How about the one you wrote for *Startling?*"

I said, "Fred, it's only forty thousand words. And it's a stinker."

He said, "So if they like it, you can lengthen it. And if you don't tell them it's a stinker, they might not find out."

But I didn't want to go through another rejection on the story, so I said, "I'd rather not submit it."

"I insist," said Fred.

I was not proof against Fred's quiet pertinacity, and I let him have the story. He let Doubleday have the story. Doubleday asked me to extend it to seventy thousand words and took it. It appeared in January 1950 as *Pebble in the Sky,* and it has earned me money in each of the seventy-four Doubleday statements I have received since then.

What's more, it got Doubleday into the pleasant habit of accepting my manuscripts as a matter of course. As of today, they have published 102 of my books and have several in press.

I'm sure that I would have been a reasonably successful writer on magazine short stories alone, but I would have been far poorer than I am today if I had not written my novels, and I would be nowhere near as well known. In fact, if Fred had not insisted on submitting the story on that day in 1949, I doubt I could ever have qualified for Grand Master-craft.

Step 6—A Critic Asks a Question

In 1957, I published my novel *The Naked Sun* in book form. It was a science fiction mystery. Also, it had a rather understated love story in it, with a rather touching final scene between the lovers.

Damon Knight reviewed the book, and he wasn't in the least impressed by the science fiction or the mystery. (I suppose he's entitled to his opinion, but I don't suppose it very hard.) However, he liked the love story. "If you can write like that, Asimov," he asked rhetorically in the course of his review, "why do you bother writing science fiction?"

To which I answered in a letter that appeared in the magazine in which the review had earlier appeared, "Because I love science fiction. No matter what else happens, I will never stop writing science fiction."

And then, in 1958, the very next year, I suddenly grew tired of science fiction. A sequel to *The Naked Sun* died in the typewriter, and I realized that I was anxious to write nonfiction. And yet how could I stop? I remembered my answer to Damon's question, and I simply couldn't go back on my profession of love.

It was while I hesitated that Robert P. Mills, then editor of *The Magazine of Fantasy & Science Fiction,* asked me to write a monthly science column. I leaped at it, for that would enable me to write nonfiction and yet stay in the science fiction field. It was the perfect Talmudic solution. The first science column appeared in the November 1958 issue of *F & SF,* and the column still continues to this moment, twenty-nine years later. For twenty years after that first column, I wrote mostly nonfiction. Mind you, I didn't give up my science fiction altogether. In that interval I wrote two novels and dozens of short stories, but compared to my earlier production, it seemed like very little.

Had it not been for the *F & SF* column, which would not have come about, perhaps, without Damon's question and my answer, I surely would have been forgotten by the fans and been thought of as another David H. Keller. That column kept me going till the founding of *Isaac Asimov's Science Fiction Magazine* in 1977 and Doubleday's insistence in 1981 on my return to novels put me back in the mainstream. That column, by keeping me constantly in the public eye during the dry period, made it possible for me to earn Grand Masterness.

Step 7—I Survive

Naturally, I had my vicissitudes. There was a hemithyroidectomy in 1972 and a mild heart attack in 1977. I survived both handily. And then, in the fall of 1983, my angina suddenly got so bad I could scarcely walk the length of the hall in my apartment house.

On December 14, 1983, I had a triple bypass and came out of it in fine shape, thanks to a very clever surgeon. The morning after, I said to him, "The nurses tell me the operation went very well." And he answered, "What do you mean 'very well.' It was *perfect!*"

And so it seems to have been, and had it not been, there is scarcely any chance that an award would have been handed to me now. It was to that surgeon then that I owe my Grand Masterity.

The conclusion? Simple. I had nothing to do with it. If my parents hadn't brought me here; if my mother hadn't decided to let my name be; if a subway line hadn't existed at my very feet; if I hadn't wandered into Campbell's office at the right moment; if Fred Pohl hadn't insisted; if Damon Knight hadn't asked a question; and if a surgeon hadn't had a good day—I'd be left with nothing. As it is, I'm Grand Master—and I love it just as though I'd done it all myself.

TANGENTS

Greg Bear

In 1983 Greg Bear won the Nebula Award in two categories, novelette and novella. He has also won the Hugo Award. His novels include *Beyond Heaven's River, Hegira, Strength of Stones, The Infinity Concerto, Blood Music, Eon, Psychlone,* and the recent *Forge of God.* His short stories are collected in *The Wind from a Burning Woman.*

About his winning short story he writes:

"Years ago, when I was eleven or twelve years old, I checked Clifton Fadiman's anthology Fantasia Mathematica *out of a naval library on Kodiak Island and read most of the stories, including Martin Gardner's 'The No-Sided Professor.' Gardner introduced my impressionable mind to Möbius strips. I remember cutting my first out of a sheet of typing paper (I was already pounding on a typewriter then) and giving it a half-twist, and experiencing an intellectual high for several hours. I wondered whether this was just a fluke, and whether other dimensions could be lost, if one was sufficiently clever. Other stories in the collection twisted my mind in other ways, but I didn't lose dimensions; I gained them. I began amateur speculations in topology and dimensional mathematics, which I continue to this day, though without any formal rigor. My respect for mathematicians—especially theoretical mathematicians—is boundless. Decades later, I encountered a fascinating, tragic, and infuriating story in Andrew Hodges's biography,* Alan Turing: The Enigma. *John F. Carr, acting as fiction editor for a computer magazine, asked for a story. The new fury mixed with the old fascination, revived by Rudy Rucker's wonderful book* The Fourth Dimension. *The story was finally written and submitted, but the situation at that magazine had changed; John could not publish it, so I immediately sent it to Ellen Datlow at* Omni.

"To my mind, 'Tangents' is homage to all those wonderful stories, and an exorcism of the demons of anger raised by Turing's

brutal mistreatment at the hands of the English government, whose rule and land he helped to save in World War II."

The nut-brown boy stood in the California field, his Asian face shadowed by a hard hat, his short, stocky frame clothed in a T-shirt and a pair of brown shorts. He squinted across the hip-high grass at the spraddled old two-story ranch house, and then he whistled a few bars from a Haydn piano sonata. Out of the upper floor of the house came a man's high, frustrated "bloody hell!" and the sound of a fist slamming on a solid surface. Silence for a minute. Then, more softly, a woman's question: "Not going well?"

"No. I'm swimming in it, but I don't see it."

"The encryption?" the woman asked timidly.

"The tesseract. If it doesn't gel, it isn't aspic."

The boy squatted in the grass and listened.

"And?" the woman encouraged.

"Ah, Lauren, it's still cold broth."

The conversation stopped. The boy lay back in the grass, aware he was on private land. He had crept over the split-rail and brick-pylon fence from the new housing project across the road. School was out, and his mother—adoptive mother—did not like him around the house all day. Or at all.

He closed his eyes and imagined a huge piano keyboard and himself dancing on the keys, tapping out the Oriental-sounding D minor scale, which suited his origins, he thought. He loved music.

He opened his eyes and saw the thin, graying lady in a tweed suit leaning over him, staring down with her brows knit.

"You're on private land," she said.

He scrambled up and brushed grass from his pants. "Sorry."

"I thought I saw someone out here. What's your name?"

"Pal," he replied.

"Is that a name?" she asked querulously.

"Pal Tremont. It's not my real name. I'm Korean."

"Then what's your real name?"

"My folks told me not to use it anymore. I'm adopted. Who are you?"

The gray woman looked him up and down. "My name is Lauren Davies," she said. "You live near here?"

He pointed across the fields at the close-packed tract homes.

"I sold the land for those homes ten years ago," she said. "I don't normally enjoy children trespassing."

"Sorry," Pal said.

"Have you had lunch?"

"No."

"Will a grilled cheese sandwich do?"

He squinted at her and nodded.

In the broad, red-brick and tile kitchen, sitting at an oak table with his shoulders barely rising above the top, he ate the mildly charred sandwich and watched Lauren Davies watching him.

"I'm trying to write about a child," she said. "It's difficult. I'm a spinster and I don't know children well."

"You're a writer?" he asked, taking a swallow of milk.

She sniffed. "Not that anyone would know."

"Is that your brother, upstairs?"

"No," she said. "That's Peter. We've been living together for twenty years."

"But you said you're a spinster—isn't that someone who's never married or never loved?" Pal asked.

"Never married. And never you mind. Peter's relationship to me is none of your concern." She put together a tray with a bowl of soup and a tuna-salad sandwich. "His lunch," she said. Without being asked, Pal trailed up the stairs after her.

"This is where Peter works," Lauren explained. Pal stood in the doorway, eyes wide. The room was filled with electronics gear, computer terminals, and industrial-gray shelving with odd cardboard sculptures sharing each level, along with books and circuit boards. She put the lunch tray on top of a cart, resting precariously on a box of floppy disks.

"Still having trouble?" she asked a thin man with his back turned toward them.

The man turned around on his swivel chair, glanced briefly at Pal, then at the lunch, and shook his head. The hair on top of his head was a rich, glossy black; on the close-cut sides, the color changed abruptly to a bright, fake-looking white. He had a small, thin nose and large green eyes. On the desk before him was a computer monitor. "We haven't been introduced," he said, pointing to Pal.

"This is Pal Tremont, a neighborhood visitor. Pal, this is Peter Tuthy. Pal's going to help me with that character we discussed."

Pal looked at the monitor curiously. Red and green lines went through some incomprehensible transformation on the screen, then repeated.

"What's a tesseract?" Pal asked, remembering the words he had heard through the window as he stood in the field.

"It's a four-dimensional analog of a cube. I'm trying to find a way to teach myself to see it in my mind's eye," Tuthy said. "Have you ever tried that?"

"No," Pal admitted.

"Here," Tuthy said, handing him the spectacles. "As in the movies."

Pal donned the spectacles and stared at the screen. "So?" he said. "It folds and unfolds. It's pretty—it sticks out at you, and then it goes away." He looked around the workshop. "Oh, wow!" In the east corner of the room a framework of aluminum pipes—rather like a plumber's dream of an easel—supported a long, disembodied piano keyboard mounted in a slim, black case. The boy ran to the keyboard. "A Tronclavier! With all the switches! My mother had me take piano lessons, but I'd rather learn on this. Can you play it?"

"I toy with it," Tuthy said, exasperated. "I toy with all sorts of electronic things. But what did you see on the screen?" He glanced up at Lauren, blinking. "I'll eat the food, I'll eat it. Now please don't bother us."

"He's supposed to be helping *me*," Lauren complained.

Peter smiled at her. "Yes, of course. I'll send him downstairs in a little while."

When Pal descended an hour later, he came into the kitchen to thank Lauren for lunch. "Peter's a real flake. He's trying to see certain directions."

"I know," Lauren said, sighing.

"I'm going home now," Pal said. "I'll be back, though . . . if it's all right with you. Peter invited me."

"I'm sure that it will be fine," Lauren replied dubiously.

"He's going to let me learn the Tronclavier." With that, Pal smiled radiantly and exited through the kitchen door.

When she retrieved the tray, she found Peter leaning back in his chair, eyes closed. The figures on the screen patiently folded and unfolded, cubes continuously passing through one another.

"What about Hockrum's work?" she asked.

"I'm on it," Peter replied, eyes still closed.

Lauren called Pal's foster mother on the second day to apprise them of their son's location, and the woman assured her it was quite all right. "Sometimes he's a little pest. Send him home if he causes trouble—but not right away! Give me a rest," she said, then laughed nervously.

Lauren drew her lips together tightly, thanked her, and hung up.

Peter and the boy had come downstairs to sit in the kitchen, filling up paper with line drawings. "Peter's teaching me how to use his program," Pal said.

"Did you know," Tuthy said, assuming his highest Cambridge professorial tone, "that a cube, intersecting a flat plane, can be cut through a number of geometrically different cross sections?"

Pal squinted at the sketch Tuthy had made. "Sure," he said.

"If shoved through the plane, the cube can appear, to a

two-dimensional creature living on the plane—let's call him a Flatlander—to be either a triangle, a rectangle, a trapezoid, a rhombus, or a square. If the two-dimensional being observes the cube being pushed through all the way, what he sees is one or more of these objects growing larger, changing shape suddenly, shrinking, and disappearing."

"Sure," Pal said, tapping his sneakered toe. "It's easy. Like in that book you showed me."

"And a sphere pushed through a plane would appear to the hapless Flatlander first as an *invisible* point (the two-dimensional surface touching the sphere, tangential), then as a circle. The circle would grow in size, then shrink back to a point and disappear again." He sketched the stick figures, looking in awe at the intrusion.

"Got it," Pal said. "Can I play with the Tronclavier now?"

"In a moment. Be patient. So what would a tesseract look like, coming into our three-dimensional space? Remember the program, now—the pictures on the monitor."

Pal looked up at the ceiling. "I don't know," he said, seeming bored.

"Try to think," Tuthy urged him.

"It would . . ." Pal held his hands out to shape an angular object. "It would look like one of those Egyptian things, but with three sides . . . or like a box. It would look like a weird-shaped box, too, not square."

"And if we turned the tesseract around?"

The doorbell rang. Pal jumped off the kitchen chair. "Is that my Mom?"

"I don't think so," Lauren said. "More likely it's Hockrum." She went to the front door to answer. She returned with a small, pale man behind her. Tuthy stood and shook the man's hand. "Pal Tremont, this is Irving Hockrum," he introduced, waving his hand between them. Hockrum glanced at Pal and blinked a long, not-very-mammalian blink.

"How's the work coming?" he asked Tuthy.

"It's finished," Tuthy said. "It's upstairs. Looks like your savants are barking up the wrong logic tree." He retrieved a folder of papers and printouts and handed them to Hockrum.

Hockrum leafed through the printouts.

"I can't say this makes me happy," he said. "Still, I can't find fault. Looks like the work is up to your usual brilliant standards. I just wish you'd had it to us sooner. It would have saved me some grief—and the company quite a bit of money."

"Sorry," Tuthy said nonchalantly.

"Now I have an important bit of work for you. . . ." And Hockrum outlined another problem. Tuthy thought it over for several minutes and shook his head.

"Most difficult, Irving. Pioneering work there. It would take at least a month to see if it's even feasible."

"That's all I need to know for now—whether it's feasible. A lot's riding on this, Peter." Hockrum clasped his hands together in front of him, looking even more pale and worn than when he had entered the kitchen. "You'll let me know soon?"

"I'll get right on it," Tuthy said.

"Protégé?" he asked, pointing to Pal. There was a speculative expression on his face, not quite a leer.

"No, a friend. He's interested in music," Tuthy said. "Damned good at Mozart, in fact."

"I help with his tesseracts," Pal asserted.

"Congratulations," Hockrum said. "I hope you don't interrupt Peter's work. Peter's work is important."

Pal shook his head solemnly. "Good," Hockrum said, and then left the house to take the negative results back to his company.

Tuthy returned to his office, Pal in train. Lauren tried to work in the kitchen, sitting with fountain pen and pad of paper, but the words wouldn't come. Hockrum always worried her. She climbed the stairs and stood in the doorway of the office. She often did that; her presence did not disturb Tuthy, who could work under all sorts of conditions.

"Who was that man?" Pal was asking Tuthy.

"I work for him," Tuthy said. "He's employed by a very big

electronics firm. He loans me most of the equipment I use here—the computers, the high-resolution monitors. He brings me problems and then takes my solutions back to his bosses and claims he did the work."

"That sounds stupid," Pal said. "What kind of problems?"

"Codes, encryptions. Computer security. That was my expertise, once."

"You mean, like fencerail, that sort of thing?" Pal asked, face brightening. "We learned some of that in school."

"Much more complicated, I'm afraid," Tuthy said, grinning. "Did you ever hear of the German 'Enigma,' or the 'Ultra' project?"

Pal shook his head.

"I thought not. Don't worry about it. Let's try another figure on the screen now." He called up another routine on the four-space program and sat Pal before the screen. "So what would a hypersphere look like if it intruded into our space?"

Pal thought a moment. "Kind of weird."

"Not really. You've been watching the visualizations."

"Oh, in *our* space. That's easy. It just looks like a balloon, blowing up from nothing and then shrinking again. It's harder to see what a hypersphere looks like when it's real. Reft of us, I mean."

"Reft?" Tuthy said.

"Sure. Reft and light. Dup and owwen. Whatever the directions are called."

Tuthy stared at the boy. Neither of them had noticed Lauren in the doorway. "The proper terms are *ana* and *kata*," Tuthy said. "What does it look like?"

Pal gestured, making two wide swings with his arms. "It's like a ball, and it's like a horseshoe, depending on how you look at it. Like a balloon stung by bees, I guess, but it's smooth all over, not lumpy."

Tuthy continued to stare, then asked quietly, "You actually see it?"

"Sure," Pal said. "Isn't that what your program is supposed to do—make you see things like that?"

Tuthy nodded, flabbergasted.

"Can I play the Tronclavier now?"

Lauren backed out of the doorway. She felt she had eaves-dropped on something momentous but beyond her. Tuthy came downstairs an hour later, leaving Pal to pick out Telemann on the keyboard. He sat at the kitchen table with her. "The program works," he said. "It doesn't work for me, but it works for him. He's a bloody natural." Tuthy seldom used such language. He was clearly awed. "I've just been showing him reverse-shadow figures. There's a way to have at least a sensation of seeing something rotated through the fourth dimension. Those hollow masks they use at Disneyland . . . seem to reverse in and out, depending on the lighting? Crater pictures from the moon—resemble hills instead of holes? That's what Pal calls the reversed images—hills and holes."

"And what's special about them?"

"Well, if you go along with the game and make the hollow faces seem to reverse and poke out at you, that is similar to rotating them in the fourth dimension. The features seem to reverse left and right—right eye becomes left eye, and so on. He caught on right away, and then he went off and played Haydn. He's gone through all my sheet music. The kid's a genius."

"Musical, you mean?"

He glanced directly at her and frowned. "Yes, I suppose he's remarkable at that, too. But spatial relations—coordinates and motion in a higher dimension. . . . Did you know that if you take a three-dimensional object and rotate it in the fourth dimension, it will come back with left–right reversed? There is no fixed left–right in the fourth dimension. So if I were to take my hand—" He held up his right hand, "and lift it *dup*—or drop it *owwen*, it would come back like this?" He held his left hand over his right, balled the right up into a fist, and snuck it away behind his back.

"I didn't know that," Lauren said. "What are *dup* and *owwen*?"

"That's what Pal calls movement along the fourth dimension. *Ana* and *kata* to purists. Like up and down to a Flatlander, who only comprehends left and right, back and forth."

She thought about the hands for a moment. "I still can't see it," she said.

"Neither can I," Tuthy admitted. "Our circuits are just too hard-wired, I suppose."

Pal had switched the Tronclavier to a cathedral organ and wah-guitar combination and was playing variations on Pergolesi.

"Are you going to keep working for Hockrum?" Lauren asked. Tuthy didn't seem to hear her.

"It's remarkable," he murmured. "The boy just walked in here. You brought him in by accident. Remarkable."

"Do you think you can show me the direction—point it out to me?" Tuthy asked the boy three days later.

"None of my muscles move that way," he replied. "I can see it, in my head, but . . ."

"What is it like, seeing it? That direction?"

Pal squinted. "It's a lot bigger. Where we live is sort of stacked up with other places. It makes me feel lonely."

"Why?"

"Because I'm stuck here. Nobody out there pays any attention to us."

Tuthy's mouth worked. "I thought you were just intuiting those directions in your head. Are you telling me you're actually *seeing* out there?"

"Yeah. There's people out there, too. Well, not people, exactly. But it isn't my eyes that see them. Eyes are like muscles—they can't point those ways. But the head—the brain, I guess—can."

"Bloody hell," Tuthy said. He blinked and recovered. "Excuse me. That's rude. Can you show me the people . . . on the screen?"

"Shadows, like we were talking about."

"Fine. Then draw the shadows for me."

Pal sat down before the terminal, fingers pausing over the

keys. "I can show you, but you have to help me with something."

"Help you with what?"

"I'd like to play music for them—out there. So they'll notice us."

"The people?"

"Yeah. They look really weird. They stand on us, sort of. They have hooks in our world. But they're tall . . . high dup. They don't notice us because we're so small, compared with them."

"Lord, Pal, I haven't the slightest idea how we'd send music out to them. . . . I'm not even sure I believe they exist."

"I'm not lying," Pal said, eyes narrowing. He turned his chair to face a "mouse" perched on a black ruled pad and used it to sketch shapes on the monitor. "Remember, these are just shadows of what they look like. Next I'll draw the dup and owwen lines to connect the shadows."

The boy shaded the shapes to make them look solid, smiling at his trick but explaining it was necessary because the projection of a four-dimensional object in normal space was, of course, three dimensional.

"They look like you take the plants in a garden and give them lots of arms and fingers . . . and it's kind of like seeing things in an aquarium," Pal explained.

After a time, Tuthy suspended his disbelief and stared in open-mouthed wonder at what the boy was re-creating on the monitor.

"I think you're wasting your time, that's what I think," Hockrum said. "I needed that feasibility judgment by today." He paced around the living room before falling as heavily as his light frame permitted into a chair.

"I *have* been distracted," Tuthy admitted.

"By that boy?"

"Yes, actually. Quite a talented fellow."

"Listen, this is going to mean a lot of trouble for me. I

guaranteed the judgment would be made by today. It'll make me look bad." Hockrum screwed up his face in frustration. "What in hell are you doing with that boy?"

"Teaching him, actually. Or rather, he's teaching me. Right now, we're building a four-dimensional cone, part of a speaker system. The cone is three dimensional—the material part—but the magnetic field forms a fourth-dimensional extension."

"Do you ever think how it looks, Peter?"

"It looks very strange on the monitor, I grant you—"

"I'm talking about you and the boy."

Tuthy's bright, interested expression fell slowly into long, deep-lined dismay. "I don't know what you mean."

"I know a lot about you, Peter. Where you come from, why you had to leave. . . . It just doesn't look good."

Tuthy's face flushed crimson.

"Keep him away," Hockrum advised.

Tuthy stood. "I want you out of this house," he said quietly. "Our relationship is at an end."

"I swear," Hockrum said, his voice low and calm, staring up at Tuthy from under his brows, "I'll tell the boy's parents. Do you think they'd want their kid hanging around an old—pardon the expression—queer? I'll tell them if you don't get the feasibility judgment made. I think you can do it by the end of this week—two days. Don't you?"

"No. I don't think so," Tuthy said softly. "Leave."

"I know you're here illegally. There's no record of you entering the country. With the problems you had in England, you're certainly not a desirable alien. I'll pass word to the INS. You'll be deported."

"There isn't time to do the work," Tuthy said.

"Make time. Instead of 'educating' that kid."

"Get out of here."

"Two days, Peter."

Over dinner, Tuthy explained to Lauren the exchange he had had with Hockrum. "He thinks I'm buggering Pal. Unspeakable bastard. I will never work for him again."

"I'd better talk to a lawyer, then," Lauren said. "You're sure you can't make him . . . happy, stop all this trouble?"

"I could solve his little problem for him in just a few hours. But I don't want to see him or speak to him again."

"He'll take your equipment away."

Tuthy blinked and waved one hand through the air helplessly. "Then we'll just have to work fast, won't we? Ah, Lauren, you were a fool to bring me over here. You should have left me to rot."

"They ignored everything you did for them," Lauren said bitterly. She stared through the kitchen window at the overcast sky and woods outside. "You saved their hides during the war, and then . . . they would have shut you up in prison."

The cone lay on the table near the window, bathed in morning sun, connected to both the minicomputer and the Tronclavier. Pal arranged the score he had composed on a music stand before the synthesizer. "It's like a Bach canon," he said, "but it'll play better for them. It has a kind of counterpoint or over-rhythm that I'll play on the dup part of the speaker."

"Why are we doing this, Pal?" Tuthy asked as the boy sat down to the keyboard.

"You don't belong here, really, do you, Peter?" Pal asked. Tuthy stared at him.

"I mean, Miss Davies and you get along okay—but do you belong *here*, now?"

"What makes you think I don't belong?"

"I read some books in the school library. About the war and everything. I looked up *Enigma* and *Ultra*. I found a fellow named Peter Thornton. His picture looked like you but younger. The books made him seem like a hero."

Tuthy smiled wanly.

"But there was this note in one book. You disappeared in 1965. You were being prosecuted for something. They didn't even mention what it was you were being prosecuted for."

"I'm a homosexual," Tuthy said quietly.

"Oh. So what?"

"Lauren and I met in England, in 1964. They were going to put me in prison, Pal. We liked—love each other, so she smuggled me into the U.S. through Canada."

"But you're a homosexual. They don't like women."

"Not at all true, Pal. Lauren and I like each other very much. We could talk. She told me her dreams of being a writer, and I talked to her about mathematics and about the war. I nearly died during the war."

"Why? Were you wounded?"

"No. I worked too hard. I burned myself out and had a nervous breakdown. My lover . . . a man . . . kept me alive throughout the Forties. Things were bad in England after the war. But he died in 1963. His parents came in to settle the estate, and when I contested the settlement in court, I was arrested." The lines on his face deepened, and he closed his eyes for a long moment. "I suppose I don't really belong here."

"I don't either. My folks don't care much. I don't have too many friends. I wasn't even born here, and I don't know anything about Korea."

"Play," Tuthy said, his face stony. "Let's see if they'll listen."

"Oh, they'll listen," Pal said. "It's like the way they talk to each other."

The boy ran his fingers over the keys on the Tronclavier. The cone, connected with the keyboard through the minicomputer, vibrated tinnily. For an hour, Pal paged back and forth through his composition, repeating passages and creating variations. Tuthy sat in a corner, chin in hand, listening to the mousy squeaks and squeals produced by the cone. *How much more difficult to interpret a four-dimensional sound*, he thought. *Not even visual clues.* Finally the boy stopped and wrung his hands, then stretched his arms. "They must have heard. We'll just have to wait and see." He switched the Tronclavier to automatic playback and pushed the chair away from the keyboard.

Pal stayed until dusk, then reluctantly went home. Tuthy

stood in the office until midnight, listening to the tinny sounds issuing from the speaker cone. There was nothing more he could do. He ambled down the hall to his bedroom, shoulders slumped.

All night long the Tronclavier played through its preprogrammed selection of Pal's compositions. Tuthy lay in bed in his room, two doors down from Lauren's room, watching a shaft of moonlight slide across the wall. *How far would a four-dimensional being have to travel to get here?*

How far have I come to get here?

Without realizing he was asleep, he dreamed, and in his dream a wavering image of Pal appeared, gesturing with both arms as if swimming, eyes wide. *I'm okay,* the boy said without moving his lips. *Don't worry about me. . . . I'm okay. I've been back to Korea to see what it's like. It's not bad, but I like it better here. . . .*

Tuthy awoke sweating. The moon had gone down, and the room was pitch-black. In the office, the hypercone continued its distant, mouse-squeak broadcast.

Pal returned early in the morning, whistling disjointed selections from Mozart's Fourth Violin Concerto. Lauren opened the front door for him, and he ran upstairs to join Tuthy. Tuthy sat before the monitor, replaying Pal's sketch of the four-dimensional beings.

"Do you see them now?" he asked the boy.

Pal nodded. "They're closer. They're interested. Maybe we should get things ready, you know—be prepared." He squinted. "Did you ever think what a four-dimensional footprint would look like?"

Tuthy considered this for a moment. "That would be most interesting," he said. "It would be solid."

On the first floor, Lauren screamed.

Pal and Tuthy almost tumbled over each other getting downstairs. Lauren stood in the living room with her arms crossed above her bosom, one hand clamped over her mouth. The first intrusion had taken out a section of the living-room floor and the east wall.

"Really clumsy," Pal said. "One of them must have bumped it."

"The music," Tuthy said.

"What in *hell* is going on?" Lauren queried, her voice starting as a screech and ending as a roar.

"You'd better turn the music off," Tuthy elaborated.

"Why?" Pal asked, face wreathed in an excited smile.

"Maybe they don't like it."

A bright, filmy blue blob rapidly expanded to a diameter of a yard beside Tuthy, wriggled, froze, then just as rapidly vanished.

"That was like an elbow," Pal explained. "One of its arms. I think it's trying to find out where the music is coming from. I'll go upstairs."

"Turn it off!" Tuthy demanded.

"I'll play something else." The boy ran up the stairs. From the kitchen came a hideous hollow crashing, then the sound of vacuum being filled—a reverse pop, ending in a hiss—followed by a low-frequency vibration that set their teeth on edge.

The vibration caused by a four-dimensional creature *scraping* across their three-dimensional "floor." Tuthy's hands shook with excitement.

"Peter!" Lauren bellowed, all dignity gone. She unwrapped her arms and held clenched fists out as if she were ready to exercise or start boxing.

"Pal's attracted visitors," Tuthy explained.

He turned toward the stairs. The first four steps and a section of floor spun and vanished. The rush of air nearly drew him down the hole.

After regaining his balance, he kneeled to feel the precisely cut, concave edge. Below was the dark basement.

"Pal!" Tuthy called out. "Turn it *off!*"

"I'm playing something new for them," Pal shouted back. "I think they like it."

The phone rang. Tuthy was closest to the extension at the bottom of the stairs and instinctively reached out to answer. Hockrum was on the other end, screaming.

"I can't talk now—" Tuthy said. Hockrum screamed again, loud enough for Lauren to hear. Tuthy abruptly hung up. "He's been fired, I gather," he said. "He seemed angry." He stalked back three paces and turned, then ran forward and leapt the gap to the first intact step. "Can't talk." He stumbled and scrambled up the stairs, stopping on the landing. "Jesus," he said, as if something had suddenly occurred to him.

"He'll call the government," Lauren warned.

Tuthy waved that off. "I know what's happening. They're knocking chunks out of three-space, into the fourth. The fourth dimension. Like Pal says: clumsy brutes. They could kill us!"

Sitting before the Tronclavier, Pal happily played a new melody. Tuthy approached and was abruptly blocked by a thick green column, as solid as rock and with a similar texture. It vibrated and described an arc in the air. A section of the ceiling a yard wide was kicked out of three-space. Tuthy's hair lifted in the rush of wind. The column shrunk to a broomstick, and hairs sprouted all over it, writhing like snakes.

Tuthy edged around the hairy broomstick and pulled the plug on the Tronclavier. A cage of zeppelin-shaped brown sausages encircled the computer, spun, elongated to reach the ceiling, the floor, and the top of the monitor's table, and then pipped down to tiny strings and was gone.

"They can't see too clearly here," Pal said, undisturbed that his concert was over. Lauren had climbed the outside stairs and stood behind Tuthy. "Gee, I'm sorry about the damage."

In one smooth, curling motion, the Tronclavier and cone and all the wiring associated with them were peeled away as if they had been stick-on labels hastily removed from a flat surface.

"Gee," Pal said, his face suddenly registering alarm.

Then it was the boy's turn. He was removed more slowly, with greater care. The last thing to vanish was his head, which hung suspended in the air for several seconds.

"I think they liked the music," he said with a grin.

Head, grin and all, dropped away in a direction impossible for Tuthy or Lauren to follow. The room sucked air through the open door, then quietly sighed back to normal.

Lauren stood her ground for several minutes, while Tuthy wandered through what was left of the office, passing his hand through mussed hair.

"Perhaps he'll be back," Tuthy said. "I don't even know . . ." But he didn't finish. *Could a three-dimensional boy survive in a four-dimensional void, or whatever lay dup—or owwen?*

Tuthy did not object when Lauren took it upon herself to call the boy's foster parents and the police. When the police arrived, he endured the questions and accusations stoically, face immobile, and told them as much as he knew. He was not believed; nobody knew quite what to believe. Photographs were taken.

It was only a matter of time, Lauren told him, until one or the other or both of them were arrested. "Then we'll make up a story," he said. "You'll tell them it was my fault."

"I will *not*," Lauren said. "But where *is* he?"

"I'm not positive," Tuthy said. "I think he's all right, however."

"How do you know?"

He told her about the dream.

"But that was before," she said.

"Perfectly allowable in the fourth dimension," he explained. He pointed vaguely up, then down, then shrugged.

On the last day, Tuthy spent the early morning hours bundled in an overcoat and bathrobe in the drafty office, playing his program again and again, trying to visualize *ana* and *kata*. He closed his eyes and squinted and twisted his head, intertwined his fingers and drew odd little graphs on the monitors, but it was no use. His brain was hard-wired.

Over breakfast, he reiterated to Lauren that she must put all the blame on him.

"Maybe it will all blow over," she said. "They have no case. No evidence . . . nothing."

All blow over, he mused, passing his hand over his head and grinning ironically. *How over,* *they'll never know.*

The doorbell rang. Tuthy went to answer it, and Lauren followed a few steps behind.

Putting it all together later, she decided that subsequent events happened in the following order:

Tuthy opened the door. Three men in gray suits, one with a briefcase, stood on the porch. "Mr. Peter Tuthy?" the tallest asked.

"Yes," Tuthy acknowledged.

A chunk of the doorframe and wall above the door vanished with a roar and a hissing pop. The three men looked up at the gap. Ignoring what was impossible, the tallest man returned his attention to Tuthy and continued, "Sir, it's our duty to take you into custody. We have information that you are in this country illegally."

"Oh?" Tuthy said.

Beside him, an irregular, filmy blue blob grew to a length of four feet and hung in the air, vibrating. The three men backed away. In the middle of the blob, Pal's head emerged, and below that, his extended arm and hand. Tuthy leaned forward to study this apparition. Pal's fingers waggled at him.

"It's fun here," Pal said. "They're friendly."

"I believe you," Tuthy said calmly.

"Mr. Tuthy," the tallest man valiantly persisted, though his voice was a squeak.

"Won't you come with me?" Pal asked.

Tuthy glanced back at Lauren. She gave him a small fraction of a nod, barely understanding what she was assenting to, and he took Pal's hand. "Tell them it was all my fault," he said again.

From his feet to his head, Peter Tuthy was peeled out of this world. Air rushed in. Half of the brass lamp to one side of the door disappeared. The INS men returned to their car with damp pants and embarrassed, deeply worried expressions, and without any further questions. They drove away, leaving Lauren to contemplate the quiet.

She did not sleep for three nights, and when she did sleep, Tuthy and Pal visited her and put the question to her.

Thank you, but I prefer it here, she replied.

It's a lot of fun, the boy insisted. *They like music.*

Lauren shook her head on the pillow and awoke. Not very far away, there was a whistling, tinny kind of sound, followed by a deep vibration. To her, it sounded like applause.

She took a deep breath and got out of bed to retrieve her notebook.

SURVIVING

Judith Moffett

Judith Moffett is a professor of English at the University of Pennsylvania. She has published two books of poetry, one volume of criticism, and another volume of translations from the Swedish, for which she was honored with an award from the Swedish Academy. She has also taught at the Iowa Writers' Workshop and at the Bread Loaf Writers' Conference. Her short fiction and poetry have appeared in *Shenandoah*, *Kenyon Review*, and *The Magazine of Fantasy & Science Fiction*. *Pennterra*, her eagerly awaited first novel, has recently been published by Congdon & Weed.

"Surviving" is her first published SF story, about which she writes:

"There were probably two main drives behind this story, both of which had been reactivated by work on a long poem about Tarzan, Mowgli, 'real' feral children, Bigfoot, Darwin, fundamentalism, experiments in teaching language to the great apes, and other related themes, that I'd finished not long before beginning to plan 'Surviving.'

"First, I knew that none of the wild children of (dubious) record had ever been more than marginally integrated back into human society after they were recovered, and wondered what it would take—what factors would have to be present—in order for the socialization process to work. I also wondered how the reintegrated child would feel about it all afterwards.

"Second, I was brought up a Conservative Baptist and remain impressed by the power of the 'conversion experience' to turn a life around, thoroughly and permanently. But the missionary (political worker, dedicated friend, whatever) that prevails upon others to change their lives—while often working from the highest of conscious motives—is in an extremely tricky position, morally speaking. For such people, 'Surviving' might be viewed as a cautionary tale.

"Everything else is pure wish-fulfillment. If there were such

a person as Sally, I can imagine Janet's feelings with no effort at all."

For nearly eighteen years I've been keeping a secret to honor the memory of someone, now pretty certainly dead, who didn't want it told. Yet over those years I've come gradually to feel uncomfortable with the idea of dying without recording what I know—to believe that science would be pointlessly cheated thereby, and Sally, too; and just lately, but with a growing urgency, I've also felt the need to write an account of my own actions into the record.

Yet it's difficult to begin. The events I intend to set down have never, since they happened, been out of my mind for a day; nevertheless the prospect of reexperiencing them is painful and my silence the harder to break on that account.

I'll start, I guess, with the afternoon an exuberant colleague I scarcely knew at the time spotted me through the glass door and barged into the psychology department office calling, "Hey, Jan, you're the expert on the Chimp Child—wait'll you hear this, you're not gonna believe it!"

People were always dashing to inform me of some item, mostly inconsequential, relating to this subject. I glanced across at John from the wall of mailboxes, hands full of memos and late papers, one eyebrow probably raised. "What now?"

"We've *hired* her!" And when I continued to look blank: "No kidding, I was just at a curriculum committee meeting in the dean's office, and Raymond Lickorish in Biology was there, and he told me: they've definitely given Sally Barnes a tenure-track appointment, to replace that old guy who's retiring this year, what's his name, Ferrin. The virus man. Raymond says Barnes's Ph.D. research was something on viruses and the origin of life on earth and her published work is all first-rate and she did well in the interview—he wasn't there so he didn't meet her, but they were all talking about it afterward—and she seems eager to leave England. So the department made her an offer and she accepted! She'll be here in September, I swear to God!''

By this point I'm sure I was showing all the incredulous excitement and delight a bearer of happy tidings could possibly have wished. And no wonder: I wrote my *dissertation* on Sally Barnes; I went into psychology chiefly because of the intense interest her story held for me. In fact the Chimp Child had been a kind of obsession of mine—part hobby, part mania—for a long time. I was a college freshman, my years of Tarzan games in the woods less far behind me than you might suppose, in 1990, when poachers hauled the screeching, scratching, biting, terrified white girl into a Tanzanian village and told its head man they would be back to collect the reward. Electrified, I followed the breaking story from day to day.

The girl was quickly and positively identified as Sally, the younger daughter of Martin and Hilary Barnes, Anglican missionary teachers at a secondary school in the small central African republic of Malawi, who had been killed when the lightplane in which they and she were traveling from Kigoma had crashed in the jungle. A helicopter rescue crew found only the pilot's body in the burned-out fuselage. Scavengers may have dragged the others away and scattered the bones; improbable survivors of the crash may have tried to walk out—the plane had come down in the mountains, something less than 150 kilometers east of Lake Tanganyika—and starved, or been killed by anything from leopards to thieves to fever. However it was, nothing had been heard or seen of the Barnes family after that day in 1981; it was assumed that one way or another all three had died in the bush.

No close living relatives remained in England. An older daughter, left at home that weekend with an attack of malaria, had been sent to an Anglican school for the children of missionaries, somewhere in the Midlands. There was no one but the church to assume responsibility for her sister the wild girl, either.

The bureaucracies of two African nations and the Church of

England hummed, and after a day or two Sally was removed to the Malosa School in Southern Malawi, where the whole of her life before the accident had been lived. She could neither speak nor understand English, seemed stunned, and masturbated constantly. She showed no recognition of the school, its grounds or buildings, or the people there who had been friendly with her as a small child. But when they had cleaned her up, and cropped her matted hair, *they* recognized that child in *her;* pictures of Sally at her fourth birthday party, printed side by side in the papers with new ones of the undersized thirteen-year-old she had become, were conclusive. Hers was one of those faces that looks essentially the same at six and sixty.

But if the two faces obviously belonged to the same person, there was a harrowing difference.

A long time later Sally told me, gazing sadly at this likeness of herself: "Shock. It was nothing but shock, nothing more beastly. On top of everything else, getting captured must have uncovered my memories of the plane crash—violence; noise; confusion; my parents screaming, then not answering me—I mean, when the poachers started shooting and panicked everybody, and then killed the Old Man and flung that net over me, I fought and struggled, of course, but in the end I sort of went blank. Like the accident, but in reverse."

"Birth Trauma Number Three?" We were sitting cross-legged on the floor before the fireplace in my living room, naked under blankets, like Mohegan. I could imagine the scene vividly, had in fact imagined it over and over: the brown child blindly running, running, in the green world, the net spreading, dropping in slow motion, the child pitching with a crash into wet vegetation. Helplessness. Claustrophobia. Uttermost bowel-emptying terror. The hysterical shrieks, the rough handling . . . Sally patted my thigh, flushed from the fire's heat, then let her hand stay where it was.

"No point looking like that. What if they *hadn't* found me then? At University College, you know, they all think it was only just in time."

"And having read my book, you know I think so, too." We smiled; I must have pressed my palm flat to her hot, taut belly, or slipped my hand behind her knee or cupped her breast—some such automatic response. "The wonder is that after that double trauma they were able to get you back at all. You had to have been an awfully resilient, tough kid, as well as awfully bright. A survivor in every sense. Or you'd have died of shock and grief after the plane crashed, or of shock and grief when the poachers picked you up, or of grief and despair in England from all that testing and training, like spending your adolescence in a pressure cooker." I can remember nuzzling her shoulder, how my ear grazed the rough blanket. "You're a survivor, Sal."

In the firelight Sally smiled wanly. "Mm. Up to a point."

Any standard psych text published after 2003 will describe Sally Barnes as the only feral child in history to whom, before her final disappearance, full functional humanity had been restored. From the age of four and a half until just past her thirteenth birthday, Sally acted as a member of a troop of chimpanzees in the Tanzanian rain forest; from sixteen or seventeen onward, she was a young Englishwoman, a person. What sort of person? The books are vague on this point. Psychologists, naturally enough, were wild to know; Sally herself, who rather thought she did know, was wild to prevent them from turning her inside out all her life in the interest of Science. I was (and am) a psychologist and a partisan, but professional integrity is one thing and obsession is quite another, and if I choose finally to set the record straight it's not because I respect Sally's own choice any less.

From the very first, of course, I'd been madly infatuated with the *idea* of Sally, in whose imagined consciousness—that of a human girl accepted by wild creatures as one of themselves—I saw, I badly wished to see, myself. The extreme harshness of such a life as hers had been—with its parasites, cold rains, bullying of the weak by the strong, and so forth—got neatly edited out of this hyperromantic conception; yet the myth had amazing force. I don't know how many times I read the *Jungle Books* and the best of the Tarzan novels between the ages of eight and fifteen, while my mother hovered uneasily in the background, dropping hints about eye makeup and stylish clothes. Pah.

So that later, when a real apechild emerged from a real jungle and the Sunday supplements and popular scientific magazines were full of her story, for me it was an enthralling and fabulous thing, one that made it possible to finish growing up, at graduate school, *inside* the myth: a myth not dispelled but amplified, enhanced, by scientific scrutiny. The more one looked at what had happened to Sally, the more wonderful it seemed.

Her remarkable progress had been minutely documented, and I had read every document and published half a dozen of my own, including my dissertation. It was established that she had talked early and could even read fairly well before the accident, and that her early family history had been a happy, stable one; all we experts were agreed that these crucial factors explained how Sally, alone among feral children, had been able to develop, or reacquire normal language skills in later life. She was therefore fortunate in her precocity; fortunate, too, in her foster society of fellow primates. Almost certainly she could not have recovered, or recovered so completely, from eight years of life as a wolf or a gazelle. Unlike Helen Keller, she had never been sensually deprived; unlike Kaspar Hauser, also sensually deprived, she had not been isolated from social relations—wild chimpanzees provide one another with plenty of those; unlike the wolf girls of India, she had learned language before her period of abstention from the use of it. And like Helen Keller, Sally had a very considerable native intelligence to assist her.

It may seem odd that despite frequent trips to England, I had never tried to arrange a meeting with the subject of all this fascinated inquiry, but in some way my fixation made me shy, and I would end each visit by deciding that another year would do as well or better. That Sally might come to America, and to my own university, and to stay, was a wholly unlooked-for development. Now that chance had arranged it, however, shyness seemed absurd. Not only would we meet, we would become friends. Everyone would expect us to, and nothing seemed more natural.

My grandfather used to claim, with a forgiving chuckle, that his wedding night had been the biggest disappointment of his life. I thought bleakly of him the September evening of the annual cocktail party given by the dean of arts and sciences so that the standing faculty could make the acquaintance of their newly hired colleagues. A lot of people knew about Sally Barnes, of course, and among psychologists she was really famous, a prodigy; everybody wanted to meet her, and more than a few wanted to be there when *I* met her, to witness the encounter. I was exasperated with myself for being so nervous, as well as annoyed that the meeting would occur under circumstances so public, but when the moment arrived and I was actually being introduced to Sally—the dean had stationed himself beside her to handle the crush, and did the honors himself—these feelings all proved maddeningly beside the point.

There she stood, the Chimp Child of all my theories and fantasies: a small, utterly ordinary-seeming and -sounding young woman who touched my hand with purely mechanical courtesy. The plain black dress did less than nothing for her plain pale face and reddish hair; history's only rehabilitated feral child was a person you wouldn't look at twice in the street, or even once. That in itself meant nothing; but her expression, too, was indifferent and blank, and she spoke without any warmth at all, in an "educated" English voice pitched rather high: "How d'you do, a pleasure to meet you . . ." There she actually stood, saying her canned phrase to *me,* sipping from her clear plastic container of white wine, giving away nothing at all.

I stared at the pale, round, unfamiliar face whose shape and features I knew so well, unable to believe in it or let go of the hand that felt so hard in mine. The room had gradually grown deafening. Bright, curious eyes had gathered round us. The moment felt utterly weird and wrong. Dean Eccles, perhaps supposing his difficult charge had failed to catch my name, chirped helpfully, "Of course Janet is the author of that fascinating book about *you*," and beamed at Sally as if to say, *There* now, you lucky girl!

Only a flicker of eyelids betrayed her. "Oh, I see," she said, but her hand pulled out of mine with a little yank as she spoke, and she looked pointedly past me toward the next person in the receiving line—a snub so obvious that even the poor dean couldn't help but notice. Flustered, he started to introduce the elderly English professor Sally's attention had been transferred to.

We had hardly exchanged a dozen words. Suddenly I simply had to salvage something from the wreck of the occasion. "Look—could I call you in a week or two? Maybe we could get together for lunch or a drink or something after you're settled in?"

"Ah, I'm afraid I'll be rather busy for quite some time," said the cool voice, not exactly to me. "Possibly I might ring you if I happen to be free for an hour one afternoon." Then she was speaking to the old gentleman and I had been eased out of the circle of shoulders and that was that.

I went home thoroughly despondent and threw myself on the sofa. An hour or so later, the phone rang: John, who had witnessed the whole humiliating thing. "Listen, she acted that way with *everybody*, I watched her for an hour. Then I went through the line and she acted like that with *me*. She was probably jet-lagged or hates being on display—she was just pretending to drink that wine, by the way, sip, sip, sip, but the level never went down the whole time I was watching. You shouldn't take it personally, Jan. I doubt she had any idea who you were in that mob of freak-show tourists."

"Oh, she knew who I was, all right, but that doesn't make you wrong. O.K., thanks. I just wish the entire department hadn't been standing around with their tongues hanging out, waiting to see us fall weeping on each other's necks." Realizing I wasn't sure which I minded more, the rejection or its having been witnessed in that way, made me feel less tragic. I said good night to John, then went and pulled down the foldable attic stairs, put on the light, and scrounged among cartons till I found the scrapbook; this I brought downstairs and brooded over, soothed by a glass of rosé.

The scrapbook was fat. The Chimp Child had been an international sensation when first reclaimed from the wild, and for years thereafter picture essays and articles had regularly appeared where I could clip or copy them. I had collected dozens of photographs of Sally: arriving at Heathrow, a small, oddly garbed figure, face averted, clinging to a uniformed attendant; dressed like an English schoolgirl at fifteen, in blazer and tie, working at a table with the team of psychologists at University College, London; on holiday with the superb teacher Carol Cheswick, who had earned a place for herself in the educators' pantheon beside Jean-Marc Itard and Annie Sullivan by virtue of her brilliant achievements with Sally; greeting Jane Goodall, very old and frail, on one of Goodall's last visits to England; in her rooms at Newnham College, Cambridge, an average-looking undergraduate.

The Newnham pictures were not very good, or so I had always thought. Only now that I'd seen her in person . . . I turned back to the yellow newspaper clipping, nearly twenty years old, of a wild thing with matted, sawed-off hair; and now for the first time the blank face beneath struck me as queerly like this undergraduate's, and like the face I had just been trying to talk to at the party. The expressive adolescent's face brought into being sometime during the nineties—what had become of it? Who was Sally Barnes, after all? That precocious, verbally gifted little girl . . . I closed the cover, baffled. Whoever she was, she had long since passed the stage of being studied without her consent.

Yet I wanted so badly to know her. As fall wore on to winter, I would often see her on campus, walking briskly, buttoned up in her silver coat with a long black scarf wrapped round her, appearing to take no notice of whatever leaves or slush or plain brickwork happened to be underfoot, or of the milling, noisy students. She always carried reading equipment and a black shoulder bag. Invariably she would be alone. I doubt that I can convey more than a dim impression of the bewilderment and frustration with which the sight of her affected me throughout those slow, cold months. I knew every detail of the special education of Sally Barnes, the dedication of her teachers, her own eagerness to learn; and there had been *nothing,* nothing at all, to suggest that once "restored to human status," she would become ordinary—nothing to foreshadow this standoffish dullness. Of course it was understandable that she would not wish to be quizzed constantly about her life in the wild; rumor got round of several instances when somebody unintimidated by her manner had put some question to her and been served with a snappish "Sorry, I don't talk about that." But was it credible that the child whom this unique experience had befallen had been, as her every word and action now implied, a particularly unfriendly, unoriginal, bad-tempered child who thereafter had scuttled straight back to sour conventionality as fast as ever she could?

I simply did not believe it. She had to be deceiving us deliberately. But I couldn't imagine why, nor entirely trust my own intuition: I wanted far too badly to believe that *no* human being who had been a wild animal for a time, and then become human again, could possibly really be the sort of human Sally seemed to be.

And yet why not (I would argue with myself)? Why doubt that a person who had fought so hard for her humanity might desire, above all else, the life of an ordinary human?

But is it ordinary to be so antisocial (I would argue back)? Of course she never got in touch with me. A couple of weeks after the party, I nerved myself up enough to call her office and suggest meeting for lunch. The brusqueness of that refusal took some getting over; I let a month go by before trying again. "I'm sorry," she said. "But what was it you wanted to discuss? Perhaps we could take care of it over the phone."

"The idea wasn't to discuss anything, particularly. I only thought—new people sometimes find it hard to make their way here at first, it's not a very friendly university. And then, naturally I'd like to—well, just talk. Get acquainted. Get to know you a bit."

"Thanks, but I'm tremendously busy, and in any event there's very little I could say." And then, after a pause: "Someone's come to the door. Thanks for ringing."

It was no good, she would have nothing to do with me, beyond speaking when we met on campus—I could, and did, force her to take that much notice of me. Where was she living? I looked it up, an address in the suburbs, not awfully far from mine. Once I pedaled past the building, a shabby older high-rise, but there was no way of telling which of the hundreds of windows might be hers. I put John up to questioning his committee acquaintance in Biology, learning in this way: that Sally had cooly repulsed every social overture from people in her department, without exception; that student gossip styled her a Britishly reserved but better-than-competent lecturer; that she was hard at work in the lab on some project she never discussed with anybody. Not surprisingly, her fellow biologists had soon lost interest. She had speedily trained us all to leave her alone.

The psych department lost interest also, not without a certain tiresome belaboring of me, jokes about making silk purses out of chimps' ears and Ugly Chimplings and the like. John overheard a sample of this feeble mailbox badinage one day and retorted with some heat, "Hey, Janet only said she's *human* in that book. If education made you nice and personable, I know lots of people around here besides Sally Barnes who could stand to go back to school." But John, embroiled in a romance with a first-year graduate student, now found Sally a dull subject himself; besides, what he had said was true. My thesis had not been invalidated, nor Carol Cheswick and the team at King's College overrated. It was simply the case, in fact, that within six months of her arrival, Sally—billed in advance as an exotic ornament to the university—had compelled us all to take her for neither more nor less than the first-rate young microbiologist she had come among us to be.

My personal disappointment grew by degrees less bitter. But still I would see the silver coat and subduedly fashionable boots, all points and plastic, moving away across the quad and think: Lady, had it been given unto me to be the Chimp Child, by God I'd have made a better job of it than you do!

Spring came. Between the faculty club and the library, the campus forsythia erupted along its straggling branches, the azaleas flowered as usual a week earlier in the city than in my garden fifteen miles away. Ridley Creek, in the nearby state park, roared with rains and snowmelt and swarmed with stocked trout and bulky anglers; and cardinals and titmice, visible all winter at the feeders, abruptly began to sing. Every winter I used to lose interest in the park between the first of February and the middle of March; every spring rekindled my sense of the luck and privilege of having it so near. During the first weeks of trout season, the trails, never heavily used, were virtually deserted, and any sunny day my presence was not required in town I would stuff a sandwich, a pocket reader, and a blanket into a daypack and pedal to the park. Generally I stayed close to the trails, but would sometimes tough my way through some brambly thicket of blackberry or raspberry canes, bright with small new chartreuse-colored leaves, to find a private spot where I could take off my shirt in safety.

Searching for this sort of retreat in a tract of large beech trees one afternoon in April, I came carefully and painfully through a tangle of briars to be thunderstruck by the sight of young Professor Barnes where she seemed at once least and most likely to be: ten meters up in one of the old beeches. She was perfectly naked. She sat poised on a little branch, one shoulder set against the smooth gray bole of the bare tree, one foot dangling, the opposite knee cocked on the branch, the whole posture graced by a naturalness that smote me with envy in the surreal second or two before she caught sight of me. She was rubbing herself, and seemed to be crying.

One after another, like blows, these impressions whammed

home in the instant of my emerging. The next instant Sally's face contorted with rage, she screamed, snapped off and threw a piece of dead branch at me (and hit me, too, in the breastbone), and was down the tree and running almost faster than I could take in what had happened, what was still happening. While part of my brain noted with satisfaction, *She didn't hear me coming!* a different part galvanized my frenzied shouting: "No! Sally, for God's sake, stop! Stop! Come back here, I won't tell anybody, I won't, I swear! *Sally!*" Unable to move, to chase her, I could only go on yelling in this semihysterical vein; I felt that if she got away now, I would not be able to bear it. I'd have been heard all over that side of the park if there had been anybody to hear, outside the zone of noise created by the creek. It was the racket I was making, in fact, that made her come pelting back—that, and the afterthought that all her clothes were back there under the tree, and realizing I had recognized her.

"All right, I'm not going anywhere, now *shut up!*" she called in a low, furious voice, crashing through undergrowth. She stomped right up to me barefoot and looked me in the eye. "God damn it to hell. What will you take to keep your mouth shut?" Did she mean right now? But I *had* stopped shouting. My heart went right on lurching about like a tethered frog, though, and the next moment the view got brighter and began to drift off to the right. I sat down abruptly on something damp.

"I was scared witless you wouldn't come back. Wait a second, let me catch my breath."

"You're the one who wrote that book. Morgan," she said between her teeth. "God damn it to *hell.*" In a minute she sat down, too, first pushing aside the prickly stems unthinking. The neutral face that gave away nothing had vanished. Sally Barnes, angry and frightened, looked exactly as I had wished to see her look; incredibly, after so much fruitless fantasy, here we were in the woods together. Here she sat, scratching a bare breast with no more special regard than if it had been a nose or a shoulder. It was pretty overwhelming. I couldn't seem to pull myself together.

Sally's skin had turned much darker than mine already, all over—plainly this was not her first visit to the bare-branched woods. Her breasts were smallish, her three tufts of body hair reddish, and all her muscles large and smooth and well-molded as a gymnast's. I said what came into my head: "I was a fairly good tree-climber as a kid, but I could never have gotten up one with a trunk as thick as that, and those high, skinny branches. Do you think if I built my arms and shoulders up, lifted weights or something—I mean, would you teach me? Or maybe I'm too old," I said. "My legs aren't in such bad shape, I run a few kilometers three times a week, but the top half of my body is a flabby mess—"

"Don't play stupid games," Sally burst out furiously. "You had to come blundering in here today, you're the worst luck I ever had. I'm asking again: Will you take money not to tell anyone you saw me? Or is there something else you want? If I can get it, you can have it, only you've *got* to keep quiet about seeing me out here like this."

"That's a rotten way to talk to people!" I said, furious myself. "I was blundering around in these woods for years before you ever set foot in them. And I'm sorry if you don't like my book, or is it just me you don't like? Or just psychologists? If it weren't for you, I probably wouldn't even *be* one." My voice wobbled up and down. I'd been angry with Sally for seven months. "Don't worry, I won't say anything. You don't need to bribe me."

"Yes, but you will, you see. Sooner or later you'll be at some dinner party, and someone will ask what the Chimp Child is like, *really*"—I looked slantwise at her; this had already happened a couple of times—"and you won't be able to resist. 'There I was, walking along minding my own business, and whomever do you think I saw—stark naked and gone right up a tree like a monkey!' Christ," Sally said through her teeth, "I could *throttle* you. Everything's spoiled." She got up hastily; I could feel how badly she wanted to clobber me again.

But I was finally beginning to be able to think, and to call upon my expertise. "Well, then, make me *want* not to tell. Make it a question of self-interest. I don't want money, but I wasn't kidding: I'd absolutely love to be able to get around in a forest like a chimp does. Teach me to climb like one—like you do. If the story gets out, the deal's off. Couldn't you agree to that?"

Sally's look meant, "What kind of idiot do you take me for?" Quickly I said, "I know it sounds crazy, but all through my childhood—and most of my adolescence, too—for whatever wacky reason, I wanted in the *worst* way to be Tarzan! And for the past twenty years, I've gone on wanting even more to be *you!* I don't know why—it's irrational, one of those passions people develop for doing various weird things, being fans or collecting stamps or—I used to know a former world champion flycaster who'd actually gone fishing only a couple of times in his life!" I drew a deep breath, held it, let it out in a burst of words: "Look—even if I don't understand it, I *know* that directly behind *The Chimp Child and the Human Family*—and the whole rest of my career, for that matter—is this ten-year-old kid who'd give anything to be Tarzan swinging through the trees with the Great Apes. I can promise that so long as you were coaching me, you'd be safe. I'll never get a better chance to act out part of that fantasy, and it would be worth—just everything! One *hell* of a lot more than keeping people entertained at some dinner party, I'll tell you that!"

"You don't want to be me," said Sally in a flat voice. "I was right the first time; it's a stupid game you're playing at." She looked at me distastefully, but I could see that at any rate she believed me now.

The ground was awfully damp. I got up, starting to feel vastly better. Beech limbs webbed the sky; strong sunshine and birdsong poured through web; it was all I could do, suddenly, not to howl and dance among the trees. I could see she was going to say yes.

Sally set conditions, all of which I accepted promptly. I was not to ask snoopy professional questions, or do any nonessential talking. At school we were to go on as before, never revealing by so much as a look or gesture that an association existed between us. I was not to tell *anybody*. Sally could not, in fact, prevent my telling people, but I discovered that I hadn't any desire to tell. My close friends, none of whom lived within 150 kilometers of the city, could guess I was concealing a relationship but figured I would talk about it when I got ready; they tended to suppose a married man, reason enough for secrecy. Sally and I both taught our classes, and Sally had her work in the lab, and I my private patients.

Once in midweek and once each weekend, we met in the beech grove; and so the "lessons" got under way.

I acquired some light weights and began a program of exercise to strengthen my arms, shoulders, chest, and back, but the best way to build up the essential muscles was to climb a lot of trees. Before long the calluses at the base of each finger, which I had carried throughout my childhood, had been re-created (and I remembered then the hardness of Sally's palm when I'd shaken hands with her at the cocktail party in September). Seeing how steadily my agility and toughness increased, Sally was impressed and, in spite of herself, gratified. She was also nervous; she'd had no intention of letting herself enjoy this companionship that had been forced upon her.

It was a queer sort of blackmail. I went along patiently, working hard and trying to make my company too enjoyable to resist; and in this way the spring semester ended.

Sally was to teach summer school, I to prepare some articles for publication and continue to see my patients through the summer. By June all the trout had been hooked and the beech woods had grown risky; we found more inaccessible places on the riding-trail side of the park where I could be put through my training-exercise routines. By the Fourth of July my right biceps measured thirty-seven centimeters and Sally had finally begun to relax in my presence, even to trust me.

That we shortly became lovers should probably surprise nobody. All the reports describe the pre-accident Sally as an affectionate child, and her family as a loving one. From my reading I knew that in moments of anxiety or fear, chimps reassure one another by touching, and that in placid ones they reaffirm the social bond by reciprocal grooming. Yet for a decade, ever since Carol Cheswick died and she'd gone up to Cambridge, Sally had protected herself strictly against personal involvements, at the cost of denying herself all emotional and physical closeness. Cheswick, a plump, middle-aged, motherly person, had hugged and cuddled Sally throughout their years together, but after Cheswick's death—sick of the pokings and peerings of psychologists and of the curious public, resentful and guilty about the secret life she had felt compelled to create for herself—Sally had simply done without. Now she had me.

Except for the very beginning, in London, there had always been a secret life.

She abruptly started to talk about it late one horribly hot afternoon, at the end of a workout. We had dropped out of the best new training tree, a century-old white oak, then shaken out a ragged army blanket, sat on it cross-legged, and passed a plastic canteen and a bunch of seedless grapes between us. I felt sticky and spent, but elated. Sally looked me over critically. "You're filling out quite well, it's hard to believe these are the same scrawny shoulders." She kneaded the nearer shoulder with her hard hand, while I carefully concealed my intense awareness that except to correct an error, she had never touched me anywhere before. The hand slipped down, gripped my upper arm. When I "made a muscle" the backs of her brown fingers brushed my pale-tan breast; our eyes met, and I said lightly, "I owe it all to you, coach," but went warmer still with pleasure and the rightness of these gestures, which had the feeling of a course correction.

Sally plucked several grapes and popped them in her mouth, looking out over the creek valley while she chewed. After a bit she said, "They let me go all to pot in London. All anybody cared about was guiding me out of the wilderness of ignorance, grafting my life at thirteen back onto the stump of my life at four and

then making up for the lost years how they could. The lost years
. . . mind you, they had their hands full, they all worked like
navvies and so did I. But I'd got absolutely consumptive with
longing for the bush before they brought Carol in, and she noticed and made them let me out for a fortnight's holiday in the
countryside. I'd lost a lot of strength by then, but it was only just
a year so it came back quick enough."

She stopped there, and I didn't dare say anything; we ate
grapes and slapped mosquitoes. It was incredibly hot. After a bit,
desperate to hear more, I was weighing the risks of a response
when she went on without prodding:

"At University College, though, they didn't much care to
have me swinging about in trees. I think they felt, you know,
'Here *we* are, slaving away trying to drag the ape kid into the
modern world, and what does she do the minute our backs are
turned but go dashing madly back to her savage ways.' Sort of,
'Ungrateful little beast.' They *never* imagined I might miss that
benighted life, or anything about it, but when I read *Tarzan of
the Apes* myself a few years later, the part toward the end where
Tarzan strips off his suit and tie and shoes and leaps into the
branches swearing he'll never, never go back—I cried like anything."

I said, "What could you do about it, though?" breaking
Sally's no-questions rule without either of us noticing.

"Oh, on my own, not much. But Carol had a lot to say about
what I should and shouldn't do. They respected her tremendously. And she was marvelous. After I'd got so I could talk and
read pretty well, she'd take me to the South Downs on weekends
and turn me loose. We had a tacit agreement that if she didn't
ask, I needn't tell. We were so close, she certainly knew I was
getting stronger and my hands were toughening up, but *she*
never took the view that those years in the wild were best forgotten. She arranged for me to meet Jane Goodall once . . . I couldn't
have borne it without her. I never should have left England
while she lived. If it weren't for Carol—" For several minutes
Sally's hand had been moving of its own accord, short rhythmic

strokes that ceased abruptly when, becoming aware of this movement, she broke off her sentence and glanced—sharply, in alarm—at me.

I made a terrific effort to control my face and voice, a fisherman angling for the biggest trout in the pool. "She must have been remarkable."

For a wonder Sally didn't get up without a word and stalk away. Instead she said awkwardly, "I—do you mind very much my doing this? I've always done it—for comfort, I suppose—ever since I was small, and it's a bit difficult to talk about all these things . . . without . . ."

From the first day of training, I had determined never to let Sally force a contrast between us; I would adapt to her own sense of fitness out here. If she climbed naked, so would I, tender skin or not. If she urinated openly, and standing, so would I—and without a doubt there was something agreeable about spraddling beside Sally while our waters flowed. A civilized woman can still pass the whole length of her life without ever seeing another woman's urine, or genitalia, or having extended, repeated, and matter-of-fact exposure to another woman's naked body—and yet how many *men*, I had asked myself, ever gave these homely matters a second thought?

Then why on earth should we?

Certainly no woman had ever before done in my presence what Sally had been doing. Mentally, I squared my shoulders. "Why should I mind? Look, I'll keep you company"—suiting action to words with a sense of leaping in desperation into unknown waters, graceless but absolutely determined—"O.K.?"

It was the very last thing Sally had looked for. For a second I was afraid she thought I was ridiculing her in some incomprehensible way; but she only watched, briefly, before saying, "O.K. For a psychologist you're not a bad sort. The first bloody thing they did at that mission school was make me stop doing this in front of people.

"So anyway. Carol knew I was longing for the wild life, and knew it was important, not trivial or wrong, so she gave it back to me as well as she could. But she couldn't give me back"—her voice cracked as she said this—"the chimpanzees. The people I knew. And I did miss them dreadfully—certain ones, and living in the troop—the thing is, I was a child among them, and in a lot of ways it was a lovely life for a child, out there. The wild chimps are so direct and excitable, their feelings change like lightning, they're perfectly uninhibited—they squabble like schoolkids with no master about. And the babies are so sweet! But it's all very—very, you know, physical; and I missed it. I thought I should die with missing it, before Carol came." The grapes were all gone. Sally chucked the stem into the brambles and lay back on the blanket, left arm bent across her eyes, right hand rocking softly.

"Part of my training in London was manners and morals: to control myself, play fair, treat people politely whether I liked them or not. I'd *enjoyed* throwing tantrums and swatting the little ones when they got in my road, and screaming when I was furious and throwing my arms around everybody in reach when I was excited or happy, and being hugged and patted—like this," patting her genitals to demonstrate the chimpanzees' way of reassuring one another, "when I was upset. Chimps have no super-ego. It's hard to have to form one at thirteen. By then, pure selfishness without guilt is hard to conquer. Oh, I had a lot of selfishness to put up with from the others—I was very low-ranking, of course, being small and female—but I never got seriously hurt. And a knockabout life makes you tough, and then I had the Old Man for a protector as well." Sally lifted her arm and looked beneath it, up at me. "For a kid, most of the time, it was a pretty exhilarating life, and I missed it. And I missed," she said, "getting fucked. They were not providing any of that at University College, London."

"What?" My thumb stopped moving. "Ah—were you old enough? I mean, were the males interested, even though you didn't go pink?" I began to rub again, perhaps faster.

"For the last year or thereabouts—I'm not quite sure how long. It must have been, I don't know, pheromones in the mucus, or something in my urine, but I know it was quite soon after my periods started that they'd get interested in me *between* periods, when I would have been fertile, even without the swelling. I knew all about it, naturally; I'd seen plenty of copulating right along, as far back as I could remember. A pink female is a very agitating social element, so I'd needed to watch closely, because one's got to get out of the way, except while they're actually going at it. That's when all the little ones try to make them stop—don't ask me why," she added quickly, then grinned. "Sorry. That's one thing every primatologist has wanted to know." Sally's movements were freer now; watching, I was abruptly pierced by a pang of oddity, which I clamped down on as best I could. This was definitely not the moment for turning squeamish.

"It frightened me badly that first time; adult male chimps who want something don't muck about. When they work themselves up, you know, they're quite dangerous. I usually avoided them, except for the Old Man, who'd sort of adopted me not long after the troop took me in . . . any road the first time hurt, and then of course everybody always wants a piece of the action, and it went on for *days.* By the time it was over, I'd got terribly sore. But later . . . well, after I'd recovered from that first bout, I found it didn't really hurt anymore. In fact, I liked it. Quite a lot, actually, once I saw I needn't be frightened. The big males are frightfully strong, the only time I could ever dare be so close to so many of them was then, when I came in season, and one or another of them would sort of summon me over to him, and then they'd all queue up and press up behind me, one after another . . ."

More relieved than she realized at having broken the long silence at last, Sally went on telling her story; and of course, the more vividly she pictured for me her role in this scene of plausible bizarreness, elaborating, adding details, the more inevitable was the outcome of our own unusual scene. All the same, when the crisis struck us, more or less simultaneously, it left me for the moment speechless and utterly nonplussed, and Sally seemed hardly less flustered than I.

But after that momentary shock, we each glanced sidelong

at each other's flushed, flummoxed face and burst into snorts of laughter; and we laughed together—breathlessly, raggedly, probably a little hysterically—for quite a while. And pretty soon it was all right. Everything was fine.

It was all right, but common sense cautioned that if Sally's defenses were too quickly breached, she would take fright. So many barriers had collapsed at once as to make me grateful for the several days that must elapse before the next coaching session. Still, when I passed her figure in its floppy navy smockdress and dark glasses on campus the following morning, I was struck as never before by the contrast between the public Sally and the powerful glowing creature nobody here had seen but me. A different person in her situation, I thought, would surely have exploited the public's natural curiosity: made movies, written books, gone on the lecture circuit, endorsed products and causes. Instead, to please her teachers, everything that had stubbornly remained Chimp Child in Sally as she learned and grew had had to be concealed, denied.

But because the required denial was a concealment and a lie, she had paid an exorbitant price for it; too much of what was vital in her had living roots in those eight years of wildness. Sally was genuinely fond of and grateful to the zealous psychologists who had given back her humanity. At the same time she resented them quite as bitterly as she resented a public interested only in the racier parts of her life in the wild and in her humanity not at all. One group starved her, the other shamed her. Resentments and gratitudes had split her life between them. She would never consent to display herself *as* the Chimp Child on any sort of platform, yet without the secret life she would have shriveled to a husk. When I surprised her in the park, she had naturally feared and hated me. Not any more.

Success despite such odds made me ambitious. I conceived a plan. Somehow I would find a way—become a way!—to integrate the halves of Sally's divided self; one day she would walk across this quad, no longer alone, wearing her aspect of the woods (though clothed and cleaner). I'd worked clinically with self-despising homosexuals, and with the children of divorced and poisonously hostile parents; Sally's case, though unique in one way, was common enough in others. Charged with purpose, I watched as the brisk, dark shape entered a distant building and swore a sacred oath to the Principle of Human Potential: I would finish the job, I would dedicate myself to the saving of Sally Barnes. Who but I could save her now? At that fierce moment I knew exactly how Itard had felt when finally, for the first time, he had succeeded in reducing Victor to the fundamental humanity of tears.

Saturday looked threatening, but I set off anyway for the park. The mid-afternoon heat was oppressive; I cut my muscle-loosening jog to a kilometer or two, then quartered through the woods to the training oak. Early as I was, Sally had come before me. I couldn't see her, high in the now dense foliage, but her clothing was piled in the usual place and I guessed she had made a day-nest at the top of that tree or one nearby, or was traveling about up there somewhere. After a long drink from the canteen I peeled off my own sweaty shorts, toweling shirt, shoes, and the running bra of heavy spandex, smeared myself with insect repellent, and dried my hands on my shirt. Then I crouched slightly, caught a heavy limb well over two meters above the ground and pulled myself into the tree.

For ten minutes I ran through a set of upper-body warmups with care and concentration; I'd pulled one muscle in my shoulder four times and once another in my back, before finding an old book on gymnastics explaining how to prevent (and treat) such injuries. The first few weeks I had worn lightweight Keds, and been otherwise generally scraped and skinned. But now my skin had toughened—I hadn't known it would do that—and greater strength made it easier to forgo the clambering friction of calves and forearms; now, for the most part, my hands and feet were all that came in contact with the bark. A haircut had nicely solved the problems of snarling twigs and obscured vision.

Warm and loose, I quickly climbed ten meters higher and

began another series of strengthening and balancing exercises, swinging back and forth, hand over hand, along several slender horizontal limbs, standing and walking over a heavier one, keeping myself relaxed.

After half an hour of this, I descended to the massive lowest limb and practiced dropping to the ground, absorbing the shock elastically with both hands and both feet, chimp-style. Again and again I sprang into the tree, poised, and landed on the ground. I was doing quite well, but on about the fifteenth drop I bruised my hand on a rock beneath the leaf mold and decided to call it an afternoon; my hair was plastered flat with sweat, and I was as drenched as if I'd just stepped out of a shower. I had a long, tepid drink and was swabbing myself down with my shirt when Sally left the tree by the same limb, landed with a negligent, perfect pounce, came forward and—without meeting my eye—relieved me of the canteen, at the same time laying her free arm briefly across my shoulders. "That one's looking pretty good," she said, nodding at the branch to indicate my Dropping-to-the-Ground exercise. The arm slid off, she picked up the squirter of Tropikbug—"but did you ever see such monstrous mosquitoes in your life?"

"It's the humidity. I was afraid the storm would break before I could get through the drill. Maybe we better skip the rest and try to beat it home."

Sally squirted some repellent into her palm and wiped it up and down her limbs and over her brown abdomen. She squirted out some more. "Yours is all sweated off," she said, still not meeting my eye; and instantly Hugo Van Lawick's photographs of chimps soliciting grooming flashed into my mind, and I turned my shoulder toward Sally, who rubbed the bug stuff into it, then anointed the other shoulder, and my back and breasts and stomach for good measure, and then handed the flask dreamily to me, presenting her own back to be smeared with smelly goop. At that instant the first dramatic thunderclap banged above the park, making us both jump; and for a heart-stopping second Sally's outstretched arm clutched round me.

We bundled the blanket back into its plastic pouch and cached it, and pulled on clothes, while rain began to fall in torrents. My jogging shoes were clearly goners. I didn't bother to put on the bra, rolling it up on the run and sticking it inside my waistband. We floundered out of the trees in a furious commotion of wind and crackle-WHAM of lightning, and dashed in opposite directions for our parked cars. It took me fully fifteen minutes to reach mine, and twenty more to pedal home by roads several centimeters deep in rain, with the heater going full blast, and another half hour to take a hot shower and brew some tea. Then, wrapped in a bathrobe, I carried the tea tray and Jane Goodall's classic study *In the Shadow of Man* into the living room, and reread for the dozenth time the passages on the social importance of physical contact among wild chimpanzees.

Over and over, as I sat there, I relived the instant of Sally's instinctive quasi embrace in the storm, and each time it stopped my breath. What must Sally herself be feeling then? What terrifying conflict of needs? She must realize, just as I did, that a torrent had begun to build that would sweep her carefully constructed defenses away, that she could not stop it now, that she must flee or be changed by what would follow.

When I thought of *change*, it was as something about to happen to Sally, though change was moving just as inexorably down upon me. Three or four times in my life, I've experienced that sense of *courting* change, of choosing my life from moment to moment, the awareness of process and passage that exalted me that evening but never before or since with such intensity. I alone had brought us to this, slowly, over months of time, as the delicate canoe is portaged and paddled to where the white water begins. Day by day we had picked up speed; now the stream was hurtling us forward together; now, with all our skill and nerve and strength, we would ride the current—we would shoot through. There is a word for this vivid awareness: existential.

If I feared then, it was that Sally might hurl herself out of the canoe.

The next day but one was not a regular coaching day, but the pitch of nervous excitement made desk work impossible. I drove to the park in mid-afternoon to jog, and afterward decided, in preference to more disciplined routines, to practice my Traveling-from-Tree-to-Tree. My speed and style at this—that of a very elderly, very arthritic ape—was still not half bad (I thought) for a human female pushing forty, though proper brachiation still lay well beyond my powers. The run, as usual, had settled me down. The creek, still aboil with muddy runoff from the storm, was racketing along through a breezy, beautiful day. I chose an ash with a low fork, stuffed my clothes into my fanny pack, buckled it on, and started to climb.

I hadn't expected to find Sally at the training tree, but saw her without surprise—seated below me, cross-legged on the grubby blanket—when, an hour later, I had made my way that far. She stood up slowly while I descended the familiar pattern of limbs and dropped from the bottommost one. Again without surprise I saw that she looked awful, shaky and sick, that assurance had deserted her—and understood then that *whatever* happened now would not surprise me, that I was ready and would be equal to it. While I stood before Sally, breathing hard, unfastening the buckle, the world arranged itself into a patterned whole.

Then, as I let the pack fall, Sally crouched low on the blanket, whimpering and twisting with distress. I knelt at once and gathered her into my arms, holding her firmly, all of her skin close against all of mine. She clutched at me, pressed her face into my neck. Baffled moaning sounds and sobs came out of her. She moved inside this embrace; still moaning, eyes squeezed shut, her blind face searched until she had taken the nipple and end of my left breast into her mouth. As she sucked and mouthed at this, with her whole face pushed into the breast, her body gradually unknotted, relaxed, curled about mine, so I could loosen my hold to stroke her with the hand not supporting her head. Soon, to relieve the strain of the position, I pressed the fanny pack—I could just reach it—into service as a pillow and lay down on my side, still cradling Sally's head.

Time passed, or stopped. The nipple began to be sore.

At last, seemingly drained, she rolled away onto her back. Her face was smeared with mucus and tears; I worked my shirt out of the pack one-handed and dried it. At once she rolled back again, pushing herself against me with a long, groaning sigh. "The past couple of nights, God, I've had all sorts of dreams. Not bad dreams, not exactly, but—there was this old female in the troop, maybe her baby died, it must have done . . . I'd completely forgotten this. This must have been when they first found me. *She* found me, I think . . . I think I'd been alone in the forest without food long enough to be utterly petrified and apathetic with terror. But when she found me . . . I remember she held me against her chest and shoved the nipple in—maybe just to relieve her discomfort, or to replace her own child with a substitute, who knows. I think I would certainly have died except for that milk, there was such all-encompassing fear and misery. I don't know how many weeks or months she let me nurse. She couldn't have lived very long, though."

Sally weighed my breast in her hand. "Last night I dreamed I was in some terrible place, so frightened I couldn't move or open my eyes, and somebody . . . picked me up and held me, and then I was suckling milk from a sort of teat, and felt, oh, ever so much better, a great flood of relief. Then I opened my eyes and saw we were in the bush—I recognized the actual place—but it was *you,* the person holding me was you! You had a flat chest with big rubbery chimpanzee nipples"—lifting the tender breast on her palm—"and a sort of chimp face, but you were only skin all over, and I realized it was you."

I put my hand firmly over hers, moved it down along her forearm. "How did you feel when you knew it was me?"

"Uncomfortable. Confused. Angry." Then reluctantly: "Happy, too. I woke up, though, and then mostly felt just astonished to remember that that old wet nurse had saved my life and I'd not given her a single thought for twenty-five years." She lay quiet under my caressing: neck, breasts, stomach, flank; her eyes closed again. "What's queer is that I should remember *now,* but not when Carol first took charge of me, and not when I first read *Tarzan*, even though the Tarzan story's nearly the same as mine. I don't understand why now and not then."

"Do you feel you need to? I mean, does it seem important to understand?"

"I don't know." She sounded exhausted. "I certainly don't feel like even trying to sort it all out now."

"Well. It'll probably sort itself out soon enough, provided you don't start avoiding whatever makes these disturbing memories come back."

Sally opened her eyes and smiled thinly. "Start avoiding you, you mean. No. I shan't, never fear." She snuggled closer, widening and tilting herself; in my "therapist" frame of mind, I tried to resist this, but my hand—stroking on automatic for so long—slid downward at once on its own, and I ceased at the same instant to ignore a response I'd been blocking without realizing it for a good long while. I was still lying on my side, facing Sally; my top knee shifted without permission, and seconds later another afternoon had culminated in a POW that made my ears ring.

I was destined to know very well indeed the complicated space between Sally's muscular thighs, far better than I would ever know the complicated space inside her head, but that first swift unforeseen climax had a power I still recall with astonishment. My sex life, though quite varied, had all been passed in the company of men. I'd never objected to homosexuality in any of its forms, on principle and by professional conviction, but before that day no occasion of proving this personally had happened to occur. As for Sally, her isolation had allowed for no sex life at all with humans male *or* female; and though the things we did together meant, if possible, even more to her than they did to me, she didn't really view them in a sexual light. To Sally's way of thinking, *sex* was a thing that happened more or less constantly during several days each month, and had to do with dark, shaggy, undeniable maleness forcing itself upon you—with brief, rough gusto—from behind. She continued to miss this fear-laced excitement just as before. Our physical involvement, which was regularly reinforced, and which often ended as it had that afternoon, was a source of immeasurable pleasure and solace to her, but she viewed it as the natural end of a process that had more to do with social grooming than with sex.

But for me it was a revelation, and late in August, when the coarse, caterpillar-chewed foliage hung dispiritedly day after day in the torpid air, I went away for a week to remind myself of what ordinary sex was like with an ordinary man. Afterward I returned to Sally having arrived at a more accurate view of the contrast: not as pudendum versus penis, but as the mythic versus the mundane. Sleeping with my comfy old flame had been enjoyable as ever, but he was no wild thing living a split life and sharing the secret half with me alone.

"Are you in love with somebody?" Bill asked me on our last evening together. "Is that what's up with you? It's got to have something to do with your being in this incredible physical shape—wait! don't tell me! you've conceived a fatal passion for a jock!" I laughed and promised to let him in on the secret when I could, and though his eyes were sharp with curiosity, he didn't press the point. And for that, when the time came, Bill was one of half a dozen friends I finally did tell about Sally.

But even then, after it could no longer matter materially, I was unable to answer his question. Was I in love with Sally, or she with me? No. Or yes. For more than a year, I worked hard to link her with the human community, she to school me for a role in a childhood fantasy of irresistible (and doubtless neurotic) appeal. Each of us was surely fated to love what the other symbolized; how could we help it? But I've wondered since whether I was ever able to see Sally as anything but the Chimp Child, first and last. For each of us, you see, there was only *one.* In such a case, how can individual be told from type, how can the love be personal? And when not personal, what does "love" mean, anyway?

Whatever it was or meant, it absorbed us, and I was as happy that summer as ever in my life. As the season waned and the fall semester began, my skills and plans both moved forward obedient to my will. After workouts we would spread the blanket on its plastic ground sheet and ourselves across the blanket, giving our senses up to luxuriant pleasure, while the yellow leaves tapped down about us all but inaudibly.

And afterward we'd talk. It was at this stage that bit by bit I was able to breach Sally's quarantine by turning the talk to our work: her research, my theoretical interests, gifted or maddening students, departmental politics, university policy. Even then, when I encountered Sally on campus, her indifference toward me as toward everyone appeared unchanged; and at first these topics annoyed and bored her. But bit by bit I could see her begin to take an interest in the personalities we worked among, form judgments about them, distinguish among her students. To my intense delight, colorful chimp personalities began to swim up from her memory, with anecdotes to illustrate them, and she spoke often of Carol Cheswick, and—less frequently—of the team of psychologists at University College.

Cambridge provided no material of this sort, for by the time the church fellowship had sent her up, Cheswick was dead and Sally left to devise ways of coping on her own with the nosy public while protecting her privacy and the purposes it served. Antisocial behavior had proved an effective means to that end at Cambridge, as it was to do subsequently at our own university. She had concentrated fiercely on her studies. In subjects that required an intuitive understanding of people—literature, history, the social sciences—her schoolwork had always been lackluster; in mathematics and hard science, she had excelled from the first. At Cambridge she read biology. Microbiology genuinely fascinated her; now, thus late in her career, Sally was discovering the pleasures of explaining an ongoing experiment to a listener only just able to follow. In fact, she was discovering gossip and shop talk.

By the time cold temperatures and bare trees had forced me to join a fitness center and Sally to work out alone in a thermal skinsuit and thin pigskin gloves and moccasins, she

was able to say: "I remember that old mother chimpanzee because she saved me out of a killing despair, and so did you. So
did you, Jan. That day you discovered me crying in the beech,
remember? I actually believed I was coping rather well then,
but the truth is I was dying. I might really have died, I
think—like a houseplant, slowly, of heat and dryness and de-
pleted soil." And to me as well, this seemed no more than the
simple truth.

That winter, one measure of our progress was that I could
sometimes coax Sally to my house. Had close friends of mine
been living nearby, or friendly neighbors or relatives, this could
not have been possible; as it was she would leave her pedalcar
several blocks away and walk to the house by varying routes, and
nearly always after dark. But once inside, with doors locked and
curtains drawn, we could be easy, eat and read, light a fire to sit
before, snuggle in bed together. In winter, outdoor sex was im-
practical and we could never feel entirely safe from observation
in the denuded woods, whose riding trails wound through and
through it. And Sally's obsessive concealment of the fact that
she had made a friend, and that her privacy could therefore be
trespassed upon, seemed to weaken very little despite the radical
changes she had passed through.

Truly, I found myself in no hurry to weaken it. I could not
expect, nor did I wish, to have Sally to myself forever. Indeed
my success would be measured by how much more fully she
could learn to function in society—develop other friendships
and activities and so on—eventually. It is true that I could not
quite picture this, though I went on working toward it in perfect
confidence that the day would come. Yet for the time being, like
a mother who watches her child grow tall with mingled pride
and sorrow, I kept our secret willingly and thought *eventually*
would be here soon enough.

As spring drew closer, Sally began sleeping badly and to be
troubled again by dreams. She grew oddly moody also. All
through the winter she had dressed and slipped out to her car in

the dark; now I would sometimes wake in the morning to find her still beside me. Several times her mutterings and thrashings disturbed me in the night, and then I would soothe and hold her till we both dozed off again. That a crisis was brewing looked certain, but though the dreams continued for weeks, she soon stopped telling me anything about them and said little else to reveal the nature of her distress. In fact, I believed I knew what the trouble was. The first dreams, those she had described, were all about Africa and England and seemed drenched in yearning for things unutterably dear, lost beyond recall. They seemed dreams of mourning—for her parents, her lost wild life in Tanzania, her teacher. Events of the past year, I thought, had rendered the old defenses useless. She could not escape this confrontation any longer.

I was very glad. Beyond the ordeal of grief lay every possibility for synthesizing the halves of her life into one coherent human whole. I believed that Cheswick's death in Sally's twenty-third year had threatened to touch off a mourning for all these losses at once, and that to avoid this she had metamorphosed into the Cambridge undergraduate of my scrapbook: intellectual, unsociable, dull. "You're a survivor," I had told her one night that winter, and she had replied, "Up to a point." Now it seemed she felt strong enough at last to do the grieving and survive *that*, and break through to a more complete sort of health and strength.

Either that, or the year's developments had weakened her ability to compensate, and she would now be swiftly destroyed by the forces held so long in check; but I thought not.

Weeks passed while Sally brooded and sulked; our partnership, so long a source of happy relief, had acquired ambiguities she found barely tolerable. Once she did avoid me for nine days despite her promise—only to turn up, in a state of feverish lust, for a session as unlike our lazy summertime trysts as possible. Afterward she was heavy and silent, then abruptly tearful. I bore with all this patiently enough, chiefly by trying to foresee what might happen next and what it might mean, and so was not much surprised when she said finally, "I've decided not to teach this summer after all. I want to go to England for a month or so, after I've got the experiment written up."

I nodded, thinking, *Here it is.* Huge green skunk cabbages were thick now in the low places on the floor of the April woods, and fly fisherfolk thick along and in the creek; once again we had the mild, bare, windy, hairy-looking forest to ourselves, and were perched together high in a white-topped sycamore hung with balls. "Sounds like a good plan, though I'll miss you. Where to, exactly, or have you decided yet?"

"Well—London for a start, and Cambridge, and here and there. I might just pop in on my sister, not that there's much point to *that.*" Sally's sister Helen had married the vicar of a large church in Liverpool and produced four children. "But about missing me. You like England, you're always telling me. Why not come along?"

"Really?" I hadn't foreseen everything, it seemed. "Of course I'll come, I'd love to. Or no, wait a minute"—squirming round on the smooth limb to watch her face—"have you thought this through? I mean, suppose the papers get wind of it? 'Chimp Child Returns to Foster Country.' Or even: 'Chimp Child, Friend, Visit England.' If we're traveling together, people are bound to *see* us together—sure you want to risk it?"

"Oh well, so what," said the Chimp Child, for all the world as if she hadn't been creeping up to my house under cover of night all winter long. "I want to talk to the blokes at the university, Snyder and Brill and a couple of others—get them to show me the files on *me.*" She swung free of the branch and dangled by one hand to hug me with the opposite arm. "Sorry I've been such a bore lately. There's something I'm suddenly madly curious about, I've had the most appalling dreams, night after night, for weeks." She swung higher in the tree, climbing swiftly by her powerful arms alone, flashing across gaps as she worked her way to the high outermost branches and leapt outward and downward into another tree with the action I loved to see. "Right," she called back across the gulf between us, "get to work then, you lazy swine. We'll put on a show for Helen's kids that'll stop traffic all over the ruddy parish."

And so we flew to England; and now my part of the story is nearly finished.

Sally did not quite feel ready to come out, as it were, to the extent of going anywhere in my company at school, though she'd smile now with some naturalness when our paths would cross there, and even exchange a few words in passing. We arrived separately at the airport. But from that point on, we were indeed "traveling together," and she never tried to make it seem otherwise.

She had wanted a couple of days in Cambridge before tackling the records of her unique education, as if to work backward in time by bearable degrees, and so it was together that we climbed the wide stairs on a Tuesday afternoon early in June to look into her first-year room in Newnham College. Unfortunately the present occupant knew the Chimp Child had once been quartered in her room and recognized Sally immediately; she must have felt perplexed and dismayed at the grimness of the famous pilgrim, who glared round without comment, refused a cup of tea, and stalked away leaving me to render thanks/apologies on behalf of us both. I caught Sally on the stairs. Nothing was said till we had proceeded the length of two green courts bordered with flower beds and come out into the road. Then: "God, I was wretched here!" she burst out. "I went through the whole three years in a—in a chromatic daze, half unconscious except in the lab, and going through that door again—it was as if all the color and warmth began to drain out of a hole in the floor of the day, and I could only stand helplessly watching. The very *smell* of the place means nothing but death to me. What bloody, bloody waste."

And "What a waste," more thoughtfully the next morning, as we walked back to the station from our bed-and-breakfast across the river and the common with its grazing Friesians and through the Botanical Gardens. "One sees why other people could manage to be so jolly and smug here, while I'd go skulking down to Grantchester at five in the morning to work out in the only wood for miles, terrified every day I should be caught out, and skulking back to breakfast every day relieved, like an exhibitionist who thinks, 'Well, there's one more time I got away with it.' " A few minutes later she added, "Of course it got much better when I was working on my thesis . . . only those years don't seem real at *all* when I try to remember them. All I can remember is the lab, I expect that's why."

"Why it got better, or why it's unreal?"

"Both, very likely."

She was pensive on the train. I fell asleep and woke as we were pulling into Liverpool Street, feeling tired and headachy, the beginnings of the flu that put me to bed for a crucial week when I might otherwise have done something, just by staying well, to affect the course of events. By late afternoon of that Wednesday, I felt too miserable to be embarrassed at imposing myself on Dr. Snyder's wife and filling their tiny guest room with my awkward germiness. For four or five days, I had a dry, wheezy cough and a fever so high that Mrs. Snyder was beginning to talk rather worriedly of doctors; then the fever broke and my head, though the size of a basketball, no longer burned, and I rallied enough to take in that Sally was gone.

She had spent the early days of my illness at University College, reading, asking occasional questions, searching—as it seemed—for something she couldn't describe but expected to recognize when she found it. Late on the fourth day, the day my temperature was highest, she came in and sat on the bed. "Listen, Jan. I'm off to Africa tomorrow."

I swam wearily to the surface. "Africa? But . . . don't you have to get, uh, inoculations or something? Visas?" I didn't wonder, within the remoteness of my fever, why she was going. Nor did I much care that evidently she would be going without me.

"Only cholera and yellow fever, and I've had them. Before we left, just in case; and yesterday afternoon I bagged the last seat on a tourist charter to Dar es Salaam. The flight returns in a fortnight, by which time you should be fit again, and we can go on up north then or wherever you like." When I didn't reply, she added, unnecessarily, "I've got to visit the school, Malosa School, and sort of stare the forest in the face again. It's terribly important, though I can't say just why. Maybe when I've got back, when you're better. Only, I've made my mind up to take this chance while it's going, because I do feel I've absolutely got to go through with it, as quick as I can."

My eyes ached. I closed them, shutting out the floating silhouette of Sally's head and shoulders. "I know. I wish . . ."

"Never mind. It'll be all right. Sorry I didn't tell you before, but first I wanted to make sure." I felt her hand beneath my pajama jacket. "God, you're *hot,*" she said, surprised. "Perhaps I ought to leave it till you're a bit better."

Distantly amused at this display of superego, I said, "You know a fever's always highest at night, old virologist. Anyway, you can't do any good here. We'll have a doctor in soon if it doesn't go down." I made a truly tremendous effort. "It's probably a good idea, Sally, the trip. I hope you can find whatever it is you're looking for." Clumsily I patted the hand inside my pajamas. "But don't miss the plane coming back, I'll be dying to hear what happened."

"I shan't, I promise you," she said with relief; and when I woke the next morning, she had gone.

We know that Sally reached Dar es Salaam after an uneventful flight, spent the night in an airport hotel, flew Air Malawi to the Chileka airfield the next morning, and hired a driver to take her the 125 kilometers overland to Machinga and the Malosa Secondary School, where she was greeted with pleased astonishment by those of the staff who remembered her—everyone, of course, knew of her connection with the school. She stayed there nearly a week, questioning people about the details of her early childhood and of exactly what had happened when the church officials brought her in, in the weeks before she had been whisked to London. She spent hours prowling about the grounds and buildings, essentially the same as thirty years before despite some modest construction, and borrowed the school's Land-Rover several times to drive alone into the countryside of the Shire Highlands and the valley beyond. Her manner had been alternately brusque and preoccupied, and she had impressed them all as being under considerable strain.

The school staff confirmed that Sally had been driven back to Chileka by a couple, old friends of her parents, who at her request had dropped her at the terminal without coming in to see her off. She had told them she intended to fly back to Dar that evening in order to catch her charter for London the next day, and that she hated a dragged-out good-bye; the couple had no way of knowing that her ticket had specified a two-week stay abroad. Inside the terminal she bought a round-trip ticket for Ujiji, in Tanzania.

From Ujiji a helicopter shuttle took her to Kogoma on Lake Tanganyika. Once there, Sally had made inquiries, then gone straight to the town's tiny branch of Bookers Ltd., a safari agency operating out of a closet-sized cubbyhole in the VW dealership. She told the Bookers agent—a grizzled old Indian—that she wanted to hire two men to help her locate the place where a plane had crashed in the mountains east of the lake, some thirty years before. She produced detailed directions and maps; and the agent, though openly doubtful whether the wreckage would not have rusted into the ground after so long, agreed for a stiff price to outfit and provision the trip. He assigned his cousin to guide her, and a native porter. Forty-eight hours later this small expedition set off into the mountains in the agency's battered four-wheel-drive safari van.

The cousin had parked the van beside the road of ruts that had brought them as far as roads could bring them toward the area marked on Sally's maps, much nearer than any road had approached it on the day of the crash, but still not near. They had then followed a footpath into the forest for several kilometers before beginning to slash a trail away from it to the westward, toward the site where the plane had gone down. Something like fifty kilometers of rain-forested mountainous terrain had to be negotiated on foot, a difficult, unpleasant, suffocating sort of passage. Sally must have been assailed by frustration at the clumsiness of their progress; the guide called her a bad-tempered bitch, probably for good reason. On the third morning her patience had evidently snapped. When the men woke up, Sally was not in camp. They waited, then shouted, then searched, but she never replied or reappeared. And I knew what they could not: that she must have slipped away and taken to the trees, flying toward a goal now less than fifteen kilometers distant.

I had gone out to meet Sally's plane, due into Gatwick on the same day the reporters got hold of the story of her disappearance. When she proved not to be aboard, and to have sent no word, all my uneasiness broke out like sweat, and back in the city I must have hurried past any number of "newsagents" before the *Guardian* headline snatched at my attention:WILD WOMAN MISSING IN JUNGLE, SEARCH CONTINUES. I bought a paper and stood shaking on the pavement to read: "Dodoma (Tanzania), Tuesday. Sally Barnes, the wild girl brought up by chimpanzees, has been missing in the mountains of Tanzania since Friday . . . two companions state . . . no trace of the Chimp Child . . . police notified and a search party . . ." and finally: "Searchers report sighting several groups of wild chimpanzees in the bush near the point of her disappearance."

All the rest is a matter of record. Day by day the newspapers repeated it: No trace, No trace, and at last, Presumed dead. The guide and porter were questioned but never tried for murder. In print and on the video news, it was noted that Dr. Barnes had vanished into the jungle only a few kilometers east of the spot where she had emerged from it twenty years earlier. Investigators quickly discovered that Sally and I had been together in Cambridge and London, and I, too, was forced to submit to questioning; I told them we had met on the plane and spent a few days as casual traveling companions, and that when I fell ill, her friends had kindly taken me in. I denied any closer connection between us, despite my having studied her case professionally—

mentioning that she was well known at the university for her solitary ways. Sally herself had said nothing in particular to the Snyders about us, and I had been too sick. No one was alive in all the world to contradict the essential factors of this story, and, as it appeared to lead nowhere, they soon let me alone. (Some years later, however, I told Dr. Snyder the whole truth.)

It developed that no one had any idea why Sally had gone to Tanzania, why she was looking for the site of the plane crash.

For me that fall was hellish. By the time I returned to the States, only a few days before the new semester was to get under way, Sally's apartment—the apartment I had never seen, though she had called me from it two or three times during the final weeks of spring—had been stripped of its contents by strangers and her effects shipped to the Liverpool sister. At school, people were overheard to suggest, only half jokingly, that Sally had rejoined the chimps and was living now in the jungle, wild again. Such things were freely voiced in my presence; indeed, the loss of Sally, so shocking, so complete, was the more difficult to accept because not a single person on my side of the Atlantic could have the least suspicion that I had lost her.

My acting, I believe, was flawless. Though I went dazedly about my work, nobody seemed to see anything amiss. But might-have-beens tormented me. Save for my interference, Sally would almost certainly still have been alive. Or (more excruciating by far), had she not met defeat in the jungle, her search would almost certainly have left her healed of trauma, able to fit the halves of her life together. I had nearly freed her; now she was dead, the labor come to nothing, the child stillborn. I did believe she was dead. Yet I felt as angry with her, at times, as if she had purposely abandoned and betrayed me, disdained the miracle of healing I had nearly brought off—as if she had really chosen to return to the wild. For now neither of us could ever, ever complete the crossing into those worlds each had been training the other to enter for the preceding year.

I did not see how I was going to survive the disappointment, nor could I imagine what could possibly occupy, or justify, the rest of my life. The interlude with Sally had spoiled me thoroughly for journeyman work. It would not be enough, any longer, to divide my time between educating healthy minds and counseling disturbed ones. Long before that bleak winter was out, I had begun to cast about fretfully for something else to do.

This document has been prepared in snatches, over many evenings, by kerosene lanternlight in my tent in the Matangawe River Nature Reserve overlooking Lake Malawi, 750 kilometers northwest across the immense lake from Sally's birthplace. The tent is set up inside a chimp-proof cage made of Cyclone fencing and corrugated iron. Outside, eleven chimpanzees of assorted ages and stages of reacclimatization to independent survival in the wild are sleeping (all but the newest arrival, who is crying to get in). A few of these chimps were captured as infants in the wild; the rest are former subjects of language and other learning experiments, ex-laboratory animals or animals who were reared in homes until they began to grow unmanageable.

This may seem an unlikely place in which to attempt the establishment of a free-living population of rehabilitant chimpanzees, for the ape has been extinct in Malawi for a couple of centuries at least, and the human population pressure is terrific, the highest in Africa. In fact, to "stare the forest in the face," Sally was forced to go on back to Tanzania, where there was (and still is) some riverine forest left standing. Yet private funding materialized, and I've been here since the reserve was created, nearly fifteen years. Despite some setbacks and failures—well, there were bound to be some!—the project is doing very well indeed. At this writing, thirty-four chimps have mastered the course of essential survival skills and moved off to establish breeding, thriving communities on their own in the reserve. For obvious reasons these societies fascinate the primatologists, who often come to study them. We've lost a few to disease and accidents, and two to poachers, but our success, considering the problems inherent to the enterprise, might even be called spectacular. We've been written up in *National Geographic* and the

Smithsonian, which in primate studies is how you know when you've arrived, and similar projects in several more suitable West African countries have been modeled on ours.

I started alone, with three adolescent chimpanzee "graduates in psychology" from my university who, having outgrown their usefulness along with their tractable childhoods, faced long, dull lives in zoos or immediate euthanasia. Now a staff of eight works with me: my husband, John (yes, the same John), and seven graduate students from my old department and from the Department of Biology, which used to be Sally's. She would be pleased with my progress in brachiation, though arthritis in my hands and shoulders has begun to moderate my treetop traveling with my charges. (That skill, incidentally, has given me a tactical edge over every other pioneer in the field of primate rehabilitation.)

To all the foregoing I will add only that I have found this work more satisfying than I can say. And that very often as I'm swinging along through lush forest in the company of four or five young chimps, "feeding" with them on new leaves and baobab flowers, showing them how to build a sturdy nest in the branches, I know a deep satisfaction that now, at last, there's no difference that matters between Sally and me.

THE GIRL WHO FELL INTO THE SKY

Kate Wilhelm

Kate Wilhelm has won both the Nebula and Hugo Awards. Her many novels include *Where Late the Sweet Birds Sang, Welcome, Chaos, Huysman's Pets, The Clewiston Test, Fault Lines, Margaret and I,* and *Juniper Time.* Some of her best short fictions are collected in *The Downstairs Room, The Infinity Box,* and *Listen, Listen.*

About her winning novelette she writes:

"We were driving from Cheyenne, Wyoming, to Louisville, Kentucky, in August, and every day the temperature soared to over a hundred. In the back of the big, ugly station wagon the two boys had teased and fought continuously until we were all as mean as rattlesnakes. We decided to drive at night and in the early morning hours to escape the heat. Accordingly, we turned off the highway that morning onto a state road in Kansas, to a state park where we would rest until late afternoon. The highway had been a canyon bounded by corn well over the top of our car, but suddenly we were in the grasslands, the Kansas prairie, with a small lake as warm as tea, and undulating grass in all directions.

"The boys—one not yet three, the other a few months past seven—were too restless to rest. I took them for a walk around the shallow lake. Very soon the grass hid the station wagon, hid the world; it moved, although no wind stirred. And it whispered. Although I was always too far away to hear what it was saying, the whispers were all around. The grass had secrets it would not share. That was 1956. I never went back.

"Nearly thirty years later, on a train in air-conditioned comfort, I watched a storm play with the grass in Montana. Because the mind works in its own wondrous ways, the other scene came to mind, the grasslands in Kansas telling secrets all around me,

and this story was born. Where the sky is so much bigger than the land, if one falls, it must be up, I thought, mulling over the story. And the grass does have secrets. It really does, and it never forgets."

His father was a MacLaren, his mother a MacDaniel, and for forty years John had been the one thrust between them when they fought. Today they stood glaring at each other, through him, around him, his mother with her flashing green eyes and red hair that she now dyed (exactly the same color it always had been), his father with his massive face set in a scowl, thick white eyebrows drawn close together over his long nose.

"I'll take an axe to the wheels first!" she said in a low, mean voice.

"Since when do I let you tell me what I can or can't do?"

"Knock it off, both of you!" John MacLaren yelled. "For God's sake! It's a hundred and five! You'll both have heart attacks!"

"No one asked you to butt in, either," his father snapped, not shifting his glare from his wife.

She tilted her head higher and turned, marched from the room. "I asked him," she called back. "Johnny, you want a gin and tonic?"

"Please," he said quietly. "Dad, what the hell is it all about?"

The room was green and white, cool, with many growing plants, everything neat and well cared for. The entire house was like this, furnished in good pieces, each one an investment: Hepplewhite chests, Duncan Phyfe chairs, pieces over two hundred years old that had come from Scotland, or France, or England. David MacLaren was the collector; Mary accepted it, even encouraged it sometimes, but she would not walk across the street to add to the assortment that had accumulated over the forty-five years they had been married.

Now that the argument had been stopped by Mary's departure, David MacLaren smiled at his son, waved toward a wicker arrangement near a window and led the way to it. He seated himself with a soft grunt, then waited until John was seated opposite him.

"Made the mistake of telling her I plan to take a spin over to the Castleman house tomorrow, pick up that player piano and bring it home. You know, I told you about it, first one to cross the Mississippi, still in fine shape, I bet. Probably hasn't been opened in nearly thirty years, more than thirty years. It's a beauty. Cherry wood. Keys mahogany-colored and ivory, not black and white."

The words rang false to John's ears. "You mean over in Greeley County?"

"Yep."

"Dad, that's a three hundred mile drive, and it's going to be hotter tomorrow than today. It's going up to one ten before the afternoon's over."

He looked past his father, out the window at the lawn, kept green by nearly constant watering this summer. No breeze stirred; heat shimmies rose from the white concrete of the sidewalk; the leaves of the red Japanese maple drooped. And he knew where all this would lead, knew why his mother had called him at the office only half an hour ago. Of course, his father could not drive three hundred miles in this weather, could not have anything to do with moving a piano. He took a deep breath.

His mother returned with a tray, three tall sweating glasses, twists of lemon, sugar frosted rims. Her face was smooth, imperturbable as she looked at him; there was a glint of understanding in her eyes, a spark of determination that he knew quite well. She really would take the axe to the wheels if she had to. She was seventy-three, his father seventy-four.

He drank deeply. "You know you can't do that, Dad," he said then. "It'll keep. It's kept this long."

His father shook his head. "It's kept because Louis Castleman kept it. That nephew, Ross Cleveland, he'll drive in there hot as hell, take a look around, piss-poor land, isolated house, nothing there for him, and he'll head up to Goodland first thing, make a deal with Jennings and head for home again. And Jennings will put that piano in his café and let customers spill beer in it, lay cigarettes down on it."

"Dad, have you ever been over there for the past twenty-five years? How do you know it's there? And what difference can it possibly make? You don't need it. You don't have room for it. A player piano! What for?"

"It's there," his father muttered. "I saw it listed on the inventory. Just a matter of getting the nephew to let me take stuff out, accept my offer. Be worth his while, of course, but he might want a separate appraisal or something. The land's not worth a damn, but he might want to realize a little from the possessions." He looked at Mary, his eyebrows touching, and said, "And I want it because it's mine. Oh, I'll pay for it, but I intend to go over there first thing in the morning and collect the thing and bring it home as soon as Ross Cleveland shows up to inspect his inheritance."

John looked helplessly from his father to his mother. Neither of them would give an inch to the other, but they would let him propose a third alternative, the one his mother was waiting for, the one she had called him for. And his father would protest, curse a bit, maybe storm out briefly before agreeing to let John go collect the piano. For a moment he was tempted to finish his drink and leave, let them fight it out. A surge of envy came and went; he envied them their passion, their uncompromising fights, their uncompromising love. They played hard, fought hard, loved hard, and they had kept all their passion when characteristics were being handed out at his conception. He had her hair and eyes, his father's long thin nose and robust build. They had kept all the passion for themselves.

When he left his parents' house an hour later, the temperature had climbed to one hundred ten, and he was committed to driving three hundred plus miles to load an old piano into his father's truck and bring it home.

He and his father were partners in the law firm his father had started decades ago. He had called his secretary to warn her that he would be gone a few days possibly, that MacLaren Senior would handle anything that came up. There was no point now in going back to the office since it was four, a blistering afternoon, and he was driving his father's ten-year-old truck without air conditioning. He turned toward his house instead of downtown Wichita.

His house overlooked Three Oaks Golf Club; no one was on the greens that hot afternoon. The sprinklers worked day and night, it seemed, and still the grass had brown patches here and there. The groundskeepers kept moving the sprinklers in a futile attempt to cope with the heat wave and drought. John entered the house through the garage door and turned up the air conditioning on his way to the front door mail drop. No letter from Gina. He dumped the mail on the hall table and went to the kitchen to make himself a drink, and again a surge of envy swept him. His parents fought like alley brats and would kill anyone who tried to come between them. He and Gina never fought, never quarreled, never spoke sharply to each other, and she was spending the hot summer with her family in St. Louis. She did not write, did not call, and when he called, she was out somewhere. He spoke on those occasions with his son Tommy, or his daughter Amanda, but not with his wife who was always very, very busy.

Lorna Shields stood behind the heavy glass door of the Howard Johnson restaurant where she had just finished a strawberry soda and a glass of iced tea and two glasses of water. Beyond the door the heat rose crookedly from the pavement; the glare of light was painful. Ever rising heat; cruel light; and no sweat. It's not Ohio, kid, she told herself with some satisfaction. Not at all like Ohio. Oh, it got hot back there, too, but a thick, sticky, sweat-making heat, not like this inferno that sucked her dry as soon as she walked out into it. Her lips felt parched; her skin prickled; her hair had so much static electricity that when she had tried to comb it on entering the rest room earlier, it had sprung out like the hair of the bride of Frankenstein. She had laughed and another woman in the small space had eyed her warily.

Lorna was tall and lanky, boyish-looking with her short dark hair that curled back home in Ohio, but was quite straight here in Kansas. Her eyes were such a dark blue that many people thought they were black, and she tanned so deeply so easily that it always seemed that the first day of spring when the sun came out and stayed more than an hour, she got the kind of suntan that other people spent thousands of dollars on hot beaches trying to acquire. She was twenty-five.

If she kept driving, she was thinking, she could get there around ten and Elly and Ross wouldn't show up for at least a day, maybe two. Elly had said Friday night or Saturday. The thought of having a house to herself for a day or two, not having to ask questions, listen to answers, smile and be polite was overwhelmingly tempting. Back in February her instructor-advisor on her committee had taken her aside and encouraged her to apply for a grant to continue her master's project after graduation; he had even helped her with the forms, and had written an almost embarrassing letter of recommendation. To her astonishment, she was awarded the grant, to take effect in June, to run for nine months. All expenses and living money, even enough to buy her little, three-year-old Datsun. For the first time in her life she felt very rich. And with the grant the work she had been doing changed, became meaningful where it had been the result of nearly idle daydreaming, a last minute desperate attempt to find something for her project that would win approval from her committee. She was doing an oral history of religion, its importance, its rituals, its impact on people who were now over sixty-five or seventy. Not their present religion, but the religion of their youth.

Suddenly, yesterday, she had frozen, could not think what to say to the old woman waiting kindly for her to begin, could hardly remember why she was in the convalescent home in Kansas City in the first place. Last night in her motel room, she had looked about with loathing. Even the air-conditioned air smelled exactly the same in each motel she stayed in, as if they bought it in the same place that furnished the bedspreads and the pictures on the walls, and the dim lights. She had planned to stop interviewing periodically and rent an apartment, start the transcriptions that would take much longer than getting the information. The time had come for just that, she had realized, and put away her tape recorder, consulted her map, and headed for Greeley County, Kansas.

Really, the only question was, should she stop now, or continue? She could get a motel here in Topeka, but on down the road? They might all be filled later, and it was too early to stop now. Only four. She shook her head, smiling faintly at herself. She had no intention of sitting in a motel room for the next twelve or fourteen hours. She pushed the thick door open and went out into the hot air. More stuff to drink, bread, sandwich makings, fruit . . . She got into her small Datsun and started looking for a supermarket. And breakfast things, she told herself. She always woke up ravenous. Half an hour later she was on the interstate again, heading for the rendezvous with her sister and her sister's husband at the house he had inherited from an uncle he had never met. She hiked her cotton skirt up to her thighs as she drove; the wind rushed through the little car screeching maniacally, and all around her the world turned into a corn field as far as she could see. She loved it.

What she had not reckoned with, she realized later, was the lowering sun. The sky remained cloudless, clear, pale, sun-bleached to invisibility ahead, a great white nothingness with an intolerable glare at its heart. And she had been right about the motels filling up. By seven when she would have admitted her mistake, there was nothing to be found. Doggedly she drove on into the glare, looking forward to each oasis of gas station, restaurant, sometimes a motel, all huddled together as if pressured by the corn that would have reclaimed even those spots. Finally, the sun fell out of the sky, vanished without a hint of sunset. It was there, then it was not there and the sky came back, violet turning into a deep purple faster than she would have thought possible. At Goodland she made her last stop. It was ten thirty; nothing was open except a gas station. She got more water, filled her gas tank, and, consulting the notes she had made when she talked to her sister two weeks ago, recalled the instructions: "As soon as you get on the road heading south, watch the odometer; it's exactly fourteen point six miles to the turn-off. Then it's exactly four miles to the house. Mr. MacLaren said the key will be taped to the underside of the kitchen window around the back of the house. He said you can't miss it. So, if you get there first, go on inside and make yourself at home. The electricity will be on; there's well water, everything you need, even beds and bedding. See you soon, honey."

The gas-station attendant had said it was cooling off good, wasn't it, and she had thought he was making a joke, but now, heading south finally, she took a deep breath and another. It was cooling off a bit. The countryside was totally dark; no light showed anywhere, only her headlights on the strip of state road ever rushing toward her. After the traffic of the interstate, the roar of passing trucks, the uncountable trucks pulling trailers, the vans and station wagons and motorcycles, she felt suddenly as if she were completely alone. She felt tension seeping out through her pores and had not known until now that she had become tense in the long day of interstate driving.

Without the explicit directions she never would have found the turnoff. Even knowing it was there, at fourteen point six miles, she would not have found it without coming to a complete stop, backing up a hundred feet and approaching again, straining to see another road. The road she finally found was dirt.

Gingerly she turned onto it and suddenly the land changed, became hilly. She had grown so used to the corn-covered tabletop land that she hit the brake hard when the dirt road began to go downhill. She eased off the brake and slowly rolled forward. The road was narrow, white under her lights, hard-packed, not really difficult. It seemed that the last four miles were the longest miles of all. Then she saw the house and drew in a sigh of relief. The road ended at the house.

Finding the key was easier than finding her flashlight in the mess she had made of her belongings in the car. When she opened the back door, hot air rushed out. She entered, searched for lamps, switches. The electricity was on. She lighted rooms as she entered them to open windows, open the front door, open everything that could be opened. The house was not very big, two bedrooms, a spacious living room, another room off it that might have been a bedroom once but seemed a storeroom for dead furniture now, and a very large kitchen with dinette space and all electric appliances. No wood out here, she thought, nodding. Everything was neat and clean. Her sister had said that the lawyer had hired people to come in and see to things. Lorna plugged in the water heater and refrigerator and put water in the ice trays and then sat down at the kitchen table too tired to pay any more attention to her surroundings.

She roused herself enough to bring her cooler inside, make herself a sandwich, then go back out to find her sleeping bag. All she could think of now was a shower and sleep.

She dreamed of distant music and voices raised in song, laughter, more song. She found herself singing along, in her dream:

> In Scarlet town, where I was born,
> There was a fair maid dwellin'
> Made ev'ry youth cry "well-a-way";
> Her name was Barb'ra Allen.
> All in the merry month of May,
> When green buds there were swellin',
> Young Jemmy Grove on his death-bed lay,
> For love of Barb'ra Allen.

Suddenly she came wide awake and sat up. She was shivering. At last the night was cooling off. She strained to hear something, anything. Far away a lone coyote yipped. As she drifted into sleep again, the refrain played itself through her head over and over: "Henceforth take warning by the fall of cruel Barb'ra Allen."

It was after nine when she woke up again. She blinked at the ceiling, sky-blue, not a motel-room color. There was a silence so deep it was eerie, other-wordly. She thought of all the things the silence excluded: maids with cleaning carts, automobiles revving up, trucks shifting gears, showers running. . . . She hugged herself and ran to the outside kitchen door where she came to an abrupt stop and caught her breath sharply, then walked very slowly out onto the porch barefoot, in her flimsy short gown. The world had turned blue and gold while she slept.

Everywhere golden grass stretched out under a sky so blue it looked like an inverted lake. There were hills, all grass-covered, the grass gold, brown, ocher. She felt no breeze, yet the golden grass responded to something that was like a shadow passing over it, shading it, moving on, restoring the shining gold. As she stood motionless, her gaze taking in the landscape, she began slowly to make out other details: the grass ended at outcroppings of rock that were also golden, or tan, ocher. There were rocky ridges outlining hills in the distance, and now she saw that the grass was not the lush carpet she had thought it to be at first. It was sparse, in places yielding to the rocky ground, in a few places high and thick, but there were few of those stands. And she could see paths winding through the grass. Leading where? She hurried back inside, eager to dress, have something quick to eat, and get back out to follow a trail or two before the sun got much higher, before the heat returned.

The drive across the state was as hot and tedious as John Mac-Laren had known it would be. His father had had the truck serviced, even had a new battery in it, but the monster was thirteen years old and cranky. Although his father claimed it was his hunting and fishing truck, actually he had bought it for hauling pieces of furniture from barn sales, estate sales, garage sales. And he had been willing to travel a thousand miles to attend such sales. Not for the past five or six years, John thought then, not since a heart attack had slowed him down a little, and he was glad again that he was the one in the truck, and not his father. The fact that the truck had been tuned up, the battery replaced, the tires checked meant that his father had fully intended to take this trip himself. He returned to the question that had bothered him all night: Why? What was so damned important about one more piano, one more antique?

There was something, he knew. Castleman's death two weeks ago had stirred a darkness in his father that usually was so deeply buried that few people suspected its presence. John had sensed it now and then, and had seen it only yesterday. He could almost envy his father that, he thought bleakly. His own life had no secrets, no past best left unexplored. He had married the girl most suitable for him according to her family and his. An exemplary citizen, an exemplary husband and father with no darkness in him, no crazy hermit pal to beckon and stir the darkness that didn't exist anyway.

He knew the two old men had known each other for fifty years or more, and had assumed that they never saw each other only because Castleman had been a recluse, three hundred miles away, and not entirely sane.

When John was fifteen, his father had taken him along when he visited Castleman to draw up his will. Even then Castleman had been a crank, raving incoherencies. John had stayed outside while they talked, argued, yelled at each other in the end, and he was certain that his father had not been back since that day; he himself had never been back. He had not even seen the piano then. After the legal work was completed, he and his father had walked in the ruins of the commune that had been built and then abandoned on the property.

His head was starting to ache from the heat and the glare of the sun. He had left early enough, he had thought, to avoid having the lowering sun in his face, but there it was, almost like a physical presence pushing against the visor, burning his chest, his arms. He made his turn north before it slipped below the visor, but it was almost worse having it on the side of his face.

He missed the dirt road. When he finally was certain he had missed it, and maneuvered the truck in a U-turn, headed back very slowly, he remembered his father's curses from the distant past, when he too had missed it. "Made it hard to find on purpose," he had muttered. John crept along, found the turn, and followed the dirt road to the house. It was going on six.

He felt disoriented then because it looked exactly the same as twenty-five years before. The poplars shading the house looked unchanged, neither taller nor older; the house itself was just like the memory of it: tan with green trim, well-maintained. The surrounding hills were covered with drought-stricken grass, as they had been then. Maybe the grass came up brown and never changed, he thought, almost wildly. He saw the Datsun in the driveway, back by the rear of the house, and felt disappointment. He had hoped to have one evening alone before negotiating for the stupid piano, had planned on entering the house, inspecting it, snooping around for papers, letters, anything to shed some light on the mystery in which his father had had some unfathomable part.

Resignedly he left the truck, ran his hand through his hair, gritty with road dirt, and went up to the front porch. He did not knock. There were voices clearly audible on the porch. An old woman was talking.

". . . didn't dare laugh or even smile, nothing. I did like the singing though. Mamie Eglin could sing like someone on radio or television today. Pretty! Ma's favorite was 'The Old Rugged Cross.' Makes me soup up every time I hear it even now."

They were not in the living room. He could see the empty room through the screen door. The kitchen, he decided, and backed away from the front door. He walked around the house slowly, not in a hurry to break up the conversation. No breeze blew, yet the grass moved slightly, stirred by pressure perhaps, the lifting and falling of the blanket of heat that pushed hard against the land. He stood at the corner of the house and let his gaze follow the shadows of the invisible something that played over the responsive grass.

He no longer listened to the words of the old woman; her voice was a droning in the background of his thoughts. How had Castleman stood it? So alone, so far from anyone else, just him and the grass and heat in summer, blizzards in the winter. Why had he stayed? What had he done with his time day after day, year after year? A hawk rode an air current into his field of vision and he watched it out of sight. It did not fly away, it merged with the sky, vanished.

Suddenly he was jolted by the sound of a truck rumbling by, close enough, it seemed, to hit him. He jerked away from the house at the same time a clear, young voice said:

"Shit!"

The other voice continued without pause, apparently not bothered by the noise. ". . . preached to scare us, meant to scare us. And did scare us near to death. And Aunt Lodi, she scared us to death. Not my aunt, but everyone called her that. She told us girls stories that scared us to death. About being turned into a mule and being rode all night, things like that. Such terrible things. We was scared all the time. Most of us didn't pay much mind to the sermons unless he hollered and then we sat up and listened until one of the boys would wiggle his fingers at us, or one of the girls would have a coughing fit and then all of us would have to cough and Brother Dale would thunder that the devil was there with us and please, God Almighty, give us strength to put him out of our hearts, and we'd be scared again."

John looked in the window then and at first glance thought the person he saw was an Indian youth. Short, windblown dark hair, dark skin. A girl? Who? He moved to the door and looked in. No one was with her and he realized she was listening to a tape recording, transcribing the words into a portable computer.

". . . wouldn't have missed it for nothing. You see, there wasn't nothing else to do. It took all day just to get to church and back home and make dinner for a crowd, and clean it up again, and by then it was time to go to bed. But it might of been the only time for weeks on end that we'd even see another soul."

Another truck roared by; the girl scowled and tapped her fingers on the table top, waiting. John knocked on the door.

What intrigued him the most was that although she obviously had been startled by him, she just as obviously was not afraid. She looked up with widening eyes, then squinting, with her head tilted slightly as if trying to get him in focus. He spoke; she responded, and he stepped inside.

"John MacLaren—"

"Oh, the lawyer?"

"One of them. Mrs. Cleveland?"

"No. She's my sister. I'm waiting for them to show up."

"Oh."

"I'm Lorna Shields."

"Ah," he said, nodding, as if that explained a lot.

She looked around guiltily. Probably he had come to make sure everything was neat and clean for the new owner, and she had managed to create a mess everywhere. The table was covered with her tapes and papers. Her cooler was on the floor, dirty dishes in the sink. Actually she had decided that Elly and Ross would not arrive until Saturday evening, and by then she would have straightened it all up again. She glanced back at John MacLaren and forgot the rush of guilt.

"I wasn't expecting company or anything."

"I suppose not. I wasn't expecting to find anyone here."

She wanted him to go away, John realized uncomfortably. She looked very young, wearing shorts, a tank top, barefooted, too young to be out here alone at night. Her skin was deeply tanned all over, as far as he could tell, but her high cheekbones, her nose, the tops of her shoulders all glowed redder than the rest of her. She must not understand about the prairie sun, he thought, must not know how dangerous it could be. He looked past her toward the refrigerator.

"May I have a drink of water?"

Now her whole face glowed with embarrassment. "Sorry," she said. "Sure. Water's about it. Or coffee, or apple juice."

"I've got some cold beer in the truck. Would you like one?"

She nodded and he turned and left the kitchen. As soon as he was off the back porch, she raced through the room, into the living room where she picked up a stack of papers from the sofa and looked around for a place to deposit them. There was no good place. She went into the smaller of the two bedrooms and dumped the papers on her sleeping bag on the floor, folded the bag over to hide them, and returned to the kitchen.

She had started to read the stuff that afternoon and then put it off until night, but one of the names she had found in the early papers was MacLaren. Surely not this MacLaren, but she did not want him leafing through the material, and she did not want him to think she had been snooping.

He brought in the beer and they sat at the kitchen table drinking it. She told him briefly about her project, amused that he had thought the conversation was in real time.

"That's the problem with taping," she said. "You have to listen to it in real time, and transcribe it in real time before you can do a thing about editing. It's going to be a bitch to get on paper."

He realized how closely she was watching him when he finished his beer and she stood up, her own can still virtually untouched. Reluctantly he rose also. He offered her another beer and she refused, politely and firmly. When he asked if he could look around she shook her head.

"You'd better wait for Ross, don't you think? I mean, I don't have the authority to give permission or anything."

Still he hesitated, and then, surprising himself, he asked her to have dinner with him.

Her eyes widened as they had done before in startlement. She shook her head.

"I really do have work to get to. I guess Ross and Elly will be here tomorrow by this time. Why don't you drop in then?"

He could find no other excuse to stay. He went to the truck, turned it, and started back up the dirt road, and he began to chuckle. He was acting like a damn schoolboy, a lovesick, love-stricken junior-high-school boy. At the highway, he stopped and stared at the landscape and thought what fine cheekbones she had, what lovely eyes. He thought briefly of Gina and could not visualize her; it was as if she were in another universe. The face before his mind's eye had high sunburned cheekbones and wide, dark-blue eyes, straight dark hair swept back carelessly. The eyes looked at him directly without a hint of flirtation.

As soon as the truck made the first turn and vanished from sight, Lorna had hurried to change her clothes. Jeans, sneakers, a long-sleeved shirt that she did not put on, but carried to the kitchen. She already had checked her camera, and found her flashlight. She looked around, remembered the papers, and went back to the bedroom, collected them and took them out to her car where she locked them up in the trunk. She did not expect Mr. MacLaren to return, but then she had not expected anyone in the first place. She took the house key with her when she started her walk.

It was still too hot for this, too hot for jeans, but the heat did not have the intensity that had driven her inside earlier that day. She had learned that unless she stayed on the well-beaten trails, the grass cut her legs; in some places it was high enough to cut into her arms. That morning her walk had taken her to a ridge overlooking a valley perfectly enclosed on all sides, and in the valley she had seen ruins. There had not been a trail down to the valley as far as she could tell, and she had known even then that was wrong. If people had gone down there to build anything, there was a way to get down now. She had started over at the house, first searching for a map, then studying her road map, and finally examining the road that stopped so abruptly out in front of the house. And she had seen that the road at one time had continued, that it had been bulldozed and the grass had invaded, but it was discernible to anyone really looking for it. By then the sun had been too high to continue. But now the shadows were lengthening and, although the air was inferno-hot, it was impossible for it to become any hotter. The temperature could only go down from now until dark. She had a canteen of water clipped to her belt, her camera slung from her neck, a notebook and pencil in her pocket, and the shirt. Presently she tied the arms together and draped it over her shoulders; she did not need it yet.

She learned the feel of walking on the ruined road, how it differed from walking on the grass that never had been disturbed. The grass was sparser on the old road, rocks more numerous, sometimes making a trail of their own. After some minutes of walking steadily she turned to look at the house and could see only the tips of the poplars. For the first time she hesitated. She supposed it was possible to get lost in the grass, to wander aimlessly until thirst and then dehydration claimed one. She laughed softly. All she had to do was head east, she knew, and within minutes she would come across the highway. She continued.

There was no warning, no indication that the land dipped, formed the valley. One moment it appeared fairly level with hills in the distance, and then she was on a ridge again overlooking the round valley below. This time, she could see where the road had gone down the side of the sloping hill, where the bulldozer had knocked the land over onto it, tried to eradicate it. She nodded and started to pick her way down through the boulders and the grass that grew around them, between them, hid them from view. The boulders and the ground and the grass were all the same color, all gold in the lowering sunlight. She paused often; too hot for strenuous activity, she told herself, and wished she could sweat, could help cool herself that way. The sweat evaporated as fast as it formed. People always had told her that this dry heat was manageable, not bad at all, that it was the humidity that hurt. She took a sip of water and let it trickle down her throat, then another, and continued downward. She could not even take pictures from here, not facing into the sun as she was.

Then she was in the valley and it seemed even hotter than it had been up above. Nothing stirred. The ruins were of houses; foundations of stone and brick, fireplaces remained, nothing else. No wood. In some places the land had collapsed in areas fifteen feet wide, twenty feet. Sod houses, she realized, and tried to find an entrance to one. Only stones, boulders indicated where they had been; the earth had reclaimed its own.

The valley was much larger than she had thought; she would not be able to explore it all before dark, but already a pattern was emerging. Here there had been a big building, bigger than the houses, and directly opposite it, all the way across the valley floor there had been another large building. The houses lined a path between the two. She squinted, could almost see how it had been laid out. She shook her head; there was only grass and stones and bricks, nothing else. She turned and saw a stone fireplace standing over a cave of shade that was longer than the fireplace was tall. Wearily she sank to the ground in the shade to rest. She drank again, then leaned her head back against the bricks and closed her eyes. She had not known how exhausting the heat could be. After she rested a minute or two, she would go back to the house, she decided, and in the morning she would set her clock for five and come down here at dawn, before the heat was so bad.

And then she began to hear the grass. First a soft sighing, a whisper on one side then the other, a long-drawn-out exhalation, a rustling. Singing? No words, just a hum, so low it was felt even more than heard.

"Lorna! Lorna!"

She opened her eyes to a deep violet twilight without shadows. Around her the unmoving grass had turned to silver. The voice came again:

"Lorna!"

Then she saw him, the lawyer, clambering down the slope. She could not for the moment remember his name. She stood up and started to walk toward him. MacLaren. John MacLaren.

"What the devil are you doing down here? You know it's going to be dark within ten minutes? Come on, let's get out of here."

He was afraid, she thought in wonder. His face looked

pinched and his voice was rough with fear. She glanced behind herself at the silver grass, stiff and still, and could not understand his fear. He grasped her hand and began the climb back up, pulling her along with him. When she stumbled, he simply pulled more strongly.

"Wait," she gasped, unable to breathe.

"We're almost there," he said brusquely. "Come on."

Then he was hauling her up over the last boulder that started the ridge and finally he let her rest. She dropped to her knees and drew in long shuddering breaths. Her heart was pounding; her chest hurt and she could not get enough air.

"Take a sip," he said.

She felt the canteen against her mouth and took a drink, coughed, drank again and gradually began to breathe normally.

"Okay now?"

"Yes. Thanks, I think." She began to get to her feet, his hand firm on her arm, helping her, and she realized that it was fast getting dark. But the sun had been out, there had been shadows. She looked at him then, her own eyes widening with fear, and his gaze was troubled.

"Let's move while we can still see," he said.

His voice was normal again, no longer harsh and brusque, but his hand on her arm was tight.

They walked silently for several minutes. The violet deepened; the horizon in the east vanished. Wall of night, she thought. In the west the sky was the color of bad picture postcards from the Florida Keys or someplace like that. An uncanny blue, the blue of peacock feathers. She looked up at the sky overhead where stars were appearing out of the void like magic: not there, there. When she looked at the horizon again, it had deepened to midnight blue, and she marveled at the speed of nightfall here. Then a constellation of lights appeared in a tight cluster, a galaxy straight ahead. It could have been a ship far out to sea; or it could have been a warning buoy signaling danger, rocks, shoals. John MacLaren grunted his satisfaction and eased up on the fast pace he had set for them.

"What were you doing out there at dark?" he asked.

She bit back her retort that she had not intended being there at dark and said, "I fell asleep. Why did you come back? Why did you go to the valley?"

He was walking ahead of her now, a shadow against the shadowed sky, merging with the grass from his waist down, grass man, shadow man, floating above the grass that was as dark as a magician's cape, and she thought that was right. There was so little to work with here, grass, sky, stones, the tricks of the land had to be accomplished with few props; the illusions demanded magic. The illusion of a cool cave of shadows by the fireplace in the valley, the illusion of voices humming, sighing. The illusion of sky beneath her.

She stopped and caught her breath and let it out slowly, started to walk again. He had gone on, unaware that she had paused. She had forgotten her questions, forgotten that he had not answered, might never answer, when his voice floated back to her.

"I was worried about you," he said, sounding very far away. "Funny things happen out on the prairie to people not used to it. Visual distortions happen, make you think something's near enough to reach in a couple of minutes, when actually it might be a hundred miles away. It's so quiet people provide noises, and sometimes are frightened by the noises their own heads create."

"How did you know where I was?"

"I followed your trail," he said and the brusqueness was again in his voice. He did not say the grass told him because that sounded too crazy. The Judge—his grandfather—had taught him to read the grass the way a sea captain could read the open sea, follow another ship across the ocean without ever sighting it by following its wake. A subtle change in water color, a flattening of waves, a smoothing out peculiar to that one passage. And so it was with the grass. Her trail had been arrow sharp. He also did not tell her the other crazy things he had felt, thought, had known out on the prairie: how, when the sky vanished, as it had done this evening, it took all space, all distance with it. Then he could reach into the firmament and touch the stars, the moon; he could reach across space from horizon to horizon. He did not tell how the grass could play with sound so that a whisper uttered miles away could be the warm breath from lips not quite touching your ear; or how the grass could banish sound so that the one you touched could not be heard without effort.

Ahead, the house formed around the lights; the trees arranged themselves in tree shapes. She was almost sorry. The magic was gone.

"Have you eaten yet?" she asked as they drew near the house.

"No. Have you?"

"No. It was too hot."

"I bought a very big steak and some lettuce. Share it with me?"

"You're on," she said cheerfully. "All I have is peanut butter and sardines."

He laughed and she joined in and they entered the house. He apologized for letting himself in earlier when he realized she was gone. He had a key, of course, and had put the steak in the refrigerator. She nodded. Of course.

She waited until they had finished eating and were having coffee before she asked about the valley. "What was it? What happened?"

He frowned and looked past her, considering.

"You don't have to tell me," she said quickly. "Not if it bothers you."

He brought his gaze back to her, puzzled. "Why would it bother me?"

She shrugged and did not say she had seen the name Mac-Laren on the papers she had hidden away.

"I'm just not sure where to start," he said then.

"Start at the beginning, go to the end, and stop."

He grinned and nodded. "Right. My grandfather was the beginning. Everyone called him the Judge. Before him this was all Indian country. How he got hold of this land no one knows

for sure. He used to tell half a dozen different stories about it.
Maybe he won it at cards. That was one of his stories anyway.
So he came out here from New Orleans back in eighteen ninety-
seven, owner of twenty-five hundred acres of scrub prairie, and
he saw right off that he was not going to make it on the land.
He never had farmed or run a ranch or anything like it. He
became a preacher at first, traveled all over the state, over into
Colorado, back. Then he went into politics, settled down in
Wichita and started to raise a family. Somewhere in there he was
appointed a circuit judge. And he still had this land that he was
paying taxes on."

His voice was almost dreamy as he told the story; his gaze
was distant, perhaps even amused, as if he was proud of his
grandfather. Lorna poured more coffee for both of them and
wished vaguely that she had turned on her tape recorder.

"Anyway, during his many travels meting out justice, the
Judge met Josiah Wald. No one talks much about this particular
period, you understand. I doubt that anyone even knows what
went on. Josiah was being tried for something or other; my
grandfather was the judge, and when it was all over, Josiah had
bought himself twenty-five hundred acres of scrub prairie, and
he did not go to jail.

"The time was the mid-twenties," he said, bringing his gaze
back, seeing her again. He liked the way she listened, as attentive
as a schoolgirl with a test coming along any minute. And he
wished that thought had not intruded because he wanted to
think of her as a woman past the age of consent. He sighed and
looked out the window again and went on with his story.

"It was the boom swing of the cycle, a dress rehearsal for
the sixties, wild, amoral; the devil walked the earth gathering
in his own. And Josiah was a prophet, a showman, a tent reviv-
alist who suddenly was a landowner with a following. So he
started a commune down in the valley. A religious community." Her eyes widened the way they did when she was surprised. He shrugged and spread his hands as if to say, don't
blame me. "So far this is all pretty much on public record.

Nothing else really is recorded until nineteen forty-one when there was a fire in the valley and Louis Castleman became the owner of the land. Somehow they had survived the dust bowl conditions and the depression, but it seems the fire ended it all. The commune simply vanished after that. Six people died in the fire; Josiah was not listed as one of them. He vanished, one of the mysteries of the prairie. Castleman salvaged what he could, built this house, and tried to destroy the road down to the valley. Finis."

"Wow!" she said softly. Then she got up and started to clear the table.

"What? No questions?"

"Hundreds. But I'm not sure what they are yet. Where are you going to sleep?"

"Dad keeps camping gear in the truck at all times. I'll sleep out under the stars."

She nodded and did not protest, and he thought it was a victory of some sort that she seemed to assume he had a right to stay around. He liked the way she accepted things without fussing. He felt certain she would have had the same acceptance if he had said in the bedroom, or the living room. Just not her room, he added, also certain of that.

She began to wash the few dishes. "Why did you tell me all that?"

"I'm not sure. Probably because you went down there. Maybe because I don't think you should go back."

"Do you believe in ghosts, evil spirits? Any spirits at all?"

"No."

"Are you religious?"

He hesitated this time. Then he said slowly, "My wife takes our kids to Sunday School and church, and I go along much of the time. We have church weddings and funerals in my family. I support our church financially."

She turned to give him a long searching look and he added, "No. I'm not religious. Are you?"

She shook her head, still gazing at him, almost absently.

"Why are you here? Elly told me the legalities were all settled. They just want to look around and make decisions about what to do with things."

He stood up and walked to the door. "I'm on an errand for my father. To buy the old player piano, if your brother-in-law will sell it."

She turned back to the dishes. "Is there music for it?"

"I guess so. I don't know." He had his hand on the screen door, yet did not push it open, did not want to go out, go to sleep. "You're asking the wrong questions," he said.

"Are you and your wife together?"

Now he pushed the door open. "Good night," he said and walked out into the warm dark air.

She dreamed. She was on a stage wearing a filmy blue dress, fastened only with one pearl clasp at the waist. She had nothing on under it. She sang to an audience of men and women who stared silently with vacant expressions.

"I will never more deceive you, or of happiness bereave you,
But I'll die a maid to grieve you. Oh! you naughty, naughty
*   men;*
You may talk of love, and, sighing, say for us you're nearly
*   dying;*
All the while you know you're trying to deceive, you
*   naughty men;*
You may talk of love, and, sighing, say for us you're nearly
*   dying;*
All the while you know you're trying to deceive, you
*   naughty, naughty men."*

She sang almost demurely, with innocent flirtatiousness, not moving. Then the music changed, the piano started over, but this time it was different and when she went on to the next verses, she moved obscenely, lewdly, and the audience stirred, seemed to come awake, out of trance.

*"And when married how you treat us, and of each
  fond hope defeat us,
And there's some will even beat us, oh! you naughty,
  naughty men;
You take us from our mothers, from our sisters and our
  brothers, oh! you naughty, cruel, wicked men."*

Two men were with her, fondling her, and she sang, smiling
at one, then the other, accessible to their hands. She twisted
away as one of them started to force her down, but it was a game
she was playing with them for the audience, all hooting and
whistling, clapping to the mad music. One of the men on stage
with her had his belt in his hand; men and women were coupling
on tables, on the floor, and she knew he was going to beat her,
beat her, beat her . . . She tried to run away; the other man caught
her and held her and the belt whistled through the air and she
woke up, drenched.

She was tangled in her sleeping bag, fighting to be free of it;
the music was still there, still in her head. She jammed her hands
against her ears. Silence returned.

She crawled free of the sleeping bag and got to her feet, made
her way to the kitchen for a drink of water, an aspirin, coffee,
anything. No more sleep, she thought almost wildly. No more
dreams, not that night.

"What in hell have you been doing?" John MacLaren demanded, motionless in the center of the kitchen.

"What did you do? Why—" She stopped, clutching the door
frame. "You heard it?"

Shock, he thought distantly. She was shiny with sweat;
when he took her arm to move her to a chair, she felt clammy.
He went to the room she was using and found a short terry robe,
went by the bathroom and picked up a towel and returned to her.
She had not moved. He wiped her face and arms and got the robe
on her, and then made coffee. By the time it was ready, she
looked better, bewildered and frightened.

"What happened?" she asked in a low voice. "I was dreaming. What did you hear? Was I making noise?"

"I heard music," he said bluntly. "I thought you were playing the piano and singing." He poured coffee and she held her cup with both hands. "Were you?"

She shook her head.

"I want to look at that damn piano." When he stood up, she did too, and he did not try to dissuade her. Together they went through the living room. She pointed silently at the door to the adjoining room.

He felt baffled by her. Crazy? She did not look or act like any of the crazies he had known, yet . . . He knew he had heard her playing the piano and singing and that was crazy in the middle of the night. He felt curiously betrayed, even angry, the way he was angered when he caught a client lying to him. He opened the door and felt the wall for the light switch.

There was another television, an ancient model, one of the earliest. There was a rocking chair with the rocker aslant. There were boxes; an open one was stuffed full of clothes, apparently. A kitchen chair, painted blue, a chest of drawers with one drawer gone, charred-looking. And behind it was the piano against the far wall. Things had been moved so that it was possible to get to it, but he no longer believed she had played it that night. She would have had to be in here in the dark, he realized; he would have seen this light from outside when the music woke him up. Silently they stared at the piano.

The keyboard cover was down, dusty, the way everything out here was during the drought. He worked his way to the piano and touched it, opened the compartment where the music rolls went in. Empty. He pulled the piano bench out and tried to open it. Locked. That was where the music rolls would be, he thought, locked away. Finally he recrossed the room, looked back, then turned off the light and closed the door.

"I think there's a bottle of booze in the truck. Right back."

"I put some papers in my car," she said quickly. "I'll get them. Castleman's papers," she added.

He thought she simply did not want to remain alone in the house for even a minute, and waited for her to slip on sandals and get her car keys. He found a bottle of bourbon in the truck;

she retrieved a stack of papers from her car, and they returned to the kitchen.

He made them both drinks and they started to sort through the papers. There was very little of any use, he thought after several minutes. A few newspaper clippings, a few letters, receipts.

"Mr. MacLaren," Lorna said a bit later, "is your father's name David?"

"Yes. Why?"

"He already owns the piano. Look."

She held out a slip of paper, a bill of sale. It was signed by Louis Castleman, who had sold the piano to David MacLaren for one dollar. Twenty-five years ago, the summer John had come to this house with his father, the day they had gone down into the valley to look at the ruins.

But that was not where she had seen the name before, Lorna knew. "MacLaren" had been on a full sheet of paper. There were not many left to examine; she picked up the next one in her pile.

"Lorna, please call me John," he said. "In this part of the world only the senior male member of the family is Mister."

She looked up at him in the direct way she had. "Are you having a midlife crisis?"

He snatched his glass and stood up, went to the sink where he had left the bottle and poured himself another drink. Only then did he look at her. "Isn't that a bit impertinent?" he asked coldly.

"Sure it is." She finished scanning a sheet of paper, put it down, picked up another one. "I found it," she said in satisfaction and leaned back to read.

He looked out the window where he could see the eastern horizon, lightening in streaks. In an hour it would be sunrise, and he suspected that neither of them would sleep any more that night. He began to make more coffee.

When he glanced at her again, she was sitting very still, staring at the wall.

"Coffee, *Miss* Shields?" His voice was quite impersonal, he thought. He looked more closely. "What is it? What's wrong?"

She started, and pushed her chair away from the table, not looking at him. "You'd better read it," she said, and left the kitchen. Before he reached the table, he heard water running in the bathroom.

The paper was a letter written on Judge MacLaren's stationery, addressed to Louis Castleman. It was written in the kind of legalese that attorneys sometimes used to obfuscate an issue, language designed to bury the meaning in so many layers of verbal garbage that only a very persistent, or trained, reader could possibly grasp the contents. John MacLaren read it twice, then sat down and read it a third time.

His grandfather, the Judge, had been blackmailed by Louis Castleman, had yielded to his demands. He stated that he was satisfied that the unfortunate deaths had been the result of a disastrous fire, which was clearly an act of God. He had brought the weight of his good office to bear on the official investigation and the matter was now closed.

The last paragraph said: "David left this morning to be sworn in in the armed forces. I have no forwarding address for him; therefore I am returning your letter to him. I believe this concludes all our business."

He let the sheet of paper fall to the table and went out on the porch. In a few minutes Lorna joined him.

"I brought you coffee," she said. "Black, the way you had it last time. It does finally cool off a little, doesn't it?"

"Thanks. A little. When the weather changes, it'll be on the storm front. Black clouds gather like a phalanx and march across the land. I used to stay down in Tribune with the Judge quite a bit. We watched a tornado once and he said it was the devil pissing on earth." He sipped the coffee. "He died when I was seven."

"Did he teach you to love the prairie?"

"You can't teach that, just learn it."

"One of the women I interviewed back in West Virginia said people there had the mountains in their eyes. I didn't know what she meant. I think I do now. You have the prairie in your eyes."

They were silent for several minutes. John spoke first. "Think you could sleep an hour or so?"

"No!"

"I don't mean inside. Out in the grass in your sleeping bag. I won't sleep. I'll stand guard. An hour's about all the time you'll have before the sun will be up, the heat back."

"I'll collapse later, I guess, but right now I don't feel at all sleepy. You could go find someone to help with the piano and just take it, couldn't you? Since your father really owns it."

"Afraid not. As executor he had someone come out and make an inventory and send a copy to your brother-in-law. The piano's listed. And the question really is why is the bill of sale here. Why did Castleman keep it? Let's sit down."

They had been standing at the porch rail; now they went to the steps and sat on the top one, his back to one of the railing uprights, hers to the opposite. The sky was definitely getting brighter. No stars were visible any longer. It was as if the sky were simply retreating farther and farther away.

"I'm not going to make a pass," John said. "Might have yesterday, but not now, now that I know you."

She nodded. There had been a moment yesterday when she thought he would make a pass, and she had realized that he didn't know how to start and had felt safe. Keeping her eyes on the brightening sky, she said, "I'd like to tell you the dream I had."

She related the dream matter-of-factly, distancing herself from it as if she were retelling a story she had read a long time ago. When she was done, she said, "I never heard that song before, and now I know it. It's flirty and innocent at the same time, not like music now. No innuendoes, nothing like that, just a little teasing, but what I dreamed was grotesquely obscene. I think the song's among the music rolls. That and the other one I dreamed."

"God," he muttered. "This is crazy. Do you walk in your sleep, have you ever? Could you have played the piano in your sleep?"

She gave him one of her long level looks and shook her head.

"Okay. I heard that song and assumed it was you. It sounded like your voice, but it was dark. Let's go have a look at that goddamn piano."

"I'll go shower and get dressed. It'll be light by then, I think."

Dusk was yielding to daylight although the sun had not yet appeared. No clouds reflected the sunrise.

The clear, sharp light was all about them when they returned to the storage room. John moved junk to make a path and together they pushed the piano through it into the living room. He opened the cover—mahogany and ivory keys, just as his father had said. The piano was out of tune, and when he stooped to examine the bellows behind the foot pump, he found them brittle and useless. Obviously the piano had not been played for decades.

He went back for the bench and brought it out, then forced the lock with his pocket knife. The music was so brittle that when he tried to open a roll, a piece of paper broke off in his hand and he looked at it dumbly, paper with many holes punched in it, nothing more than that. He dropped the roll down among several dozen others and closed the lid. He was angry, his anger directed at himself this time. He had expected to solve a little mystery and instead had simply revealed a larger one. It would have been neat to prove that she might have been up playing the piano in her sleep—he had abandoned the idea that she had done it consciously—and instead he had proven that no one could have played the thing. When he turned his glare to her, she was frowning almost absently in his direction, not at him.

"Let's eat," he said, trying to submerge his frustration. His voice came out brusque and harsh.

"Peanut butter and sardines and fruit," she said, trying to achieve the same light-hearted teasing tone that she had come by so naturally the day before. It sounded false this morning.

They settled for the peanut butter and fruit and more coffee.

"You should pack up your stuff and go up to Goodland, get

a motel room and get some sleep," he said. "I'll be here when your sister and her husband come. I'll tell them."

"Tell them what? That's the problem, isn't it? There's nothing to tell anyone. And I can't let Elly and Ross just walk in on . . . on—I have to be here."

She packed up her computer and tapes and tape recorder and straightened the room she had slept in, and there was nothing else to do. The papers they had examined were still on the kitchen table.

"If I were you," she said slowly, "I'd sort through that stuff and take out things that really don't concern Ross. If I were you."

He nodded. She moved to the door and looked out.

"I'm going to take a walk before it gets any hotter."

"You're not going back down there?"

She shuddered. "Never! Don't worry about me. I'll stay on the trails."

He watched until she was out of sight, heading directly away from the ruins, on a well-defined trail that first rose, then dipped; her shiny dark hair was like a sail vanishing over the edge of the sea. The grass, shadowed without wind, disguised the point of origin of a faint "Chuketa, chuketa," the hoarse call of a quail. Above, where the sky should have been, there was only the vastness of empty space stretching away forever.

When he went back to the table and the papers, the house seemed preternaturally quiet. What had Louis Castleman done out here every day for over forty years? How had he paid his bills, bought food, paid taxes? He began to read the papers again, this time sorting them as he went, searching for clues.

Lorna walked aimlessly, needing to be away from the house, away from the piano, the papers that hinted at terrible things. She heard the sounds in the grass all around her without identifying them. Birds, quail probably, but she was not sure. Snakes? If there were birds, mice, and voles, then there would be snakes and hawks and coyotes, she told herself, and tried to follow the food chain higher, but lost track. How had he managed to keep so many trails clear of grass, she wondered. The trails were not very wide, but they were easy to follow, well trodden down, so clear that it seemed he must have spent most of his time just maintaining them. Why?

She had been going downward for some time until now she was at the bottom of a ravine, a snow run-off possibly. The trail went through, out the other end, up a steep hill, over its crest. She stopped at a boulder large enough to cast shade and rested. And now the thoughts that she had denied surged back. The nightmare, the singing the first night, her lethargy down in the ruins. There was a pattern, she thought, and just by admitting it was there, she was jeopardizing everything she had ever thought she knew. That was what frightened people: Not that strange things happen, everyone admitted that readily, joked about it, used strange happenings as anecdotal material at cocktail parties. And then they all denied any meaning, any pattern and went on to other things. Because, she went on, if you admit the pattern, a meaning, you are saying the world isn't what you thought it was, what you were taught from earliest infancy. All the stories had to be treated alike, with the same value, and that was no value at all, except as amusements.

She thought of the many elderly people she had interviewed already for her oral history of religious experiences. How easily they had accepted the various superstitions, the Aunt Lodies being turned into mules, the magical cures and powers they talked about. One woman had said, "Well, we went to any church being held. Didn't make no difference. They's all about the same."

And another: "Oh, we was scared to death all the time."

Fear of the inexplicable was channeled into religious fear that merely doubled its effect. And when religion became rational, the fear of the inexplicable had to be denied; there was nothing left to incorporate it. The inexplicable became small talk at cocktail parties. One event was caused by indigestion, one by misinterpreting the signals, one by a psychological problem. That was the only way to handle the inexplicable.

Her instructor had been surprised, then elated with the ease with which she managed to get people to talk about their experiences. It was because, he told her finally, she had no strong system of belief that she used to challenge whatever she heard. She did not threaten anyone with contradictory dogma.

"I'm an uncritical listener," she had admitted cheerfully. "I believe that they believe and that's enough for me."

"And all women are twits," he had said.

She had stiffened with instant anger, and then realized what he had done.

"You see, until you feel threatened personally, you don't pose a threat to anyone else. The people you're interviewing sense that and confide in you."

She had listened to so many stories with uncritical interest, had felt no terror and had discounted the terror of others. That was a long time ago, she had thought, when people were still superstitious. And she had known those people had brought the fears upon themselves by admitting to the supernatural, to magic, to witchcraft. Where would one draw the line, she had asked herself. If you believe one such story, why not the next and the next?

Her world was defined by air travel and moon walks and computers, by wonder drugs and heart transplants, by instant communication. Life was defined by the first brain waves of a fetus in the womb and the flattening of the EEG line that marked brain death. The fears were of things that people did to people, fear of disability, of incurable disease, of accidents, war. Fear of tornadoes and hurricanes and blizzards. There was no place in her world for the terrors of the inexplicable, no place for the terror of sensing a pattern that would mean the end of the world she knew. Admitting that such a pattern might exist created a void, and the void filled itself with terror.

"We was scared to death all the time."

She got up then and looked at the ravine, up the far side, back the way she had come. She had been out longer than she had intended; the sun was high and hot already. Out here with the white-hot sky, the golden grasses withering from a lack of water, the quiet air, it was impossible to believe in the ghost piano playing by itself in the middle of the night. And she wouldn't believe it, she told herself.

John had put the papers for Ross Cleveland in the living room, and the others in his pocket, the ones he never intended to show anyone. Twice he had gone to look at the prairie to see if Lorna was in sight, not actually worried about her, just wishing she would come back. When he heard the automobile out front, he assumed it was Ross and Elly at last, and was stunned when he went to the front door to see his father approaching.

"The Buick's air conditioned and the office is closed," David MacLaren growled as he entered the house.

He stopped, gazing at the piano still in the living room. He looked old and frail, John realized. Even when his father had suffered a warning heart attack—that was what they all called it—he had not looked frail. And now he did.

"What are you doing here?"

"Restless. Wanted to see to this myself after all. Got up at five and here I am. Not bad time actually. Anything cold to drink?"

"Water."

"Water's fine," the father said mildly. He had not yet moved, had not shifted his gaze from the piano.

John took his arm and steered him to the kitchen, saw him to a chair, glad now that Lorna had not returned. He put ice in a glass and filled it with water, thinking furiously. His father could clam up tighter than anyone he knew, and if he took that tack, nothing would budge him. He put the glass on the table and sat down.

"Before the others show up," he said, "there are things I have to know. They'll have questions—"

His father was looking with great interest at Lorna's purse on the counter. "Seems to me someone has already showed up," he said.

"Lorna Shields," John said, and then plunged in, knowing if he had decided wrong, he never would learn anything. "She's convinced the piano's haunted." He told his father about Lorna.

"Romantic schoolgirl nonsense," David MacLaren said, and drank his water without looking at his son.

"I'd like to think so, but I heard the music too, and neither of us ever heard that song in our lives before last night." He drew in a long breath. "And I found a letter from the Judge to Louis Castleman, virtually acknowledging blackmail. You were here when the commune burned. You told me it burned while you were in the army."

David shook his head. "Never said that. I said when I came home it was all gone, done with. And it was."

"Tell me about it. What went on here? Why is that damn piano so important? What was your connection with Josiah Wald?"

"Give me a minute." He drained the glass and John took it, refilled it while he was making up his mind. When he went to the table again, his father said, "Sit down, son."

He drank, and wiped his mouth with his hand. "Even with air conditioning that's one hell of a dry drive this kind of weather. You know, John, there are things you just never get around to telling your kids. There must be a thing or two you haven't brought up with yours." He was facing the open door, his gaze on the prairie beyond. "Well, there are things I never got around to talking about. I was eighteen when the crash came and the Judge was wiped out, and he never got around to mentioning it to me. Father to son, father to son, the same pattern again and again. Anyway it was time for me to go to college, the way my brothers had done, and the Judge was broke. Then Josiah Wald appeared. And Josiah had money and was on the run. Next thing he owned the land here, and I was off for Lawrence, no questions asked. I was too ignorant to know what to ask, I guess. And Josiah started building down in the valley, got his people coming in, was off and running, and I never knew a thing about him, or what was going on here. The Judge managed to get me a summer job at City Hall in Kansas City, and I was in school the rest of the year, and just not home much at all until I got out of school. And that summer I learned what Josiah Wald meant."

His father's voice had become almost a monotone and grew flatter as he continued. "I was bone ignorant when I graduated from college. Bone dumb. I never had had a girl. The first girl I kissed thought she'd get pregnant from open mouth kissing and wouldn't do it. That's how ignorant we all were those days. And Josiah Wald had a little Sodom and Gomorrah and Eden all wrapped up in one package in the valley. You have to remember there was the dust bowl and ruination and people jumping off buildings, only here there wasn't anything high enough to matter and they just picked up and left. There was Prohibition and the devil was on the earth everywhere you looked. Josiah prospered. You wanted a hideout, you had it. You wanted dope, no problem. Girls, they were there. Anything you wanted, if you had the price, it was there. And he mixed in religion. His message was that no one can choose good who hasn't experienced evil. And he provided the evil. The devil was loose on earth, all right."

He drew in a long breath and looked at John. "If I ever had found you in a place like that I would have killed whoever took you there. Anyway, the Judge found out I was sneaking off there when I could and he sent me packing to Kansas City again, to work part time, starve, whatever. And he tried to run Josiah Wald out. Didn't work, though. By then Josiah had other, even more influential backers. Along about then I met Louis Castleman, and we came over together one week, and he stayed. He played the piano in the hotel. There was one building they called the hotel, and one they called the church. The hotel was a gambling casino, whorehouse, God knows what all. It was all a perversion. They turned everything into mockery and blasphemy. What Josiah was especially good at was corrupting the innocent. He got me and he got Louis even worse. What saved me was my state of finances. Down around zero most of the time, and I couldn't play the piano worth a damn. I thought he was being good to me but I know now that he let me in just to taunt the Judge. He never let me stay, only long enough to spend every cent I'd scraped together, then he'd kick me out. So I wasn't around the year that Louis was hired on. Then Louis wrote me that he was in love with a girl there and that he was going to kidnap her, to save her, and would I help him. A man doesn't get many chances in this life to wear the shining armor and ride the white horse," he said reflectively, and took a deep breath.

"You saw the valley, one road down there and that was it. No one ever went in there without an invitation and no one ever left without permission. I went in on the north side, sliding on my belly in the grass most of the way. And no one saw me. Louis sneaked me into his room and we plotted for three days and made one plan after another until we finally had it down pat. The girl was a singer, pretty as an angel, and thoroughly corrupt. She hadn't been, Louis said, when someone brought her there. She had been frightened and innocent, a virgin. I don't know how much he made up, how much he actually knew, but he was in love with her and that was the truth."

He stood up and went to the sink for more water, not bothering with ice this time. Then he stood with his back to the room.

"The act was supposed to be funny," he said. "The stage was a copy of an Old West saloon with a piano player and a girl singer, nothing else. He plays and she sings and then he leaves the piano and falls on his knees in front of her, and the piano keeps on playing by itself. The audience loved it usually. She kicks him away and he crawls back to the piano and takes up where it left off. They had music from back in eighteen sixty-five or so, a comic song from a Broadway musical, one of the first to strip the girls, I guess. Anyway, she sang it pretty nearly stripped. They had an electric motor rigged up to work the bellows. And that gave him the idea. After the act, the piano was out of sight, but he was supposed to keep on playing for the next hour or so. He planned to turn on the motor, grab the girl and tie her up and hand her over to me. I was to carry her to the high grass on the north slope and hide with her there and wait for him. He'd continue to play his usual numbers until he was through and by then she would have been missed, of course, but he'd be in the clear, and later he planned to join me and drag or carry her up over the top and save her."

John felt frozen in that brilliant, hot kitchen as he listened to his father. His mouth was so dry he could not have spoken.

"We were all a little crazy." His father went on as if he had rehearsed all of it over and over, waiting for a chance to perform, keeping his voice dispassionate as if long ago he had severed any connection between himself and the events. "The girl was the craziest of all. Louis told her he wanted to save her and she told Josiah, because she loved him and she thought he'd be nicer to her then, and that night the show was changed without anyone mentioning it. I was outside, keeping out of sight at the start. She sang and he played all right, but then the new action began. Two men joined her and at first it looked like a mock rape, but it didn't stay like that. I ran in when she screamed and others were screaming by then and some running out wanting no part of what was happening up there, and some liking it just fine. They beat the living hell out of her on stage while two goons held Louis just off stage and the piano never stopped playing. The girl died."

He said it so simply, so emotionlessly that it took a second or two for John to realize what he had said, what it meant.

"Oh my God."

His father turned, his face a dark blur against the glare of light. He came back to the table and sat down and his voice was brisk now.

"Louis went crazy. Everyone was crazy, leaving the valley as fast as they could get their cars started, get up the hill. Louis carried her out and got in someone's car and drove off with her. I got myself out of there the same way I had gone in, up the north side and walked the twenty-two miles to the Judge's house before daylight. The next day there were rumors but nothing concrete, and that night the fire broke out and more people died and

Josiah vanished. Well, that was too much to cover up. We all knew the war was coming fast and the day after the valley burned the Judge gave me an ultimatum. I could join the army that day and get the hell out or I'd be indicted along with half a dozen others as accomplices to murder. No one ever was indicted for murder. The girl's death was laid to the fire along with the others'. No one disputed Louis's claim to the land. He took what he wanted and bulldozed the road and lived in this godforsaken place until he died.''

"The piano?'' John said after a moment. "What is that all about?''

"I never was sure. The day I brought you here with me, he said he wanted it in his will, that he wanted me to have it, and I said chances were about even that I'd go first and then what? I told you he was crazy. He went wild then and sold it to me for a dollar and kept the bill of sale. If I went first he'd tear it up, and if he went first, it was legally mine.''

"He killed Josiah Wald,'' John said slowly.

"Yes. He buried the girl and went back to the valley and started the fire. When Josiah came running he pulled a gun on him and took him out. I never knew that until the day I came back with you.'' He looked at his son shrewdly and said, "You heard something that day and denied it. I always wondered how much you heard, what it meant to you.''

"I thought it was the raving of a madman. It scared me. All that talk about the girl on the prairie.'' He glanced at his watch and abruptly stood up. Lorna! He had forgotten her and she had left more than two hours ago.

Lorna sat in the high grass and tried to think what to do. Long ago she had made herself a hat of sorts, woven grass held on by strips torn from her shirt. What else could she do? What did animals do when the sun got so high and hot? Burrow into the ground and wait for shadows, wait for cooler air? Wait for water next month or the next? She pressed her forehead against her knees. No tears, not now. She could not afford to waste the water that went into tears. Presently she pulled herself up and started to walk again. It seemed incredible that she could be lost when the trails were so clear and easy to follow, when she knew that if she went east she would reach the highway. She had gone east over and over, but she had not reached the highway. Once she had seen half a dozen red-winged blackbirds, wounded-looking, bloodied with the bright red on their shoulders, and she had started to run after them. They would be heading for the corn-fields, east, the highway. Then, panic-stricken, the birds lost from view, she had jolted to a stop, surrounded by high grass, no sign of a trail anywhere. She had forced herself not to move, to think first. What had John MacLaren said? You can read the grass if you really look at it. She made herself study it all around and only then began to pick her way back to the trail. It had taken a long time to find it again, and if the grass had been less brittle, if she had not crashed through it so roughly, she might never have found the trail again. Now she left it only to rest in the grass from time to time.

Why were there so many trails? Louis Castleman must have been mad. Some of the trails wandered as aimlessly as a leaf miner on foliage, twisting and turning, going nowhere, crossing themselves. Landmarks meant nothing. They changed or van-ished or receded continually. And there was only the grass left. The next rise, she thought, the next high place where she could look out over the countryside, there she would find a flat rock and make a map or something . . . then she heard voices.

"For God's sake, just shoot me and be done with it!" A hoarse male voice slurred the words.

Lorna dropped to her knees in the grass, crouched as low as she could.

"Haven't decided yet," a second voice said. It was almost as hoarse and raspy as the first.

"God! Just cut me loose. We'll both end up dead out here."

"Shut up!"

Then she could see them, two men, one with his hands bound behind his back, the other holding a rope attached to him,

leading him as if he were a horse. The bound man stumbled and
fell; the other one continued to walk, dragging him through the
grass until he regained his feet, sobbing and cursing. Suddenly
he rushed the man leading him, and that man veered off, let him
dash by, and jerked the rope. The bound man crashed to the
ground, then scrambled to get up again as the other walked in
the new direction.

Lorna held her breath until they were out of sight. Cautiously she raised her head and listened, and more cautiously she
crept after them, following the beaten grass. When she saw them
again, they were in a shallow gully, the bound man tied to a
boulder, the other one vanishing over the crest of the opposite
ridge.

"Don't leave me here! Louis, don't leave me here!"

She must have made a noise. He swung his head around and
saw her.

"Get down! Don't let him see you! He's crazy, a madman."

His voice was a harsh whisper that seemed to be in her head,
not across the gully. Desperately he looked up the ridge, then
back to her, and he caught and held her gaze with his own. His
eyes were the incredible blue of high mountain lakes, and even
now, unshaven and filthy, he was beautiful, she thought, and
found herself moving toward him.

"Get down! Duck behind the boulders and come to me that
way!"

She took a hesitant step.

"Listen. I've got money. Lots of it, more than you dreamed
of. I'll give it to you, all of it. Please help me! Untie me!"

She moved another step, another.

"He intends to drag me through the grass in the heat until
we both drop dead. Do you know what it's going to be like dying
of thirst under that sun, tied to a dead man, or a raving maniac?
Help me!"

"He won't die," she whispered, so softly her words failed to
reach her own ears. "He'll live and walk this trail every day for
the rest of his life."

A shriek of insane laughter came from the ridge. "You hear that, Josiah? I told you we'd get a sign. If she wants to help you, I won't stop her. Otherwise, we keep walking, Josiah, you and me."

She looked up the ridge where he was a black shadow against the brilliance of the void. Then she was falling, falling into the sky.

John MacLaren walked steadily up a hill to scan the surrounding prairie. Strange, he thought, how he had put out of mind the day he had come here with his father, twenty-five years ago. He had decided Louis Castleman was a nut, and with the arrogance of youth, he had dismissed him entirely.

That day he had been under the poplar trees, bored, hot, and the voices had carried out clearly, the way they sometimes did on the prairie. Castleman had raved and his father had yelled from time to time.

"Wanted to shoot him and I had the gun, but I just couldn't do it. Couldn't bring myself to do it. He was the devil and you know it and he deserved shooting and I couldn't."

"Why didn't you just turn him over to the sheriff, you damn fool?"

"Couldn't do that either. We made a deal, the Judge and me. And that devil would have brought in everyone, you, the Judge, my girl, everyone, made filth of everything he talked about, everything he touched. He would have done that, the devil. So we walked and I tried to pray and forgot the words and she came. God knew she was innocent, the devil couldn't take away that innocence no matter what he did to her. God knew and sent her to me as a sign and she told me the price I'd have to pay and that was all right. A fair enough price to get the devil off the face of the earth. And then God took her back up to His heaven."

He had heard talk like that all his life, John thought, and had always dismissed it without considering what personal tragedies might lie behind it, what real terrors it concealed. He reached the crest of the hill and looked out over the prairie at the crazy, meandering trails that went nowhere in particular and briefly tried to find a pattern to them. There was none. Then he saw Lorna moving through the grass. She was not on a trail, but was walking directly toward the house as if she knew exactly where it was.

He watched her for several minutes. She had asked, mockingly he thought, if he was having a midlife crisis. Yes, he thought at her as she moved easily through the grass. He liked the loose jointedness of her walk, the way she held her head. It pleased him that she had had enough sense to make herself a sunhat out of grass. She would do, he thought nodding as the phrase came to him, revived from the Judge's pronouncement made more years ago than this girl had lived.

He waved then and she waved back. He joined her at the foot of the hill.

"Are you okay? I got worried, after all."

"I'm okay. I got lost for a while, then I . . . I reached a high place that let me see the house." She realized she could not tell him. She did not know him well enough; she did not understand enough to tell anyone, and she could not turn what had happened into small talk. Suddenly the silence between them became awkward and they walked to the house without speaking again.

He watched her drink thirstily, watched his father's careful neutrality turn into acceptance, and he knew the girl he had first met here, the girl he had yearned for like a schoolboy, was gone, lost on the prairie perhaps. He was very much afraid that he was in love with the woman who had replaced her.

After her thirst had been satisfied, David MacLaren said he wanted to take the piano out to the middle of the dirt road and burn it. No one objected. There was a dolly and straps in the truck; the truck could be backed up to the porch and he didn't give a damn how they dumped the thing into it. An hour later they stood and watched as the first flames caught and flared straight up. They had brought out buckets of water and a broom and a rake, even blankets that had been soaked and were already drying out. They knew that if the prairie caught fire it would all burn. No one had mentioned it and they watched the fire silently. The back of the piano popped off and stacks of money fell out, caught fire and burned. No one made a motion to salvage any of it.

The devil's money, John thought, watching it curl up, blaze, turn to ash. He wanted to take nothing with him, nothing that belonged here.

She had not earned it, Lorna thought as she watched it burn. Had there been a choice? Could she have intervened? Not having an answer had put shadows in her eyes although she was not yet aware of them.

When the fire was little more than smoldering ashes, John dug a pit in the road. It was too hard-packed to go very deep, but it was enough to rake the ashes into, to let him pour water over them, and finally to cover them with the pale, sun-bleached dirt.

"Will you come to visit us?" David MacLaren asked Lorna, holding her hand. "I'd like my wife to meet you."

"Yes," she said. "Thank you."

He would take it easy, he assured John. The Buick was comfortable and he was not in a hurry now. He wanted thinking time, a lot of thinking time.

Lorna and John sat on the top step of the front porch where the poplars cast deep shade. They would keep an eye on the hot spot in the road, they had told his father.

"Hungry?" he asked, thinking of her peanut butter and sardines. She looked surprised, then nodded, and he went in and brought out everything edible he could find. The silence was companionable now, not awkward.

"I'd like to have your address," he said after they had eaten.

"Yes. It's not fixed at the moment, though."

"Mine is."

She turned to give him one of her long searching looks and then nodded. She was glad that he realized they could meet now in an ageless relationship, wherever it might lead eventually. She was glad that they could move with the unhurried rhythms of the prairie itself, take the time they both needed before decisions had to be made. She was most glad that none of them had demanded answers, that they had by silent consent agreed that first they had to find the right questions, and that might take a lifetime. She leaned her head against the newel post and listened to the rustlings of the grass and did not know that he heard the sounds as a singing that his heart could not contain.

LISTENING TO BRAHMS

Suzy McKee Charnas

Suzy McKee Charnas is a past Nebula Award winner in the novella category. Her graceful but infrequent short fictions have appeared in *New Dimensions, Omni,* and *New Voices.* She is best known for her novels, *Walk to the End of the World* (her first novel, which received favorable attention from Marge Piercy and William S. Burroughs), *The Vampire Tapestry, Motherlines,* and the recent *Dorothea Dreams.*

About "Listening to Brahms" she writes:

"I can hardly call myself a writer of short fiction on the basis of my output, but from time to time something less bulky than a novel finds a way to get itself written by me. 'Brahms' is a case in point. This tale began with a conversation that I overheard at a concert in 1981. What I had heard struck me deeply at the time and would not go away afterward. I knew it signified something but I could not put my finger on exactly what, and when I tried writing it out as straightforward narration, I ended up with a mere anecdote. So I put the whole thing away and tried to forget it, not very successfully. Because it did signify.

"Prompted by impulse, I ran it through the typewriter again in the spring of 1985 and found myself writing, very quickly and easily, what I later recognized as the guts and bones of a long, bitter, melancholy novel, tightly compressed. This brevity was essential, so that the grimmer aspects of the story could be lightly brushed in—danced in, almost—and leave the reader affected (I hoped) but alive, not bludgeoned to death with expansive horrors and lavish gloom. I see this with hindsight, of course; at the time I structured nothing, just let my narrator tell his tale. It was done in two weeks and sold in two more, in direct contradiction to the aforesaid known fact that I am not a writer of short fiction.

"Some weeks later I happened to be looking through some notes that I keep of the dreams that I remember and I found the account of a dream (which predated the writing of 'Brahms' by

about a month) in which an upright, lizard-like humanoid and I sat engaged in a lengthy conversation of which not one word remained in my waking mind. But maybe it all stuck in the part of the brain that attends to such things, so that in effect I had already been told (or had told myself) the story, which I then retrieved in this very tight, boiled-down form, on paper.

"Whatever the mechanism, I think the novelette form suits the material nicely, and I congratulate myself on having gotten away with producing a novel without having had to sink the usual three years of my life into making a full-scale book. I'd love to be able to do something like it again (process, I mean, not product), but given my pattern of pattern-avoidance, it's not too likely that I will. But it was a great feeling while it lasted, and I like to think that the result goes some little way toward paying the debt I owe to the music that has fed and sustained me for so many years."

Entry 1: They had already woken up Chandler and Ross. They did me third. I was supposed to be up first so I could check the data on the rest of our crew during their cold sleep, but how would a bunch of aliens know that?

Our ship is full of creatures with peculiar eyes and wrinkled skin covered with tiny scales, a lot like lizards walking around on their hind legs. Their skins are grayish or greenish or even bluish sometimes. They have naked-looking faces—no hair—with features that seem polished smooth. The first ones I met had wigs on, and they wore evening clothes and watered-silk sashes with medals. I was too numb brained to laugh, and now I don't feel like it. They all switched to jumpsuits once the formalities were over. I keep waiting for them to unzip their jumpsuits and then their lizard suits and climb out, regular human beings. I keep waiting for the joke to be over.

They speak English, some with accents, some not. They have breathy voices and talk very softly to us. That may be because of what they have to say. They say Earth burned itself up, which is why we never got our wake-up signal and were still in the freezer when they found us. Chandler believes them. Ross doesn't. I won't know what the others think until they're unfrozen.

I sit looking through the viewplate at Earth, such as it is. I know what the lizards say is true, but I don't think I really believe it. I think mostly that I'm dead or having a terrible dream.

Entry 2: Steinbrunner killed himself (despite their best efforts to prevent anything like that, the lizards say). Sue Anne Beamish, fifth to be thawed, won't talk to anybody. She grits her teeth all the time. I can hear them grinding whenever she's around. It's very annoying.

The lead lizard's name is Captain Midnight. He says he knows it's not the most appropriate name for a spaceflight commander, but he likes the sound of it.

It seems that on their home planet the lizards have been fielding our various Earth transmissions, both radio and TV, and they borrow freely from what they've found there. They are given native names, but if they feel like it later they take Earth-type names instead. Those on Captain Midnight's ship all have Earth-type names. Luckily the names are pretty memorable, because I can't tell one alien from another except by the name badges they wear on their jumpsuits. I look at them sometimes and I wonder if I'm crazy. Can't afford to be, not if I've got to deal on a daily basis with things that look as if they walked out of a Walt Disney cartoon feature.

They revive us one by one and try to make sure nobody else cuts their wrists like Steinbrunner. He cut the long way that can't be fixed.

I look out the viewplate at what's left of the Earth and let the talk slide over me. We can't raise anything from down there. I can't raise anything inside me either. I can only look and look and let the talk slide over me. Could I be dead after all? I feel dead.

Entry 3: Captain Midnight says now that we're all up he would be honored beyond expression if we would consent to come back to Kondra with him and his crew in their ship. *Kondra* is their name for their world. Chu says she's worked out where and what it is in our terms, and she keeps trying to show me on the star charts. I don't look; I don't care. I came up here to do studies on cryogenic nutrition in space, not to look at star charts.

It doesn't matter what I came up here to do. Earth is a moon with a moon now. *Nutrition* doesn't mean anything, not in connection with anything human. There's nothing to nourish. There's just this airless rock, like all the other airless rocks rolling around in space.

I took the data the machines recorded about us while we slept and I junked it. Chu says I did a lot of damage to some of our equipment in the process. I didn't set out to do that, but it felt good, or something like good, to go on from wiping out information to smashing metal. I've assured everybody that I won't break out like that again. It doesn't accomplish anything, and I felt foolish afterward. I'm not sure they believe me. I'm not sure I believe my own promise.

Morris and Myers say they won't go with the Kondrai. They say they want to stay here in our vessel just in case something happens down there or in case some other space mission survived and shows up looking for whatever's left, which is probably only us.

Captain Midnight says they can rig a beacon system on our craft to attract anybody who does come around and let them know where we've gone. I can tell the lizards are not going to let Morris and Myers stay here and die.

They say, the Kondrai do, that they didn't actually come here for us. After several generations of receiving and enjoying Earth's transmissions, Kondran authorities decided to borrow a ship from a neighboring world and send Earth an embassy from Kondra, a mission of goodwill.

First contact at last, and there's nobody here but the seven of us. Tough on the Kondrai. They expected to find a whole worldful of us, glued to our screens and speakers. Tough shit all around.

I have dreams so terrible there are no words.

Entry 4: There's nothing for us to do on the Kondran ship, which is soft and leathery inside its alloy shell. I have long talks with Walter Drake, who is head of mission. Walter Drake is female, I think. Walter Duck.

If I can make a joke, does that mean I'm crazy?

It took me a while to figure out what was wrong with the name. Then I said, "Look, it's Sir Walter *Raleigh* or Sir *Francis* Drake."

She said, "But we don't always just copy. I have chosen to commemorate two great voyagers."

I said, "And they were both males."

She said, "That's why I dropped the *Sir.*"

Afterward I can't believe these conversations. I resent the end of the world, my world, coming on as a bad joke with Edgar Rice Burroughs aliens.

Myers and Morris play chess with each other all day and won't talk to anybody. Most of us don't like to talk to each other right now. We can't look in each other's eyes, for some reason. There's an excuse in the case of not looking the lizards in the eyes. They have this nictitating membrane. It's unsettling to look at that.

All the lizards speak English and at least one other Earth language. Walter Drake says there are several native languages on Kondra, but they aren't spoken in the population centers anymore. Kondran culture, in its several major branches, is very old. It was once greater and more complex than our own, she says, but then it got simple again and the population began to drop. The whole species was, in effect, beginning to close down. When our signals were first picked up, something else began to happen: a growing trend toward population increase and a young generation fascinated by Earth culture.

The older Kondrai, who had gone back to living like their

ancestors in the desert, didn't object. They said fine, let the youngsters do as they choose as long as they let the oldsters do likewise.

I had to walk away when Walter Drake told me about this. It started me thinking about my own people I left back on Earth, all dead now. I won't put their names down. I was crying. Now I've stopped, and I don't want to start again. It makes my eyes hurt.

Walter Drake brought me some tapes of music that they've recorded from our broadcasts. They collect our signals, every thing they can, through something they call the Retrieval Project. They reconstruct the broadcasts and record them and store the recordings in a huge library for study. Our classical music has a great following there.

I've been listening to some Bach partitas. My mother played the piano. She sometimes played Bach.

Entry 5: Sibelius, Symphony No. 2 in D, Op. 43; Tchaikovsky, Variations on a Rococo Theme, Op. 33; Rachmaninoff, Symphonic Dances, Op. 45; Mozart, Clarinet Quintet in A major, K581; Sibelius, Symphony No. 2 in D, Op. 43; Sibelius Symphony No. 2 in D, Op. 43.

Entry 6: Chandler is alive, Ross is alive, Beamish is alive, Chu is alive, Morris is alive, Myers is alive, and I am alive. But that doesn't count. I mean I can't count it. Up. To mean anything. *Why* are we alive?

Entry 7: Myers swallowed a chess piece. The lizards operated on him somehow and saved his life.

Entry 8: Woke up from a dream wondering if maybe we did die in our ship and my "waking life" in the Kondran ship is really just some kind of after-death hallucination. Suppose I died, suppose we all actually died at the same moment Earth died? It wouldn't make any difference. Earth's people are all dead and someplace else or nowhere, but we are *here*. We are separate.

They're in contact with their home planet all the time. Chu is fascinated by their communications technology, which is wild, she says. Skips over time or folds up space—I don't know,

I'm just a nutrition expert. Apparently on Kondra now they are making up their own human-style names instead of lifting them ready-made. (Walter Drake was a pioneer in this, I might point out.) Captain Midnight has changed his name. He is henceforth to be known as Vernon Zeno Ellerman.

Bruckner and Mahler symphonies, over and over, fill a lot of time. Walter Drake says she is going to get me some fresh music, though I haven't asked for any.

Entry 9: Beamish came and had a talk with me. She looked fierce.

"Listen, Flynn," she said, "we're not going to give up."

"Give up what?" I said.

"Don't be so obtuse," she said between her teeth. "The human race isn't ended as long as even a handful of us are still alive and kicking."

I am alive, though I don't know why (I now honestly do not recall the exact nature of the experiments I was on board our craft to conduct). I'm not sure I'm kicking, and I told her so.

She grinned and patted my knee. "Don't worry about it, Flynn. I don't mean you should take up where you left off with Lily Chu." That happened back in training. I didn't even remember it until Beamish said this. "Nobody's capable right now, which is just as well. Besides, the women in this group are not going to be anybody's goddamn brood mares, science-fiction traditions to the contrary."

"Oh," I said. I think.

She went on to say that the Kondrai have or can borrow the technology to develop children for us in vitro. All we have to do is furnish the raw materials.

I said fine. I had developed another terrible headache. I've been having headaches lately.

After she left I tried some music. Walter Drake got me *Boris Godunov*, but I can't listen to it. I can't listen to anything with people's voices. I don't know how to tell this to Walter Drake. Don't want to tell her. It's none of her business anyhow.

Entry 10: Chu and Morris are sleeping together. So much for

Beamish's theory that nobody is capable. With Myers not up to playing chess yet, I guess Morris had to find something to do.

Chu said to me, "I'm sorry, Michael."

I felt this little, far-off sputtering like anger somewhere deep down, and then it went out. "That's okay," I said. And it is.

Chandler has been spending all his time in the communications cell of the ship with another lizard, one with a French name that I can't remember. Chandler tells us he's learning a lot about Kondran life. I tune him out when he talks like this. I never go to the communications cell. The whole thing gives me a headache. Everything gives me a headache except music.

Entry 11: I was sure it would be like landing in some kind of imitation world, a hodgepodge of phony bits and pieces copied from Earth. That's why I wouldn't go out for two K-days after we landed.

Everybody was very understanding. Walter Drake stayed on-board with me.

"We have fixed up a nice hotel where you can all be together," she told me, "like the honored guests that you are."

I finally got off and went with the others when she gave me the music recordings to take with me. She got me a playback machine. I left the Mozart clarinet quintet behind, and she found it and brought it after me. But I won't listen to it. The clarinet sound was made by somebody's living breath, somebody who's dead now, like all of them. I can't stand to hear that sound.

The hotel was in a suburb of a city, which looked a little like L.A., though not as much as I had expected. Later sometime I should try to describe the city. There's a hilly part, something like San Francisco, by the sea. We asked to go over there instead. They found us a sort of rooming house of painted wood with a basement. Morris and Chu have taken the top floor, though I don't think they sleep together anymore.

Ross has the apartment next door to me. She's got her own problems. She threw up when she first set foot on Kondra. She throws up almost every day, says she can't help it.

There are invitations for us to go meet the locals and partici-
pate in this and that, but the lizards do not push. They are so
damned considerate and respectful. I don't go anywhere. I stay
in my room and listen to music. Handel helps me sleep.

Entry 12: Four and a half K-years have passed. I stopped
doing this log because Chandler showed me his. He was keeping
a detailed record of what was happening to us, what had happened, what he thought was going to happen. Then Beamish
circulated her version, and Dr. Birgit Nilson, the lizard in charge
of our mental health, started encouraging us all to contribute
what we could to a "living history" project.

I was embarrassed to show anybody my comments. I am not
a writer or an artist like Myers has turned out to be. (His pictures
are in huge demand here, and he has a whole flock of Kondran
students.) If Chandler and Beamish were writing everything
down, why should I waste my time doing the same thing?

Living history of what, for whom?

Also I didn't like what Chandler wrote about me and Walter
Drake. Yes, I slept with her. One of us would have tried it, sooner
or later, with one lizard or another. I just happened to be the one
who did. I had better reasons than any of the others. Walter
Drake had been very kind to me.

I was capable all right (still am). But the thought of going
to bed with Lily or Sue Anne made my skin creep, though I
couldn't have said why. On the Kondran ship I used to jerk off
and look at the stuff in my hand and wonder what the hell it was
doing there: Didn't my body know that my world is gone, my
race, my species?

Sex with Walter Drake is different from sex with a woman.
That's part of what I like about it. And another thing. Walter
Drake doesn't cry in her sleep.

Walter and I did all right. For a couple of years I went
traveling alone, at the government's expense—like everything
we do here—all over Kondra. Walter was waiting when I got
back. So we went to live together away from the rooming house.
The time passed like a story or a dream. Not much sticks in my

head now from that period. We listened to a lot of music together. Nothing with flutes or clarinet, though. String music, percussion, piano music, horns only if they're blended with other sounds—that's what I like. Lots of light stuff, Dukas and Vivaldi and Milhaud.

Anyway, that period is over. After all this time Chu and Morris have committed suicide together. They used a huge old pistol one of them must have smuggled all this way. Morris, probably. He always had a macho hang-up.

Beamish goes around saying, "Why? Why?" At first I thought this was the stupidest question I'd ever heard. I was seriously worried that maybe these years on Kondran food and water had addled her mind through some weird allergic reaction.

Then she said, "We're so close, Flynn. Why couldn't they have waited? I wouldn't have let them down."

I keep forgetting about her in vitro project. It's going well, she says. She works very hard with a whole team of Kondrai under Dr. Boleslav Singh, preparing a cultural surround for the babies she's developing. She comes in exhausted from long discussions with Dr. Boleslav Singh and Dr. Birgit Nilson and others about the balance of Earth information and Kondran information to be given to the human babies. Beamish wants to make little visitors out of the babies. She says it's providential that we were found by the Kondrai—a race that has neatly caught and preserved everything transmitted by us about our own culture and our past. So now all that stuff is just waiting to be used, she says, to bridge the gap in our race's history. "The gap," that's what she calls it. She has a long-range plan of getting a ship for the in vitros to use when they grow up and want to go find a planet they can turn into another Earth. This seems crazy to me. But she is entitled. We all are.

I've moved back into the rooming house. I feel it's my duty, now that we're so few. Walter has come with me.

Entry 13: Mozart's piano concertos, especially Alfred Brendel's renditions, all afternoon. I have carried out my mission after all—to answer the question: What does a frozen Earthman eat for breakfast? The answer is music. For lunch? Music. Dinner? Music. This frozen Earthman stays alive on music.

Entry 14: A year and a half together in the rooming house, and Walter Drake and I have split up. Maybe it has nothing to do with being in the rooming house with the other humans. Divorce is becoming very common among young Kondrai. So is something like hair. They used to wear wigs. Now they have developed a means of growing featherlike down on their heads and in their armpits, etc.

When Walter came in with a fine dusting of pale fuzz on her pate, I told her to pack up and get out. She says she understands, she's not bitter. She doesn't understand one goddamned thing.

Entry 15: Beamish's babies, which I never went to see, have died of an infection that whipped through the whole lot of them in three days. The Kondran medical team taking care of them caught it, too, though none of them died. A few are blind from it, perhaps permanently.

Myers took pictures of the little corpses. He is making paintings from his photos. Did I put it in here that swallowing a chess piece did not kill Myers? Maybe it should have, but it seems nothing can kill Myers. He is as tough as rawhide. But he doesn't play chess, not since Morris killed himself. There are Kondrai who play very well, but Myers refuses their invitations. You can say that for him at least.

He just takes photographs and paints.

I'm not really too sorry about the babies. I don't know which would be worse, seeing them grow up as a little clutch of homeless aliens among the lizards or seeing them adapt and become pseudo-Kondrai. I don't like to think about explaining to them how the world they really belong to blew itself to hell. (Lily Chu is the one who went over the signals the Kondrai salvaged about that and sorted out the sequence of events. That was right before she killed herself.) We slept through the end of our world. Bad enough to do it, worse to have to talk about it. I never talk about it now, not even with the Kondrai. With Dr. Birgit Nilson I discuss food, of course, and health. I find these boring and absurd subjects, though I cooperate out of politeness. I also don't want to get stuck on health problems, like Chandler, who has gone through one hypochondriacal frenzy after another in the past few years.

Beamish says she will try again. Nothing will stop her. She confided to Ross that she thinks the Kondrai deliberately let the babies die, maybe even infected them on purpose. "They don't want us to revive our race," she said to Ross. "They're trying to take our place. Why should they encourage the return of the real thing?"

Ross told me Beamish wants her to help arrange some kind of escape from Kondra, God knows to where. Ross is worried about Beamish. "What," she says, "if she goes off the deep end and knifes some innocent lizard medico? They might lock us all up permanently."

Ross does not want to be locked up. She plays the cello all the time, which used to be a hobby of hers. The lizards were only too pleased to furnish her an instrument. A damn good one, too, she says. What's more, she now has three Kondrai studying with her.

I don't care what she does. I walk around watching the Kondrai behave like us.

I have terrible dreams, still.

Symphonic music doesn't do it for me anymore, not even Sibelius. I can't hear enough of the music itself; there are too many voices. I listen to chamber pieces. There you can hear each sound, everything that happens between each sound and each other sound near it.

They gave me a free pass to the Library of the Retrieval Project. I spend a lot of time there, listening.

Entry 16: Fourteen K-years later. Beamish eventually did get three viable Earth-style children out of her last lot. Two of them drowned in a freak accident at the beach a week ago. The third one, a girl named Melissa, ran away. They haven't been able to find her.

Our tissue contributions no longer respond, though Beamish

keeps trying. She calls the Kondrai "snakefaces" behind their backs.

Her hair is gray. So is mine.

Kondran news is all about the growing tensions between Kondra and the neighbor world it does most of its trading with. I don't know how that used to work in economic terms, but apparently it's begun to break down. I never saw any of the inhabitants of that world, called Chadondal, except in pictures and Kondran TV news reports. Now I guess I never will. I don't care.

Something funny happened with the flu that killed all of Beamish's first babies. It seems to have mutated into something that afflicts the Kondrai the way cancer used to afflict human beings. This disease doesn't respond to the cure human researchers developed once they figured out that our cancer was actually a set of symptoms of an underlying disease. Kondran cancer is something all their own.

They are welcome to it.

Entry 17: I went up into the sandhills to have a look at a few of the Old Kondrai, the ones who never did buy into imitating Earth ways. Most of them don't talk English (they don't even talk much Kondran to each other), but they don't seem to mind if you hang around and watch them awhile.

They live alone or else in very small settlements on a very primitive level, pared down to basics. Your individual Old Kondran will have a small, roundish stone house or even a burrow or cave and will go fetch water every day and cook on a little cell-powered stove or a wood fire. They usually don't even have TV. They walk around looking at things or sit and meditate or dig in their flower gardens or carve things out of the local wood. Once in a while they'll get together for a dance or a sort of mass bask in the sun or to put on plays and skits and so on. These performances can go on for days. They have a sort of swap economy, which is honored elsewhere when they travel. You sometimes see these pilgrims in the city streets, just wandering around. They never stay long.

Some of the younger Kondrai have begun harking back to this sort of life, trying to create the same conditions in the cities, which is ridiculous. These youngsters act as if it's something absolutely basic they have to try to hang on to in the face of an invasion of alien ways. Earth ways.

This is obviously a backlash against the effects of the Retrieval Project. I keep an eye on developments. It's all fascinating and actually creepy. To me the backlash is uncannily reminiscent of those fundamentalist-nationalist movements—Christian American or Middle-Eastern Muslim or whatever—that made life such hell for so many people toward the end of our planet's life. But if you point this resemblance out, the anti-Retrieval Kondrai get furious because, after all, anything Earth-like is what they're reacting against.

I sometimes bring this up in conversation just to get a rise out of them.

If I'm talking to Kondrai who are part of the backlash, they invariably get furious. "No," they say, "we're just trying to turn back to our old, native ways!" They don't recognize this passion itself as something that humans, not Kondrai, were prone to. From what I can gather and observe, fervor, either reactionary or progressive, is something alien to native Kondran culture as it was before they started retrieving our signals. Their life was very quiet and individualized and pretty dull, as a matter of fact.

Sometimes I wish we'd found it like that instead of the way it had already become by the time we got here. Of course the Old Kondrai never would have sent us an embassy in the first place.

I talk to Dr. Birgit Nilson about all this a lot. We aren't exactly friends, but we communicate pretty well for a man and a lizard.

She says they have simply used human culture to revitalize themselves.

I think about the Old Kondrai I saw poking around, growing the kind of flowers that attract the flying grazers they eat, or just sitting. I like that better. If they were a dying culture they should have just gone ahead and died.

Entry 18: Ross has roped Chandler into her music making. Turns out he played the violin as a kid. They practice a lot in the rooming house. Sometimes Ross plays the piano, too. She's better on the cello. I sit on my porch, looking at the bay, and I listen.

Ross says the Kondrai as a group are fascinated by performance. Certainly they perform being human better and better all the time. They think of Earth's twentieth century as the Golden Age of Human Performance. How would they know? It's all secondhand here, everything.

I've been asked to join a nutritional-study team heading for Kondra-South, where some trouble spots are developing. I have declined. I don't care if they starve or why they starve. I had enough of looking at images of starvation on Earth, where we did it on a terrific scale. What a performance that was!

Also I don't want to leave here because then I wouldn't get to hear Ross and Chandler play. They do sonatas and duets and they experiment, not always very successfully, with adapting music written for other instruments. It's very interesting. Now that Ross is working on playing the piano as well as the cello, their repertoire has been greatly expanded.

They aren't nearly as good as the great musical performers of the Golden Age, of course. But I listen to them anyway whenever I can. There's something about live music. You get a hunger for it.

Entry 19: Myers has gone on a world tour. He is so famous as an artist that he has rivals, and there are rival schools led by artists he himself has trained. He spends all his time with the snakes now, the ones masquerading as artists and critics and aesthetes. He hardly ever stops at the rooming house or comes by here to visit.

Sue Anne Beamish and I have set up house together across the bay from the rooming house. She's needed somebody around her ever since they found the desiccated corpse of little Melissa in the rubbish dump and worked out what had been done to her.

The Kondran authorities say they think some of the Kondrachalikipon (as the anti-Retrieval-backlash members call themselves now, meaning "return to Kondran essence") were responsible. The idea is that these Kondracha meant what they did as a symbolic rejection of everything the Retrieval Project has retrieved and a warning that Kondra will not be turned into an imitation Earth without a fight.

When Dr. Birgit Nilson and I talked about this, I pointed out that the Kondracha, if it was them, didn't get it right. They should have dumped the kid's body on the Center House steps and then called a press conference. Next time they'll do it better, though, being such devoted students of our ways.

"I know that," she said. "What is becoming of us?"

Us meant "us Kondrai," of course, not her and me. She likes to think that we Earth guests have a special wisdom that comes from our loss and from a mystical blood connection with the culture that the Kondrai are absorbing. As if I spend my time thinking about that kind of thing. Dr. Birgit Nilson is a romantic.

I don't talk to Sue Anne about Melissa's death. I don't feel it enough, and she would know that. So many died before, what's one more kid's death now? A kid who could never have been human anyway because a human being is born on Earth and raised in a human society, like Sue Anne and me.

"We should have blown their ship up and us with it," she says, "on the way here."

She won't come with me to the rooming house to listen to Ross and Chandler play. They give informal concert evenings now. I go, even though the audience is ninety-eight percent lizard, because by now I know every recording of chamber music in the Retrieval Library down to the last scrape of somebody's chair during a live recital. The recordings are too faithful. I can just about tolerate the breath intake you hear sometimes when the first violinist cues a phrase. It's different with Ross and Chandler. Their live music makes the live sounds all right.

Concerts are given by Kondran "artists" all the time, but I won't go to those.

For one thing, I know perfectly well that we don't hear sounds, we human beings, not sounds from outside. Our inner ear vibrates to the sound from outside, and we hear the sound that our own ear creates inside the head in response to that vibration. Now, how can the Kondran ear be exactly the same as ours? No matter how closely they've learned to mimic the sounds that our musicians produced, Kondran ears can't be hearing what human ears do when human music is played. A Kondran concert of human music is a farce.

Poor Myers. He missed the chance to take pictures of Melissa's dead body so he could make paintings of it later.

Entry 20: They are saying that the reason there's so much crime and violence now on Kondra isn't because of the population explosion at all. Some snake who calls himself Swami Nanda has worked out how the demographic growth is only a sign of the underlying situation.

According to him Kondra made an "astral agreement" to take in not only us living human survivors but the souls of all the dead of Earth. Earth souls on the astral plane, seeing that there were soon going to be no more human bodies on Earth to get born into, sent out a call for new bodies and a new world to inhabit. The Kondran souls on the astral plane, having pretty much finished their work on the material world of Kondra, agreed to let human souls take over the physical plant here, as it were. Now the younger generation is all Earth souls reborn as Kondrai on this planet, and they're re-creating conditions familiar to them from Earth.

I have sent this "Swami" four furious letters. He answered the last one very politely and at great length, explaining it all very clearly with the words he has stolen for his stolen metaphysical concepts.

Oh, yes: Another dozen K-years have passed. I might as well just say *years*. Kondran years are only a few days off our own, and Chandler has stopped keeping his Earth-time calendar since he's gotten so deep into music.

Chandler is now doing some composing, Ross tells me.

Ross rebukes me when I call the Kondrai snakes, talking to me as gently and reasonably as the Kondrai themselves always talk to us. That makes me sick, which is pretty funny when I recall how she used to vomit every day when we first came here. So she can stop telling me how to talk and warning me that it's no good to be a recluse. No good for what? And what would be better?

Nobody ever taught me to play any instrument. My parents said I had no talent, and they were right. I'm a listener, so I listen. I'm doing my job. I wouldn't go to the rooming house and talk to Ross at all except for the music. They are getting really good. It's amazing. Once in a while I spend a week at the Retrieval Library listening to the really great performances that are recorded there, to make sure my taste hasn't become degraded.

It hasn't. My two crew mates are converting themselves, by some miracle of dedication, into fine performers.

Last night I had to walk out in the middle of a Beethoven sonata to be alone.

Entry 21: Sue Anne had a stroke last week. She is paralyzed down her left side. I am staying with her almost constantly because I know she can't stand having the snakes around her anymore.

She blames me, I know, for having cooperated with them. We all spent hours and hours with their researchers, filling out their information about our dead planet. How could we have refused? In the face of their courtesy and considering how worried we all were about forgetting Earth ourselves, how could we? Besides, we really had nothing else to do.

She blames me anyhow, but I don't mind.

A wave of self-immolation is going on among young Kondrai. They find themselves an audience and set themselves afire, and the watching Kondrai generally stand there as if hypnotized by the flames and do nothing.

Dr. Birgit Nilson told me, "Your entire population died out; many of them burnt up in an instant. This created much karma, and those who are responsible must be allowed to pay."

"You're a Nandist, then," I said. "Swami Nanda and his reincarnation crap."

"I see no other explanation," she said.

"It all makes sense to you?" I said.

"Yes." She stroked her cheek with her orange-polished talons. "It's a loan: We have lent our beautiful material world and our species' bodies in exchange for your energetic souls and your rich, passionate culture."

They are the crazy ones, not us.

Entry 22: Some wild-eyed young snake with his top feathers dyed blue took a shot at the swami this morning with an old-fashioned thorn gun.

They caught him. We watched on the news. The would-be assassin sneers at the camera like a real Earth punk. Sue Anne glares back and snorts derisively.

Entry 23: Dreamed of my mother at her piano, but her hands were Kondran hands. The fingers were too long and the nails were set like claws, and her skin was covered in minute, grayish scales.

I think she was playing Chopin.

Entry 24: Sometimes I wish I were a writer, to do all this justice. I might have some function as a survivor.

Look at Sue Anne: Except for some terrible luck, she would have created out of us a new posterity.

Myers is doing prints these days, but not on Earth themes anymore, though the Kondrai beg him to concentrate on what's "native" to him. He says his memory of Earth is no longer trustworthy, and besides, images of Kondra are native to the eyes of reborn Earth souls now. He accepts Nandism openly and goes around doing Kondran landscapes and portraits and so on. Well, nobody will have to miss any of that in my account, then. They can always look at Myers's pictures.

Walter Drake died last winter of Kondran cancer. I went to the funeral. For the first time I wore makeup.

Myers, the arrogant son of a bitch, condescended to share a secret with me. He uses this face paint, plus a close haircut or a feathered cap, to go out incognito among the snakes so he can observe them undisturbed. Age has smoothed his features and made him thin, like most Kondrai, and he's been getting away with it for years. Well, good for him. Look at what *they're* trying to get away with along those lines!

Being disguised has its advantages. I hadn't realized the pressure of being stared at all the time in public until I moved around without it.

They said, "Ashes to ashes and dust to dust," and I got dizzy and had to sit down on a bench.

Entry 25: Four more years. My heart still checks out, Dr. Birgit Nilson tells me. I put on makeup and hang out in the bars, watching TV with the Kondrai, but not too often. Sometimes they make me so damn nervous, even after so long here. I forget what they are and what I am. I forget myself. I get scared that I'm turning senile.

When I get home Sue Anne gives me this cynical look, and my perspective is restored. I play copy-tapes of Dvořák for her. Also Schubert. She likes the French, though. I find them superficial.

To hear Brahms and Beethoven and Mozart, I go to the rooming house. I go whenever Ross and Chandler play. While the music sounds the constant crying inside me gets so big and so painful and beautiful that I can't contain it. So it moves outside me for a while, and I feel rested and changed. This is only an illusion, but wonderful.

Entry 26: Poor Myers got caught in a religious riot on the other side of the world. He was beaten to death by a Kondracha mob. I guess his makeup job was careless. Dr. Birgit Nilson, much aged and using a cane, came to make a personal apology, which I accepted for old times' sake.

"We caught two of them," she said, "the ringleaders of the Kondracha group that killed your poor Mr. Myers."

"Kondrachalations," I said. Couldn't help myself.

Dr. Birgit looked at me. "Forgive me," she said. "I shouldn't have come."

When I told Sue Anne about this, she slapped my face. She

hasn't much strength even in her good arm these days. But I resented being hit and asked her why she did it.

"Because you were smiling, Michael."

"You can't cry all the time," I said.

"No," she said. "I wish we could."

Dr. Birgit Nilson says that Kondrai are now composing music in classical, popular, and "primitive" styles, all modeled on Earth music. I have not heard any of this new music. I do not want to.

Entry 27: At least Sue Anne didn't live to see this: They are now grafting lobes onto their ugly ear holes.

No, that's not the real news. The real news is about Kondra-South, where a splinter group of Kondracha extremists set up a sort of purist, Ur-Kondran state some years ago. They use only their version of Old Kondran farming methods, which is apparently not an accurate version. Their topsoil has been rapidly washing away in the summer floods.

Now they are killing newborns down there to have fewer mouths to feed. The pretext is that these newborns look like humans and are part of the great taint that everything Earthish represents to the pure. The official Kondrachalikipon line is that they are feeding themselves just fine, thank you. The truth seems to be mass starvation and infanticide.

After Sue Anne died I moved back into the rooming house. I have a whole floor to myself and scarcely ever go out. I watch Kondran TV a lot, which is how I keep track of their politics and so on. I keep looking for false notes that would reveal to any intelligent observer the hollowness of their performance of humanity. There isn't much except for my gut reaction. The Kondran claim to have preserved human culture by making it their own would be very convincing to anyone who didn't know better. Even their game shows look familiar. Young Kondrai go mad for music videos and deafening concerts by their own groups like the Bear Minimum and Dead Boring. I stare and stare at the screen, looking for slipups. I am not sure that I would recognize one now if I saw one.

I hate the lizards. I miss her. I hate them.

Entry 28: Ross and Chandler have done the unthinkable. At last night's musicale they sprang one hell of a surprise.

They have trained two young Kondrai to a degree that satisfies them (particularly Gillokan Chukchonturanfis, who plays both violin and viola).

Now the four of them are planning to go out and perform in public together as the Retrieval String Quartet.

The Lost Earth String Quartet I could stomach, maybe. Or the Ghost String Quartet, or the Remnant String Quartet. But then, of course, how could Kondran musicians be in it?

I walked out in protest.

Ross says I am being unreasonable and cutting off my nose to spite my face, since as a quartet they have so much more music they can play. To hell with Ross. The traitress. Chandler, too.

Entry 29: I cut my hair and put on my makeup and managed to get myself one ticket, not as Michael Flynn the Earthman but as a nameless Kondran. The debut concert of the Retrieval String Quartet is the event of the year in the city: a symbol of the passing of the torch of human culture, they say. An outrage, the Kondracha scream. I keep my thoughts to myself and lay my plans.

Lizards are pouring into the city for the event. Two bombings have already occurred, credit for them claimed by the Kondrachalikipon, of course.

As long as the scaly bastards don't blow me up before I do my job.

The gun is in my pocket, Morris's gun that I took after he and Chu killed themselves. I was a good shot once. My seat is close to the stage and on the aisle, leaving my right hand free. I have had too much bitterness in my life. I will not be mocked and betrayed in the one place where I find some comfort.

Entry 30: Now I know who I wrote all this for. Dear Dr. Herbert Akonditichilka: You do not know me. Until a little while ago I didn't know you either. I am the man who sat next to you in Carnegie Hall last night. Your Kondran version of

Carnegie Hall, that is: constructed from TV pictures; all sparkling in crystal and cream and red velvet—handsomer than the real place was, but in my judgment slightly inferior acoustically.

You didn't notice me, Doctor, because of my makeup. I noticed you. All evening I noticed everything, starting with the police and the Kondracha demonstration outside the hall. But you I noticed in particular. You managed to wreck my concentration during the last piece of fine music I expected to hear in my life.

It was the Haydn String Quartet Number One in G, Opus 77. I sat trying to hear the effect of having two Kondrai among the players, but your damned fidgeting distracted me.

Just my luck, I thought. *A Kondran who came for a historic event, though he has no feeling for classical Earth music at all.* All through the Haydn you sat locked tight except for these tiny, spasmodic movements of your head, arms, and hands. It was a great relief to me when the music ended and you joined the crashing applause. I was so busy glaring at you that I missed seeing the musicians leave the stage.

I watched you all through the interval. I needed something to fix my attention on while I waited. The second piece was to be one of my favorites, the Brahms String Quartet Number Two in A minor, Opus 51. I had chosen the opening of that quartet as my signal. I meant to see to it that the Brahms would never be played by the traitors Ross and Chandler and the two snakes they had trained. In fact, no one was ever going to hear Ross and Chandler play anything again.

What would happen to me afterward I didn't know or care (though it crossed my mind in a farcical moment that I might be rescued as a hero by the Kondracha).

I wondered if you would be a problem—an effective interference, once the first note of the Brahms piece sounded and I began to make my move. I thought not.

You were small and thin, Dr. Akonditichilka, neatly dressed in your fake blazer with the fake gold buttons; a thick thatch of white top feathers; a round face, for a lizard; and glasses that made your eyes enormous. I wondered if you had ruined your eyesight studying facsimile texts taken from Earth transmissions. I could see by the grayed-off skin color that you were elderly, like so many in this audience, though probably not as old as I am.

You fell into conversation with the Kondran on your left. I realized from what I could overhear that the two of you had met for the first time earlier that same day. She was now exploring the contact. "Oh," she said, "you're a doctor?"

"Retired," you said.

"You must meet Mischa Two Hawks," she said, "my escort tonight. He's a retired doctor, too."

The seat to her left was empty. Retired doctor Mischa Two Hawks may have withdrawn to the men's room or gone out in the lobby for a smoke.

You must understand, my mind made automatic translations as fast as the thought finished: Imitation retired, imitation doctor Mischa S. (for Stolen names) Two Hawks was in the imitation men's room or smoking an imitation cigarette.

His companion, an imitation woman in a green, imitation wool dress, wore a white wig with a blue-rinse tint. God, how Beamish used to rage over the tendency of Kondran females to choose the most traditional women's styles as models! Beamish would have been proud of my work tonight, I thought.

Green Wool Dress, whose name I had not caught, said to you, "The lady with you this afternoon at the gallery—is she your wife? And where is she tonight?"

You shook your head, and your glasses flashed. It pleases me that the nictitating membrane prevents you snakes from wearing contact lenses.

"We used to go to every concert in the city together," you said. "We both love good music, and there is no replacement for hearing it live. But she's been losing her hearing. She doesn't go anymore; it's too painful for her."

"What a pity," Green Wool Dress said. "To miss such a great event! Wasn't the first violinist wonderful just now? And so young, too. It was amazing to hear him."

Damned right it was. Chandler had literally played second fiddle to his own student, Chukchonturanfis. For that alone I could have killed my old crew mate.

I shut my eyes and thought about the gun in my pocket. It was a heavy goddamned thing. I thought about the danger of getting it caught in the cloth as I pulled it out, of missing my aim, of my elderly self being jumped by you two elderly aliens before I could complete my job. I thought of Chandler and Ross, no spring chickens themselves anymore, soon to die and leave me alone among you. The whole thing was a sort of doddering comedy.

Another Kondran, heavyset for a lizard and bald, worked his way along the row of seats. He hovered next to Green Wool Dress, clearly wanting to sit down. She wouldn't let him until she had made introductions. This was, of course, retired doctor Mischa Two Hawks.

"Akonditichilka," you said with a little bow. "Herbert." And the two of you shook hands across Green Wool Dress. All three of you settled back to chat.

Suddenly I heard your voices as music. You, Doctor, were the first violin, with your clear, light tenor. Dr. Two Hawks's lower register made a reasonable cello. Green Wool Dress, who scarcely spoke, was second violin, of course, noodling busily along among her own thoughts. And I was the viola, hidden and dark.

If this didn't stop I knew I would use the gun right now, on you and then on myself. I listened to the words you were saying instead of your voices. I grabbed onto the words to keep control.

"A beautiful piece, the Haydn," you were saying. "I have played it. Oh, not like these musicians, of course. But I used to belong to an amateur chamber group." (How like you thieving snakes, to mimic our own medical doctors' affinity for music making as a hobby!) You went on to explain how it was that you no longer played. Some slow, crippling Kondran bone disease. Of course—your lizard claws were never meant to handle a bow and strings. What was your instrument? I missed that. You said you had not played for six or seven years now. No wonder you had twitched all through the Haydn, remembering.

Some snake in a velvet suit pushed past, managing to step on both my feet. We traded insincere apologies, and he went on to trample past you and your companions. They were all hurrying back in now. My moment was coming. The row was fully occupied, so I sat down and pretended to skim the program notes for the next piece.

On you went, in that clear, distantly regretful tone. I couldn't stop hearing. "It's been a terrible season for me," you said. "My only grandchild died last month. He was fifteen."

Your voice was not music. It was just a voice, taking a tone I remembered from when I and my crew mates first began to be able to say to each other, "Well, it's all gone, blown up—mankind and womankind and whalekind and everykind smashed to smithereens while we were sleeping." It's how you sound instead of screaming. You have no more actual screaming left in your throat, but you can't stop talking about what is making you scream, because the screaming of your spirit is going on and on.

My eyes locked on the page in front of me. Had you really spoken this way, to two strangers, at a concert? The other two were making sounds of shock and sympathy.

"Cancer," you said, though of course you meant not our kind of cancer but Kondran cancer, and of course even if you were screaming inside it wasn't the same as the spirit of a human being screaming that way.

You leaned forward in your seat to talk across Green Wool Dress to Dr. Two Hawks. "It was terrible," you said. "It started in his right leg. None of the therapy even slowed it down. They did three operations."

I sneaked a look at you to see what kind of expression you wore on your imitation human face while you recited your afflictions. But you were leaning outward to address your fellow doctor, and the back of your narrow lizard shoulders was turned toward me.

Between you two, Green Wool Dress sat with a blank social

smile, completely withdrawn into herself. I tried to follow what you were saying, but you got into technical terms, one doctor to another.

The musicians were tuning up their instruments backstage. The gun felt like a battleship in my pocket. Under the dimming lights I could make out the face of Dr. Two Hawks, sympathetic and earnest. Amazing, I thought, how they've learned to produce the effect of expressions like our own with their alien musculature and their alien skin.

"But it's better now than it was at first," Dr. Two Hawks protested (I thought of Beamish's babies and the death of Walter Drake). "I can remember when there was nothing to do but cut and cut, and even then—there was a young patient I remember, we removed the entire hip—oh, we were desperate. Dreadful things were done. It's better now."

All around, oblivious, members of the audience settled expectantly into their seats, whispering to each other, rustling program pages. Apparently I was your only involuntary eavesdropper, and soon that ordeal would be over.

The audience quieted, and here they came: Ross first, then Chandler (the Kondran players didn't matter). Ross first: You wouldn't see the blood on her red dress. No one would understand exactly what was happening, and that would give me time to get Chandler, too. I needed my concentration. My moment was here.

On you went, inexorably, in your quiet, melancholy tone: "As a last resort they castrated him. He lost most of his skin at the end, and he was too weak to sip fluids through a tube. I think now it was all a mistake. We should never have fought so hard. We should have let him die at the start."

"But we can't just give up!" cried Dr. Two Hawks over the applause for the returning musicians. "We must do *something!*"

And you sighed, Dr. Akonditichilka. "Aaah," you said softly, a long curve of sounded breath in the silence before the players began. You leaned there an instant longer, looking across at him.

Then you said gently (and how clearly your voice still sounds in my mind)—each word a steep, sweet fall in pitch from the one before—"Let's listen to Brahms."

And you sat back slowly in your seat as the first notes rippled into the hall. After a little I managed to uncramp my fingers from around the gun and take my empty hand out of my pocket. We sat there together in the dimness, our eyes stinging with tears past shedding, and we listened.

R & R

Lucius Shepard

Lucius Shepard recently won the John W. Campbell Award for Best New Writer, yet his achievements seem to belong to a writer who has spent many years at his craft. His books include the novel *Green Eyes* and a collection of stories, *The Jaguar Hunter.* Readers of this anthology series will recall that he graced the pages of *Nebula Awards 20* with the wonderfully self-assured fantasy "The Man Who Painted the Dragon Griaule." New stories by Shepard may be found in *Universe, Isaac Asimov's Science Fiction Magazine, Playboy,* and *The Magazine of Fantasy & Science Fiction. Life During Wartime* is his newest novel.

This year he was nominated in two categories, novella and novelette, and won his first Nebula in the novella. He writes:

"I really can't think of anything worth saying concerning either 'R & R' or 'Aymara' that is not implicit in the material itself, except to comment that both are attempts to make plain my feeling that science fiction is well suited to creating a literature of witness in that it's capable of treating the immediate future as though it were the immediate past, and thus achieving a poignancy of effect inaccessible to 'mainstream' fiction."

1.

One of the new Sikorsky gunships, an element of the First Air Cavalry with the words Whispering Death painted on its side, gave Mingolla and Gilbey and Baylor a lift from the Ant Farm to San Francisco de Juticlan, a small town located inside the green zone which on the latest maps was designated Free Occupied Guatemala. To the east of this green zone lay an undesignated band of yellow that crossed the country from the Mexican border to the Caribbean. The Ant Farm was a firebase on the eastern edge of the yellow band, and it was from there that Mingolla—an artillery specialist not yet twenty-one years old—lobbed shells into an area which the maps depicted in black and white terrain markings. And thus it was that he often thought of himself as engaged in a struggle to keep the world safe for primary colors.

Mingolla and his buddies could have taken their r&r in Río or Caracas, but they had noticed that the men who visited these cities had a tendency to grow careless upon their return; they understood from this that the more exuberant your r&r, the more likely you were to wind up a casualty, and so they always opted for the lesser distractions of the Guatemalan towns. They were not really friends: they had little in common, and under different circumstances they might well have been enemies. But taking their r&r together had come to be a ritual of survival, and once they had reached the town of their choice, they would go their separate ways and perform further rituals. Because they had survived so much already, they believed that if they continued to perform these same rituals they would complete their tours unscathed. They had never acknowledged their belief to one another, speaking of it only obliquely—that, too, was part of the ritual—and had this belief been challenged they would have admitted its irrationality; yet they would also have pointed out that the strange character of the war acted to enforce it.

The gunship set down at an airbase a mile west of town, a cement strip penned in on three sides by barracks and offices, with the jungle rising behind them. At the center of the strip another Sikorsky was practicing take-offs and landings—a drunken, camouflage-colored dragonfly—and two others were hovering overhead like anxious parents. As Mingolla jumped out a hot breeze fluttered his shirt. He was wearing civvies for the first time in weeks, and they felt flimsy compared to his combat gear; he glanced around, nervous, half-expecting an unseen enemy to take advantage of his exposure. Some mechanics were lounging in the shade of a chopper whose cockpit had been destroyed, leaving fanglike shards of plastic curving from the charred metal. Dusty jeeps trundled back and forth between the buildings; a brace of crisply starched lieutenants were making a brisk beeline toward a fork-lift stacked high with aluminum coffins. Afternoon sunlight fired dazzles on the seams and handles of the coffins, and through the heat haze the distant line of barracks shifted like waves in a troubled olive-drab sea. The incongruity of the scene—its What's-Wrong-With-This-Picture mix of the horrid and the commonplace—wrenched at Mingolla. His left hand trembled, and the light seemed to grow brighter, making him weak and vague. He leaned against the Sikorsky's rocket pod to steady himself. Far above, contrails were fraying in the deep blue range of the sky: XL-16s off to blow holes in Nicaragua. He stared after them with something akin to longing, listening for their engines, but heard only the spacy whisper of the Sikorskys.

Gilbey hopped down from the hatch that led to the computer deck behind the cockpit; he brushed imaginary dirt from his jeans and sauntered over to Mingolla and stood with hands on hips: a short muscular kid whose blond crewcut and petulant mouth gave him the look of a grumpy child. Baylor stuck his head out of the hatch and worriedly scanned the horizon. Then he, too, hopped down. He was tall and raw-boned, a couple of years older than Mingolla, with lank black hair and pimply olive skin and features so sharp that they appeared to have been hatcheted into shape. He rested a hand on the side of the Sikorsky, but almost instantly, noticing that he was touching the flaming letter W in Whispering Death, he jerked the hand away as if he'd been scorched. Three days before there had been an all-out assault on the Ant Farm, and Baylor had not recovered from it. Neither had Mingolla. It was hard to tell whether or not Gilbey had been affected.

One of the Sikorsky's pilots cracked the cockpit door. "Y'all can catch a ride into 'Frisco at the PX," he said, his voice muffled by the black bubble of his visor. The sun shined a white blaze on the visor, making it seem that the helmet contained night and a single star.

"Where's the PX?" asked Gilbey.

The pilot said something too muffled to be understood.

"What?" said Gilbey.

Again the pilot's response was muffled, and Gilbey became angry. "Take that damn thing off!" he said.

"This?" The pilot pointed to his visor. "What for?"

"So I can hear what the hell you sayin'."

"You can hear now, can'tcha?"

"Okay," said Gilbey, his voice tight. "Where's the goddamn PX?"

The pilot's reply was unintelligible; his faceless mask regarded Gilbey with inscrutable intent.

Gilbey balled up his fists. "Take that son of a bitch off!"

"Can't do it, soldier," said the second pilot, leaning over so that the two black bubbles were nearly side by side. "These here doobies"—he tapped his visor—"they got microcircuits that beams shit into our eyes. 'Fects the optic nerve. Makes it so we can see the beaners even when they undercover. Longer we wear 'em, the better we see."

Baylor laughed edgily, and Gilbey said, "Bull!" Mingolla naturally assumed that the pilots were putting Gilbey on, or else their reluctance to remove the helmets stemmed from a superstition, perhaps from a deluded belief that the visors actually did bestow special powers. But given a war in which combat drugs were issued and psychics predicted enemy movements, anything was possible, even microcircuits that enhanced vision.

"You don't wanna see us, nohow," said the first pilot. "The beams mess up our faces. We're deformed-lookin' mothers."

" 'Course you might not notice the changes," said the second pilot. "Lotsa people don't. But if you did, it'd mess you up."

Imagining the pilots' deformities sent a sick chill mounting from Mingolla's stomach. Gilbey, however, wasn't buying it. "You think I'm stupid?" he shouted, his neck reddening.

"Naw," said the first pilot. "We can *see* you ain't stupid. We can see lotsa stuff other people can't, 'cause of the beams."

"All kindsa weird stuff," chipped in the second pilot. "Like souls."

"Ghosts."

"Even the future."

"The future's our best thing," said the first pilot. "You guys wanna know what's ahead, we'll tell you."

They nodded in unison, the blaze of sunlight sliding across both visors: two evil robots responding to the same program.

Gilbey lunged for the cockpit door. The first pilot slammed it shut, and Gilbey pounded on the plastic, screaming curses. The second pilot flipped a switch on the control console, and a moment later his amplified voice boomed out: "Make straight past that fork-lift 'til you hit the barracks. You'll run right into the PX."

It took both Mingolla and Baylor to drag Gilbey away from the Sikorsky, and he didn't stop shouting until they drew near the fork-lift with its load of coffins: a giant's treasure of enormous silver ingots. Then he grew silent and lowered his eyes. They wangled a ride with an MP corporal outside the PX, and as the jeep hummed across the cement, Mingolla glanced over at the Sikorsky that had transported them. The two pilots had spread a canvas on the ground, had stripped to shorts and were sunning themselves. But they had not removed their helmets. The weird juxtaposition of tanned bodies and shiny black heads disturbed Mingolla, reminding him of an old movie in which a guy had gone through a matter transmitter along with a fly and had ended up with the fly's head on his shoulders. Maybe, he thought, the helmets were like that, impossible to remove. Maybe the war had gotten that strange.

The MP corporal noticed him watching the pilots and let out a barking laugh. "Those guys," he said, with the flat emphatic tone of a man who knew whereof he spoke, "are fuckin' nuts!"

Six years before, San Francisco de Juticlan had been a scatter of thatched huts and concrete block structures deployed among palms and banana leaves on the east bank of the Río Dulce, at the junction of the river and a gravel road that connected with the Pan American Highway; but it had since grown to occupy substantial sections of both banks, increased by dozens of bars and brothels: stucco cubes painted all the colors of the rainbow, with a fantastic bestiary of neon signs mounted atop their tin roofs. Dragons; unicorns; fiery birds; centaurs. The MP corporal told Mingolla that the signs were not advertisements but coded symbols of pride; for example, from the representation of a winged red tiger crouched amidst green lilies and blue crosses, you could deduce that the owner was wealthy, a member of a Catholic secret society, and ambivalent toward government policies. Old signs were constantly being dismantled, and larger, more ornate ones erected in their stead as testament to improved profits, and this warfare of light and image was appropriate to the time and place, because San Francisco de Juticlan was less a town than a symptom of war. Though by night the sky above it was radiant, at ground level it was mean and squalid. Pariah dogs foraged in piles of garbage, hardbitten whores spat from the windows, and according to the corporal, it was not unusual to stumble across a corpse, probably a victim of the gangs of abandoned children who lived in the fringes of the jungle. Narrow streets of tawny dirt cut between the bars, carpeted with a litter of flattened cans and feces and broken glass; refugees begged at every corner, displaying burns and bullet wounds. Many of the buildings had been thrown up with such haste that their walls were tilted, their roofs canted, and this made the shadows they cast appear exaggerated in their jaggedness, like shadows in the work of a psychotic artist, giving visual expression to a pervasive undercurrent of tension. Yet as Mingolla moved along, he felt at ease, almost happy. His mood was due in part to his hunch that it was going to be one hell of an r&r (he had learned to trust his hunches); but it mainly spoke to the fact that towns like this had become for him a kind of afterlife, a reward for having endured a harsh term of existence.

The corporal dropped them off at a drugstore, where Mingolla bought a box of stationery, and then they stopped for a drink at the Club Demonio: a tiny place whose whitewashed walls were shined to faint phosphorescence by the glare of purple light bulbs dangling from the ceiling like radioactive fruit. The club was packed with soldiers and whores, most sitting at tables around a dance floor not much bigger than a king-size mattress. Two couples were swaying to a ballad that welled from a jukebox encaged in chicken wire and two-by-fours; veils of cigarette smoke drifted with underwater slowness above their heads. Some of the soldiers were mauling their whores, and one whore was trying to steal the wallet of a soldier who was on the verge of passing out; her hand worked between his legs, encouraging him to thrust his hips forward, and when he did this, with her other hand she pried at the wallet stuck in the back pocket of his tight-fitting jeans. But all the action seemed listless, half-hearted, as if the dimness and syrupy music had thickened the air and were hampering movement. Mingolla took a seat at the bar. The bartender glanced at him inquiringly, his pupils becoming cored with purple reflections, and Mingolla said, "Beer."

"Hey, check that out!" Gilbey slid onto an adjoining stool and jerked his thumb toward a whore at the end of the bar. Her skirt was hiked to mid-thigh, and her breasts, judging by their fullness and lack of sag, were likely the product of elective surgery.

"Nice," said Mingolla, disinterested. The bartender set a bottle of beer in front of him, and he had a swig; it tasted sour, watery, like a distillation of the stale air.

Baylor slumped onto the stool next to Gilbey and buried his face in his hands. Gilbey said something to him that Mingolla didn't catch, and Baylor lifted his head. "I ain't goin' back," he said.

"Aw, Jesus!" said Gilbey. "Don't start that crap."

In the half-dark Baylor's eye sockets were clotted with shadows. His stare locked onto Mingolla. "They'll get us next time," he said. "We should head downriver. They got boats in Livingston that'll take you to Panama."

"Panama!" sneered Gilbey. "Nothin' there 'cept more bean-ers."

"We'll be okay at the Farm," offered Mingolla. "Things get too heavy, they'll pull us back."

" 'Too heavy'?" A vein throbbed in Baylor's temple. "What the fuck you call 'too heavy'?"

"Screw this!" Gilbey heaved up from his stool. "You deal with him, man," he said to Mingolla; he gestured at the big-breasted whore. "I'm gonna climb Mount Silicon."

"Nine o'clock," said Mingolla. "The PX. Okay?"

Gilbey said, "Yeah," and moved off. Baylor took over his stool and leaned close to Mingolla. "You know I'm right," he said in an urgent whisper. "They almost got us this time."

"Air Cav'll handle 'em," said Mingolla, affecting noncha-lance. He opened the box of stationery and unclipped a pen from his shirt pocket.

"You *know* I'm right," Baylor repeated.

Mingolla tapped the pen against his lips, pretending to be distracted.

"Air Cav!" said Baylor with a despairing laugh. "Air Cav ain't gonna do squat!"

"Why don't you put on some decent tunes?" Mingolla sug-gested. "See if they got any Prowler on the box."

"Dammit!" Baylor grabbed his wrist. "Don't you under-stand, man? This shit ain't workin' no more!"

Mingolla shook him off. "Maybe you need some change," he said coldly; he dug out a handful of coins and tossed them on the counter. "There! There's some change."

"I'm tellin' you . . ."

"I don't wanna hear it!" snapped Mingolla.

"You don't wanna hear it?" said Baylor, incredulous. He was on the verge of losing control. His dark face slick with sweat, one eyelid fluttering. He pounded the countertop for emphasis. "Man, you better hear it! 'Cause we don't pull somethin' to-gether soon, *real* soon, we're gonna die! You hear that, don't-cha?"

Mingolla caught him by the shirtfront. "Shut up!"

"I ain't shuttin' up!" Baylor shrilled. "You and Gilbey, man, you think you can save your ass by stickin' your head in the sand. But I'm gonna make you listen." He threw back his head, his voice rose to a shout. "We're gonna die!"

The way he shouted it—almost gleefully, like a kid yelling a dirty word to spite his parents—pissed Mingolla off. He was sick of Baylor's scenes. Without planning it, he punched him, pulling the punch at the last instant. Kept a hold of his shirt and clipped him on the jaw, just enough to rock back his head. Baylor blinked at him, stunned, his mouth open. Blood seeped from his gums. At the opposite end of the counter, the bartender was leaning beside a choirlike arrangement of liquor bottles, watching Mingolla and Baylor, and some of the soldiers were watching too: they looked pleased, as if they had been hoping for a spot of violence to liven things up. Mingolla felt debased by their attentiveness, ashamed of his bullying. "Hey, I'm sorry, man," he said. "I . . ."

"I don't give a shit 'bout you're sorry," said Baylor, rubbing his mouth. "Don't give a shit 'bout nothin' 'cept gettin' the hell outta here."

"Leave it alone, all right?"

But Baylor wouldn't leave it alone. He continued to argue, adopting the long-suffering tone of someone carrying on bravely in the face of great injustice. Mingolla tried to ignore him by studying the label on his beer bottle: a red and black graphic portraying a Guatemalan soldier, his rifle upheld in victory. It was an attractive design, putting him in mind of the poster work he had done before being drafted; but considering the unreliability of Guatemalan troops, the heroic pose was a joke. He gouged a trench through the center of the label with his thumbnail.

At last Baylor gave it up and sat staring down at the warped veneer of the counter. Mingolla let him sit a minute; then, without shifting his gaze from the bottle, he said, "Why don't you put on some decent tunes?"

Baylor tucked his chin onto his chest, maintaining a stubborn silence.

"It's your only option, man," Mingolla went on. "What else you gonna do?"

"You're crazy," said Baylor; he flicked his eyes toward Mingolla and hissed it like a curse. "Crazy!"

"You gonna take off for Panama by yourself? Un-unh. You know the three of us got something going. We come this far together, and if you just hang tough, we'll go home together."

"I don't know," said Baylor. "I don't know anymore."

"Look at it this way," said Mingolla. "Maybe we're all three of us right. Maybe Panama *is* the answer, but the time just isn't ripe. If that's true, me and Gilbey will see it sooner or later."

With a heavy sigh, Baylor got to his feet. "You ain't never gonna see it, man," he said dejectedly.

Mingolla had a swallow of beer. "Check if they got any Prowler on the box. I could relate to some Prowler."

Baylor stood for a moment, indecisive. He started for the jukebox, then veered toward the door. Mingolla tensed, preparing to run after him. But Baylor stopped and walked back over to the bar. Lines of strain were etched deep in his forehead. "Okay," he said, a catch in his voice. "Okay. What time tomorrow? Nine o'clock?"

"Right," said Mingolla, turning away. "The PX."

Out of the corner of his eye he saw Baylor cross the room and bend over the jukebox to inspect the selections. He felt relieved. This was the way all their r&rs had begun, with Gilbey chasing a whore and Baylor feeding the jukebox, while he wrote a letter home. On their first r&r he had written his parents about the war and its bizarre forms of attrition; then, realizing that the letter would alarm his mother, he had torn it up and written another, saying merely that he was fine. He would tear this letter up as well, but he wondered how his father would react if he were to read it. Most likely with anger. His father was a firm believer in God and country, and though Mingolla understood the futility of adhering to any moral code in light of the insanity around him, he had found that something of his father's tenets had been ingrained in him: he would never be able to desert as Baylor kept insisting. He knew it wasn't that simple, that other factors, too, were responsible for his devotion to duty; but since his father would have been happy to accept the responsibility, Mingolla tended to blame it on him. He tried to picture what his parents were doing at that moment—father watching the Mets on TV, mother puttering in the garden—and then, holding those images in mind, he began to write.

"Dear Mom and Dad,
    In your last letter you asked if I thought we were winning the war. Down here you'd get a lot of blank stares in response to that question, because most people have a perspective on the war to which the overall result isn't relevant. Like there's a guy I know who has this rap about how the war is a magical operation of immense proportions, how the movements of the planes and troops are inscribing a mystical sign on the surface of reality, and to survive you have to figure out your location within the design and move accordingly. I'm sure that sounds crazy to you, but down here everyone's crazy the same way (some shrink's actually done a study on the incidence of superstition among the occupation forces). They're looking for a magic that will ensure their survival. You may find it hard to believe that I subscribe to this sort of thing, but I do. I carve my initials on the shell casings, wear parrot feathers inside my helmet . . . and a lot more.
    "To get back to your question, I'll try to do better than a blank stare, but I can't give you a simple Yes or No. The matter can't be summed up that neatly. But I can illustrate the situation by telling you a story and let you draw your own conclusions. There are hundreds of stories that would do, but the one that comes to mind now concerns the Lost Patrol . . ."

A Prowler tune blasted from the jukebox, and Mingolla broke off writing to listen: it was a furious, jittery music, fueled—it seemed—by the same aggressive paranoia that had generated the war. People shoved back chairs, overturned tables, and began dancing in the vacated spaces: they were crammed together, able to do no more than shuffle in rhythm, but their tread set the light bulbs jiggling at the end of their cords, the purple glare slopping over the walls. A slim acne-scarred whore came to dance in front of Mingolla, shaking her breasts, holding out her arms to him. Her face was corpse-pale in the unsteady light, her smile a dead leer. Trickling from one eye, like some exquisite secretion of death, was a black tear of sweat and mascara. Mingolla couldn't be sure he was seeing her right. His left hand started trembling, and for a couple of seconds the entire scene lost its cohesiveness. Everything looked scattered, unrecognizable, embedded in a separate context from everything else: a welter of meaningless objects bobbing up and down on a tide of deranged music. Then somebody opened the door, admitting a wedge of sunlight, and the room settled back to normal. Scowling, the whore danced away. Mingolla breathed easier. The tremors in his hand subsided. He spotted Baylor near the door talking to a scruffy Guatemalan guy . . . probably a coke connection. Coke was Baylor's panacea, his remedy for fear and desperation. He always returned from r&r bleary-eyed and prone to nosebleeds, boasting about the great dope he'd scored. Pleased that he was following routine, Mingolla went back to his letter.

". . . Remember me telling you that the Green Berets took drugs to make them better fighters? Most everyone calls the drugs 'Sammy,' which is short for 'samurai.' They come in ampule form, and when you pop them under your nose, for the next thirty minutes or so you feel like a cross between a Medal-of-Honor winner and Superman. The trouble is that a lot of Berets overdo them and flip out. They sell them on the black market, too, and some guys use them for sport. They take the ampules and fight each other in pits . . . like human cockfights.

"Anyway, about two years ago a patrol of Berets went on patrol up in Fire Zone Emerald, not far from my base, and they didn't come back. They were listed MIA. A month or so after they'd disappeared, somebody started ripping off ampules from various dispensaries. At first the crimes were chalked up to guerrillas, but then a doctor caught sight of the robbers and said they were Americans. They were wearing rotted fatigues, acting nuts. An artist did a sketch of their leader according to the doctor's description, and it turned out to be a dead ringer for the sergeant of that missing patrol. After that they were sighted all over the place. Some of the sightings were obviously false, but others sounded like the real thing. They were said to have shot down a couple of our choppers and to have knocked over a supply column near Zacapas.

"I'd never put much stock in the story, to tell you the truth, but about four months ago this infantryman came walking out of the jungle and reported to the firebase. He claimed he'd been captured by the Lost Patrol, and when I heard his story, I believed him. He said they had told him that they weren't Americans anymore but citizens of the jungle. They lived like animals, sleeping under palm fronds, popping the ampules night and day. They were crazy, but they'd become geniuses at survival. They knew everything about the jungle. When the weather was going to change, what animals were near. And they had this weird religion based on the beams of light that would shine down through the canopy. They'd sit under those beams, like saints being blessed by God, and rave about the purity of the light, the joys of killing, and the new world they were going to build.

"So that's what occurs to me when you ask your questions, mom and dad. The Lost Patrol. I'm not attempting to be circumspect in order to make a point about the horrors of war. Not at all. When I think about the Lost Patrol I'm not thinking about how sad and crazy they are. I'm wondering what it is they see in that light, wondering if it might be of help to me. And maybe therein lies your answer . . ."

It was coming on sunset by the time Mingolla left the bar to begin the second part of his ritual, to wander innocent as a tourist through the native quarter, partaking of whatever fell to hand, maybe having dinner with a Guatemalan family, or buddying up with a soldier from another outfit and going to church, or hanging out with some young guys who'd ask him about America. He had done each of these things on previous r&rs, and his pretense of innocence always amused him. If he were to follow his inner directives, he would burn out the horrors of the firebase with whores and drugs; but on that first r&r—stunned

by the experience of combat and needing solitude—a protracted walk had been his course of action, and he was committed not only to repeating it but also to recapturing his dazed mental set: it would not do to half-ass the ritual. In this instance, given recent events at the Ant Farm, he did not have to work very hard to achieve confusion.

The Río Dulce was a wide blue river, heaving with a light chop. Thick jungle hedged its banks, and yellowish reed beds grew out from both shores. At the spot where the gravel road ended was a concrete pier, and moored to it a barge that served as a ferry; it was already loaded with its full complement of vehicles—two trucks—and carried about thirty pedestrians. Mingolla boarded and stood in the stern beside three infantry-men who were still wearing their combat suits and helmets, holding double-barreled rifles that were connected by flexible tubing to backpack computers; through their smoked faceplates he could see green reflections from the read-outs on their visor displays. They made him uneasy, reminding him of the two pilots, and he felt better after they had removed their helmets and proved to have normal human faces. Spanning a third of the way across the river was a sweeping curve of white cement sup-ported by slender columns, like a piece fallen out of a Dali landscape: a bridge upon which construction had been halted. Mingolla had noticed it from the air just before landing and hadn't thought much about it; but now the sight took him by storm. It seemed less an unfinished bridge than a monument to some exalted ideal, more beautiful than any finished bridge could be. And as he stood rapt, with the ferry's oily smoke farting out around him, he sensed there was an analogue of that beautiful curving shape inside him, that he, too, was a road ending in mid-air. It gave him confidence to associate himself with such loftiness and purity, and for a moment he let himself believe that he also might have—as the upward-angled terminus of the bridge implied—a point of completion lying far beyond the one anticipated by the architects of his fate.

On the west bank past the town the gravel road was lined

with stalls: skeletal frameworks of brushwood poles roofed with palm thatch. Children chased in and out among them, pretending to aim and fire at each other with stalks of sugar cane. But hardly any soldiers were in evidence. The crowds that moved along the road were composed mostly of Indians: young couples too shy to hold hands; old men who looked lost and poked litter with their canes; dumpy matrons who made outraged faces at the high prices; shoeless farmers who kept their backs ramrod-straight and wore grave expressions and carried their money knotted in handkerchiefs. At one of the stalls Mingolla bought a sandwich and a Coca-Cola. He sat on a stool and ate contentedly, relishing the hot bread and the spicy fish cooked inside it, watching the passing parade. Gray clouds were bulking up and moving in from the south, from the Caribbean; now and then a flight of XL-16s would arrow northward toward the oil fields beyond Lake Ixtabal, where the fighting was very bad. Twilight fell. The lights of the town began to be picked out sharply against the empurpling air. Guitars were plucked, hoarse voices sang, the crowds thinned. Mingolla ordered another sandwich and Coke. He leaned back, sipped and chewed, steeping himself in the good magic of the land, the sweetness of the moment. Beside the sandwich stall, four old women were squatting by a cooking fire, preparing chicken stew and corn fritters; scraps of black ash drifted up from the flames, and as twilight deepened, it seemed these scraps were the pieces of a jigsaw puzzle that were fitting together overhead into the image of a starless night.

Darkness closed in, the crowds thickened again, and Mingolla continued his walk, strolling past stalls with necklaces of light bulbs strung along their frames, wires leading off them to generators whose rattle drowned out the chirring of frogs and crickets. Stalls selling plastic rosaries, Chinese switchblades, tin lanterns; others selling embroidered Indian shirts, flour-sack trousers, wooden masks; others yet where old men in shabby suit coats sat cross-legged behind pyramids of tomatoes and melons and green peppers, each with a candle cemented in melted wax atop them, like primitive altars. Laughter, shrieks, vendors shouting. Mingolla breathed in perfume, charcoal smoke, the scents of rotting fruit. He began to idle from stall to stall, buying a few souvenirs for friends back in New York, feeling part of the hustle, the noise, the shining black air, and eventually he came to a stall around which forty or fifty people had gathered, blocking all but its thatched roof from view. A woman's amplified voice cried out, *"LA MARIPOSA!"* Excited squeals from the crowd. Again the woman cried out, *"EL CUCHILLO!"* The two words she had called—the butterfly and the knife—intrigued Mingolla, and he peered over heads.

Framed by the thatch and rickety poles, a dusky-skinned young woman was turning a handle that spun a wire cage: it was filled with white plastic cubes, bolted to a plank counter. Her black hair was pulled back from her face, tied behind her neck, and she wore a red sundress that left her shoulders bare. She stopped cranking, reached into the cage, and without looking plucked one of the cubes; she examined it, picked up a microphone and cried, *"LA LUNA!"* A bearded guy pushed forward and handed her a card. She checked the card, comparing it to some cubes that were lined up on the counter; then she gave the bearded guy a few bills in Guatemalan currency.

The composition of the game appealed to Mingolla. The dark woman; her red dress and cryptic words; the runelike shadow of the wire cage; all this seemed magical, an image out of an occult dream. Part of the crowd moved off, accompanying the winner, and Mingolla let himself be forced closer by new arrivals pressing in from behind. He secured a position at the corner of the stall, fought to maintain it against the eddying of the crowd, and on glancing up, he saw the woman smiling at him from a couple of feet away, holding out a card and a pencil stub. "Only ten cents Guatemalan," she said in American-sounding English.

The people flanking Mingolla urged him to play, grinning and clapping him on the back. But he didn't need urging. He knew he was going to win: it was the clearest premonition he had ever had, and it was signaled mostly by the woman herself. He felt a powerful attraction to her. It was as if she were a source of heat . . . not of heat alone but also of vitality, sensuality, and now that he was within range, that heat was washing over him, making him aware of a sexual tension developing between them, bringing with it the knowledge that he would win. The strength of the attraction surprised him, because his first impression had been that she was exotic-looking but not beautiful. Though slim, she was a little wide-hipped, and her breasts, mounded high and served up in separate scoops by her tight bodice, were quite small. Her face, like her coloring, had an East Indian cast, its features too large and voluptuous to suit the delicate bone structure; yet they were so expressive, so finely cut, that their disproportion came to seem a virtue. Except that it was thinner, it might have been the face of one of those handmaidens you see on Hindu religious posters, kneeling beneath Krishna's throne. Very sexy, very serene. That serenity, Mingolla decided, wasn't just a veneer. It ran deep. But at the moment he was more interested in her breasts. They looked nice pushed up like that, gleaming with a sheen of sweat. Two helpings of shaky pudding.

The woman waggled the card, and he took it: a simplified Bingo card with symbols instead of letters and numbers. "Good luck," she said, and laughed, as if in reaction to some private irony. Then she began to spin the cage.

Mingolla didn't recognize many of the words she called, but an old man cozied up to him and pointed to the appropriate square whenever he got a match. Soon several rows were almost complete. *"LA MANZANA!"* cried the woman, and the old man tugged at Mingolla's sleeve, shouting, *"Se ganó!"*

As the woman checked his card, Mingolla thought about the mystery she presented. Her calmness, her unaccented English and the upper class background it implied, made her seem out of place here. Maybe she was a student, her education interrupted by the war . . . though she might be a bit too old for that. He figured her to be twenty-two or twenty-three. Graduate school, maybe. But there was an air of worldliness about her that didn't support that theory. He watched her eyes dart back and forth between the card and the plastic cubes. Large, heavy-lidded eyes. The whites stood in such sharp contrast to her dusky skin that they looked fake: milky stones with black centers.

"You see?" she said, handing him his winnings—about three dollars—and another card.

"See what?" Mingolla asked, perplexed.

But she had already begun to spin the cage again.

He won three of the next seven cards. People congratulated him, shaking their heads in amazement; the old man cozied up further, suggesting in sign language that he was the agency responsible for Mingolla's good fortune. Mingolla, however, was nervous. His ritual was founded on a principle of small miracles, and though he was certain the woman was cheating on his behalf (that, he assumed, had been the meaning of her laughter, her "You see?"), though his luck was not really luck, its excessiveness menaced that principle. He lost three cards in a row, but thereafter won two of four and grew even more nervous. He considered leaving. But what if it *were* luck? Leaving might run him afoul of a higher principle, interfere with some cosmic process and draw down misfortune. It was a ridiculous idea, but he couldn't bring himself to risk the faint chance that it might be true.

He continued to win. The people who had congratulated him became disgruntled and drifted off, and when there were only a handful of players left, the woman closed down the game. A grimy street kid materialized from the shadows and began dismantling the equipment. Unbolting the wire cage, unplugging the microphone, boxing up the plastic cubes, stuffing it all into a burlap sack. The woman moved out from behind the stall and leaned against one of the roofpoles. Half-smiling, she cocked her head, appraising Mingolla, and then—just as the silence between them began to get prickly—she said, "My name's Debora."

"David." Mingolla felt as awkward as a fourteen-year-old; he had to resist the urge to jam his hands into his pockets and look away. "Why'd you cheat?" he asked; in trying to cover his nervousness, he said it too loudly and it sounded like an accusation.

"I wanted to get your attention," she said. "I'm . . . interested in you. Didn't you notice?"

"I didn't want to take it for granted."

She laughed. "I approve! It's always best to be cautious."

He liked her laughter; it had an easiness that made him think she would celebrate the least good thing.

Three men passed by arm-in-arm, singing drunkenly. One yelled at Debora, and she responded with an angry burst of Spanish. Mingolla could guess what had been said, that she had been insulted for associating with an American. "Maybe we should go somewhere," he said. "Get off the streets."

"After he's finished." She gestured at the kid, who was now taking down the string of light bulbs. "It's funny," she said. "I have the gift myself, and I'm usually uncomfortable around anyone else who has it. But not with you."

"The gift?" Mingolla thought he knew what she was referring to, but was leery about admitting to it.

"What do you call it? ESP?"

He gave up the idea of denying it. "I never put a name on it," he said.

"It's strong in you. I'm surprised you're not with Psicorp."

He wanted to impress her, to cloak himself in a mystery equal to hers. "How do you know I'm not?"

"I could tell." She pulled a black purse from behind the counter. "After drug therapy there's a change in the gift, in the way it comes across. It doesn't feel as hot, for one thing." She glanced up from the purse. "Or don't you perceive it that way? As heat."

"I've been around people who felt hot to me," he said. "But I didn't know what it meant."

"That's what it means . . . sometimes." She stuffed some bills into the purse. "So, why aren't you with Psicorp?"

Mingolla thought back to his first interview with a Psicorp agent: a pale, balding man with the innocent look around the eyes that some blind people have. While Mingolla had talked, the agent had fondled the ring Mingolla had given him to hold, paying no mind to what was being said, and had gazed off distractedly, as if listening for echoes. "They tried hard to recruit me," Mingolla said. "But I was scared of the drugs. I heard they had bad side-effects."

"You're lucky it was voluntary," she said. "Here they just snap you up."

The kid said something to her; he swung the burlap sack over his shoulder, and after a rapid-fire exchange of Spanish he ran off toward the river. The crowds were still thick, but more than half the stalls had shut down; those that remained open looked—with their thatched roofs and strung lights and be-shawled women—like crude nativity scenes ranging the darkness. Beyond the stalls, neon signs winked on and off: a chaotic menagerie of silver eagles and crimson spiders and indigo dragons. Watching them burn and vanish, Mingolla experienced a wave of dizziness. Things were starting to look disconnected as they had at the Club Demonio.

"Don't you feel well?" she asked.

"I'm just tired."

She turned him to face her, put her hands on his shoulders. "No," she said. "It's something else."

The weight of her hands, the smell of her perfume, helped to steady him. "There was an assault on the firebase a few days ago," he said. "It's still with me a little, y'know."

She gave his shoulders a squeeze and stepped back. "Maybe I can do something." She said this with such gravity, he thought she must have something specific in mind. "How's that?" he asked.

"I'll tell you at dinner . . . that is, if you're buying." She took his arm, jollying him. "You owe me that much, don't you think, after all your good luck?"

"Why aren't *you* with Psicorp?" he asked as they walked.

She didn't answer immediately, keeping her head down, nudging a scrap of cellophane with her toe. They were moving along an uncrowded street, bordered on the left by the river—a

channel of sluggish black lacquer—and on the right by the windowless rear walls of some bars. Overhead, behind a latticework
of supports, a neon lion shed a baleful green nimbus. "I was in
school in Miami when they started testing here," she said at last.
"And after I came home, my family got on the wrong side of
Department Six. You know Department Six?"

"I've heard some stuff."

"Sadists don't make efficient bureaucrats," she said. "They
were more interested in torturing us than in determining our
value."

Their footsteps crunched in the dirt; husky jukebox voices
cried out for love from the next street over. "What happened?"
Mingolla asked.

"To my family?" She shrugged. "Dead. No one ever bothered to confirm it, but it wasn't necessary. Confirmation, I
mean." She went a few steps in silence. "As for me . . ." A muscle
bunched at the corner of her mouth. "I did what I had to."

He was tempted to ask for specifics, but thought better of it.
"I'm sorry," he said, and then kicked himself for having made
such a banal comment.

They passed a bar lorded over by a grinning red-and-purple
neon ape. Mingolla wondered if these glowing figures had meaning for guerrillas with binoculars in the hills: gone-dead tubes
signaling times of attack or troop movements. He cocked an eye
toward Debora. She didn't look despondent as she had a second
before, and that accorded with his impression that her calmness
was a product of self-control, that her emotions were strong but
held in tight check and only let out for exercise. From out on the
river came a solitary splash, some cold fleck of life surfacing
briefly, then returning to its long ignorant glide through the dark
. . . and his life no different really, though maybe less graceful.
How strange it was to be walking beside this woman who gave
off heat like a candle-flame, with earth and sky blended into a
black gas, and neon totems standing guard overhead.

"Shit," said Debora under her breath.

It surprised him to hear her curse. "What is it?"

"Nothing," she said wearily. "Just 'shit.' " She pointed ahead and quickened her pace. "Here we are."

The restaurant was a working-class place that occupied the ground floor of a hotel: a two-story building of yellow concrete block with a buzzing Fanta sign hung above the entrance. Hundreds of moths swarmed about the sign, flickering whitely against the darkness, and in front of the steps stood a group of teenage boys who were throwing knives at an iguana. The iguana was tied by its hind legs to the step railing. It had amber eyes, a hide the color of boiled cabbage, and it strained at the end of its cord, digging its claws into the dirt and arching its neck like a pint-size dragon about to take flight. As Mingolla and Debora walked up, one of the boys scored a hit in the iguana's tail and it flipped high into the air, shaking loose the knife. The boys passed around a bottle of rum to celebrate.

Except for the waiter—a pudgy young guy leaning beside a door that opened onto a smoke-filled kitchen—the place was empty. Glaring overhead lights shined up the grease spots on the plastic tablecloths and made the uneven thicknesses of yellow paint appear to be dripping. The cement floor was freckled with dark stains that Mingolla discovered to be the remains of insects. However, the food turned out to be pretty good, and Mingolla shoveled down a plateful of chicken and rice before Debora had half-finished hers. She ate deliberately, chewing each bite a long time, and he had to carry the conversation. He told her about New York, his painting, how a couple of galleries had showed interest even though he was just a student. He compared his work to Rauschenberg, to Silvestre. Not as good, of course. Not yet. He had the notion that everything he told her—no matter its irrelevance to the moment—was securing the relationship, establishing subtle ties: he pictured the two of them enwebbed in a network of luminous threads that acted as conduits for their attraction. He could feel her heat more strongly than ever, and he wondered what it would be like to make love to her, to be swallowed by that perception of heat. The instant he wondered this, she glanced up and smiled, as if sharing the thought. He wanted to ratify his sense of intimacy, to tell her something he had told no one else, and so—having only one important secret—he told her about the ritual.

She laid down her fork and gave him a penetrating look. "You can't really believe that," she said.

"I know it sounds . . ."

"Ridiculous," she broke in. "That's how it sounds."

"It's the truth," he said defiantly.

She picked up her fork again, pushed around some grains of rice. "How is it for you," she said, "when you have a premonition? I mean, what happens? Do you have dreams, hear voices?"

"Sometimes I just know things," he said, taken aback by her abrupt change of subject. "And sometimes I see pictures. It's like with a TV that's not working right. Fuzziness at first, then a sharp image."

"With me, it's dreams. And hallucinations. I don't know what else to call them." Her lips thinned; she sighed, appearing to have reached some decision. "When I first saw you, just for a second, you were wearing battle gear. There were inputs on the gauntlets, cables attached to the helmet. The faceplate was shattered, and your face . . . it was pale, bloody." She put her hand out to cover his. "What I saw was very clear, David. You can't go back."

He hadn't described artilleryman's gear to her, and no way could she have seen it. Shaken, he said, "Where am I gonna go?"

"Panama," she said. "I can help you get there."

She suddenly snapped into focus. You find her, dozens like her, in any of the r&r towns. Preaching pacifism, encouraging desertion. Do-gooders, most with guerrilla connections. And that, he realized, must be how she had known about his gear. She had probably gathered information on the different types of units in order to lend authenticity to her dire pronouncements. His opinion of her wasn't diminished; on the contrary, it went up a notch. She was risking her life by talking to him. But her mystery had been dimmed.

"I can't do that," he said.

"Why not? Don't you believe me?"

"It wouldn't make any difference if I did."

"I . . ."

"Look," he said. "This friend of mine, he's always trying to convince me to desert, and there've been times I wanted to. But it's just not in me. My feet won't move that way. Maybe you don't understand, but that's how it is."

"This childish thing you do with your two friends," she said after a pause. "That's what's holding you here, isn't it?"

"It isn't childish."

"That's exactly what it is. Like a child walking home in the dark and thinking that if he doesn't look at the shadows, nothing will jump out at him."

"You don't understand," he said.

"No, I suppose I don't." Angry, she threw her napkin down on the table and stared intently at her plate as if reading some oracle from the chicken bones.

"Let's talk about something else," said Mingolla.

"I have to go," she said coldly.

"Because I won't desert?"

"Because of what'll happen if you don't." She leaned toward him, her voice burred with emotion. "Because knowing what I do about your future, I don't want to wind up in bed with you."

Her intensity frightened him. Maybe she *had* been telling the truth. But he dismissed the possibility. "Stay," he said. "We'll talk some more about it."

"You wouldn't listen." She picked up her purse and got to her feet.

The waiter ambled over and laid the check beside Mingolla's plate; he pulled a plastic bag filled with marijuana from his apron pocket and dangled it in front of Mingolla. "Gotta get her in the mood, man," he said. Debora railed at him in Spanish. He shrugged and moved off, his slow-footed walk an advertisement for his goods.

"Meet me tomorrow then," said Mingolla. "We can talk more about it tomorrow."

"No."

"Why don't you gimme a break?" he said. "This is all coming down pretty fast, y'know. I get here this afternoon, meet you, and an hour later you're saying, 'Death is in the cards, and Panama's your only hope.' I need some time to think. Maybe by tomorrow I'll have a different attitude."

Her expression softened but she shook her head, No.

"Don't you think it's worth it?"

She lowered her eyes, fussed with the zipper of her purse a second, and let out a rueful hiss. "Where do you want to meet?"

"How 'bout the pier on this side? 'Round noon."

She hesitated. "All right." She came around to his side of the table, bent down and brushed her lips across his cheek. He tried to pull her close and deepen the kiss, but she slipped away. He felt giddy, overheated. "You really gonna be there?" he asked.

She nodded but seemed troubled, and she didn't look back before vanishing down the steps.

Mingolla sat a while, thinking about the kiss, its promise. He might have sat even longer, but three drunken soldiers staggered in and began knocking over chairs, giving the waiter a hard time. Annoyed, Mingolla went to the door and stood taking in hits of the humid air. Moths were loosely constellated on the curved plastic of the Fanta sign, trying to get next to the bright heat inside it, and he had a sense of relation, of sharing their yearning for the impossible. He started down the steps but was brought up short. The teenage boys had gone; however, their captive iguana lay on the bottom step, bloody and unmoving. Bluish-gray strings spilled from a gash in its throat. It was such a clear sign of bad luck, Mingolla went back inside and checked into the hotel upstairs.

The hotel corridors stank of urine and disinfectant. A drunken Indian with his fly unzipped and a bloody mouth was pounding on one of the doors. As Mingolla passed him, the Indian bowed and made a sweeping gesture, a parody of welcome. Then he went back to his pounding. Mingolla's room was a windowless cell five feet wide and coffin-length, furnished with a sink and a cot and a chair. Cobwebs and dust clotted the glass of the transom, reducing the hallway light to a cold bluish-white glow. The walls were filmy with more cobwebs, and the sheets were so dirty that they looked to have a pattern. He lay down and closed his eyes, thinking about Debora. About ripping off that red dress and giving her a vicious screwing. How she'd cry out. That both made him ashamed and gave him a hard-on. He tried to think about making love to her tenderly. But tenderness, it seemed, was beyond him. He went flaccid. Jerking-off wasn't worth the effort, he decided. He started to unbutton his shirt, remembered the sheets and figured he'd be better off with his clothes on. In the blackness behind his lids he began to see explosive flashes, and within those flashes were images of the assault on the Ant Farm. The mist, the tunnels. He blotted them out with the image of Debora's face, but they kept coming back. Finally he opened his eyes. Two . . . no, three fuzzy-looking black stars were silhouetted against the transom. It was only when they began to crawl that he recognized them to be spiders. Big ones. He wasn't usually afraid of spiders, but these particular spiders terrified him. If he hit them with his shoe he'd break the glass and they'd eject him from the hotel. He didn't want to kill them with his hands. After a while he sat up, switched on the overhead and searched under the cot. There weren't any more spiders. He lay back down, feeling shaky and short of breath. Wishing he could talk to someone, hear a familiar voice. "It's okay," he said to the dark air. But that didn't help. And for a long time, until he felt secure enough to sleep, he watched the three black stars crawling across the transom, moving toward the center, touching each other, moving apart, never making any real progress, never straying from their area of bright confinement, their universe of curdled, frozen light.

2.

In the morning Mingolla crossed to the west bank and walked toward the airbase. It was already hot, but the air still held a trace of freshness and the sweat that beaded on his forehead felt clean and healthy. White dust was settling along the gravel road, testifying to the recent passage of traffic; past the town and the cut-off that led to the uncompleted bridge, high walls of vegetation crowded close to the road, and from within them he heard monkeys and insects and birds: sharp sounds that enlivened him, making him conscious of the play of his muscles. About halfway to the base he spotted six Guatemalan soldiers coming out of the jungle, dragging a couple of bodies; they tossed them onto the hood of their jeep, where two other bodies were lying. Drawing near, Mingolla saw that the dead were naked children, each with a neat hole in his back. He had intended to walk on past, but one of the soldiers—a gnomish, copper-skinned man in dark blue fatigues—blocked his path and demanded to check his papers. All the soldiers gathered around to study the papers, whispering, turning them sideways, scratching their heads. Used to such hassles, Mingolla paid them no attention and looked at the dead children.

They were scrawny, sun-darkened, lying face down with their ragged hair hanging in a fringe off the hood; their skins were pocked by infected mosquito bites, and the flesh around the bullet holes was ridged-up and bruised. Judging by their size, Mingolla guessed them to be about ten years old; but then he noticed that one was a girl with a teenage fullness to her buttocks, her breasts squashed against the metal. That made him indignant. They were only wild children who survived by robbing and killing, and the Guatemalan soldiers were only doing their duty: they performed a function comparable to that of the birds that hunted ticks on the hide of a rhinoceros, keeping their American beast pest-free and happy. But it wasn't right for the children to be laid out like game.

The soldier gave back Mingolla's papers. He was now all smiles, and—perhaps in the interest of solidifying Guatemalan-American relations, perhaps because he was proud of his work—he went over to the jeep and lifted the girl's head by the hair so Mingolla could see her face. *"Bandita!"* he said, arranging his features into a comical frown. The girl's face was not unlike the soldier's, with the same blade of a nose and prominent cheekbones. Fresh blood glistened on her lips, and the faded tattoo of a coiled serpent centered her forehead. Her eyes were open, and staring into them—despite their cloudiness—Mingolla felt that he had made a connection, that she was regarding him sadly from somewhere behind those eyes, continuing to die past the point of clinical death. Then an ant crawled out of her nostril, perching on the crimson curve of her lip, and the eyes merely looked vacant. The soldier let her head fall and wrapped his hand in the hair of a second corpse; but before he could lift it, Mingolla turned away and headed down the road toward the airbase.

There was a row of helicopters lined up at the edge of the landing strip, and walking between them, Mingolla saw the two pilots who had given him a ride from the Ant Farm. They were stripped to shorts and helmets, wearing baseball gloves, and they were playing catch, lofting high flies to one another. Behind them, atop their Sikorsky, a mechanic was fussing with the main rotor housing. The sight of the pilots didn't disturb Mingolla as it had the previous day; in fact, he found their weirdness somehow comforting. Just then, the ball eluded one of them and bounced Mingolla's way. He snagged it and flipped it back to the nearer of the pilots, who came loping over and stood pounding the ball into the pocket of his glove. With his black reflecting face and sweaty, muscular torso, he looked like an eager young mutant.

"How's she goin'?" he asked. "Seem like you a little tore down this mornin'."

"I feel okay," said Mingolla defensively. " 'Course"—he smiled, making light of his defensiveness—"maybe you see something I don't."

The pilot shrugged; the sprightliness of the gesture seemed to convey good humor.

Mingolla pointed to the mechanic. "You guys broke down, huh?"

"Just overhaul. We're goin' back up early tomorrow. Need a lift?"

"Naw, I'm here for a week."

An eerie current flowed through Mingolla's left hand, setting up a palsied shaking. It was bad this time, and he jammed
the hand into his hip pocket. The olive-drab line of barracks
appeared to twitch, to suffer a dislocation and shift farther away;
the choppers and jeeps and uniformed men on the strip looked
toylike: pieces in a really neat GI Joe Airbase kit. Mingolla's
hand beat against the fabric of his trousers like a sick heart.

"I gotta get going," he said.

"Hang in there," said the pilot. "You be awright."

The words had a flavor of diagnostic assurance that almost
convinced Mingolla of the pilot's ability to know his fate, that
things such as fate could be known. "You honestly believe what
you were saying yesterday, man?" he asked. " 'Bout your helmets? 'Bout knowing the future?"

The pilot bounced the ball on the cement, snatched it at the
peak of its rebound and stared down at it. Mingolla could see the
seams and brand name reflected in the visor, but nothing of
the face behind it, no evidence either of normalcy or deformity.
"I get asked that a lot," said the pilot. "People raggin' me,
y'know. But you ain't raggin' me, are you, man?"

"No," said Mingolla. "I'm not."

"Well," said the pilot, "it's this way. We buzz 'round up in
the nothin', and we see shit down on the ground, shit nobody
else sees. Then we blow that shit away. Been doin' it like that
for ten months, and we're still alive. Fuckin' A, I believe it!"

Mingolla was disappointed. "Yeah, okay," he said.

"You hear what I'm sayin'?" asked the pilot. "I mean we're
livin' goddamn proof."

"Uh-huh." Mingolla scratched his neck, trying to think of
a diplomatic response, but thought of none. "Guess I'll see you."
He started toward the PX.

"Hang in there, man!" the pilot called after him. "Take it
from me! Things gonna be lookin' up for you real soon!"

The canteen in the PX was a big, barnlike room of unpainted
boards; it was of such recent construction that Mingolla could

still smell sawdust and resin. Thirty or forty tables; a jukebox; bare walls. Behind the bar at the rear of the room, a sour-faced corporal with a clipboard was doing a liquor inventory, and Gilbey—the only customer—was sitting by one of the east windows, stirring a cup of coffee. His brow was furrowed, and a ray of sunlight shone down around him, making it look that he was being divinely inspired to do some soul-searching.

"Where's Baylor?" asked Mingolla, sitting opposite him.

"Fuck, I dunno," said Gilbey, not taking his eyes from the coffee cup. "He'll be here."

Mingolla kept his left hand in his pocket. The tremors were diminishing, but not quickly enough to suit him; he was worried that the shaking would spread as it had after the assault. He let out a sigh, and in letting it out he could feel all his nervous flutters. The ray of sunlight seemed to be humming a wavery golden note, and that, too, worried him. Hallucinations. Then he noticed a fly buzzing against the windowpane. "How was it last night?" he asked.

Gilbey glanced up sharply. "Oh, you mean Big Tits. She lemme check her for lumps." He forced a grin, then went back to stirring his coffee.

Mingolla was hurt that Gilbey hadn't asked about his night; he wanted to tell him about Debora. But that was typical of Gilbey's self-involvement. His narrow eyes and sulky mouth were the imprints of a mean-spiritedness that permitted few concerns aside from his own well-being. Yet despite his insensitivity, his stupid rages and limited conversation, Mingolla believed that he was smarter than he appeared, that disguising one's intelligence must have been a survival tactic in Detroit, where he had grown up. It was his craftiness that gave him away: his insights into the personalities of adversary lieutenants; his slickness at avoiding unpleasant duty; his ability to manipulate his peers. He wore stupidity like a cloak, and perhaps he had worn it for so long that it could not be removed. Still, Mingolla envied him its virtues, especially the way it had numbed him to the assault.

"He's never been late before," said Mingolla after a while.

"So what he's fuckin' late!" snapped Gilbey, glowering. "He'll be here!"

Behind the bar, the corporal switched on a radio and spun the dial past Latin music, past Top Forty, then past an American voice reporting the baseball scores. "Hey!" called Gilbey. "Let's hear that, man! I wanna see what happened to the Tigers." With a shrug, the corporal complied.

". . . White Sox six, A's three," said the announcer. "That's eight in a row for the Sox . . ."

"White Sox are kickin' some ass," said the corporal, pleased.

"The White Sox!" Gilbey sneered. "What the White Sox got 'cept a buncha beaners hittin' two hunnerd and some coke-sniffin' niggers? Shit! Every spring the White Sox are flyin', man. But then 'long comes summer and the good drugs hit the street and they fuckin' die!"

"Yeah," said the corporal, "but this year . . ."

"Take that son of a bitch Caldwell," said Gilbey, ignoring him. "I seen him coupla years back when he had a trial with the Tigers. Man, that guy could hit! Now he shuffles up there like he's just feelin' the breeze."

"They ain't takin' drugs, man," said the corporal testily. "They can't take 'em 'cause there's these tests that show if they's on somethin'."

Gilbey barreled ahead. "White Sox ain't gotta chance, man! Know what the guy on TV calls 'em sometimes? The Pale Hose! The fuckin' Pale Hose! How you gonna win with a name like that? The Tigers, now, they got the right kinda name. The Yankees, the Braves, the . . ."

"Bullshit, man!" The corporal was becoming upset; he set down his clipboard and walked to the end of the bar. "What 'bout the Dodgers? They gotta wimpy name and they're a good team. Your name don't mean shit!"

"The Reds," suggested Mingolla; he was enjoying Gilbey's rap, its stubbornness and irrationality. Yet at the same time he was concerned by its undertone of desperation: appearances to the contrary, Gilbey was not himself this morning.

"Oh, yeah!" Gilbey smacked the table with the flat of his

hand. "The Reds! Lookit the Reds, man! Lookit how good they been doin' since the Cubans come into the war. You think that don't mean nothin'? You think their name ain't helpin' 'em? Even if they get in the Series, the Pale Hose don't gotta prayer against the Reds." He laughed—a hoarse grunt. "I'm a Tiger fan, man, but I gotta feelin' this ain't their year, y'know. The Reds are tearin' up the NL East, and the Yankees is comin' on, and when they get together in October, man, then we gonna find out alla 'bout everything. Alla 'bout fuckin' everything!" His voice grew tight and tremulous. "So don't gimme no trouble 'bout the candyass Pale Hose, man! They ain't shit and they never was and they ain't gonna be shit 'til they change their fuckin' name!"

Sensing danger, the corporal backed away from confrontation, and Gilbey lapsed into a moody silence. For a while there were only the sounds of chopper blades and the radio blatting out cocktail jazz. Two mechanics wandered in for an early morning beer, and not long after that three fatherly-looking sergeants with potbellies and thinning hair and quartermaster insignia on their shoulders sat at a nearby table and started up a game of rummy. The corporal brought them a pot of coffee and a bottle of whiskey, which they mixed and drank as they played. Their game had an air of custom, of something done at this time every day, and watching them, taking note of their fat, pampered ease, their old-buddy familiarity, Mingolla felt proud of his palsied hand. It was an honorable affliction, a sign that he had participated in the heart of the war as these men had not. Yet he bore them no resentment. None whatsoever. Rather it gave him a sense of security to know that three such fatherly men were here to provide him with food and liquor and new boots. He basked in the dull, happy clutter of their talk, in the haze of cigar smoke that seemed the exhaust of their contentment. He believed that he could go to them, tell them his problems and receive folksy advice. They were here to assure him of the rightness of his purpose, to remind him of simple American values, to lend an illusion of fraternal involvement to the war, to make clear that it was merely an exercise in good fellowship and tough-mindedness, an initiation rite that these three men had long ago passed through, and after the war they would all get rings and medals and pal around together and talk about bloodshed and terror with head-shaking wonderment and nostalgia, as if bloodshed and terror were old, lost friends whose natures they had not fully appreciated at the time . . . Mingolla realized then that a smile had stretched his facial muscles taut, and that his train of thought had been leading him into spooky mental territory. The tremors in his hand were worse than ever. He checked his watch. It was almost ten o'clock. *Ten o'clock!* In a panic, he scraped back his chair and stood.

"Let's look for him," he said to Gilbey.

Gilbey started to say something but kept it to himself. He tapped his spoon hard against the edge of the table. Then he, too, scraped back his chair and stood.

Baylor was not to be found at the Club Demonio or any of the bars on the west bank. Gilbey and Mingolla described him to everyone they met, but no one remembered him. The longer the search went on, the more insecure Mingolla became. Baylor was necessary, an essential underpinning of the platform of habits and routines that supported him, that let him live beyond the range of war's weapons and the laws of chance, and should that underpinning be destroyed . . . In his mind's eye he saw the platform tipping, him and Gilbey toppling over the edge, cartwheeling down into an abyss filled with black flames. Once Gilbey said, "Panama! The son of a bitch run off to Panama." But Mingolla didn't think this was the case. He was certain that Baylor was close at hand. His certainty had such a valence of clarity that he became even more insecure, knowing that this sort of clarity often heralded a bad conclusion.

The sun climbed higher, its heat an enormous weight pressing down, its light leaching color from the stucco walls, and Mingolla's sweat began to smell rancid. Only a few soldiers were on the streets, mixed in with the usual run of kids and beggars, and the bars were empty except for a smattering of drunks still on a binge from the night before. Gilbey stumped along, grabbing people by the shirt and asking his questions. Mingolla, however, terribly conscious of his trembling hand, nervous to the point of stammering, was forced to work out a stock approach whereby he could get through these brief interviews. He would amble up, keeping his right side forward, and say, "I'm looking for a friend of mine. Maybe you seen him? Tall guy. Olive skin, black hair, thin. Name's Baylor." He came to be able to let this slide off his tongue in a casual unreeling.

Finally Gilbey had had enough. "I'm gonna hang out with Big Tits," he said. "Meet'cha at the PX tomorrow." He started to walk off, but turned and added, "You wanna get in touch 'fore tomorrow, I'll be at the Club Demonio." He had an odd expression on his face. It was as if he were trying to smile reassuringly, but—due to his lack of practice with smiles—it looked forced and foolish and not in the least reassuring.

Around eleven o'clock Mingolla wound up leaning against a pink stucco wall, watching out for Baylor in the thickening crowds. Beside him, the sun-browned fronds of a banana tree were feathering in the wind, making a crispy sound whenever a gust blew them back into the wall. The roof of the bar across the street was being repaired: patches of new tin alternating with narrow strips of rust that looked like enormous strips of bacon laid there to fry. Now and then he would let his gaze drift up to the unfinished bridge, a great sweep of magical whiteness curving into the blue, rising above the town and the jungle and the war. Not even the heat haze rippling from the tin roof could warp its smoothness. It seemed to be orchestrating the stench, the mutter of the crowds, and the jukebox music into a tranquil unity, absorbing those energies and returning them purified, enriched. He thought that if he stared at it long enough, it would speak to him, pronounce a white word that would grant his wishes.

Two flat cracks—pistol shots—sent him stumbling away from the wall, his heart racing. Inside his head the shots had spoken the two syllables of Baylor's name. All the kids and beggars had vanished. All the soldiers had stopped and turned to face the direction from which the shots had come: zombies who had heard their master's voice.

Another shot.

Some soldiers milled out of a side street, talking excitedly. ". . . fuckin' nuts!" one was saying, and his buddy said, "It was Sammy, man! You see his eyes?"

Mingolla pushed his way through them and sprinted down the side street. At the end of the block a cordon of MPs had sealed off access to the right-hand turn, and when Mingolla ran up one of them told him to stay back.

"What is it?" Mingolla asked. "Some guy playing Sammy?"

"Fuck off," the MP said mildly.

"Listen," said Mingolla. "It might be this friend of mine. Tall, skinny guy. Black hair. Maybe I can talk to him."

The MP exchanged glances with his buddies, who shrugged and acted otherwise unconcerned. "Okay," he said. He pulled Mingolla to him and pointed out a bar with turquoise walls on the next corner down. "Go on in there and talk to the captain."

Two more shots, then a third.

"Better hurry," said the MP. "Ol' Captain Haynesworth there, he don't have much faith in negotiations."

It was cool and dark inside the bar; two shadowy figures were flattened against the wall beside a window that opened onto the cross-street. Mingolla could make out the glint of automatic pistols in their hands. Then, through the window, he saw Baylor pop up from behind a retaining wall: a three-foot-high structure of mud bricks running between a herbal drugstore and another bar. Baylor was shirtless, his chest painted with reddish-brown smears of dried blood, and he was standing in a nonchalant pose, with his thumbs hooked in his trouser pockets. One of the men by the window fired at him. The report was deafening, causing Mingolla to flinch and close his eyes. When he looked out the window again, Baylor was nowhere in sight.

"Fucker's just tryin' to draw fire," said the man who had shot at Baylor. "Sammy's fast today."

"Yeah, but he's slowin' some," said a lazy voice from the

darkness at the rear of the bar. "I do believe he's outta dope."

"Hey," said Mingolla. "Don't kill him! I know the guy. I can talk to him."

"Talk?" said the lazy voice. "You kin talk 'til yo' ass turns green, boy, and Sammy ain't gon' listen."

Mingolla peered into the shadows. A big, sloppy-looking man was leaning on the counter; brass insignia gleamed on his beret. "You the captain?" he asked. "They told me outside to talk to the captain."

"Yes, indeed," said the man. "And I'd be purely delighted to talk with you, boy. What you wanna talk 'bout?"

The other men laughed.

"Why are you trying to kill him?" asked Mingolla, hearing the pitch of desperation in his voice. "You don't have to kill him. You could use a trank gun."

"Got one comin'," said the captain. "Thing is, though, yo' buddy got hisself a coupla hostages back of that wall, and we get a chance at him 'fore the trank gun 'rives, we bound to take it."

"But . . ." Mingolla began.

"Lemme finish, boy." The captain hitched up his gunbelt, strolled over, and draped an arm around Mingolla's shoulder, enveloping him in an aura of body odor and whiskey breath. "See," he went on, "we had everything under control. Sammy there . . ."

"Baylor!" said Mingolla angrily. "His name's Baylor."

The captain lifted his arm from Mingolla's shoulder and looked at him with amusement. Even in the gloom Mingolla could see the network of broken capillaries on his cheeks, the bloated alcoholic features. "Right," said the captain. "Like I's sayin', yo' good buddy Mister Baylor there wasn't doin' no harm. Just sorta ravin' and runnin' round. But then 'long comes a coupla our Marine brothers. Seems like they'd been givin' our beaner friends a demonstration of the latest combat gear, and they was headin' back from said demonstration when they seen our little problem and took it 'pon themselves to play hero. Wellsir, puttin' it in a nutshell, Mister Baylor flat kicked their ass. Stomped all over their *esprit de corps.* Then he drags 'em back of that wall and starts messin' with one of their guns. And . . .''

Two more shots.

"Shit!" said one of the men by the window.

"And there he sits," said the captain. "Fuckin' with us. Now either the gun's outta ammo or else he ain't figgered out how it works. If it's the latter case, and he does figger it out . . ." The captain shook his head dolefully, as if picturing dire consequences. "See my predicament?"

"I could try talking to him," said Mingolla. "What harm would it do?"

"You get yourself killed, it's your life, boy. But it's my ass that's gonna get hauled up on charges." The captain steered Mingolla to the door and gave him a gentle shove toward the cordon of MPs. " 'Preciate you volunteerin', boy."

Later Mingolla was to reflect that what he had done had made no sense, because—whether or not Baylor had survived—he would never have been returned to the Ant Farm. But at the time, desperate to preserve the ritual, none of this occurred to him. He walked around the corner and toward the retaining wall. His mouth was dry, his heart pounded. But the shaking in his hand had stopped, and he had the presence of mind to walk in such a way that he blocked the MPs' line of fire. About twenty feet from the wall he called out, "Hey, Baylor! It's Mingolla, man!" And as if propelled by a spring, Baylor jumped up, staring at him. It was an awful stare. His eyes were like bulls-eyes, white showing all around the irises; trickles of blood ran from his nostrils, and nerves were twitching in his cheeks with the regularity of watchworks. The dried blood on his chest came from three long gouges; they were partially scabbed over but were oozing a clear fluid. For a moment he remained motionless. Then he reached down behind the wall, picked up a double-barreled rifle from whose stock trailed a length of flexible tubing, and brought it to bear on Mingolla.

He squeezed the trigger.

No flame, no explosion. Not even a click. But Mingolla felt that he'd been dipped in ice water. "Christ!" he said. "Baylor! It's me!" Baylor squeezed the trigger again, with the same result. An expression of intense frustration washed over his face, then lapsed into that dead man's stare. He looked directly up into the sun, and after a few seconds he smiled: he might have been receiving terrific news from on high.

Mingolla's senses had become wonderfully acute. Somewhere far away a radio was playing a country and western tune, and with its plaintiveness, its intermittent bursts of static, it seemed to him the whining of a nervous system on the blink. He could hear the MPs talking in the bar, could smell the sour acids of Baylor's madness, and he thought he could feel the pulse of Baylor's rage, an inconstant flow of heat eddying around him, intensifying his fear, rooting him to the spot. Baylor laid the gun down, laid it down with the tenderness he might have shown toward a sick child, and stepped over the retaining wall. The animal fluidity of the movement made Mingolla's skin crawl. He managed to shuffle backward a pace and held up his hands to ward Baylor off. "C'mon, man," he said weakly. Baylor let out a fuming noise—part hiss, part whimper—and a runner of saliva slid between his lips. The sun was a golden bath drenching the street, kindling glints and shimmers from every bright surface, as if it were bringing reality to a boil.

Somebody yelled, "Get down, boy!"

Then Baylor flew at him, and they fell together, rolling on the hard-packed dirt. Fingers dug in behind his Adam's apple. He twisted away, saw Baylor grinning down, all staring eyes and yellowed teeth. Strings of drool flapping from his chin. A Halloween face. Knees pinned Mingolla's shoulders, hands gripped his hair and bashed his head against the ground. Again, and again. A keening sound switched on inside his ears. He wrenched an arm free and tried to gouge Baylor's eyes; but Baylor bit his thumb, gnawing at the joint. Mingolla's vision dimmed, and he couldn't hear anything anymore. The back of his head felt mushy. It seemed to be rebounding very slowly from the dirt, higher and slower after each impact. Framed by blue sky, Baylor's face looked to be receding, spiraling off. And then, just as Mingolla began to fade, Baylor disappeared.

Dust was in Mingolla's mouth, his nostrils. He heard shouts, grunts. Still dazed, he propped himself onto an elbow. A little ways off, khaki arms and legs and butts were thrashing around in a cloud of dust. Like a comic strip fight. You expected asterisks and exclamation points overhead to signify profanity. Somebody grabbed his arm, hauled him upright. The MP captain, his beefy face flushed. He frowned reprovingly as he brushed dirt from Mingolla's clothes. "Real gutsy, boy," he said. "And real, real stupid. He hadn't been at the end of his run, you'd be drawin' flies 'bout now." He turned to a sergeant standing nearby. "How stupid you reckon that was, Phil?"

The sergeant said that it beat him.

"Well," the captain said, "I figger if the boy here was in combat, that's be 'bout Bronze-Star stupid."

That, allowed the sergeant, was pretty goddamn stupid.

" 'Course here in 'Frisco''—the captain gave Mingolla a final dusting—"it don't get you diddley-shit."

The MPs were piling off Baylor, who lay on his side, bleeding from his nose and mouth. Blood thick as gravy filmed over his cheeks.

"Panama," said Mingolla dully. Maybe it *was* an option. He saw how it would be . . . a night beach, palm shadows a lacework on the white sand.

"What say?" asked the captain.

"He wanted to go to Panama," said Mingolla.

The captain gave an amused snort. "Don't we all."

One of the MPs rolled Baylor onto his stomach and handcuffed him; another manacled his feet. Then they rolled him back over. Yellow dirt had mired with the blood on his cheeks and forehead, fitting him with a blotchy mask. His eyes snapped open in the middle of that mask, widening when he felt the restraints. He started to hump up and down, trying to bounce his way to freedom. He kept on humping for almost a minute; then he went rigid and—his gone eyes fixed on the molten disc of the sun—he let out a roar. That was the only word for it. It wasn't a scream or a shout, but a devil's exultant roar, so loud and full of fury, it seemed to be generating all the blazing light and heat-dance. Listening to it had a seductive effect, and Mingolla began to get behind it, to feel it in his body like a good rock 'n' roll tune, to sympathize with its life-hating exuberance.

"Whoo-ee!" said the captain, marveling. "They gon' have to build a whole new zoo for that boy."

After giving his statement, letting a Corpsman check his head, Mingolla caught the ferry to meet Debora on the east bank. He sat in the stern, gazing out at the unfinished bridge, this time unable to derive from it any sense of hope or magic. Panama kept cropping up in his thoughts. Now that Baylor was gone, was it really an option? He knew he should try to figure things out, plan what to do, but he couldn't stop seeing Baylor's bloody, demented face. He'd seen worse, Christ yes, a whole lot worse. Guys reduced to spare parts, so little of them left that they didn't need a shiny silver coffin, just a black metal can the size of a cookie jar. Guys scorched and one-eyed and bloody, clawing blindly at the air like creatures out of a monster movie. But the idea of Baylor trapped forever in some raw, red place inside his brain, in the heart of that raw, red noise he'd made, maybe that idea was worse than anything Mingolla had seen. He didn't want to die; he rejected the prospect with the impassioned stubbornness a child displays when confronted with a hard truth. Yet he would rather die than endure madness. Compared to what Baylor had in store, death and Panama seemed to offer the same peaceful sweetness.

Someone sat down beside Mingolla: a kid who couldn't have been older than eighteen. A new kid with a new haircut, new boots, new fatigues. Even his face looked new, freshly broken from the mold. Shiny, pudgy cheeks; clear skin; bright, unused blue eyes. He was eager to talk. He asked Mingolla about his home, his family, and said, Oh, wow, it must be great living in

New York, wow. But he appeared to have some other reason for initiating the conversation, something he was leading up to, and finally he spat it out.

"You know the Sammy that went animal back there?" he said. "I seen him pitted last night. Little place in the jungle west of the base. Guy name Chaco owns it. Man, it was incredible!"

Mingolla had only heard of the pits third- and fourth-hand, but what he had heard was bad, and it was hard to believe that this kid with his air of homeboy innocence could be an affi-cionado of something so vile. And, despite what he had just witnessed, it was even harder to believe that Baylor could have been a participant.

The kid didn't need prompting. "It was pretty early on," he said. "There'd been a coupla bouts, nothin' special, and then this guy walks in lookin' real twitchy. I knew he was Sammy by the way he's starin' at the pit, y'know, like it's somethin' he's been wishin' for. And this guy with me, friend of mine, he gives me a poke and says, 'Holy shit! That's the Black Knight, man! I seen him fight over in Reunion awhile back. Put your money on him,' he says. 'The guy's an ace!' "

Their last r&r had been in Reunion. Mingolla tried to frame a question but couldn't think of one whose answer would have any meaning.

"Well," said the kid, "I ain't been down long, but I'd even heard 'bout the Knight. So I went over and kinda hung out near him, thinkin' maybe I can get a line on how he's feelin', y'know, 'cause you don't wanna just bet the guy's rep. Pretty soon Chaco comes over and asks the Knight if he wants some action. The Knight says, 'Yeah, but I wanna fight an animal. Somethin' fierce, man. I wanna fight somethin' fierce.' Chaco says he's got some monkeys and shit, and the Knight says he hears Chaco's got a jaguar. Chaco he hems and haws, says Maybe so, maybe not, but it don't matter 'cause a jaguar's too strong for Sammy. And then the Knight tells Chaco who he is. Lemme tell ya, Chaco's whole attitude changed. He could see how the bettin' was gonna go for somethin' like the Black Knight versus a jaguar.

And he says, 'Yes sir, Mister Black Knight sir! Anything you want!' And he makes the announcement. Man, the place goes nuts. People wavin' money, screamin' odds, drinkin' fast so's they can get ripped in time for the main event, and the Knight's just standin' there, smilin', like he's feedin' off the confusion. Then Chaco lets the jaguar in through the tunnel and into the pit. It ain't a full-growed jaguar, half-growed maybe, but that's all you figure even the Knight can handle.''

The kid paused for breath; his eyes seemed to have grown brighter. ''Anyway, the jaguar's sneakin' 'round and 'round, keepin' close to the pit wall, snarlin' and spittin', and the Knight's watchin' him from up above, checkin' his moves, y'know. And everybody starts chantin', 'Sam-mee, Sam-mee, Sam-mee,' and after the chant builds up loud the Knight pulls three ampules outta his pocket. I mean, shit, man! Three! I ain't never been 'round Sammy when he's done more'n two. Three gets you clear into the fuckin' sky! So when the Knight holds up these three ampules, the crowd's tuned to burn, howlin' like they's playin' Sammy themselves. But the Knight, man, he keeps his cool. He is *so* cool! He just holds up the ampules and lets 'em take the shine, soakin' up the noise and energy, gettin' strong off the crowd's juice. Chaco waves everybody quiet and gives the speech, y'know, 'bout how in the heart of every man there's a warrior-soul waitin' to be loosed and shit. I tell ya, man, I always thought that speech was crap before, but the Knight's makin' me buy it a hunnerd percent. He is so goddamn cool! He takes off his shirt and shoes, and he ties this piece of black silk 'round his arm. Then he pops the ampules, one after another, real quick, and breathes it all in. I can see it hittin', catchin' fire in his eyes. Pumpin' him up. And soon as he's popped the last one, he jumps into the pit. He don't use the tunnel, man! He jumps! Twenty-five feet down to the sand, and lands in a crouch.''

Three other soldiers were leaning in, listening, and the kid was now addressing all of them, playing to his audience. He was so excited that he could barely keep his speech coherent, and Mingolla realized with disgust that he, too, was excited by the image of Baylor crouched on the sand. Baylor, who had cried after the assault. Baylor, who had been so afraid of snipers that he had once pissed in his pants rather than walk from his gun to the latrine.

Baylor, the Black Knight.

"The jaguar's screechin' and snarlin' and slashin' at the air," the kid went on. "Tryin' to put fear into the Knight. 'Cause the jaguar knows in his mind the Knight's big trouble. This ain't some jerk like Chaco, this is Sammy. The Knight moves to the center of the pit, still in a crouch." Here the kid pitched his voice low and dramatic. "Nothin' happens for a coupla minutes, 'cept it's tense. Nobody's hardly breathin'. The jaguar springs a coupla times, but the Knight dances off to the side and makes him miss, and there ain't no damage either way. Whenever the jaguar springs, the crowd sighs and squeals, not just 'cause they's scared of seein' the Knight tore up, but also 'cause they can see how fast he is. Silky fast, man! Unreal. He looks 'bout as fast as the jaguar. He keeps on dancin' away, and no matter how the jaguar twists and turns, no matter if he comes at him along the sand, he can't get his claws into the Knight. And then, man . . . oh, it was so smooth! Then the jaguar springs again, and this time 'stead of dancin' away, the Knight drops onto his back, does this half roll onto his shoulders, and when the jaguar passes over him, he kicks up with both feet. Kicks up hard! And smashes his heels into the jaguar's side. The jaguar slams into the pit wall and comes down screamin', snappin' at his ribs. They was busted, man. Pokin' out the skin like tentposts."

The kid wiped his mouth with the back of his hand and flicked his eyes toward Mingolla and the other soldiers to see if they were into the story. "We was shoutin', man," he said. "Poundin' the top of the pit wall. It was so loud, the guy I'm with is yellin' in my ear and I can't hear nothin'. Now maybe it's the noise, maybe it's his ribs, whatever . . . the jaguar goes berserk. Makin' these scuttlin' lunges at the Knight, tryin' to get close 'fore he springs so the Knight can't pull that same trick. He's snarlin' like a goddamn chainsaw! The Knight keeps leapin' and spinnin' away. But then he slips, man, grabs the air for balance, and the jaguar's on him, clawin' at his chest. For a second they're like waltzin' together. Then the Knight pries loose the paw that's hooked him, pushes the jaguar's head back and smashes his fist into the jaguar's eye. The jaguar flops onto the sand, and the Knight scoots to the other side of the pit. He's checkin' the scratches on his chest, which is bleedin' wicked. Meantime, the jaguar gets to his feet, and he's fucked up worse than ever. His one eye's fulla blood, and his hindquarters is all loosey-goosey. Like if this was boxin', they'd call in the doctor. The jaguar figures he's had enough of this crap, and he starts tryin' to jump outta the pit. This one time he jumps right up to where I'm leanin' over the edge. Comes so close I can smell his breath, I can see myself reflected in his good eye. He's clawin' for a grip, wantin' to haul hisself up into the crowd. People are freakin', thinkin' he might be gonna make it. But 'fore he gets the chance, the Knight catches him by the tail and slings him against the wall. Just like you'd beat a goddamn rug, that's how he's dealin' with the jaguar. And the jaguar's a real mess, now. He's quiverin'. Blood's pourin' outta his mouth, his fangs is all red. The Knight starts makin' these little feints, wavin' his arms, growlin'. He's toyin' with the jaguar. People don't believe what they're seein', man. Sammy's kickin' a jaguar's ass so bad he's got room to toy with it. If the place was nuts before, now it's a fuckin' zoo. Fights in the crowd, guys singin' the Marine Hymn. Some beaner squint's takin' off her clothes. The jaguar tries to scuttle up close to the Knight again, but he's too fucked up. He can't keep it together. And the Knight he's still growlin' and feintin'. A guy behind me is booin', claimin' the Knight's defamin' the purity of the sport by playin' with the jaguar. But hell, man, I can see he's just timin' the jaguar, waitin' for the right moment, the right move."

Staring off downriver, the kid wore a wistful expression: he might have been thinking about his girlfriend. "We all knew it was comin'," he said. "Everybody got real quiet. So quiet you could hear the Knight's feet scrapin' on the sand. You could feel it in the air, and you knew the jaguar was savin' up for one big effort. Then the Knight slips again, 'cept he's fakin'. I could see that, but the jaguar couldn't. When the Knight reels sideways, the jaguar springs. I thought the Knight was gonna drop down like he did the first time, but he springs, too. Feetfirst. And he catches the jaguar under the jaw. You could hear bone splinterin', and the jaguar falls in a heap. He struggles to get up, but no way! He's whinin', and he craps all over the sand. The Knight walks up behind him, takes his head in both hands and gives it a twist. Crack!''

As if identifying with the jaguar's fate, the kid closed his eyes and sighed. ''Everybody'd been quiet 'til they heard that crack, then all hell broke loose. People chantin', 'Sam-mee, Sam-mee,' and people shovin', tryin' to get close to the pit wall so they can watch the Knight take the heart. He reaches into the jaguar's mouth and snaps off one of the fangs and tosses it to somebody. Then Chaco comes in through the tunnel and hands him the knife. Right when he's 'bout to cut, somebody knocks me over and by the time I'm back on my feet, he's already took the heart and tasted it. He's just standin' there with the jaguar's blood on his mouth and his own blood runnin' down his chest. He looks kinda confused, y'know. Like now the fight's over and he don't know what to do. But then he starts roarin'. He sounds the same as the jaguar did 'fore it got hurt. Crazy fierce. Ready to get it on with the whole goddamn world. Man, I lost it! I was right with that roar. Maybe I was roarin' with him, maybe everybody was. That's what it felt like, man. Like bein' in the middle of this roar that's comin' outta every throat in the universe.'' The kid engaged Mingolla with a sober look. ''Lotsa people go 'round sayin' the pits are evil, and maybe they are. I don't know. How you s'posed to tell 'bout what's evil and what's not down here? They say you can go to the pits a thousand times and not see nothin' like the jaguar and the Black Knight. I don't know 'bout that, either. But I'm goin' back just in case I get lucky. 'Cause what I saw last night, if it was evil, man, it was so fuckin' evil it was beautiful, too.''

3.

Debora was waiting at the pier, carrying a picnic basket and wearing a blue dress with a high neckline and a full skirt: a schoolgirl dress. Mingolla homed in on her. The way she had her hair, falling about her shoulders in thick, dark curls, made him think of smoke turned solid, and her face seemed the map of a beautiful country with black lakes and dusky plains, a country in which he could hide. They walked along the river past the town and came to a spot where ceiba trees with slick green leaves and whitish bark and roots like alligator tails grew close to the shore, and there they ate and talked and listened to the water gulping against the clay bank, to the birds, to the faint noises from the airbase that at this distance sounded part of nature. Sunlight dazzled the water, and whenever wind riffled the surface, it looked as if it were spreading the dazzles into a crawling crust of diamonds. Mingolla imagined that they had taken a secret path, rounded a corner on the world, and reached some eternally peaceful land. The illusion of peace was so profound that he began to see hope in it. Perhaps, he thought, something was being offered here. Some new magic. Maybe there would be a sign. Signs were everywhere if you knew how to read them. He glanced around. Thick white trunks rising into greenery, dark leafy avenues leading off between them . . . nothing there, but what about those weeds growing at the edge of the bank? They cast precise fleur-de-lis shadows on the clay, shadows that didn't have much in common with the ragged configurations of the weeds themselves. Possibly a sign, though not a clear one. He lifted his gaze to the reeds growing in the shallows. Yellow reeds with jointed stalks bent akimbo, some with clumps of insect eggs like seed pearls hanging from loose fibers, and others dappled by patches of algae. That's how they looked one moment. Then Mingolla's vision rippled, as if the whole of reality had shivered, and the reeds were transformed into rudimentary shapes: yellow sticks poking up from flat blue. On the far side of the river, the jungle was a simple smear of Crayola green; a speedboat passing with a red slash unzippering the blue. It seemed that the rippling had jostled every element of the landscape a fraction out of kilter, revealing each one to be as characterless as a building block. Mingolla gave his head a shake. Nothing changed. He rubbed his brow. No effect. Terrified, he squeezed his eyes shut. He felt like the only meaningful piece in a nonsensical puzzle, vulnerable by virtue of his uniqueness. His breath came rapidly, his left hand fluttered.

"David? Don't you want to hear it?" Debora sounded peeved.

"Hear what?" He kept his eyes closed.

"About my dream. Weren't you listening?"

He peeked at her. Everything was back to normal. She was sitting with her knees tucked under her, all her features in sharp focus. "I'm sorry," he said. "I was thinking."

"You looked frightened."

"Frightened?" He put on a bewildered face. "Naw, just had a thought is all."

"It couldn't have been pleasant."

He shrugged off the comment and sat up smartly to prove his attentiveness. "So tell me 'bout the dream."

"All right," she said doubtfully. The breeze drifted fine strands of hair across her face, and she brushed them back. "You were in a room the color of blood, with red chairs and a red table. Even the paintings on the wall were done in shades of red, and . . ." She broke off, peering at him. "Do you want to hear this? You have that look again."

"Sure," he said. But he was afraid. How could she have known about the red room? She must have had a vision of it, and . . . Then he realized that she might not have been talking about the room itself. He'd told her about the assault, hadn't he? And if she had guerrilla contacts, she would know that the emergency lights were switched on during an assault. That had to be it! She was trying to frighten him into deserting again, psyching him the way preachers played upon the fears of sinners with images of fiery rivers and torture. It infuriated him. Who the hell was she to tell him what was right or wise? Whatever he did, it was going to be *his* decision.

"There were three doors in the room," she went on. "You wanted to leave the room, but you couldn't tell which of the doors was safe to use. You tried the first door, and it turned out to be a façade. The knob of the second door turned easily, but the door itself was stuck. Rather than forcing it, you went to the third door. The knob of this door was made of glass and cut your hand. After that you just walked back and forth, unsure what to do." She waited for a reaction, and when he gave none, she said, "Do you understand?"

He kept silent, biting back anger.

"I'll interpret it for you," she said.

"Don't bother."

"The red room is war, and the false door is the way of your childish . . ."

"Stop!" He grabbed her wrist, squeezing it hard.

She glared at him until he released her. "Your childish magic," she finished.

"What is it with you?" he asked. "You have some kinda quota to fill? Five deserters a month, and you get a medal?"

She tucked her skirt down to cover her knees, fiddled with a loose thread. From the way she was acting, you might have thought he had asked an intimate question and she was framing an answer that wouldn't be indelicate. Finally she said, "Is that who you believe I am to you?"

"Isn't that right? Why else would you be handing me this bullshit?"

"What's the matter with you, David?" She leaned forward, cupping his face in her hands. "Why . . ."

He pushed her hands away. "What's the matter with me? This"—his gesture included the sky, the river, the trees—"that's what's the matter. You remind me of my parents. They ask the same sorta ignorant questions." Suddenly he wanted to injure her with answers, to find an answer like acid to throw in her face and watch it eat away her tranquility. "Know what I do for my parents?'' he said. ''When they ask dumb-ass questions like 'What's the matter?', I tell 'em a story. A war story. You wanna hear a war story? Something happened a few days back that'll do for an answer just fine.''

''You don't have to tell me anything,'' she said, discouraged.

''No problem,'' he said. ''Be my pleasure.''

The Ant Farm was a large sugar-loaf hill overlooking dense jungle on the eastern border of Fire Zone Emerald; jutting out from its summit were rocket and gun emplacements that at a distance resembled a crown of thorns jammed down over a green scalp. For several hundred yards around, the land had been cleared of all vegetation. The big guns had been lowered to maximum declension and in a mad moment had obliterated huge swaths of jungle, snapping off regiments of massive tree trunks a couple of feet above the ground, leaving a moat of blackened stumps and scorched red dirt seamed with fissures. Tangles of razor wire had replaced the trees and bushes, forming surreal blue-steel hedges, and buried beneath the wire were a variety of mines and detection devices. These did little good, however, because the Cubans possessed technology that would neutralize most of them. On clear nights there was little likelihood of trouble; but on misty nights trouble could be expected. Under cover of the mist Cuban and guerrilla troops would come through the wire and attempt to infiltrate the tunnels that honeycombed the interior of the hill. Occasionally one of the mines would be triggered, and you would see a ghostly fireball bloom in the swirling whiteness, tiny black figures being flung outward from its center. Lately some of these casualties had been found to be wearing red berets and scorpion-shaped brass pins, and from this it was known that the Cubans had sent in the Alacran Division, which had been instrumental in routing the American Forces in Miskitia.

There were nine levels of tunnels inside the hill, most lined with little round rooms that served as living quarters (the only exception being the bottom level, which was given over to the computer center and offices); all the rooms and tunnels were coated with a bubbled white plastic that looked like hardened seafoam and was proof against anti-personnel explosives. In Mingolla's room, where he and Baylor and Gilbey bunked, a scarlet paper lantern had been hung on the overhead light fixture, making it seem that they were inhabiting a blood cell: Baylor had insisted on the lantern, saying that the overhead was too bright and hurt his eyes. Three cots were arranged against the walls, as far apart as space allowed. The floor around Baylor's cot was littered with cigarette butts and used Kleenex; under his pillow he kept a tin box containing a stash of pills and marijuana. Whenever he lit a joint he would always offer Mingolla a hit, and Mingolla always refused, feeling that the experience of the firebase would not be enhanced by drugs. Taped to the wall above Gilbey's cot was a collage of beaver shots, and each day after duty, whether or not Mingolla and Baylor were in the room, he would lie beneath them and masturbate. His lack of shame caused Mingolla to be embarrassed by his own secretiveness in the act, and he was also embarrassed by the pimply-youth quality of the objects taped above his cot: a Yankee pennant; a photograph of his old girlfriend, and another of his senior-year high school basketball team; several sketches he had made of the surrounding jungle. Gilbey teased him constantly about this display, calling him "the boy-next-door," which struck Mingolla as odd, because back home he had been considered something of an eccentric.

It was toward this room that Mingolla was heading when the assault began. Large cargo elevators capable of carrying up to sixty men ran up and down just inside the east and west slopes of the hill; but to provide quick access between adjoining levels, and also as a safeguard in case of power failures, an auxiliary tunnel corkscrewed down through the center of the hill like a huge coil of white intestine. It was slightly more than twice as wide as the electric carts that traveled it, carrying officers and VIPs on tours. Mingolla was in the habit of using the tunnel for his exercise. Each night he would put on sweat clothes and jog up and down the entire nine levels, doing this out of a conviction

that exhaustion prevented bad dreams. That night, as he passed
Level Four on his final leg up, he heard a rumbling: an explosion,
and not far off. Alarms sounded, the big guns atop the hill began
to thunder. From directly above came shouts and the stutter of
automatic fire. The tunnel lights flickered, went dark, and the
emergency lights winked on.

Mingolla flattened against the wall. The dim red lighting
caused the bubbled surfaces of the tunnel to appear as smooth
as a chamber in a gigantic nautilus, and this resemblance intensi-
fied his sense of helplessness, making him feel like a child
trapped in an evil undersea palace. He couldn't think clearly,
picturing the chaos around him. Muzzle flashes, armies of ant-
men seething through the tunnels, screams spraying blood, and
the big guns bucking, every shellburst kindling miles of sky. He
would have preferred to keep going up, to get out into the open
where he might have a chance to hide in the jungle. But down
was his only hope. Pushing away from the wall, he ran full-tilt,
arms waving, skidding around corners, almost falling, past Level
Four, Level Five. Then, halfway between Levels Five and Six, he
nearly tripped over a dead man: an American lying curled up
around a belly wound, a slick of blood spreading beneath him
and a machete by his hand. As Mingolla stooped for the machete, he thought nothing about the man, only about how weird
it was for an American to be defending himself against Cubans
with such a weapon. There was no use, he decided, in going any
farther. Whoever had killed the man would be somewhere
below, and the safest course would be to hide out in one of the
rooms on Level Five. Holding the machete before him, he moved
cautiously back up the tunnel.

Levels Five through Seven were officer country, and though
the tunnels were the same as the ones above—gently curving
tubes eight feet high and ten feet wide—the rooms were larger
and contained only two cots. The rooms Mingolla peered into
were empty, and this, despite the sounds of battle, gave him a
secure feeling. But as he passed beyond the tunnel curve, he
heard shouts in Spanish from his rear. He peeked back around

the curve. A skinny black soldier wearing a red beret and gray fatigues was inching toward the first doorway; then, rifle at the ready, he ducked inside. Two other Cubans—slim bearded men, their skins sallow-looking in the bloody light—were standing by the arched entranceway to the auxiliary tunnel; when they saw the black soldier emerge from the room, they walked off in the opposite direction, probably to check the rooms at the far end of the level.

Mingolla began to operate in a kind of luminous panic. He realized that he would have to kill the black soldier. Kill him without any fuss, take his rifle and hope that he could catch the other two off-guard when they came back for him. He slipped into the nearest room and stationed himself against the wall to the right of the door. The Cuban, he had noticed, had turned left on entering the room; he would have been vulnerable to someone positioned like Mingolla. Vulnerable for a split-second. Less than a count of one. The pulse in Mingolla's temple throbbed, and he gripped the machete tightly in his left hand. He rehearsed mentally what he would have to do. Stab; clamp a hand over the Cuban's mouth; bring his knee up to jar loose the rifle. And he would have to perform these actions simultaneously, execute them perfectly.

Perfect execution.

He almost laughed out loud, remembering his paunchy old basketball coach saying, "Perfect execution, boys. That's what beats a zone. Forget the fancy crap. Just set your screens, run your patterns, and get your shots down."

Hoops ain't nothin' but life in short pants, huh, Coach?

Mingolla drew a deep breath and let it sigh out through his nostrils. He couldn't believe he was going to die. He had spent the past nine months worrying about death, but when it got right down to it, when the circumstances arose that made death likely, it was hard to take that likelihood seriously. It didn't seem reasonable that a skinny black guy should be his nemesis. His death should involve massive detonations of light, special Mingolla-killing rays, astronomical portents. Not some scrawny little shit with a rifle. He drew another breath and for the first time registered the contents of the room. Two cots; clothes strewn everywhere; taped-up polaroids and pornography. Officer country or not, it was your basic Ant Farm decor; under the red light it looked squalid, long-abandoned. He was amazed by how calm he felt. Oh, he was afraid all right! But fear was tucked into the dark folds of his personality like a murderer's knife hidden inside an old coat on a closet shelf. Glowing in secret, waiting its chance to shine. Sooner or later it would skewer him, but for now it was an ally, acting to sharpen his senses. He could see every bubbled pucker on the white walls, could hear the scrape of the Cuban's boots as he darted into the room next door, could feel how the Cuban swung the rifle left-to-right, paused, turned . . .

He *could* feel the Cuban! Feel his heat, his heated shape, the exact position of his body. It was as if a thermal imager had been switched on inside his head, one that worked through walls.

The Cuban eased toward Mingolla's door, his progress tangible, like a burning match moving behind a sheet of paper. Mingolla's calm was shattered. The man's heat, his fleshy temperature, was what disturbed him. He had imagined himself killing with a cinematic swiftness and lack of mess; now he thought of hogs being butchered and piledrivers smashing the skulls of cows. And could he trust this freakish form of perception? What if he couldn't? What if he stabbed too late? Too soon? Then the hot, alive thing was almost at the door, and having no choice, Mingolla timed his attack to its movements, stabbing just as the Cuban entered.

He executed perfectly.

The blade slid home beneath the Cuban's ribs, and Mingolla clamped a hand over his mouth, muffling his outcry. His knee nailed the rifle stock, sending it clattering to the floor. The Cuban thrashed wildly. He stank of rotten jungle air and cigarettes. His eyes rolled back, trying to see Mingolla. Crazy animal eyes, with liverish whites and expanded pupils. Sweat beads glittered redly on his brow. Mingolla twisted the machete, and the Cuban's eyelids fluttered down. But a second later they snapped open, and he lunged. They went staggering deeper into the room and teetered beside one of the cots. Mingolla wrangled the Cuban sideways and rammed him against the wall, pinning him there. Writhing, the Cuban nearly broke free. He seemed to be getting stronger, his squeals leaking out from Mingolla's hand. He reached behind him, clawing at Mingolla's face; he grabbed a clump of hair, yanked it. Desperate, Mingolla sawed with the machete. That tuned the Cuban's squeals higher, louder. He squirmed and clawed at the wall. Mingolla's clamped hand was slick with the Cuban's saliva, his nostrils full of the man's rank scent. He felt queasy, weak, and he wasn't sure how much longer he could hang on. The son of a bitch was never going to die, he was deriving strength from the steel in his guts, he was changing into some deathless force. But just then the Cuban stiffened. Then he relaxed, and Mingolla caught a whiff of feces.

He let the Cuban slump to the floor, but before he could turn loose of the machete, a shudder passed through the body, flowed up the hilt and vibrated his left hand. It continued to shudder inside his hand, feeling dirty, sexy, like a post-coital tremor. Something, some animal essence, some oily scrap of bad life, was slithering around in there, squirting toward his wrist. He stared at the hand, horrified. It was gloved in the Cuban's blood, trembling. He smashed it against his hip, and that seemed to stun whatever was inside it. But within seconds it had revived and was wriggling in and out of his fingers with the mad celerity of a tadpole.

"*Teo!*" someone called. "*Vamos!*"

Electrified by the shout, Mingolla hustled to the door. His foot nudged the Cuban's rifle. He picked it up, and the shaking of his hand lessened—he had the idea it had been soothed by a familiar texture and weight.

"*Teo! Donde estás?*"

Mingolla had no good choices, but he realized it would be far more dangerous to hang back than to take the initiative. He grunted *"Aquí!"* and walked out into the tunnel, making lots of noise with his heels.

"Dete prisa, hombre!"

Mingolla opened fire as he rounded the curve. The two Cubans were standing by the entrance to the auxiliary tunnel. Their rifles chattered briefly, sending a harmless spray of bullets off the walls; they whirled, flung out their arms and fell. Mingolla was too shocked by how easy it had been to feel relief. He kept watching, expecting them to do something. Moan, or twitch.

After the echoes of the shots had died, though he could hear the big guns jolting and the crackle of firefights, a heavy silence seemed to fill in through the tunnel, as if his bullets had pierced something that had dammed silence up. The silence made him aware of his isolation. No telling where the battle lines were drawn . . . if, indeed, they existed. It was conceivable that small units had infiltrated every level, that the battle for the Ant Farm was in microcosm the battle for Guatemala: a conflict having no patterns, no real borders, no orderly confrontations, but like a plague could pop up anywhere at any time and kill you. That being the case, his best bet would be to head for the computer center, where friendly forces were sure to be concentrated.

He walked to the entrance and stared at the two dead Cubans. They had fallen blocking his way, and he was hesitant about stepping over them, half-believing they were playing possum, that they would reach up and grab him. The awkward attitudes of their limbs made him think they were holding a difficult pose, waiting for him to try. Their blood looked purple in the red glow of the emergencies, thicker and shinier than ordinary blood. He noted their moles and scars and sores, the crude stitching of their fatigues, gold fillings glinting from their open mouths. It was funny, he could have met these guys while they were alive and they might have made only a vague impression; but seeing them dead, he had catalogued their physical worth in a single glance. Maybe, he thought, death revealed your essentials as life could not. He studied the dead men, wanting to read them. Couple of slim, wiry guys. Nice guys, into rum and the ladies and sports. He'd bet they were baseball players, infielders, a double-play combo. Maybe he should have called to them, Hey, I'm a Yankee fan. Be cool! Meet'cha after the war for a game of flies and grounders. Fuck this killing shit. Let's play some ball.

He laughed, and the high, cracking sound of his laughter startled him. Christ! Standing around here was just asking for it. As if to second that opinion, the thing inside his hand exploded into life, eeling and frisking about. Swallowing back his fear, Mingolla stepped over the two dead men, and this time, when nothing clutched at his trouser legs, he felt very, very relieved.

Below Level Six, there was a good deal of mist in the auxiliary tunnel, and from this Mingolla understood that the Cubans had penetrated the hillside, probably with a borer mine. Chances were the hole they had made was somewhere close, and he decided that if he could find it he would use it to get the hell out of the Farm and hide in the jungle. On Level Seven the mist was extremely thick; the emergency lights stained it pale red, giving it the look of surgical cotton packing a huge artery. Scorchmarks from grenade bursts showed on the walls like primitive graphics, and quite a few bodies were visible beside the doorways. Most of them Americans, badly mutilated. Uneasy, Mingolla picked his way among them, and when a man spoke behind him, saying, "Don't move," he let out a hoarse cry and dropped his rifle and spun around, his heart pounding.

A giant of a man—he had to go six-seven, six-eight, with the arms and torso of a weightlifter—was standing in a doorway, training a forty-five at Mingolla's chest. He wore khakis with lieutenant's bars, and his babyish face, though cinched into a frown, gave an impression of gentleness and stolidity: he conjured for Mingolla the image of Ferdinand the Bull weighing a knotty problem. "I told you not to move," he said peevishly.

"It's okay," said Mingolla. "I'm on your side."

The lieutenant ran a hand through his thick shock of brown

hair; he seemed to be blinking more than was normal. "I'd better check," he said. "Let's go down to the storeroom."

"What's to check?" said Mingolla, his paranoia increasing.

"Please!" said the lieutenant, a genuine wealth of entreaty in his voice. "There's been too much violence already."

The storeroom was a long, narrow L-shaped room at the end of the level; it was ranged by packing crates, and through the gauzy mist the emergency lights looked like a string of dying red suns. The lieutenant marched Mingolla to the corner of the L, and turning it, Mingolla saw that the rear wall of the room was missing. A tunnel had been blown into the hillside, opening onto blackness. Forked roots with balls of dirt attached hung from its roof, giving it the witchy appearance of a tunnel into some world of dark magic; rubble and clods of earth were piled at its lip. Mingolla could smell the jungle, and he realized that the big guns had stopped firing. Which meant that whoever had won the battle of the summit would soon be sending down mop-up squads. "We can't stay here," he told the lieutenant. "The Cubans'll be back."

"We're perfectly safe," said the lieutenant. "Take my word." He motioned with the gun, indicating that Mingolla should sit on the floor.

Mingolla did as ordered and was frozen by the sight of a corpse, a Cuban corpse, lying between two packing crates opposite him, its head propped against the wall. "Jesus!" he said, coming back up to his knees.

"He won't bite," said the lieutenant. With the lack of self-consciousness of someone squeezing into a subway seat, he settled beside the corpse; the two of them neatly filled the space between the crates, touching elbow to shoulder.

"Hey," said Mingolla, feeling giddy and scattered. "I'm not sitting here with this fucking dead guy, man!"

The lieutenant flourished his gun. "You'll get used to him."

Mingolla eased back to a sitting position, unable to look away from the corpse. Actually, compared to the bodies he had just been stepping over, it was quite presentable. The only signs of damage were blood on its mouth and bushy black beard, and a mire of blood and shredded cloth at the center of its chest. Its beret had slid down at a rakish angle to cover one eyebrow; the brass scorpion pin was scarred and tarnished. Its eyes were open, reflecting glowing red chips of the emergency lights, and this gave it a baleful semblance of life. But the reflections made it appear less real, easier to bear.

"Listen to me," said the lieutenant.

Mingolla rubbed at the blood on his shaking hand, hoping that cleaning it would have some good effect.

"Are you listening?" the lieutenant asked.

Mingolla had a peculiar perception of the lieutenant and the corpse as dummy and ventriloquist. Despite its glowing eyes, the corpse had too much reality for any trick of the light to gloss over for long. Precise crescents showed on its fingernails, and because its head was tipped to the left, blood had settled into that side, darkening its cheek and temple, leaving the rest of the face pallid. It was the lieutenant, with his neat khakis and polished shoes and nice haircut, who now looked less than real.

"Listen!" said the lieutenant vehemently. "I want you to understand that I have to do what's right for me!" The bicep of his gun arm bunched to the size of a cannonball.

"I understand," said Mingolla, thoroughly unnerved.

"Do you? Do you really?" The lieutenant seemed aggravated by Mingolla's claim to understanding. "I doubt it. I doubt you could possibly understand."

"Maybe I can't," said Mingolla. "Whatever you say, man. I'm just trying to get along, y'know."

The lieutenant sat silent, blinking. Then he smiled. "My name's Jay," he said. "And you are . . . ?"

"David." Mingolla tried to bring his concentration to bear on the gun, wondering if he could kick it away, but the sliver of life in his hand distracted him.

"Where are your quarters, David?"

"Level Three."

"I live here," said Jay. "But I'm going to move. I couldn't bear to stay in a place where . . ." He broke off and leaned forward, adopting a conspiratorial stance. "Did you know it takes a long time for someone to die, even after their heart has stopped?"

"No, I didn't." The thing in Mingolla's hand squirmed toward his wrist, and he squeezed the wrist, trying to block it.

"It's true," said Jay with vast assurance. "None of these people"—he gave the corpse a gentle nudge with his elbow, a gesture that conveyed to Mingolla a creepy sort of familiarity— "have finished dying. Life doesn't just switch off. It fades. And these people are still alive, though it's only a half-life." He grinned. "The half-life of life, you might say."

Mingolla kept the pressure on his wrist and smiled, as if in appreciation of the play on words. Pale red tendrils of mist curled between them.

"Of course you aren't attuned," said Jay. "So you wouldn't understand. But I'd be lost without Eligio."

"Who's Eligio?"

Jay nodded toward the corpse. "We're attuned, Eligio and I. That's how I know we're safe. Eligio's perceptions aren't limited to the here and now any longer. He's with his men at this very moment, and he tells me they're all dead or dying."

"Uh-huh," said Mingolla, tensing. He had managed to squeeze the thing in his hand back into his fingers, and he thought he might be able to reach the gun. But Jay disrupted his plan by shifting the gun to his other hand. His eyes seemed to be growing more reflective, acquiring a ruby glaze, and Mingolla realized this was because he had opened them wide and angled his stare toward the emergency lights.

"It makes you wonder," said Jay. "It really does."

"What?" said Mingolla, easing sideways, shortening the range for a kick.

"Half-lives," said Jay. "If the mind has a half-life, maybe our separate emotions do, too. The half-life of love, of hate. Maybe they still exist somewhere." He drew up his knees, shielding the gun. "Anyway, I can't stay here. I think I'll go back to Oakland." His tone became whispery. "Where are you from, David?"

"New York."

"Not my cup of tea," said Jay. "But I love the Bay Area. I own an antique shop there. It's beautiful in the mornings. Peaceful. The sun comes through the window, creeping across the floor, y'know, like a tide, inching up over the furniture. It's as if the original varnishes are being reborn, the whole shop shining with ancient lights."

"Sounds nice," said Mingolla, taken aback by Jay's lyricism.

"You seem like a good person." Jay straightened up a bit. "But I'm sorry. Eligio tells me your mind's too cloudy for him to read. He says I can't risk keeping you alive. I'm going to have to shoot."

Mingolla set himself to kick, but then listlessness washed over him. What the hell did it matter? Even if he knocked the gun away, Jay could probably break him in half. "Why?" he said. "Why do you have to?"

"You might inform on me." Jay's soft features sagged into a sorrowful expression. "Tell them I was hiding."

"Nobody gives a shit you were hiding," said Mingolla. "That's what I was doing. I bet there's fifty other guys doing the same damn thing."

"I don't know." Jay's brow furrowed. "I'll ask again. Maybe your mind's less cloudy now." He turned his gaze to the dead man.

Mingolla noticed that the Cuban's irises were angled upward and to the left—exactly the same angle to which Jay's eyes had drifted earlier—and reflected an identical ruby glaze.

"Sorry," said Jay, leveling the gun. "I have to." He licked his lips. "Would you please turn your head? I'd rather you weren't looking at me when it happens. That's how Eligio and I became attuned."

Looking into the aperture of the gun's muzzle was like peering over a cliff, feeling the chill allure of falling, and it was more out of contrariness than a will to survive that Mingolla popped his eyes at Jay and said, "Go ahead."

Jay blinked but he held the gun steady. "Your hand's shaking," he said after a pause.

"No shit," said Mingolla.

"How come it's shaking?"

"Because I killed someone with it," said Mingolla. "Because I'm as fucking crazy as you are."

Jay mulled this over. "I was supposed to be assigned to a gay unit," he said finally. "But all the slots were filled, and when I had to be assigned here they gave me a drug. Now I . . . I . . ." He blinked rapidly, his lips parted, and Mingolla found that he was straining toward Jay, wanting to apply Body English, to do something to push him over this agonizing hump. "I can't . . . be with men anymore," Jay finished, and once again blinked rapidly; then his words came easier. "Did they give you a drug, too? I mean I'm not trying to imply you're gay. It's just they have drugs for everything these days, and I thought that might be the problem."

Mingolla was suddenly, inutterably sad. He felt that his emotions had been twisted into a thin black wire, that the wire was frayed and spraying black sparks of sadness. That was all that energized him, all his life. Those little black sparks.

"I always fought before," said Jay. "And I was fighting this time. But when I shot Eligio . . . I just couldn't keep going."

"I really don't give a shit," said Mingolla. "I really don't."

"Maybe I *can* trust you." Jay sighed. "I just wish you were attuned. Eligio's a good soul. You'd appreciate him."

Jay kept on talking, enumerating Eligio's virtues, and Mingolla tuned him out, not wanting to hear about the Cuban's love for his family, his posthumous concerns for them. Staring at his bloody hand, he had a magical overview of the situation. Sitting in the root cellar of this evil mountain, bathed in an eerie red glow, a scrap of a dead man's life trapped in his flesh, listening to a deranged giant who took his orders from a corpse, waiting for scorpion soldiers to pour through a tunnel that appeared to lead into a dimension of mist and blackness. It was insane to look at it that way. But there it was. You couldn't reason it away; it had a brutal glamour that surpassed reason, that made reason unnecessary.

". . . and once you're attuned," Jay was saying, "you can't ever be separated. Not even by death. So Eligio's always going to be alive inside me. Of course I can't let them find out. I mean"—he chuckled, a sound like dice rattling in a cup—"talk about giving aid and comfort to the enemy!"

Mingolla lowered his head, closed his eyes. Maybe Jay would shoot. But he doubted that. Jay only wanted company in his madness.

"You swear you won't tell them?" Jay asked.

"Yeah," said Mingolla. "I swear."

"All right," said Jay. "But remember, my future's in your hands. You have a responsibility to me."

"Don't worry."

Gunfire crackled in the distance.

"I'm glad we could talk," said Jay. "I feel much better."

Mingolla said that he felt better, too.

They sat without speaking. It wasn't the most secure way to pass the night, but Mingolla no longer put any store in the concept of security. He was too weary to be afraid. Jay seemed entranced, staring at a point above Mingolla's head, but Mingolla made no move for the gun. He was content to sit and wait and let fate take its course. His thoughts uncoiled with vegetable sluggishness.

They must have been sitting a couple of hours when Mingolla heard the whisper of helicopters and noticed that the mist had thinned, that the darkness at the end of the tunnel had gone gray. "Hey," he said to Jay. "I think we're okay now." Jay offered no reply, and Mingolla saw that his eyes were angled upward and to the left just like the Cuban's eyes, glazed over with ruby reflection. Tentatively, he reached out and touched the gun. Jay's hand flopped to the floor, but his fingers remained clenched around the butt. Mingolla recoiled, disbelieving. It couldn't be! Again he reached out, feeling for a pulse. Jay's wrist was cool, still, and his lips had a bluish cast. Mingolla had a flutter of hysteria, thinking that Jay had gotten it wrong about being attuned: instead of Eligio becoming part of his life, he had become part of Eligio's death. There was a tightness in Mingolla's chest, and he thought he was going to cry. He would have welcomed tears, and when they failed to materialize he grew both annoyed at himself and defensive. Why should he cry? The guy had meant nothing to him . . . though the fact that he could be so devoid of compassion was reason enough for tears. Still, if you were going to cry over something as commonplace as a single guy dying, you'd be crying every minute of the day, and what was the future in that? He glanced at Jay. At the Cuban. Despite the smoothness of Jay's skin, the Cuban's bushy beard, Mingolla could have sworn they were starting to resemble each other the way old married couples did. And, yep, all four eyes were fixed on exactly the same point of forever. It was either a hell of a coincidence or else Jay's craziness had been of such magnitude that he had willed himself to die in this fashion just to lend credence to his theory of half-lives. And maybe he was still alive. Half alive. Maybe he and Mingolla were now attuned, and if that were true, maybe . . . Revolted by the prospect of joining Jay and the Cuban in their deathwatch, Mingolla scrambled to his feet and ran into the tunnel. He might have kept running, but on coming out into the dawn light he was brought up short by the view from the tunnel entrance.

At his back, the green dome of the hill swelled high, its sides brocaded with shrubs and vines, an infinity of pattern as eye-catching as the intricately carved façade of a Hindu temple; atop it, one of the gun emplacements had taken a hit: splinters of charred metal curved up like peels of black rind. Before him lay the moat of red dirt with its hedgerows of razor wire, and beyond that loomed the blackish-green snarl of the jungle. Caught on the wire were hundreds of baggy shapes wearing blood-stained fatigues; frays of smoke twisted up from the fresh craters beside them. Overhead, half-hidden by the lifting gray mist, three Sikorskys were hovering. Their pilots were invisible behind layers of mist and reflection, and the choppers themselves looked like enormous carrion flies with bulging eyes and whirling wings. Like devils. Like gods. They seemed to be whispering to one another in anticipation of the feast they were soon to share.

The scene was horrid yet it had the purity of a stanza from a ballad come to life, a ballad composed about tragic events in some border hell. You could never paint it, or if you could the canvas would have to be as large as the scene itself, and you would have to incorporate the slow boil of the mist, the whirling of the chopper blades, the drifting smoke. No detail could be omitted. It was the perfect illustration of the war, of its secret magical splendor, and Mingolla, too, was an element of the design, the figure of the artist painted in for a joke or to lend scale and perspective to its vastness, its importance. He knew that he should report to his station, but he couldn't turn away from this glimpse into the heart of the war. He sat down on the hillside, cradling his sick hand in his lap, and watched as—with the ponderous aplomb of idols floating to earth, fighting the cross-draft, the wind of their descent whipping up furies of red dust— the Sikorskys made skillful landings among the dead.

4.

Halfway through the telling of his story, Mingolla had realized that he was not really trying to offend or shock Debora, but rather was unburdening himself; and he further realized that by telling it he had to an extent cut loose from the past, weakened its hold on him. For the first time he felt able to give serious consideration to the idea of desertion. He did not rush to it, embrace it, but he did acknowledge its logic and understand the terrible illogic of returning to more assaults, more death, without any magic to protect him. He made a pact with himself: he would pretend to go along as if desertion were his intent and see what signs were offered.

When he had finished, Debora asked whether or not he was over his anger. He was pleased that she hadn't tried to offer sympathy. "I'm sorry," he said. "I wasn't really angry at you . . . at least that was only part of it."

"It's all right." She pushed back the dark mass of her hair

so that it fell to one side and looked down at the grass beside her knees. With her head inclined, eyes half-lidded, the graceful line of her neck and chin like a character in some exotic script, she seemed a good sign herself. "I don't know what to talk to you about," she said. "The things I feel I have to tell you make you mad, and I can't muster any small-talk."

"I don't want to be pushed," he said. "But believe me, I'm thinking about what you've told me."

"I won't push. But I still don't know what to talk about." She plucked a grass blade, chewed on the tip. He watched her lips purse, wondered how she'd taste. Mouth sweet in the way of a jar that had once held spices. She tossed the grass blade aside. "I know," she said brightly. "Would you like to see where I live?"

"I'd just as soon not go back to 'Frisco yet." Where you live, he thought; I want to touch where you live.

"It's not in town," she said. "It's a village downriver."

"Sounds good." He came to his feet, took her arm and helped her up. For an instant they were close together, her breasts grazing his shirt. Her heat coursed around him, and he thought if anyone were to see them, they would see two figures wavering as in a mirage. He had an urge to tell her he loved her. Though most of what he felt was for the salvation she might provide, part of his feelings seemed real and that puzzled him, because all she had been to him was a few hours out of the war, dinner in a cheap restaurant, and a walk along the river. There was no basis for consequential emotion. Before he could say anything, do anything, she turned and picked up her basket.

"It's not far," she said, walking away. Her blue skirt swayed like a rung bell.

They followed a track of brown clay overgrown by ferns, overspread by saplings with pale translucent leaves, and soon came to a grouping of thatched huts at the mouth of a stream that flowed into the river. Naked children were wading in the stream, laughing and splashing each other. Their skins were the color of amber, and their eyes were as wet-looking and purplish-dark as plums. Palms and acacias loomed above the huts, which were constructed of sapling trunks lashed together by nylon cord; their thatch had been trimmed to resemble bowl-cut hair. Flies crawled over strips of meat hung on a clothesline stretched between two of the huts. Fish heads and chicken droppings littered the ocher ground. But Mingolla scarcely noticed these signs of poverty, seeing instead a sign of the peace that might await him in Panama. And another sign was soon forthcoming. Debora bought a bottle of rum at a tiny store, then led him to the hut nearest the mouth of the stream and introduced him to a lean, white-haired old man who was sitting on a bench outside it. Tio Moises. After three drinks Tio Moises began to tell stories.

The first story concerned the personal pilot of an ex-president of Panama. The president had made billions from smuggling cocaine into the States with the help of the CIA, whom he had assisted on numerous occasions, and was himself an addict in the last stages of mental deterioration. It had become his sole pleasure to be flown from city to city in his country, to sit on the landing strips, gaze out the window and do cocaine. At any hour of night or day, he was likely to call the pilot and order him to prepare a flight plan to Colon or Bocas del Toro or Penonome. As the president's condition worsened, the pilot realized that soon the CIA would see he was no longer useful and would kill him. And the most obvious manner of killing him would be by means of an airplane crash. The pilot did not want to die alongside him. He tried to resign, but the president would not permit it. He gave thought to mutilating himself, but being a good Catholic, he could not flout God's law. If he were to flee, his family would suffer. His life became a nightmare. Prior to each flight, he would spend hours searching the plane for evidence of sabotage, and upon each landing, he would remain in the cockpit, shaking from nervous exhaustion. The president's condition grew even worse. He had to be carried aboard the plane and have the cocaine administered by an aide, while a second aide stood by with cotton swabs to attend his nosebleeds. Knowing his life could be measured in weeks, the pilot asked his priest for guidance. "Pray," the priest advised. The pilot had been praying all along, so this was no help. Next he went to the commandant of his military college, and the commandant told him he must do his duty. This, too, was something the pilot had been doing all along. Finally he went to the chief of the San Blas Indians, who were his mother's people. The chief told him he must accept his fate, which—while not something he had been doing all along— was hardly encouraging. Nonetheless, he saw it was the only available path and he did as the chief had counseled. Rather than spending hours in a pre-flight check, he would arrive minutes before take-off and taxi away without even inspecting the fuel gauge. His recklessness came to be the talk of the capitol. Obeying the president's every whim, he flew in gales and in fogs, while drunk and drugged, and during those hours in the air, suspended between the laws of gravity and fate, he gained a new appreciation of life. Once back on the ground, he engaged in living with a fierce avidity, making passionate love to his wife, carousing with friends and staying out until dawn. Then one day as he was preparing to leave for the airport, an American man came to his house and told him he had been replaced. "If we let the president fly with so negligent a pilot, we'll be blamed for anything that happens," said the American. The pilot did not have to ask whom he had meant by "we." Six weeks later the president's plane crashed in the Darien Mountains. The pilot was overjoyed. Panama had been ridded of a villain, and his own life had not been forfeited. But a week after the crash, after the new president—another smuggler with CIA connections—had been appointed, the commandant of the air force summoned the pilot, told him that the crash would never have occurred had he been on the job, and assigned him to fly the new president's plane.

All through the afternoon Mingolla listened and drank, and drunkenness fitted a lens to his eyes that let him see how these stories applied to him. They were all fables of irresolution, cautioning him to act, and they detailed the core problems of the Central American people who—as he was now—were trapped between the poles of magic and reason, their lives governed by the politics of the ultra-real, their spirits ruled by myths and legends, with the rectangular computerized bulk of North America above and the conch-shell-shaped continental mystery of South America below. He assumed that Debora had orchestrated the types of stories Tio Moises told, but that did not detract from their potency as signs: they had the ring of truth, not of something tailored to his needs. Nor did it matter that his hand was shaking, his vision playing tricks. Those things would pass when he reached Panama.

Shadows blurred, insects droned like tambouras, and twilight washed down the sky, making the air look grainy, the chop on the river appear slower and heavier. Tio Moises' granddaughter served plates of roast corn and fish, and Mingolla stuffed himself. Afterward, when the old man signaled his weariness, Mingolla and Debora strolled off along the stream. Between two of the huts, mounted on a pole, was a warped backboard with a netless hoop, and some young men were shooting baskets. Mingolla joined them. It was hard dribbling on the bumpy dirt, but he had never played better. The residue of drunkenness fueled his game, and his jump shots followed perfect arcs down through the hoop. Even at improbable angles, his shots fell true. He lost himself in flicking out his hands to make a steal, in feinting and leaping high to snag a rebound, becoming—as dusk faded—the most adroit of ten arm-waving, jitter-stepping shadows.

The game ended and the stars came out, looking like holes punched into fire through a billow of black silk overhanging the palms. Flickering chutes of lamplight illuminated the ground in front of the huts, and as Debora and Mingolla walked among them, he heard a radio tuned to the Armed Forces Network giving a play-by-play of a baseball game. There was a crack of the bat, the crowd roared, the announcer cried, "He got it all!" Mingolla imagined the ball vanishing into the darkness above the stadium, bouncing out into parking-lot America, lodging under a tire where some kid would find it and think it a miracle, or rolling across the street to rest under a used car, shimmering there, secretly white and fuming with home run energies. The score was three-to-one, top of the second. Mingolla didn't know who was playing and didn't care. Home runs were happening for him, mystical jump shots curved along predestined tracks. He was at the center of incalculable forces.

One of the huts was unlit, with two wooden chairs out front, and as they approached, the sight of it blighted Mingolla's mood. Something about it bothered him: its air of preparedness, of being a little stage set. Just paranoia, he thought. The signs had been good so far, hadn't they? When they reached the hut, Debora sat in the chair nearest the door and looked up at him. Starlight pointed her eyes with brilliance. Behind her, through the doorway, he made out the shadowy cocoon of a strung hammock, and beneath it, a sack from which part of a wire cage protruded. "What about your game?" he asked.

"I thought it was more important to be with you," she said.

That, too, bothered him. It was all starting to bother him, and he couldn't understand why. The thing in his hand wiggled. He balled the hand into a fist and sat next to Debora. "What's going on between you and me?" he asked, nervous. "Is anything gonna happen? I keep thinking it will, but . . ." He wiped sweat from his forehead and forgot what he had been driving at.

"I'm not sure what you mean," she said.

A shadow moved across the yellow glare spilling from the hut next door. Rippling, undulating. Mingolla squeezed his eyes shut.

"If you mean . . . romantically," she said, "I'm confused about that myself. Whether you return to your base or go to Panama, we don't seem to have much of a future. And we certainly don't have much of a past."

It boosted his confidence in her, in the situation, that she didn't have an assured answer. But he felt shaky. Very shaky. He gave his head a twitch, fighting off more ripples. "What's it like in Panama?"

"I've never been there. Probably a lot like Guatemala, except without the fighting."

Maybe he should get up, walk around. Maybe that would help. Or maybe he should just sit and talk. Talking seemed to steady him. "I bet," he said, "I bet it's beautiful, y'know. Panama. Green mountains, jungle waterfalls. I bet there's lots of birds. Macaws and parrots. Millions of 'em."

"I suppose so."

"And hummingbirds. This friend of mine was down there once on a hummingbird expedition, said there was a million kinds. I thought he was sort of a creep, y'know, for being into collecting hummingbirds." He opened his eyes and had to close them again. "I guess I thought hummingbird collecting wasn't very relevant to the big issues."

"David?" Concern in her voice.

"I'm okay." The smell of her perfume was more cloying than he remembered. "You get there by boat, right? Must be a pretty big boat. I've never been on a real boat, just this rowboat my uncle had. He used to take me fishing off Coney Island, we'd tie up to a buoy and catch all these poison fish. You shoulda seen some of 'em. Like mutants. Rainbow-colored eyes, weird growths all over. Scared the hell outta me to think about eating fish."

"I had an uncle who . . ."

"I used to think about all the ones that must be down there too deep for us to catch. Giant blowfish, genius sharks, whales with hands. I'd see 'em swallowing the boat, I'd . . ."

"Calm down, David." She kneaded the back of his neck, sending a shiver down his spine.

"I'm okay, I'm okay." He pushed her hand away; he did not need shivers along with everything else. "Lemme hear some more 'bout Panama."

"I told you, I've never been there."

"Oh, yeah. Well, how 'bout Costa Rica? You been to Costa Rica." Sweat was popping out all over his body. Maybe he should go for a swim. He'd heard there were manatees in the Río Dulce. "Ever seen a manatee?" he asked.

"David!"

She must have leaned close, because he could feel her heat spreading all through him, and he thought maybe that would help, smothering in her heat, heavy motion, get rid of this shakiness. He'd take her into that hammock and see just how hot she got. *How* hot *she got, how* hot *she got.* The words did a train rhythm in his head. Afraid to open his eyes, he reached out blindly and pulled her to him. Bumped faces, searched for her mouth. Kissed her. She kissed back. His hand slipped up to cup a breast. Jesus, she felt good! She felt like salvation, like Panama, like what you fall into when you sleep.

But then it changed, changed slowly, so slowly that he didn't notice until it was almost complete, and her tongue was squirming in his mouth, as thick and stupid as a snail's foot, and her breast, oh shit, her breast was jiggling, trembling with the same wormy juices that were in his left hand. He pushed her off, opened his eyes. Saw crude-stitch eyelashes sewn to her cheeks. Lips parted, mouth full of bones. Blank face of meat. He got to his feet, pawing the air, wanting to rip down the film of ugliness that had settled over him.

"David?" She warped his name, gulping the syllables as if she were trying to swallow and talk at once.

Frog voice, devil voice.

He spun around, caught an eyeful of black sky and spiky trees and a pitted bone-knob moon trapped in a weave of branches. Dark warty shapes of the huts, doors into yellow flame with crooked shadow men inside. He blinked, shook his head. It wasn't going away, it was real. What was this place? Not a village in Guatemala, naw, un-uh. He heard a strangled wildman grunt come from his throat, and he backed away, backed away from everything. She walked after him, croaking his name. Wig of black straw, dabs of shining jelly for eyes. Some of the shadow men were herky-jerking out of their doors, gathering behind her, talking about him in devil language. Long-legged licorice-skinned demons with drumbeat hearts, faceless nothings from the dimension of sickness. He backed another few steps.

"I can see you," he said. "I know what you are."

"It's all right, David," she said, and smiled.

Sure! She thought he was going to buy the smile, but he wasn't fooled. He saw how it broke over her face the way something rotten melts through the bottom of a wet grocery sack after it's been in the garbage for a week. Gloating smile of the Queen Devil Bitch. She had done this to him, had teamed up with the bad life in his hand and done witchy things to his head. Made him see down to the layer of shit-magic she lived in.

"I see you," he said.

He tripped, went backward flailing, stumbling, and came out of it running toward the town.

Ferns whipped his legs, branches cut at his face. Webs of shadow fettered the trail, and the shrilling insects had the sound of a metal edge being honed. Up ahead, he spotted a big moon-struck tree standing by itself on a rise overlooking the water. A grandfather tree, a white magic tree. It summoned to him. He stopped beside it, sucking air. The moonlight cooled him off, drenched him with silver, and he understood the purpose of the tree. Fountain of whiteness in the dark wood, shining for him alone. He made a fist of his left hand. The thing inside the hand eeled frantically as if it knew what was coming. He studied the deeply grooved, mystic patterns of the bark and found the point of confluence. He steeled himself. Then he drove his fist into the trunk. Brilliant pain lanced up his arm, and he cried out. But he hit the tree again, hit it a third time. He held the hand tight against his body, muffling the pain. It was already swelling, becoming a knuckle-less cartoon hand; but nothing moved inside it. The riverbank, with its rustlings and shadows, no longer menaced him; it had been transformed into a place of ordinary lights, ordinary darks, and even the whiteness of the tree looked unmagically bright.

"David!" Debora's voice, and not far off.

Part of him wanted to wait, to see whether or not she had changed for the innocent, for the ordinary. But he couldn't trust her, couldn't trust himself, and he set out running once again.

Mingolla caught the ferry to the west bank, thinking that he would find Gilbey, that a dose of Gilbey's belligerence would ground him in reality. He sat in the bow next to a group of five other soldiers, one of whom was puking over the side, and to avoid a conversation he turned away and looked down into the black water slipping past. Moonlight edged the wavelets with silver, and among those gleams it seemed he could see reflected the broken curve of his life: a kid living for Christmas, drawing pictures, receiving praise, growing up mindless to high school, sex, and drugs, growing beyond that, beginning to draw pictures again, and then, right where you might expect the curve to assume a more meaningful shape, it was sheared off, left hanging, its process demystified and explicable. He realized how foolish the idea of the ritual had been. Like a dying man clutching a vial of holy water, he had clutched at magic when the logic of existence had proved untenable. Now the frail linkages of that magic had been dissolved, and nothing supported him: he was falling through the dark zones of the war, waiting to be snatched by one of its monsters. He lifted his head and gazed at the west bank. The shore toward which he was heading was as black as a bat's wing and inscribed with arcana of violent light. Rooftops and palms were cast in silhouette against a rainbow haze of neon; gassy arcs of blood red and lime green and indigo were visible between them: fragments of glowing beasts. The wind bore screams and wild music. The soldiers beside him laughed and cursed, and the one guy kept on puking. Mingolla rested his forehead on the wooden rail, just to feel something solid.

At the Club Demonio, Gilbey's big-breasted whore was lounging by the bar, staring into her drink. Mingolla pushed through the dancers, through heat and noise and veils of lavender smoke; when he walked up to the whore, she put on a professional smile and made a grab for his crotch. He fended her off. "Where's Gilbey?" he shouted. She gave him a befuddled look; then the light dawned. "Meen-golla?" she said. He nodded. She fumbled in her purse and pulled out a folded paper. "Ees frawm Geel-bee," she said. "Forr me, five dol-larrs."

He handed her the money and took the paper. It proved to be a Christian pamphlet with a pen-and-ink sketch of a rail-thin, aggrieved-looking Jesus on the front, and beneath the sketch, a tract whose first line read, "The last days are in season." He turned it over and found a handwritten note on the back. The note was pure Gilbey. No explanation, no sentiment. Just the basics.

> I'm gone to Panama. You want to make that trip, check out a guy named Ruy Barros in Livingston. He'll fix you up. Maybe I'll see you. G.

Mingolla had believed that his confusion had peaked, but the fact of Gilbey's desertion wouldn't fit inside his head, and when he tried to make it fit he was left more confused than ever. It wasn't that he couldn't understand what had happened. He understood it perfectly; he might have predicted it. Like a crafty rat who had seen his favorite hole blocked by a trap, Gilbey had simply chewed a new hole and vanished through it. The thing that confused Mingolla was his total lack of referents. He and Gilbey and Baylor had seemed to triangulate reality, to locate each other within a coherent map of duties and places and events; and now that they were both gone, Mingolla felt utterly bewildered. Outside the club, he let the crowds push him along and gazed up at the neon animals atop the bars. Giant blue rooster, green bull, golden turtle with fiery red eyes. Great identities regarding him with disfavor. Bleeds of color washed from the signs, staining the air to a garish paleness, giving everyone a mealy complexion. Amazing, Mingolla thought, that you could breathe such grainy discolored stuff, that it didn't start you choking. It was all amazing, all nonsensical. Everything he saw struck him as unique and unfathomable, even the most commonplace of sights. He found himself staring at people—at whores, at street kids, at an MP who was talking to another MP, patting the fender of his jeep as if it were his big olive-drab pet—and trying to figure out what they were really doing, what special significance their actions held for him, what clues they presented that might help him unravel the snarl of his own existence. At last, realizing that he needed peace and quiet, he set out toward the airbase, thinking he would find an empty bunk and sleep off his confusion; but when he came to the cut-off that led to the unfinished bridge, he turned down it, deciding that he wasn't ready to deal with gate sentries and duty officers. Dense thickets buzzing with insects narrowed the cut-off to a path, and at its end stood a line of sawhorses. He climbed over them and soon was mounting a sharply inclined curve that appeared to lead to a point not far below the lumpish silver moon.

Despite a litter of rubble and cardboard sheeting, the concrete looked pure under the moon, blazing bright, like a fragment of snowy light not quite hardened to the material; and as he ascended he thought he could feel the bridge trembling to his footsteps with the sensitivity of a white nerve. He seemed to be walking into darkness and stars, a solitude the size of creation. It felt good and damn lonely, maybe a little too much so, with the wind flapping pieces of cardboard and the sounds of the insects left behind.

After a few minutes he glimpsed the ragged terminus ahead. When he reached it, he sat down carefully, letting his legs dangle. Wind keened through the exposed girders, tugging at his ankles; his hand throbbed and was fever-hot. Below, multicolored brilliance clung to the black margin of the east bank like a colony of bioluminescent algae. He wondered how high he was. Not high enough, he thought. Faint music was fraying on the wind—the inexhaustible delirium of San Francisco de Juticlan—and he imagined that the flickering of the stars was caused by this thin smoke of music drifting across them.

He tried to think what to do. Not much occurred to him. He pictured Gilbey in Panama. Whoring, drinking, fighting. Doing just as he had in Guatemala. That was where the idea of desertion failed Mingolla. In Panama he would be afraid; in Panama, though his hand might not shake, some other malignant twitch would develop; in Panama he would resort to magical cures for his afflictions, because he would be too imperiled by the real to derive strength from it. And eventually the war would come to Panama. Desertion would have gained him nothing. He stared out across the moon-silvered jungle, and it seemed that some essential part of him was pouring from his eyes, entering the flow of the wind and rushing away past the Ant Farm and its smoking craters, past guerrilla territory, past the seamless join of sky and horizon, being irresistibly pulled toward a point into which the world's vitality was emptying. He felt himself emptying as well, growing cold and vacant and slow. His brain became incapable of thought, capable only of recording perceptions. The wind brought green scents that made his nostrils flare. The sky's blackness folded around him, and the stars were golden pinpricks of sensation. He didn't sleep, but something in him slept.

A whisper drew him back from the edge of the world. At first he thought it had been his imagination, and he continued staring at the sky, which had lightened to the vivid blue of pre-dawn. Then he heard it again and glanced behind him. Strung out across the bridge, about twenty feet away, were a dozen or so children. Some standing, some crouched. Most were clad in rags, a few wore coverings of vines and leaves, and others were naked. Watchful, silent. Knives glinted in their hands. They were all emaciated, their hair long and matted, and Mingolla, recalling the dead children he had seen that morning, was for a moment afraid. But only for a moment. Fear flared in him like a coal puffed to life by a breeze and died an instant later, suppressed not by any rational accommodation but by a perception of those ragged figures as an opportunity for surrender. He wasn't eager to die, yet neither did he want to put forth more effort in the cause of survival. Survival, he had learned, was not the soul's ultimate priority. He kept staring at the children. The way they were posed reminded him of a Neanderthal grouping in the Museum of Natural History. The moon was still up, and they cast vaguely defined shadows like smudges of graphite. Finally Mingolla turned away, the horizon was showing a distinct line of green darkness.

He had expected to be stabbed or pushed, to pinwheel down and break against the Río Dulce, its waters gone a steely color beneath the brightening sky. But instead a voice spoke in his ear: "Hey, macho." Squatting beside him was a boy of fourteen or fifteen, with a swarthy monkeylike face framed by tangles of shoulder-length dark hair. Wearing tattered shorts. Coiled serpent tattooed on his brow. He tipped his head to one side, then the other. Perplexed. He might have been trying to see the true Mingolla through layers of false appearance. He made a growly noise in his throat and held up a knife, twisting it this way and that, letting Mingolla observe its keen edge, how it channeled the moonlight along its blade. An army-issue survival knife with a brass-knuckle grip. Mingolla gave an amused sniff.

The boy seemed alarmed by this reaction; he lowered the knife and shifted away. "What you doing here, man?" he asked.

A number of answers occurred to Mingolla, most demanding too much energy to voice; he chose the simplest. "I like it here. I like the bridge."

The boy squinted at Mingolla. "The bridge is magic," he said. "You know this?"

"There was a time I might have believed you," said Mingolla.

"You got to talk slow, man." The boy frowned. "Too fast, I can't understan'."

Mingolla repeated his comment, and the boy said, "You believe it, gringo. Why else you here?" With a planing motion of his arm he described an imaginary continuance of the bridge's upward course. "That's where the bridge travels now. Don't have not'ing to do wit' crossing the river. It's a piece of white stone. Don't mean the same t'ing a bridge means."

Mingolla was surprised to hear his thoughts echoed by someone who so resembled a hominid.

"I come here," the boy went on. "I listen to the wind, hear it sing in the iron. And I know t'ings from it. I can see the future." He grinned, exposing blackened teeth, and pointed south toward the Caribbean. "Future's that way, man."

Mingolla liked the joke; he felt an affinity for the boy, for anyone who could manage jokes from the boy's perspective, but he couldn't think of a way to express his good feeling. Finally he said, "You speak English well."

"Shit! What you think? 'Cause we live in the jungle, we talk like animals? Shit!" The boy jabbed the point of his knife into the concrete. "I talk English all my life. Gringos they too stupid to learn Spanish."

A girl's voice sounded behind them, harsh and peremptory. The other children had closed to within ten feet, their savage faces intent upon Mingolla, and the girl was standing a bit forward of them. She had sunken cheeks and deep-set eyes; ratty cables of hair hung down over her single-scoop breasts. Her hipbones tented up a rag of a skirt, which the wind pushed back between her legs. The boy let her finish, then gave a prolonged response, punctuating his words by smashing the brass-knuckle grip of his knife against the concrete, striking sparks with every blow.

"Gracela," he said to Mingolla, "she wants to kill you. But I say, some men they got one foot in the worl' of death, and if you kill them, death will take you, too. And you know what?"

"What?" said Mingolla.

"It's true. You and death"—the boy clasped his hands—"like this."

"Maybe," Mingolla said.

"No 'maybe.' The bridge tol' me. Tol' me I be t'ankful if I let you live. So you be t'ankful to the bridge. That magic you don't believe, it save your ass." The boy lowered out of his squat and sat cross-legged. "Gracela, she don' care 'bout you live or die. She jus' go 'gainst me 'cause when I leave here, she going to be chief. She's, you know, impatient."

Mingolla looked at the girl. She met his gaze coldly: a witch-child with slitted eyes, bramble hair, and ribs poking out. "Where are you going?" he asked the boy.

"I have a dream I will live in the south; I dream I own a warehouse full of gold and cocaine."

The girl began to harangue him again, and he shot back a string of angry syllables.

"What did you say?" Mingolla asked.

"I say, 'Gracela, you give me shit, I going to fuck you and t'row you in the river.' " He winked at Mingolla. "Gracela she a virgin, so she worry 'bout that firs' t'ing."

The sky was graying, pink streaks fading in from the east; birds wheeled up from the jungle below, forming into flocks above the river. In the half-light Mingolla saw that the boy's chest was cross-hatched with ridged scars: knife wounds that hadn't received proper treatment. Bits of vegetation were trapped in his hair, like primitive adornments.

"Tell me, gringo," said the boy. "I hear in America there is a machine wit' the soul of a man. This is true?"

"More or less," said Mingolla.

The boy nodded gravely, his suspicions confirmed. "I hear also America has builded a metal worl' in the sky."

"They're building it now."

"In the house of your president, is there a stone that holds the mind of a dead magician?"

Mingolla gave this due consideration. "I doubt it," he said. "But it's possible."

Wind thudded against the bridge, startling him. He felt its freshness on his face and relished the sensation. That—the fact that he could still take simple pleasure from life—startled him more than had the sudden noise.

The pink streaks in the east were deepening to crimson and fanning wider; shafts of light pierced upward to stain the bellies of some low-lying clouds to mauve. Several of the children began to mutter in unison. A chant. They were speaking in Spanish, but the way their voices jumbled the words, it sounded guttural and malevolent, a language for trolls. Listening to them, Mingolla imagined them crouched around fires in bamboo thickets. Bloody knives lifted sunwards over their fallen prey. Making love in the green nights among fleshy Rousseau-like vegetation, while pythons with ember eyes coiled in the branches above their heads.

"Truly, gringo," said the boy, apparently still contemplating Mingolla's answers. "These are evil times." He stared gloomily down at the river; the wind shifted the heavy snarls of his hair.

Watching him, Mingolla grew envious. Despite the bleakness of his existence, this little monkey king was content with his place in the world, assured of its nature. Perhaps he was deluded, but Mingolla envied his delusion, and he especially envied his dream of gold and cocaine. His own dreams had been dispersed by the war. The idea of sitting and daubing colors onto canvas no longer held any real attraction for him. Nor did the thought of returning to New York. Though survival had been his priority all these months, he had never stopped to consider what survival portended, and now he did not believe he could return. He had, he realized, become acclimated to the war, able to breathe its toxins; he would gag on the air of peace and home. The war was his new home, his newly rightful place.

Then the truth of this struck him with the force of an illumination, and he understood what he had to do.

Baylor and Gilbey had acted according to their natures, and he would have to act according to his, which imposed upon him the path of acceptance. He remembered Tio Moises' story about the pilot and laughed inwardly. In a sense his friend—the guy he had mentioned in his unsent letter—had been right about the war, about the world. It was full of designs, patterns, coincidences, and cycles that appeared to indicate the workings of some magical power. But these things were the result of a subtle natural process. The longer you lived, the wider your experience, the more complicated your life became, and eventually you were bound in the midst of so many interactions, a web of circumstance and emotion and event, that nothing was simple anymore and everything was subject to interpretation. Interpretation, however, was a waste of time. Even the most logical of interpretations was merely an attempt to herd mystery into a cage and lock the door on it. It made life no less mysterious. And it was equally pointless to seize upon patterns, to rely on them, to obey the mystical regulations they seemed to imply. Your one effective course had to be entrenchment. You had to admit to mystery, to the incomprehensibility of your situation, and protect yourself against it. Shore up your web, clear it of blind corners, set alarms. You had to plan aggressively. You had to become the monster in your own maze, as brutal and devious as the fate you sought to escape. It was the kind of militant acceptance that Tio Moises' pilot had not had the opportunity to display, that Mingolla himself—though the opportunity had been his—had failed to display. He saw that now. He had merely reacted to danger and had not challenged or used forethought against it. But he thought he would be able to do that now.

He turned to the boy, thinking he might appreciate this insight into "magic," and caught a flicker of movement out of the corner of his eye. Gracela. Coming up behind the boy, her knife held low, ready to stab. In reflex, Mingolla flung out his injured hand to block her. The knife nicked the edge of his hand, deflected upward and sliced the top of the boy's shoulder.

The pain in Mingolla's hand was excruciating, blinding him momentarily; and then as he grabbed Gracela's forearm to prevent her from stabbing again, he felt another sensation, one almost covered by the pain. He had thought the thing inside his hand was dead, but now he could feel it fluttering at the edges of the wound, leaking out in the rich trickle of blood that flowed over his wrist. It was trying to worm back inside, wriggling against the flow, but the pumping of his heart was too strong, and soon it was gone, dripping on the white stone of the bridge.

Before he could feel relief or surprise or any way absorb what had happened, Gracela tried to pull free. Mingolla got to his knees, dragged her down and dashed her knife hand against the bridge. The knife skittered away. Gracela struggled wildly, clawing at his face, and the other children edged forward. Mingolla levered his left arm under Gracela's chin, choking her; with his right hand, he picked up the knife and pressed the point into her breast. The children stopped their advance, and Gracela went limp. He could feel her trembling. Tears streaked the grime on her cheeks. She looked like a scared little girl, not a witch.

"Puta!" said the boy. He had come to his feet, holding his shoulder, and was staring daggers at Gracela.

"Is it bad?" Mingolla asked. "The shoulder?"

The boy inspected the bright blood on his fingertips. "It hurts," he said. He stepped over to stand in front of Gracela and smiled down at her; he unbuttoned the top button of his shorts.

Gracela tensed.

"What are you doing?" Mingolla suddenly felt responsible for the girl.

"I going to do what I tol' her, man." The boy undid the rest of the buttons and shimmied out of his shorts; he was already half-erect, as if the violence had aroused him.

"No," said Mingolla, realizing as he spoke that this was not at all wise.

"Take your life," said the boy sternly. "Walk away."

A long powerful gust of wind struck the bridge; it seemed to Mingolla that the vibration of the bridge, the beating of his heart, and Gracela's trembling were driven by the same shimmering pulse. He felt an almost visceral commitment to the moment, one that had nothing to do with his concern for the girl. Maybe, he thought, it was an implementation of his new convictions.

The boy lost patience. He shouted at the other children, herding them away with slashing gestures. Sullenly, they moved off down the curve of the bridge, positioning themselves along the railing, leaving an open avenue. Beyond them, beneath a lavender sky, the jungle stretched to the horizon, broken only by the rectangular hollow made by the airbase. The boy hunkered at Gracela's feet. "Tonight," he said to Mingolla, "the bridge have set us together. Tonight we sit, we talk. Now, that's over. My heart say to kill you. But 'cause you stop Gracela from cutting deep, I give you a chance. She mus' make a judgmen'. If she say she go wit' you, we"—he waved toward the other children—"will kill you. If she wan' to stay, then you mus' go. No more talk, no bullshit. You jus' go. Understan'?"

Mingolla wasn't afraid, and his lack of fear was not born of an indifference to life, but of clarity and confidence. It was time to stop reacting away from challenges, time to meet them. He came up with a plan. There was no doubt that Gracela would choose him, choose a chance at life, no matter how slim. But before she could decide, he would kill the boy. Then he would run straight at the others: without their leader, they might not hang together. It wasn't much of a plan and he didn't like the idea of hurting the boy; but he thought he might be able to pull it off. "I understand," he said.

The boy spoke to Gracela; he told Mingolla to release her. She sat up, rubbing the spot where Mingolla had pricked her with the knife. She glanced coyly at him, then at the boy; she pushed her hair back behind her neck and thrust out her breasts as if preening for two suitors. Mingolla was astonished by her behavior. Maybe, he thought, she was playing for time. He stood and pretended to be shaking out his kinks, edging closer to the boy, who remained crouched beside Gracela. In the east a red fireball had cleared the horizon; its sanguine light inspired Mingolla, fueled his resolve. He yawned and edged closer yet, firming his grip on the knife. He would yank the boy's head back by the hair, cut his throat. Nerves jumped in his chest. A pressure was building inside him, demanding that he act, that he move now. He restrained himself. Another step should do it, another step to be absolutely sure. But as he was about to take that step, Gracela reached out and tapped the boy on the shoulder.

Surprise must have showed on Mingolla's face, because the boy looked at him and grunted laughter. "You t'ink she pick you?" he said. "Shit! You don' know Gracela, man. Gringos burn her village. She lick the devil's ass 'fore she even shake hands wit' you." He grinned, stroked her hair. " 'Sides, she t'ink if she fuck me good, maybe I say, 'Oh, Gracela, I got to have some more of that!' And who knows? Maybe she right."

Gracela lay back and wriggled out of her skirt. Between her legs, she was nearly hairless. A smile touched the corners of her mouth. Mingolla stared at her, dumbfounded.

"I not going to kill you, gringo," said the boy without looking up; he was running his hand across Gracela's stomach. "I tol' you I won' kill a man so close wit' death.'' Again he laughed. ''You look pretty funny trying to sneak up. I like watching that.''

Mingolla was stunned. All the while he had been gearing himself up to kill, shunting aside anxiety and revulsion, he had merely been providing an entertainment for the boy. The heft of the knife seemed to be drawing his anger into a compact shape, and he wanted to carry out his attack, to cut down this little animal who had ridiculed him; but humiliation mixed with the anger, neutralizing it. The poisons of rage shook him; he could feel every incidence of pain and fatigue in his body. His hand was throbbing, bloated and discolored like the hand of a corpse. Weakness pervaded him. And relief.

''Go,'' said the boy. He lay down beside Gracela, propped on an elbow, and began to tease one of her nipples erect.

Mingolla took a few hesitant steps away. Behind him, Gracela made a mewling noise and the boy whispered something. Mingolla's anger was rekindled—they had already forgotten him!—but he kept going. As he passed the other children, one spat at him and another shied a pebble. He fixed his eyes on the white concrete slipping beneath his feet.

When he reached the mid-point of the curve, he turned back. The children had hemmed in Gracela and the boy against the terminus, blocking them from view. The sky had gone bluish-gray behind them, and the wind carried their voices. They were singing: a ragged, chirpy song that sounded celebratory. Mingolla's anger subsided, his humiliation ebbed. He had nothing to be ashamed of; though he had acted unwisely, he had done so from a posture of strength and no amount of ridicule could diminish that. Things were going to work out. Yes they were! He would make them work out.

For a while he watched the children. At this remove, their singing had an appealing savagery and he felt a trace of wistfulness at leaving them behind. He wondered what would happen after the boy had done with Gracela. He was not concerned, only curious. The way you feel when you think you may have to leave a movie before the big finish. Will our heroine survive? Will justice prevail? Will survival and justice bring happiness in their wake? Soon the end of the bridge came to be bathed in the golden rays of the sunburst; the children seemed to be blackening and dissolving in heavenly fire. That was a sufficient resolution for Mingolla. He tossed Gracela's knife into the river and went down from the bridge in whose magic he no longer believed, walking toward the war whose mystery he had accepted as his own.

5.

At the airbase, Mingolla took a stand beside the Sikorsky that had brought him to San Francisco de Juticlan; he had recognized it by the painted flaming letters of the words Whispering Death. He rested his head against the letter g and recalled how Baylor had recoiled from the letters, worried that they might transmit some deadly essence. Mingolla didn't mind the contact. The painted flames seemed to be warming the inside of his head, stirring up thoughts as slow and indefinite as smoke. Comforting thoughts that embodied no images or ideas. Just a gentle buzz of mental activity, like the idling of an engine. The base was coming to life around him. Jeeps pulling away from barracks; a couple of officers inspecting the belly of a cargo plane; some guy repairing a fork-lift. Peaceful, homey. Mingolla closed his eyes, lulled into a half-sleep, letting the sun and the painted flames bracket him with heat real and imagined.

Some time later—how much later, he could not be sure—a voice said, "Fucked up your hand pretty good, didn'tcha?"

The two pilots were standing by the cockpit door. In their black flight suits and helmets they looked neither weird nor whimsical, but creatures of functional menace. Masters of the Machine. "Yeah," said Mingolla. "Fucked it up."

"How'd ya do it?" asked the pilot on the left.

"Hit a tree."

"Musta been goddamn crocked to hit a tree," said the pilot on the right. "Tree ain't goin' nowhere if you hit it."

Mingolla made a non-committal noise. "You guys going up to the Farm?"

"You bet! What's the matter, man? Had enough of them wild women?" Pilot on the right.

"Guess so. Wanna gimme a ride?"

"Sure thing," said the pilot on the left. "Whyn't you climb on in front. You can sit back of us."

"Where your buddies?" asked the pilot on the right.

"Gone," said Mingolla as he climbed into the cockpit.

One of the pilots said, "Didn't think we'd be seein' them boys again."

Mingolla strapped into the observer's seat behind the co-pilot's position. He had assumed there would be a lengthy instrument check, but as soon as the engines had been warmed, the Sikorsky lurched up and veered northward. With the exception of the weapons systems, none of the defenses had been activated. The radar, the thermal imager and terrain display, all showed blank screens. A nervous thrill ran across the muscles of Mingolla's stomach as he considered the varieties of danger to which the pilots' reliance upon their miraculous helmets had laid them open; but his nervousness was subsumed by the whispery rhythms of the rotors and his sense of the Sikorsky's power. He recalled having a similar feeling of secure potency while sitting at the controls of his gun. He had never let that feeling grow, never let it rule him, empower him. He had been a fool.

They followed the northeasterly course of the river, which coiled like a length of blue-steel razor wire between jungle hills. The pilots laughed and joked, and the ride came to have the air of a ride with a couple of good ol' boys going nowhere fast and full of free beer. At one point the co-pilot piped his voice through the on-board speakers and launched into a dolorous country song.

"Whenever we kiss, dear, our two lips meet,
And whenever you're not with me, we're apart.
When you sawed my dog in half, that was depressin',
But when you shot me in the chest, you broke my heart."

As the co-pilot sang, the pilot rocked the Sikorsky back and forth in a drunken accompaniment, and after the song ended, he called back to Mingolla, "You believe this here son of a bitch wrote that? He did! Picks a guitar, too! Boy's a genius!"

"It's a great song," said Mingolla, and he meant it. The song had made him happy, and that was no small thing.

They went rocking through the skies, singing the first verse over and over. But then, as they left the river behind, still maintaining a northeasterly course, the co-pilot pointed to a section of jungle ahead and shouted, "Beaners! Quadrant Four! You got 'em?"

"Got 'em!" said the pilot. The Sikorsky swerved down toward the jungle, shuddered, and flame veered from beneath them. An instant later, a huge swath of jungle erupted into a gout of marbled smoke and fire. "Whee-oo!" the co-pilot sang out, jubilant. "Whisperin' Death strikes again!" With guns blazing, they went swooping through blowing veils of dark smoke. Acres of trees were burning, and still they kept up the attack. Mingolla gritted his teeth against the noise, and when at last the firing stopped, dismayed by this insanity, he sat slumped, his head down. He suddenly doubted his ability to cope with the insanity of the Ant Farm and remembered all his reasons for fear.

The co-pilot turned back to him. "You ain't got no call to look so gloomy, man," he said. "You're a lucky son of a bitch, y'know that?"

The pilot began a bank toward the east, toward the Ant Farm. "How you figure that?" Mingolla asked.

"I gotta clear sight of you, man," said the co-pilot. "I can tell you for true you ain't gonna be at the Farm much longer. It ain't clear why or nothin'. But I 'spect you gonna be wounded. Not bad, though. Just a goin'-home wound."

As the pilot completed the bank, a ray of sun slanted into the cockpit, illuminating the co-pilot's visor, and for a split-second Mingolla could make out the vague shadow of the face beneath. It seemed lumpy and malformed. His imagination added details. Bizarre growths, cracked cheeks, an eye webbed shut. Like a face out of a movie about nuclear mutants. He was tempted to believe that he had really seen this; the co-pilot's deformities would validate his prediction of a secure future. But Mingolla rejected the temptation. He was afraid of dying, afraid of the terrors held by life at the Ant Farm, yet he wanted no more to do with magic . . . unless there was magic involved in being a good soldier. In obeying the disciplines, in the practice of fierceness.

"Could be his hand'll get him home," said the pilot. "That hand looks pretty fucked up to me. Looks like a million-dollar wound, that hand."

"Naw, I don't get it's his hand," said the co-pilot. "Somethin' else. Whatever, it's gonna do the trick."

Mingolla could see his own face floating in the black plastic of the co-pilot's visor; he looked warped and pale, so thoroughly unfamiliar that for a moment he thought the face might be a bad dream the co-pilot was having.

"What the hell's with you, man?" the co-pilot asked. "You don't believe me?"

Mingolla wanted to explain that his attitude had nothing to do with belief or disbelief, that it signaled his intent to obtain a safe future by means of securing his present; but he couldn't think how to put it into words the co-pilot would accept. The co-pilot would merely refer again to his visor as testimony to a magical reality or perhaps would point up ahead where—because the cockpit plastic had gone opaque under the impact of direct sunlight—the sun now appeared to hover in a smoky darkness: a distinct fiery sphere with a streaming corona, like one of those cabalistic emblems embossed on ancient seals. It was an evil, fearsome-looking thing, and though Mingolla was unmoved by it, he knew the pilot would see in it a powerful sign.

"You think I'm lyin'?" said the co-pilot angrily. "You think I'd be bullshittin' you 'bout somethin' like this? Man, I ain't lyin'! I'm givin' you the good goddamn word!"

They flew east into the sun, whispering death, into a world disguised as a strange bloody enchantment, over the dark green wild where war had taken root, where men in combat armor fought for no good reason against men wearing brass scorpions on their berets, where crazy, lost men wandered the mystic light of Fire Zone Emerald and mental wizards brooded upon things not yet seen. The co-pilot kept the black bubble of his visor angled back toward Mingolla, waiting for a response. But Mingolla just stared, and before too long the co-pilot turned away.

SALVAGE

Orson Scott Card

Orson Scott Card, this year's winner in the novel category for *Speaker for the Dead*, also won last year for *Ender's Game*, to which *Speaker for the Dead* is a sequel. The only other writer to win the Nebula in the same category two years in a row is Frederik Pohl, but Card is the first to win for a sequel to a previous winner. Card has won the Hugo Award and the John W. Campbell Award for Best New Writer. His other novels include *Songmaster, Hart's Hope, The Worthing Chronicle,* and *A Woman of Destiny.*

Card was also nominated this year for the novelette "Hatrack River" (about which he writes below). However, because this story has been reprinted elsewhere and is part of a book-length work, he and I felt that he should be represented by a less visible work—a novelette from the preliminary Nebula ballot.

The author writes about his work:

"The protagonists of my earlier novels were isolated individuals, connected only tenuously with the characters around them. They had few family connections that mattered in the story. They always had to cope with the frustration and uncertainty of a world of unreliable people.

"Such isolation is a common human condition, and exploring it is valid. It is the natural condition of the adolescent, who has cut himself adrift from his parents and has not yet established a new family connection of his own.

"But as my own family grew—the children older, my wife and I more firmly identified with each other—the unconnected protagonists of my earlier novels were no longer interesting to me. It was time to connect my heroes in those irrevocable bonds of commitment that make family a nearly universal hunger in the human heart.

"A tiny first step was to give Ender Wiggin, in Ender's Game, *a brother and sister who had not existed in the novelette version of that tale; siblings who shaped his life, even though he was cut off from them very young.* Speaker for the Dead *represented my*

first attempt to create a fully developed family, and to show how their network of relationships shifted when Ender entered the family, every individual being forced to redefine himself in light of the new presence in the house."

(On "Hatrack River") "The American frontier is a period virtually untouched by SF and fantasy; American folk magic has been extensively used, to my knowledge, only by Manly Wade Wellman. As I learned more about the frontier period west of the Appalachians, I found folk beliefs and historical and biographical events that opened up thousands of story possibilities.

"There's nothing more fun than to explore a half-familiar, brand-new world. Fenimore Cooper's footprints are here and there in the landscape; I keep running into real yet bigger-than-life figures like Mike Fink, Davy Crockett, Daniel Boone, Ben Franklin, George Washington, Tecumseh, William 'Tippecanoe' Harrison. In the process of reinventing America, I get to redefine all these characters and the meaning of their lives. And, with luck, these tales will give their audience the pleasure I have felt, of discovering America with new eyes."

(On "Salvage") "The manuscript of 'Salvage' was born of the creative maelstrom of the first Sycamore Hill Writers Workshop, sponsored by John Kessel and Mark Van Name. But the story itself came from an image in my mind of the Salt Lake Temple under water. To Mormons, all our temples are sacred places, but the Salt Lake Temple has resonances far beyond the rites performed there. We built it of stone and sweat in a desert land that was the only place where America would allow us to practice our religion, not free of interference—never that—but free of murder and mob violence. The Salt Lake Temple is the ensign that we raised in the tops of the mountains; it is our symbol of defiance, of endurance, of hope. To see it drown, to lose the use of it, would be a terrible blow. But, as Deaver Teague learns in 'Salvage,' the Mormon people have a way of surviving all such blows and shocks.

"So, for that matter, does Deaver Teague."

The road began to climb steeply right from the ferry, so the truck couldn't build up any speed. Deaver just kept shifting down, wincing as he listened to the grinding of the gears. Sounded like the transmission was chewing itself to gravel. He'd been nursing it all the way across Nevada, and if the Wendover ferry hadn't carried him these last miles over the Mormon Sea, he would have had a nice long hike. Lucky. It was a good sign. Things were going to go Deaver's way for a while.

The mechanic frowned at him when he rattled in to the loading dock. "You been ridin' the clutch, boy?"

Deaver got down from the cab. "Clutch? What's a clutch?"

The mechanic didn't smile. "Couldn't you hear the transmission was shot?"

"I had mechanics all the way across Nevada askin' to fix it for me, but I told 'em I was savin' it for you."

The mechanic looked at him like he was crazy. "There ain't no mechanics in Nevada."

If you wasn't dumb as your thumb, thought Deaver, you'd know I was joking. These old Mormons were so straight they couldn't sit down, some of them. But Deaver didn't say anything. Just smiled.

"This truck's gonna stay here a few days," said the mechanic.

Fine with me, thought Deaver. I got plans. "How many days you figure?"

"Take three for now, I'll sign you off."

"My name's Deaver Teague."

"Tell the foreman, he'll write it up." The mechanic lifted the hood to begin the routine checks while the dockboys loaded off the old washing machines and refrigerators and other stuff Deaver had picked up on his trip. Deaver took his mileage reading to the window and the foreman paid him off.

Seven dollars for five days of driving and loading, sleeping in the cab, and eating whatever the farmers could spare. It was better than a lot of people lived on, but there wasn't any future in it. Salvage wouldn't go on forever. Someday he'd pick up the last broken-down dishwasher left from the old days, and then he'd be out of a job.

Well, Deaver Teague wasn't going to wait around for that. He knew where the gold was, he'd been planning how to get it for weeks, and if Lehi had got the diving equipment like he promised, then tomorrow morning they'd do a little freelance salvage work. If they were lucky they'd come home rich.

Deaver's legs were stiff but he loosened them up pretty quick and broke into an easy, loping run down the corridors of the Salvage Center. He took a flight of stairs two or three steps at a time, bounded down a hall, and when he reached a sign that said SMALL COMPUTER SALVAGE, he pushed off the doorframe and rebounded into the room. "Hey Lehi!" he said. "Hey, it's quittin' time!"

Lehi McKay paid no attention. He was sitting in front of a TV screen, jerking at a black box he held on his lap.

"You do that and you'll go blind," said Deaver.

"Shut up, carpface." Lehi never took his eyes off the screen. He jabbed at a button on the black box and twisted on the stick that jutted up from it. A colored blob on the screen blew up and split into four smaller blobs.

"I got three days off while they do the transmission on the truck," said Deaver. "So tomorrow's the temple expedition."

Lehi got the last blob off the screen. More blobs appeared.

"That's real fun," said Deaver, "like sweepin' the street and then they bring along another troop of horses."

"It's an Atari. From the sixties or seventies or something. Eighties. Old. Can't do much with the pieces, it's only eight-bit stuff. All these years in somebody's attic in Logan, and the sucker still runs."

"Old guy probably didn't even know they had it."

"Probably."

Deaver watched the game. Same thing over and over again. "How much a thing like this use to cost?"

"A lot. Maybe fifteen, twenty bucks."

"Makes you want to barf. And here sits Lehi McKay, too-dling his noodle like the old guys used to. All it ever got *them* was a sore noodle, Lehi. And slag for brains."

"Drown it. I'm trying to concentrate."

The game finally ended. Lehi set the black box on the workbench, turned off the machine, and stood up.

"You got everything ready to go underwater tomorrow?" asked Deaver.

"That was a good game. Having fun must've took up a lot of their time in the old days. Mom says the kids used to not even be able to get jobs till they was sixteen. It was the law."

"Don't you wish," said Deaver.

"It's true."

"You don't know your own tongue from dung, Lehi. You don't know your heart from a fart."

"You want to get us both kicked out of here, talkin' like that?"

"I don't have to follow school rules now, I graduated sixth grade, I'm nineteen years old, I been on my own for five years." He pulled his seven dollars out of his pocket, waved them once, stuffed them back in carelessly. "I do okay, and I talk like I want to talk. Think I'm afraid of the Bishop?"

"Bishop don't scare me. I don't even go to church except to make Mom happy. It's a bunch of bunny turds."

Lehi laughed, but Deaver could see that he was a little scared to talk like that. Sixteen years old, thought Deaver, he's big and he's smart but he's such a little kid. He don't understand how it's like to be a man. "Rain's comin'."

"Rain's always comin'. What the hell do you think filled up the lake?" Lehi smirked as he unplugged everything on the workbench.

"I meant *Lor*raine Wilson."

"I know what you meant. She's got her boat?"

"And she's got a mean set of fenders." Deaver cupped his hands. "Just need a little polishing."

"Why do you always talk dirty? Ever since you started driving salvage, Deaver, you got a gutter mouth. Besides, she's built like a sack."

"She's near fifty, what do you expect?" It occurred to Deaver that Lehi seemed to be stalling. Which probably meant he botched up again as usual. "Can you get the diving stuff?"

"I already got it. You thought I'd screw up." Lehi smirked again.

"You? Screw up? You can be trusted with *anything*." Deaver started for the door. He could hear Lehi behind him, still shutting a few things off. They got to use a lot of electricity in here. Of course they had to, because they needed computers all the time, and salvage was the only way to get them. But when Deaver saw all that electricity getting used up at once, to him it looked like his own future. All the machines he could ever want, new ones, and all the power they needed. Clothes that nobody else ever wore, his own horse and wagon or even a car. Maybe he'd be the guy who started *making* cars again. He didn't need stupid blob-smashing games from the past. "That stuff's dead and gone, duck lips, dead and gone."

"What're you talkin' about?" asked Lehi.

"Dead and gone. All your computer things."

It was enough to set Lehi off, as it always did. Deaver grinned and felt wicked and strong as Lehi babbled along behind him. About how we use the computers more than they ever did in the old days, the computers kept everything going, on and on and on, it was cute, Deaver liked him, the boy was so *intense.* Like everything was the end of the world. Deaver knew better. The world was dead, it had already ended, so none of it mattered, you could sink all this stuff in the lake.

They came out of the Center and walked along the retaining wall. Far below them was the harbor, a little circle of water in the bottom of a bowl, with Bingham City perched on the lip. They used to have an open-pit copper mine here, but when the water rose they cut a channel to it and now they had a nice harbor on Oquirrh Island in the middle of the Mormon Sea, where the factories could stink up the whole sky and no neighbors ever complained about it.

A lot of other people joined them on the steep dirt road that led down to the harbor. Nobody lived right in Bingham City itself, because it was just a working place, day and night. Shifts in, shifts out. Lehi was a shift boy, lived with his family across the Jordan Strait on Point of the Mountain, which was as rotten a place to live as anybody ever devised, rode the ferry in every day at five in the morning and rode it back every afternoon at four. He was supposed to go to school after that for a couple of hours but Deaver thought that was stupid, he told Lehi that all the time, told him again now. School is too much time and too little of everything, a waste of time.

"I gotta go to school," said Lehi.

"Tell me two plus two, you haven't got two plus two yet?"

"*You* finished, didn't you?"

"Nobody needs anything after fourth grade." He shoved Lehi a little. Usually Lehi shoved back, but not this time.

"Just try getting a real job without a sixth grade diploma, okay? And I'm pretty close now." They were at the ferry slip. Lehi got out his pass.

"You with me tomorrow or not?"

Lehi made a face. "I don't know, Deaver. You can get arrested for going around there. It's a dumb thing to do. They say there's real weird things in the old skyscrapers."

"We aren't going *in* the skyscrapers."

"Even worse in *there*, Deaver. I don't want to go there."

"Yeah, the Angel Moroni's probably waiting to jump out and say booga-booga-booga."

"Don't talk about it, Deaver." Deaver was tickling him; Lehi laughed and tried to shy away. "Cut it out, chiggerhead. Come on. Besides, the Moroni statue was moved to the Salt Lake Monument up on the mountain. And that has a guard all the time."

"The statue's just gold plate anyway. I'm telling you those old Mormons hid tons of the stuff in the Temple, just waitin' for somebody who isn't scared of the ghost of Bigamy Young to—"

"Shut *up*, snotsucker, okay? People can hear! Look around, we're not alone!"

It was true, of course. Some of the older people were glaring at them. But then, Deaver noticed that older people liked to glare at younger ones. It made the old farts feel better about kicking off. It was like they were saying, okay, I'm dying, but at least you're stupid. So Deaver looked right at a woman who was glaring at him and murmured, "Okay, I'm stupid, but at least I won't die."

"Deaver, do you always have to say that where they can hear you?"

"It's true."

"In the first place, Deaver, they aren't dying. And in the second place, you're definitely stupid. And in the third place, the ferry's here." Lehi punched Deaver lightly in the stomach.

Deaver bent over in mock agony. "Ay, the laddie's ungrateful, he is, I give him me last croost of bread and this be the thanks I gets."

"*Nobody* has an accent like that, Deaver!" shouted Lehi. The boat began to pull away.

"Tomorrow at five-thirty!" shouted Deaver.

"You'll never get up at four-thirty, don't give me that, you never get up . . ." But the ferry and the noise of the factories and machines and trucks swallowed up the rest of his insults. Deaver knew them all, anyway. Lehi might be only sixteen, but he was okay. Someday Deaver'd get married but his wife would like Lehi, too. And Lehi'd even get married, and his wife would like Deaver. She'd better, or she'd have to swim home.

He took the trolley home to Fort Douglas and walked to the ancient barracks building where Rain let him stay. It was supposed to be a storage room, but she kept the mops and soap stuff in her place so that there'd be room for a cot. Not much else, but it was on Oquirrh Island without being right there in the stink and the smoke and the noise. He could sleep and that was enough, since most of the time he was out on the truck.

Truth was, his room wasn't home anyway. Home was pretty much Rain's place, a drafty room at the end of the barracks with a dumpy, frowzy lady who served him good food and plenty of it. That's where he went now, walked right in and surprised her in the kitchen. She yelled at him for surprising her, yelled at him for being filthy and tracking all over her floor, and let him get a slice of apple before she yelled at him for snitching before supper.

He went around and changed light bulbs in five rooms before supper. The families there were all crammed into two rooms each, and most of them had to share kitchens and eat in shifts. Some of the rooms were nasty places, family warfare held off only as long as it took him to change the light, and sometimes even that truce wasn't observed. Others were doing fine, the place was small but they liked each other. Deaver was pretty sure his family must have been one of the nice ones, because if there'd been any yelling he would have remembered.

Rain and Deaver ate and then turned off all the lights while she played the old record player Deaver had wangled away from Lehi. They really weren't supposed to have it, but they figured as long as they didn't burn any lights it wasn't wasting electricity, and they'd turn it in as soon as anybody asked for it.

In the meantime, Rain had some of the old records from when she was a girl. The songs had strong rhythms, and tonight, like she sometimes did, Rain got up and moved to the music, strange little dances that Deaver didn't understand unless he imagined her as a lithe young girl, pictured her body as it must have been then. It wasn't hard to imagine, it was there in her eyes and her smile all the time, and her movements gave away secrets that years of starchy eating and lack of exercise had disguised.

Then, as always, his thoughts went off to some of the girls he saw from his truck window, driving by the fields where they bent over, hard at work, until they heard the truck and then they stood and waved. Everybody waved at the salvage truck, sometimes it was the only thing with a motor that ever came by, their only contact with the old machines. All the tractors, all the electricity were reserved for the New Soil Lands; the old places were dying. And they turned and waved at the last memories. It made Deaver sad and he hated to be sad, all these people clinging to a past that never existed.

"It never existed," he said aloud.

"Yes it did," Rain whispered. "Girls just wanna have fun," she murmured along with the record. "I hated this song when I was a girl. Or maybe it was my Mama who hated it."

"You lived here then?"

"Indiana," she said. "One of the states, way east."

"Were you a refugee, too?"

"No. We moved here when I was sixteen, seventeen, can't remember. Whenever things got scary in the world, a lot of Mormons moved home. This was always home, no matter what."

The record ended. She turned it off, turned on the lights.

"Got the boat all gassed up?" asked Deaver.

"You don't want to go there," she said.

"If there's gold down there, I want it."

"If there was gold there, Deaver, they would've taken it out before the water covered it. It's not as if nobody got a warning, you know. The Mormon Sea wasn't a flash flood."

"If it isn't down there, what's all the hush-hush about? How come the Lake Patrol keeps people from going there?"

"I don't know, Deaver. Maybe because a lot of people feel like it's a holy place."

Deaver was used to this. Rain never went to church, but she still talked like a Mormon. Most people did, though, when you scratched them in the wrong place. Deaver didn't like it when they got religious. "Angels need police protection, is that it?"

"It used to be real important to the Mormons in the old days, Deaver." She sat down on the floor, leaning against the wall under the window.

"Well it's nothin' now. They got their other temples, don't they? And they're building the new one in Zarahemla, right?"

"I don't know, Deaver. The one here, it was always the real one. The center." She bent sideways, leaned on her hand, looked down at the floor. "It still is."

Deaver saw she was getting really somber now, really sad. It happened to a lot of people who remembered the old days. Like a disease that never got cured. But Deaver knew the cure. For Rain, anyway. "Is it true they used to kill people in there?"

It worked. She glared at him and the languor left her body "Is that what you truckers talk about all day?"

Deaver grinned. "There's stories. Cuttin' people up if they told where the gold was hid."

"You know Mormons all over the place now, Deaver, do you really think we'd go cuttin' people up for tellin' secrets?"

"I don't know. Depends on the secrets, don't it?" He was sitting on his hands, kind of bouncing a little on the couch.

He could see that she was a little mad for real, but didn't want to be. So she'd pretend to be mad for play. She sat up, reached for a pillow to throw at him.

"No! No!" he cried. "Don't cut me up! Don't feed me to the carp!"

The pillow hit him and he pretended elaborately to die.

"Just don't joke about things like that," she said.

"Things like what? You don't believe in the old stuff anymore. Nobody does."

"Maybe not."

"Jesus was supposed to come again, right? There was atom bombs dropped here and there, and he was supposed to come."

"Prophet said we was too wicked. He wouldn't come 'cause we loved the things of the world too much."

"Come on, if he was comin' he would've come, right?"

"Might still," she said.

"Nobody believes that," said Deaver. "Mormons are just the government, that's all. The Bishop gets elected judge in every town, right? The president of the elders is always mayor, it's just the government, just politics, nobody believes it now. Zarahemla's the capital, not the holy city."

He couldn't see her because he was lying flat on his back on the couch. When she didn't answer, he got up and looked for her. She was over by the sink, leaning on the counter. He snuck up behind her to tickle her, but something in her posture changed his mind. When he got close, he saw tears down her cheeks. It was crazy. All these people from the old days got crazy a lot.

"I was just teasin'," he said.

She nodded.

"It's just part of the old days. You know how I am about that. Maybe if I remembered, it'd be different. Sometimes I wish I remembered." But it was a lie. He never wished he remembered. He didn't like remembering. Most stuff he couldn't remember even if he wanted to. The earliest thing he could bring to mind was riding on the back of a horse, behind some man who sweated a lot, just riding and riding and riding. And then it was all recent stuff, going to school, getting passed around in people's homes, finally getting busy one year and finishing school and getting a job. He didn't get misty-eyed thinking about any of it, any of those places. Just passing through, that's all he was ever doing, never belonged anywhere until maybe now. With Lehi and Rain, the two of them, they were both home. He belonged here. "I'm sorry," he said.

"It's fine," she said.

"You still gonna take me there?"

"I said I would, didn't I?"

She sounded just annoyed enough that he knew it was okay to tease her again. "You don't think they'll have the Second Coming while we're there, do you? If you think so, I'll wear my tie."

She smiled, then turned to face him and pushed him away. "Deaver, go to bed."

"I'm getting up at four-thirty, Rain, and then you're one girl who's gonna have fun."

"I don't think the song was about early morning boat trips."

She was doing the dishes when he left for his little room.

Lehi was waiting at five-thirty, right on schedule. "I can't believe it," he said. "I thought you'd be late."

"Good thing you were ready on time," said Deaver, " 'cause if you didn't come with us you wouldn't get a cut."

"We aren't going to find any gold, Deaver Teague."

"Then why're you comin' with me? Don't give me that stuff, Lehi, you know the future's with Deaver Teague, and you don't want to be left behind. Where's the diving stuff?"

"I didn't bring it *home,* Deaver. You don't think my Mom'd ask questions then?"

"She's always askin' questions," said Deaver.

"It's her job," said Rain.

"I don't want anybody askin' about everything I do," said Deaver.

"Nobody has to ask," said Rain. "You always tell us whether we want to hear or not."

"If you don't want to hear, you don't have to," said Deaver.

"Don't get touchy," said Rain.

"You guys are both gettin' wet-headed on me, all of a sudden. Does the temple make you crazy, is that how it works?"

"I don't mind my Mom askin' me stuff. It's okay."

The ferries ran from Point to Bingham day and night, so they had to go north a ways before cutting west to Oquirrh Island. The smelter and the foundries put orange-bellied smoke clouds into the night sky, and the coal barges were getting offloaded just like in daytime. The coal dust cloud that was so grimy and black in the day looked like white fog under the floodlights.

"My dad died right there, about this time of day," said Lehi.

"He loaded coal?"

"Yeah. He used to be a car salesman. His job kind of disappeared on him."

"You weren't there, were you?"

"I heard the crash. I was asleep, but it woke me up. And then a lot of shouting and running. We lived on the island back then, always heard stuff from the harbor. He got buried under a ton of coal that fell from fifty feet up."

Deaver didn't know what to say about that.

"You never talk about your folks," said Lehi. "I always remember my dad, but you never talk about your folks."

Deaver shrugged.

"He doesn't remember 'em," Rain said quietly. "They found him out on the plains somewhere. The mobbers got his family, however many there was, he must've hid or something, that's all they can figure."

"Well, what was it?" asked Lehi. "Did you hide?"

Deaver didn't feel comfortable talking about it, since he didn't remember anything except what people told him. He knew that other people remembered their childhood, and he didn't like how they always acted so surprised that he didn't. But Lehi was asking, and Deaver knew that you don't keep stuff back from friends. "I guess I did. Or maybe I looked too dumb to kill or somethin'." He laughed. "I must've been a real dumb little kid, I didn't even remember my own name. They figure I was five or six years old, most kids know their names, but not me. So the two guys that found me, their names were Teague and Deaver."

"You gotta remember somethin'."

"Lehi, I didn't even know how to talk. They tell me I didn't even say a word till I was nine years old. We're talkin' about a slow learner here."

"Wow." Lehi was silent for a while. "How come you didn't say anything?"

"Doesn't matter," said Rain. "He makes up for it now, Deaver the talker. Champion talker."

They coasted the island till they got past Magna. Lehi led them to a storage shed that Underwater Salvage had put up at the north end of Oquirrh Island. It was unlocked and full of diving equipment. Lehi's friend had filled some tanks with air. They got two diving outfits and underwater flashlights. Rain wasn't going underwater, so she didn't need anything.

They pulled away from the island, out into the regular shipping lane from Wendover. In that direction, at least, people had sense enough not to travel at night, so there wasn't much traffic. After a little while they were out into open water. That was when Rain stopped the little outboard motor Deaver had scrounged for her and Lehi had fixed. "Time to sweat and slave," said Rain.

Deaver sat on the middle bench, settled the oars into the locks, and began to row.

"Not too fast," Rain said. "You'll give yourself blisters."

A boat that might have been Lake Patrol went by once, but otherwise nobody came near them as they crossed the open stretch. Then the skyscrapers rose up and blocked off large sections of the starry night.

"They say there's people who was never rescued still livin' in there," Lehi whispered.

Rain was disdainful. "You think there's anything left in there to keep anybody alive? And the water's still too salty to drink for long."

"Who says they're alive?" whispered Deaver in his most mysterious voice. A couple of years ago, he could have spooked Lehi and made his eyes go wide. Now Lehi just looked disgusted.

"Come on, Deaver, I'm not a kid."

It was Deaver who got spooked a little. The big holes where pieces of glass and plastic had fallen off looked like mouths, waiting to suck him in and carry him down under the water, into the city of the drowned. He sometimes dreamed about thousands and thousands of people living under water, still driving their cars around, going about their business, shopping in stores, going to movies. In his dreams they never did anything bad, just went about their business. But he always woke up sweating and frightened. No reason. Just spooked him. "I think they should blow up these things before they fall down and hurt somebody," said Deaver.

"Maybe it's better to leave 'em standing," said Rain. "Maybe there's a lot of folks like to remember how tall we once stood."

"What's to remember? They built tall buildings and then they let 'em take a bath, what's to brag for?"

Deaver was trying to get her not to talk about the old days, but Lehi seemed to like wallowing in it. "You ever here before the water came?"

Rain nodded. "Saw a parade go right down this street. I can't remember if it was Third South or Fourth South. Third I guess.

I saw twenty-five horses all riding together. I remember that I thought that was really something. You didn't see many horses in those days."

"I seen too many myself," said Lehi.

"It's the ones I don't see that I hate," said Deaver. "They ought to make 'em wear diapers."

They rounded a building and looked up a north-south passage between towers. Rain was sitting in the stern and saw it first. "There it is. You can see it. Just the tall spires now."

Deaver rowed them up the passage. There were six spires sticking up out of the water, but the four short ones were under so far that only the pointed roofs were dry. The two tall ones had windows in them, not covered at all. Deaver was disappointed. Wide open like that meant that anybody might have come here. It was all so much less dangerous than he had expected. Maybe Rain was right, and there was nothing there.

They tied the boat to the north side and waited for daylight. "If I knew it'd be so easy," said Deaver, "I could've slept another hour."

"Sleep now," said Rain.

"Maybe I will," said Deaver.

He slid off his bench and sprawled in the bottom of the boat.

He didn't sleep, though. The open window of the steeple was only a few yards away, a deep black surrounded by the starlit grey of the temple granite. It was down there, waiting for him; the future, a chance to get something better for himself and his two friends. Maybe a plot of ground in the south where it was warmer and the snow didn't pile up five feet deep every winter, where it wasn't rain in the sky and lake everywhere else you looked. A place where he could live for a very long time and look back and remember good times with his friends, that was all waiting down under the water.

Of course they hadn't *told* him about the gold. It was on the road, a little place in Parowan where truckers knew they could stop in because the iron mine kept such crazy shifts that the diners never closed. They even had some coffee there, hot and bitter, because there weren't so many Mormons there and the miners didn't let the Bishop push them around. In fact they even called him Judge there instead of Bishop. The other drivers didn't talk to Deaver, of course, they were talking to each other when the one fellow told the story about how the Mormons back in the gold rush days hoarded up all the gold they could get and hid it in the upper rooms of the temple where nobody but the prophet and the twelve apostles could ever go. At first Deaver didn't believe him, except that Bill Horne nodded like he knew it was true, and Cal Silber said you'd never catch him messin' with the Mormon temple, that's a good way to get yourself dead. The way they were talking, scared and quiet, told Deaver that they believed it, that it was true, and he knew something else, too: if anyone was going to get that gold, it was him.

Even if it *was* easy to get here, that didn't mean anything. He knew how Mormons were about the temple. He'd asked around a little, but nobody'd talk about it. And nobody ever went there, either, he asked a lot of people if they ever sailed on out and looked at it, and they all got quiet and shook their heads no or changed the subject. Why should the Lake Patrol guard it, then, if everybody was too scared to go? Everybody but Deaver Teague and his two friends.

"Real pretty," said Rain.

Deaver woke up. The sun was just topping the mountains; it must've been light for some time. He looked where Rain was looking. It was the Moroni tower on the top of the mountain above the old capitol, where they'd put the temple statue a few years back. It was bright and shiny, the old guy and his trumpet. But when the Mormons wanted that trumpet to blow, it had just stayed silent and their faith got drowned. Now Deaver knew they only hung onto it for old times' sake. Well, Deaver lived for new times.

Lehi showed him how to use the underwater gear, and they practiced going over the side into the water a couple of times, once without the weight belts and once with. Deaver and Lehi swam like fish, of course—swimming was the main recreation that everybody could do for free. It was different with the mask and the air hose, though.

"Hose tastes like a horse's hoof," Deaver said between dives.

Lehi made sure Deaver's weight belt was on tight. "You're the only guy on Oquirrh Island who knows." Then he tumbled forward off the boat. Deaver went down too straight and the air tank bumped the back of his head a little, but it didn't hurt too much and he didn't drop his light either.

He swam along the outside of the temple, shining his light on the stones. Lots of underwater plants were rising up the sides of the temple, but it wasn't covered much yet. There was a big metal plaque right in the front of the building, about a third of the way down. THE HOUSE OF THE LORD it said. Deaver pointed it out to Lehi.

When they got up to the boat again, Deaver asked about it. "It looked kind of goldish," he said.

"Used to be another sign there," said Rain. "It was a little different. That one might have been gold. This one's plastic. They made it so the temple would still have a sign, I guess."

"You sure about that?"

"I remember when they did it."

Finally Deaver felt confident enough to go down into the temple. They had to take off their flippers to climb into the steeple window; Rain tossed them up after. In the sunlight there was nothing spooky about the window. They sat there on the sill, water lapping at their feet, and put their fins and tanks on.

Halfway through getting dressed, Lehi stopped. Just sat there.

"I can't do it," he said.

"Nothin' to be scared of," said Deaver. "Come on, there's no ghosts or nothin' down there."

"I can't," said Lehi.

"Good for you," called Rain from the boat.

Deaver turned to look at her. "What're you talkin' about!"

"I don't think you should."

"Then why'd you bring me here?"

"Because you wanted to."

Made no sense.

"It's holy ground, Deaver," said Rain. "Lehi feels it, too. That's why he isn't going down."

Deaver looked at Lehi.

"It just don't feel right," said Lehi.

"It's just stones," said Deaver.

Lehi said nothing. Deaver put on his goggles, took a light, put the breather in his mouth, and jumped.

Turned out the floor was only a foot and a half down. It took him completely by surprise, so he fell over and sat on his butt in eighteen inches of water. Lehi was just as surprised as he was, but then he started laughing, and Deaver laughed, too. Deaver got to his feet and started flapping around, looking for the stairway. He could hardly take a step, his flippers slowed him down so much.

"Walk backward," said Lehi.

"Then how am I supposed to see where I'm going?"

"Stick your face under the water and look, chiggerhead."

Deaver stuck his face in the water. Without the reflection of daylight on the surface, he could see fine. There was the stairway.

He got up, looked toward Lehi. Lehi shook his head. He still wasn't going.

"Suit yourself," said Deaver. He backed through the water to the top step. Then he put in his breathing tube and went down.

It wasn't easy to get down the stairs. They're fine when you aren't floating, thought Deaver, but they're a pain when you keep scraping your tanks on the ceiling. Finally he figured out he could grab the railing and pull himself down. The stairs wound around and around. When they ended, a whole bunch of garbage had filled up the bottom of the stairwell, partly blocking the doorway. He swam above the garbage, which looked like scrap metal and chips of wood, and came out into a large room.

His light didn't shine very far through the murky water, so

he swam the walls, around and around, high and low. Down here the water was cold, and he swam faster to keep warm. There were rows of arched windows on both sides, with rows of circular windows above them, but they had been covered over with wood on the outside; the only light was from Deaver's flashlight. Finally, though, after a couple of times around the room and across the ceiling, he figured it was just one big room. And except for the garbage all over the floor, it was empty.

Already he felt the deep pain of disappointment. He forced himself to ignore it. After all, it wouldn't be right out here in a big room like this, would it? There had to be a secret treasury.

There were a couple of doors. The small one in the middle of the wall at one end was wide open. Once there must have been stairs leading up to it. Deaver swam over there and shone his light in. Just another room, smaller this time. He found a couple more rooms, but they had all been stripped, right down to the stone. Nothing at all.

He tried examining some of the stones to look for secret doors, but he gave up pretty soon—he couldn't see well enough from the flashlight to find a thin crack even if it was there. Now the disappointment was real. As he swam along, he began to wonder if maybe the truckers hadn't known he was listening. Maybe they made it all up just so someday he'd do this. Some joke, where they wouldn't even see him make a fool of himself.

But no, no, that couldn't be it. They believed it, all right. But he knew now what they didn't know. Whatever the Mormons did here in the old days, there wasn't any gold in the upper rooms now. So much for the future. But what the hell, he told himself, I got here, I saw it, and I'll find something else. No reason not to be cheerful about it.

He didn't fool himself, and there was nobody else down here to fool. It was bitter. He'd spent a lot of years thinking about bars of gold or bags of it. He'd always pictured it hidden behind a curtain. He'd pull on the curtain and it would billow out in the water, and there would be the bags of gold, and he'd just take them out and that would be it. But there weren't any curtains, weren't any hidey-holes, there was nothing at all, and if he had a future, he'd have to find it somewhere else.

He swam back to the door leading to the stairway. Now he could see the pile of garbage better, and it occurred to him to wonder how it got there. Every other room was completely empty. The garbage couldn't have been carried in by the water, because the only windows that were open were in the steeple, and they were above the water line. He swam close and picked up a piece. It was metal. They were all metal, except a few stones, and it occurred to him that this might be it after all. If you're hiding a treasure, you don't put it in bags or ingots, you leave it around looking like garbage and people leave it alone.

He gathered up as many of the thin metal pieces as he could carry in one hand and swam carefully up the stairwell. Lehi would have to come down and help him carry it up; they could make bags out of their shirts to carry lots of it at a time.

He splashed out into the air and then walked backward up the last few steps and across the submerged floor. Lehi was still sitting on the sill, and now Rain was there beside him, her bare feet dangling in the water. When he got to them he turned around and held out the metal in his hands. He couldn't see their faces well, because the outside of the facemask was blurry with water and kept catching sunlight.

"You scraped your knee," said Rain.

Deaver handed her his flashlight, and now that his hand was free, he could pull his mask off and look at them. They were very serious. He held out the metal pieces toward them. "Look what I found down there."

Lehi took a couple of the metal pieces from him. Rain never took her eyes from Deaver's face.

"It's old cans, Deaver," Lehi said quietly.

"No it isn't," said Deaver. But he looked at his fistful of metal sheets and realized it was true. They had been cut down the side and pressed flat, but they were sure enough cans.

"There's writing on it," said Lehi. "It says, Dear Lord heal my girl Jenny please I pray."

Deaver set down his handful on the sill. Then he took one, turned it over, found the writing. "Forgive my adultery I will sin no more."

Lehi read another. "Bring my boy safe from the plains O Lord God."

Each message was scratched with a nail or a piece of glass, the letters crudely formed.

"They used to say prayers all day in the temple, and people would bring in names and they'd say the temple prayers for them," said Rain. "Nobody prays here now, but they still bring the names. On metal so they'll last."

"We shouldn't read these," said Lehi. "We should put them back."

There were hundreds, maybe thousands of those metal prayers down there. People must come here all the time, Deaver realized. The Mormons must have a regular traffic coming here and leaving these things behind. But nobody told me.

"Did you know about this?"

Rain nodded.

"You brought them here, didn't you."

"Some of them. Over the years."

"You knew what was down there."

She didn't answer.

"She told you not to come," said Lehi.

"You knew about this too?"

"I knew people came, I didn't know what they did."

And suddenly the magnitude of it struck him. Lehi and Rain had both known. All the Mormons knew, then. They all knew, and he had asked again and again, and no one had told him. Not even his friends.

"Why'd you let me come out here?"

"Tried to stop you," said Rain.

"Why didn't you tell me this?"

She looked him in the eye. "Deaver, you would've thought I was givin' you the runaround. And you would have laughed at this if I told you. I thought it was better if you saw it. Then maybe you wouldn't go tellin' people how dumb the Mormons are."

"You think I would?" He held up another metal prayer and read it aloud. "Come quickly, Lord Jesus, before I die." He shook it at her. "You think I'd laugh at these people?"

"You laugh at everything, Deaver."

Deaver looked at Lehi. This was something Lehi had never said before. Deaver would never laugh at something that was really important. And this was really important to them, to them both.

"This is yours," Deaver said. "All this stuff is yours."

"I never left a prayer here," said Lehi.

But when he said *yours* he didn't mean just them, just Lehi and Rain. He meant all of them, all the people of the Mormon Sea, all the ones who had known about it but never told him even though he asked again and again. All the people who belonged here. "I came to find something here for *me*, and you knew all the time it was only *your* stuff down there."

Lehi and Rain looked at each other, then back at Deaver.

"It isn't ours," said Rain.

"I never been here before," said Lehi.

"It's your stuff." He sat down in the water and began taking off the underwater gear.

"Don't be mad," said Lehi. "I didn't know."

"You knew more than you told me. All the time I thought we were friends, but it wasn't true. You two had this place in common with all the other people, but not with me. Everybody but me."

Lehi carefully took the metal sheets to the stairway and dropped them. They sank at once, to drift down and take their place on the pile of supplications.

Lehi rowed them through the skyscrapers to the east of the old city, and then Rain started the motor and they skimmed along the surface of the lake. The Lake Patrol didn't see them, but Deaver knew now that it didn't matter much if they did. The Lake Patrol was mostly Mormons. They undoubtedly knew about the traffic here, and let it happen as long as it was discreet. Probably the only people they stopped were the people who weren't in on it.

All the way back to Magna to return the underwater gear, Deaver sat in the front of the boat, not talking to the others, not letting them see how his eyes kept welling up. Where Deaver sat, the bow of the boat seemed to curve under him. The faster they went, the less the boat seemed to touch the water. Just skimming over the surface, never really touching deep; making a few waves, but the water always smoothed out again.

Those two people in the back of the boat, he felt kind of sorry for them. They still lived in a drowned city, they belonged down there, and the fact they couldn't go there broke their hearts. But not Deaver. His city wasn't even built yet. He blinked, and his eyes cleared. His city was tomorrow.

He'd driven a salvage truck and lived in a closet long enough. Maybe he'd go south into the New Soil Lands. Maybe qualify on a piece of land. Own something, plant in the soil, maybe he'd come to belong there. As for this place, well, he never had belonged here, just like all the foster homes and schools along the way, just one more stop for a year or two or three, he knew that all along. Never did make any friends here, but that's how he wanted it. Wouldn't be right to make friends, cause he'd just move on and disappoint them. Didn't see no good in doing that to people.

NEWTON SLEEP

Gregory Benford

Gregory Benford has won two Nebula Awards. Among his books are a collection, *In Alien Flesh*, and the novels *Artifact*, *Timescape*, *Across the Sea of Suns*, *Against Infinity*, *In the Ocean of Night*, and, with David Brin, *Heart of the Comet*. His newest novel is *Great Sky River*.

This gifted professor of physics at the University of California at Irvine belongs to that select group of scientists who write graceful prose and at the same time give us a glimpse of scientists at work. "Newton Sleep," a nominee in the novella category, is something of a departure for Benford. On the face of it, the story is a fantasy about hell; but Benford has thought about hell as if no one had ever done so before, with a scientific sensibility that tends to dig away at the "reality" with which the hero is confronted. The result is a story that may be compared to Robert A. Heinlein's "Magic Inc." for freshness and a sense of reality. Benford's own comments about his story are as fascinating as the story itself.

"In a novel published seven years ago, Timescape, *I deliberately shaped a character to resemble myself. The figure of Gregory Markham has approximately my career profile and similar details of personal life. I suspected as soon as I began writing the book that many people who knew me would immediately play spot-the-character (a game with many payoffs in* Timescape*) and search out self-glorifications.*

"It was oddly pleasurable, then, to deliberately kill Markham onstage in the novel. In one of my favorite chapters, Markham is so involved with his calculations that he does not notice that the airliner he is in is about to crash.

"But years later, Markham returned to haunt me. When Janet Morris approached me about a series of stories set in Hell, using a real person or a character from my own fiction, Markham instantly stepped forward. About this time a critic, David Ketterer, had written a piece on the persistent theme of authorial mortality in SF, and it struck odd resonances with me.

"So I posed Markham a problem: given that you wake up in Hell, how do you make sense of it? After all, Hell confounds the scientific worldview far more than it would that of any particular faith. Could Hell have any explanation which fits with what we see as an impersonal, mechanistic world?

"These questions led to 'Newton Sleep.' Though the line from Blake which opens the story usually supplies a possessive, I remembered an old edition which omits this. Somehow that rang more true, and opened the idea of an entire category of thought—the modern desire for objective forces and known laws, as shelter from the old baggage of religion.

"I intend to eventually write an entire novel about this situation. If I can manage matters, it will in the end turn out to be a work of science fiction, not fantasy. Perhaps it will even become an argument for the existence of a strange and noble kind of God."

May God us keep
From single vision
and Newton Sleep.

—William Blake

1.

The demon was a nerd.

It chewed raptly on a huge wad of yellow gum, obviously relishing the gooey smack of it, jaw muscles bunching. The white open-collar shirt, bulging belly that hung over a plastic belt, too-tight brown slacks, six pens in the shirt pocket (several marked STYX BANK in glowing red), mousy brown hair sloppily combed and parted exactly down the center of his skull, bottle-thick lenses in transparent frame glasses—all said *overaged blimpoid undergraduate* to Gregory Markham.

The thing looked like a subnormal student in Physics 3A, a certain candidate for the cut at the end of the first quarter.

Grinning, it blew a bubble. The filmy orange sphere popped, but the demon caught it with a sudden lashing of its black tongue, popped the wad back between its molars, and smacked it with delight.

"I . . . I don't follow," Markham began.

"You'll catch on." The demon's eyes widened with friendly interest, and it said enthusiastically, "How do you like these new elevators?"

"Ah . . . well, they're . . ." *Absolutely ordinary,* Markham thought. Gray steel, no carpeting, only one button on the console: THERE.

"Just got them installed. Howard Hughes did the work. Terrific!" The demon snapped its gum again as punctuation.

"And we're going . . ."

"To Hell, yeah." The demon glanced at its watch. "Right on time, too."

"What happens when I get there?"

"That's not my job. Boy, I'll tell you, these elevators are *great.* Before the Hughes contract came in—late, sure, but under the bid—we had to lead you guys up the Socophilian Stairs."

"Up?"

"Yeah, that stuff about Hell being below is just a rumor, y'know. Anyway, those stairs—what a pain! Cold granite all the way, no handrails, corners worn off so you'd slip and bust your ass."

"The pits."

The pun seemed lost on the nerd. "No foolin'. Goin' back down was the worst. Any blood at all on those worn-down steps, and *whang*—you'd roll down, ass over entrails. And likely smack into a party of lepers or saints on the way up."

"Saints?"

"Sure, we get a lot of 'em."

"But I thought—"

"That's *their* opinion, of course. Y'know—*my sainted mother,* all that. Man, it's incredible, what people think of themselves. You talk about de*lu*sions."

"Is . . . is that why I'm—"

"Don't ask me, man. I'm just a gofer."

The elevator stopped with a labored *chunka chunka.* "Ah, great. I sure don't miss them stairs."

The sliding door was dinged and smeared with something brown. *New to the demon, maybe,* Markham thought, *but I know recycled junk when I see it.* He wondered what turned brown when it dried.

The door slid open with a hiss. An absolutely featureless floor of azure stone stretched limitlessly in all directions. *Lovely.*

"C'mon, move it. I gotta go back down."

Markham stepped out. *I wonder—*

The floor was not in fact stone. It wasn't anything except the illusion of substance that comes when you look at the utterly empty sky. Markham stepped and fell straight down, suddenly feeling warm air rush past.

Falling. This was the way it had been the last instant, when the plane went into the patchwork of wintry trees, the wings snapping off barren black branches as they came in too low, too fast—

He screamed. The vicious shrieking wind blew his tie into his mouth and he spat it out, all the time tumbling, arms flailing. He had never gone skydiving, had a repressed fear of heights, but had once gone to one of those vertical wind tunnels that supposedly simulated the experience. It had been at a meeting of the American Physical Society in Las Vegas, and he had been cajoled into it by colleagues.

So—Spread your legs . . . arms out . . . turn—there. He stopped rolling and hung steady, facedown.

Ocean. He was above a fast, glinting steel-blue sea. A green landmass lay some distance away, but he was going to hit the water. Not that it made a difference. He remembered that after falling only a few hundred feet, striking water was the same as pancaking into concrete.

How can this be Hell? Falling forever?

Through his panic he tried to think. He had felt little when the plane went in, just an instant when the bulkhead crumpled and trees and steel and the head of the man in front of him came spraying back, a single flash-instant of concussion—

The air howled and he could see whitecaps lacing the sea. He had reached terminal velocity now and the hard blue surface burgeoned with detail, the sweep of hidden currents crinkling the water.

Coming up fast now—

Markham had time to scream once more.

2.

It looked like a bank president. Three-piece suit, touch of gray at the temples, the sagging jowls suntanned and well shaved. The demon clearly thought it was doing a job beneath its station.

"But how come I was just shoved out like that? That guy said—"

"I can't keep track of every customer," the demon said. "You're probably remembering something from the Other Side."

"The hell I am!"

"These fantasies will pass," the demon said stiffly. He impatiently tapped one polished black shoetip on the elevator floor, shot his cuffs, and clandestinely tried to catch his reflection in the cloudy steel walls.

"But damn it—"

Chunka chunka. Again the door hissed aside. Beyond it lay another blue featureless expanse. The blue was darker, with a deep blue-green mottling that recalled ocean depths.

"I'm not stepping out there."

"Come, come." The demon made a smile that was broad and showed perfectly regular white teeth, but the corners of the smile did not turn up. Markham had seen a similar smile once when a Merrill Lynch broker had tried to sell him a limited partnership in natural gas.

"You go out there."

A sigh. "Very well." The bank president stepped with assurance onto the shiny surface. It stood with hands behind its back, the smile twisted into a condescending smirk.

Markham took a tentative step. His foot held, so he brought the other forward—

And fell.

This time the bottom-dropped-out sensation lasted only a few seconds as the demon dwindled above, grinning with satisfaction. With a bone-cracking jolt, Markham hit the water.

He gasped, sputtered, began to dog-paddle. His glasses had fallen off, but he could see there was no land nearby. He cursed once, then choked as a wave seemed to leap deliberately into his nostrils and throat.

The water was mild, salty. Markham stripped off all his clothes. He began to swim steadily, trying to keep a straight line. Only a sullen red glow lit the clouds above; it was impossible to navigate by it. He kept going, changing regularly from breaststroke to sidestroke to backstroke. Summers when he wasn't in Europe, he swam every day in the ocean near his home in San Juan Capistrano. He could probably last a good hour this way, longer if he just floated.

He was right. His Seiko kept ticking away. He set the timer and at the very end—exhausted, purple bee-swarm dots dancing in his eyes, legs and arms numb, chest aching, mouth puckered with the taste of salt—noted that he had lasted two hours, thirteen minutes.

As he watched the digital dial, it abruptly changed to 666.

Then he drowned.

3.

Markham sagged against the gray steel. The demon was a woman.

This time he could not force his throat to work, to voice any protest. *Hell is this elevator,* he thought, fogged with fatigue. *It's that simple. Infinite death, infinitely prolonged.*

He had always been terrified of heights and he had died in

an airplane crash. They had played on that. Then they had added the ocean, knowing somehow that while he loved the sea's raw power he had also feared it, felt vaguely uneasy with the green depths. He had overcome that by taking up scuba diving. Still, those deep anxieties had come out in the long struggle to reach shore. He could feel the effects, how close he was to hysteria.

The woman gave him an empty stewardess smile. Then she slowly reached down and lifted the hem of her red dress. Tantalizingly, with the same fixed glossy smile, she lifted it to show exquisitely formed, creamy thighs. She wore black stockings fastened with a red garter belt. Markham licked his lips. *So they know I like that. So what?*

The cotton dress slid easily over her head. She wore nothing else. She simply stood, smiling and silent. Then she winked and languorously blew him a kiss. It was exactly like a hologram Markham had seen years ago, and about as erotic. She was overweight and her skin had an odd sickly cast. *Like a corpse floating underwater,* he thought. *Or the underbelly of some deep ocean fish, the kind with bulging eyes and contorted, purple mouths.*

She licked her lips and made obvious, grotesque sucking motions. Her breasts trembled like jelly, and he saw that she had something tattooed on each. He squinted. The right breast said WELCOME, the left one WOMAN. They had been seared in, like the deep brown burns on a cowhide brand.

He stepped back. She cupped the breasts and held them out to him, her mouth still making the liquid, gluttonous sucking slurps. *This,* he thought wildly, *might already be Hell.*

Chunka chunka. This time there was a sandy beach stretching away in a broad curve. An ocean nuzzled at the shore in sets of rolling breakers. *Exactly the same blue as that water I . . .*

He backed away from the door. The woman stepped toward him, offering her breasts, reaching down to finger her black pubic bush. Her left breast oozed pearly pap.

Clearly, Hell lay beyond the elevator door. So it was either her . . .

Nobody was getting him through that door, Markham knew

that much. If he could distract the woman, figure out how close the elevator—

He forced a grin. Her eyes widened with anticipation. He tentatively reached out toward her waist—and a black tongue licked out from her pubic cleft, a slick oily thing like a whip. It encircled his hand, drew it toward her. He pulled back as he caught the moist, sulfurous, rotting scent the tongue gave off. It clamped itself about his wrist, squeezing with convulsive power.

He gasped. "No!"

She caught him in an expert judo grab, one hand at his shirt collar, the other clamped into the small of his back.

Anger filled her jet-black eyes. Her spiked heel bit into his right foot. She roughly rubbed herself against him in a parody of erotic frenzy.

He started to wrench away from her rank foulness, and that gave her the momentum she needed to complete the throw. "Perhaps I can be of assistance," she said in a flat, impersonal stewardess voice, and threw him out the door.

He landed—*crunch!*—on the sand.

He rolled. Spat out grit. Sat up.

The elevator was gone.

"Hey, fella! Got a board?"

A tanned young man stood fifty yards away, holding a white fiberglass surfboard. Blond, blue-eyed, lean and muscular.

It seemed an absurd question to ask of a man in rumpled brown slacks, a camel jacket, and button-down blue shirt. "Ah . . . no."

"Too bad. Some good ones breakin' out there today."

Markham eyed the waves curling into foam about a hundred meters offshore. It *was* a good surfing spot. *So much for the old fire and brimstone.*

"What *is* today?"

Genuine puzzlement flitted across the blandly friendly face. "Why . . . today. It's always today."

One could scarcely argue with that. "I . . . Look, what's going on? I—"

"Hey, man, they're breakin'. Get outta those things and try some body surfin'."

"You go ahead. I want to . . . sunbathe for a while."

"O.K., just come out when you're ready."

"What's your name?"

"Donny."

"I'm Greg. Greg Markham."

"Brook's my last name. Good surfin' here, Greg."

"It's safe out there?"

"Sure. Sharks don't come in till night."

The man trotted into the surf. Markham was trembling, his mind churning. He sat down. He remembered a place like this on St. Thomas, where he had vacationed. At night the sharks had come in close to the beach, hunting along the edge of the Gulf Stream. From the balcony of their cabin, he could hear the splashing of the fish the sharks hunted; and if you went down to the beach, you could see the phosphorescent wakes they made in the water. At night the sharks feared nothing, and everything else fled. In the day they stayed out away from the clear white sand. Maybe this was because you could see their shadows rippling over the floury sand and get away.

He remembered that and noticed a dull glow at high noon, diffuse and red through the milky, blue-veined clouds. A midwinter sun, if he had still been in California.

Thinking about that calmed him. There was some continuity between his . . . *My life? But I still feel alive.* His life before, and . . . this. Hell.

He had died in an air crash. That much he remembered clearly. Then someone with a harsh, foul breath leering at him, hovering over his stripped and battered body, under raw, piercing orange lamps. All he could remember was that awful, green-lipped face.

His body was knotted with tension, his nerves spinning jittery along a tightrope. He had died, essentially, by falling. Then that fear had repeated in the long plummet from at least a mile up, into the sea. And the bank president demon had followed that with a real drowning.

They had his number, all right. Those were two of his greatest fears. He had been a swimmer all his life but had never overcome the feeling that eventually the ocean he loved so much would claim him.

Stop thinking about it. And don't even imagine other deaths. They can probably read your mind.

Think back further. Regain some of your own identity. That was all you had to protect yourself.

He had always retreated from the world into his delicious realm of mathematical physics. That was his profession and his dearest love. Concentration on an intricate problem could loft you into an insulated, fine-grained perspective. There were many things you could see fully only from a distance. Since childhood he had sought that sensation of slipping free, smoothly remote from the compromised churn of the raw world.

He had used his oblique humor to distance people, yes, keep them safely away from the center where he lived. It even kept away his wife, Jan, sometimes. He saw that now with a sudden pang of guilt. Was that what had sent him here?

He had used the lucid language of mathematics to overcome the battering of experience, to replace everyday life's pain and harshness and wretched dreariness with—no, not with certainty, but with an ignorance you could live with, endure. Deep ignorance, though still a kind that knew its limits.

Markham stretched out on the sand, feeling his muscles surrender to their aches.

Limits. The limits were crucial. Galileo's blocks gliding across marble Italian foyers, their slick slide obeying inertia's steady hand—they were cartoons of the world, really. Aristotle knew in his gut the awful fact that friction ruled, all things groaned to a stop. *That* was the world of man.

The wonderful childlike game of infinite planes and smooth, perfect bodies, reality unwrinkled, cast a web of consoling order, infinite trajectories and infinitesimal instants, harmonic truths. From that cartoon realm it was always necessary to slip back, cloaking exhilarating flights of imagination in a respectable, deductive style. But that did not mean—when the papers appeared in the learned journals, disguised by abstracts and references and ornate, distancing Germanic mannerisms—that did not mean you forgot being in that other place, the beautiful world where Mind met Matter, the paradise you never mentioned.

So I died scribbling mathematics on a transatlantic flight, he thought wryly. O.K. That's who I am. Professor of physics, fifty-two years old, caught in Hell, unarmed and unprepared and definitely unwise.

He sat up, brushed away clinging sand. *Odd thoughts. Not memories of Jan or friends or a world forever lost. Instead, I recalled my work. What does that mean?*

Maybe that defined most deeply just who he was. *O.K., then. That's how it damned well is.* He smiled mirthlessly at the pun.

His fear had ebbed. Nerves still jangled, muscles were stiff from spasm, but the ocean had begun to work its old magic on him.

Right, then. The first thing to do was figure out how this place worked. Reduce it to a problem.

He studied the dull ruddy glow that hung in the exact center of the sky's bowl. The sun? But it hadn't moved.

It's always today. Donny had said.

Maybe that dull glow never moved. If it was the sun, then this place was tide-locked, one face forever baked by that wan reddish radiance.

Slight offshore wind. Tall coconut palms that looked bent inshore by a trade wind.

He would've expected Hell to have a little more pizzazz. Out beyond the breaking waves, he saw gliding shadows. They flitted smoothly, never coming close to Donny.

He got up and walked to an overhang of rock at the end of the crescent beach. Donny's lifted arm looked black, scaly, like a reptile's sinewy leg and claw. Then Donny turned expertly out of the white, hissing foam and paddled for the next wave.

Markham sat on the prickly volcanic rock and dangled his legs over the drop. Below, waves battered the sheer stone face with explosions of brilliant white froth. *If this is Hell, I think I can stand it.*

He had never believed any of that kid stuff, anyway. Even if you burned forever, any mind would be driven into erasing madness after a while. They simply couldn't keep you on the edge of excruciating pain and torment forever. Elementary features of any neurological system dictated that it would saturate, overload. Protracted agony would blow away consciousness itself. There would be no *you* to suffer, because the system of memories, relations, habits, and patterns that was you would dissolve before such a battering, searing, consuming onslaught.

So it made no sense, all that childish babble the moist-eyed ministers had prattled from their pulpits. He had once listened to it, had even been an acolyte in the Episcopal Church, but the usual adolescent skepticism had ripened into a scornful contempt for such delusions.

Though there is *a Hell,* he reminded himself. *It's just not the one anybody envisioned. The Christian idea simply wouldn't have worked. To really make you suffer, they'd have to give you a break. Let the mind recuperate. Relax the spasms, cool the fevered firings of neurons. Then return that dread-drenched mind to its own personal rack, tighten screws again, begin afresh . . .*

He preferred to think of matters this way. Reduce the world to a series of mechanisms—subtle, but understandable bit by bit—and then deal with each mechanism in turn. It was comforting, it worked, and in the end—

His name is Donny Brook. Donnybrook. A free-for-all fight. From somewhere in the air around him came a low, evil snicker.

He looked down in time to see the thing come leaping up from the water. It was sleek and silvery and not a shark. It had a yawning mouth with teeth that circled the entire huge maw, spikes of glinting razor sharpness. Out of the crashing breakers it came in a stupendous leap, straight up in the air, arrow perfect and relentless. He saw the blazing little red eyes, not like those of fish at all, filled with hate and raw rage—saw it all very clearly just before the thing reached the top of its arc and the round mouth closed around his feet.

The sudden pain stopped his scream, froze every muscle in a spasm of rekindled fear. The thing shook him with a convulsive jerk; raked him from the rock ledge; pulled him down into a long, excruciating fall as it gulped in midair and then gulped again in its feeding frenzy, the lancing fire shooting up through him in agonizingly long yet infinitesimal instants before he hit the cool, watery clasp. The great throat worked and he slid in, his face a rictus, the sour, dank stench of the gullet the last thing he knew.

4.

He sat on the floor of the elevator this time.

He was a mass of bruises and aches, and lightning flashes of memory would come to him, take him back to that endless pinned agony.

He forced himself to breathe, to think of something else.

They had known of his fear of the depths, of something slick and fast and all appetite coming after him. But they had played it subtly this time. Coaxed him out with Donny Brook—and when that didn't work, had sprung the trap just as he noticed the pun.

The Welcome Woman squatted over him, trying to arouse some flagging interest. He did not have the strength to push her away. Her breasts brushed his face and he caught the sickly dank toad smell from her.

He now had an analytical understanding of this endless conveyor belt carrying him forward to his deaths. He would be forever terrified and forever taken, seized casually and put to the point. So that was to be it.

Or perhaps not. Each time had been a surprise. Maybe even this conclusion was wrong, was another way to set him up for another surprise.

Or maybe it was all a colossal infinite jest.

Sure. Or maybe this is heaven and you're just in a bad mood.

He could go on being terrified at the moment of death, brooding about it long beforehand, letting it crowd everything else from his mind.

Or he could cling to something else. But what?

His former life . . . *the* life . . . was now vague, diffuse. It slipped away eel-like when he tried to grasp it, remember his wife or their children, his friends, his small triumphs and defeats. Gone, or at least fast fading.

All that remained was his precarious sense of self.

He allowed the Welcome Woman to drag him to the elevator door and tumble him out onto a carpet of dry grass.

Getting up was too much effort. He saw trees, a somber sky . . . and slept.

He woke to find the empty, vacant, staring sky and the same scrawny trees. Mimosa, pine, eucalyptus.

He got up painfully, inspected the healing wounds in his legs and abdomen. Purple swellings oozed a clear pus. He would have to be careful of them.

Carefully, limping, he began to walk.

A long time later he staggered along a sandy roadway. He had seen several people pass but had stayed back in the pines, watching. His stomach emptied itself if he stopped to rest and think. Nothing but green bile came up, but his system insisted on going into its clenching spasm whenever he began to reflect on what happened.

A thumping in the distance grew rapidly louder. Markham leaned against a fragrant eucalyptus tree and gazed blearily down the road. Three roman chariots came charging through the rutted sand, horses struggling and sweating, their eyes wild and fever-hot as the drivers lashed them.

Markham roused himself from his sick stupor when the first chariot braked abruptly. A tall man wearing olive fatigues held up a commanding hand, stopping all three chariots. "Anyone been through here, my man?"

"Ah . . . somebody on horseback . . . I didn't see . . ."

"What did he look like?"

"I . . . Beard, blue jeans."

Two men, obviously guards, leaped from the other chariots and drew revolvers. Markham wanted to blurt out questions to them, but this didn't seem the best of times. The tall man waved a fleshy arm ahead. "Going this way?"

"Yeah. Hey, what's going on? I just—"

A guard stepped forward and clipped Markham neatly on the chin, sending him reeling. "You will speak politely to the Supreme Commander."

Markham got to his knees. The blow had not hurt him— *How can anything, after what I've been through?*—but instead sent a hot jet of anger through him. "Who are you clowns, actors from—"

The boot caught him in the shoulder, and this time it definitely did hurt. Markham struggled up slowly.

"The Commander Hadrian will order you dispatched if you sass 'im," a guard muttered softly. "Stay down if you know what's good for you."

Hadrian? Familiar, somehow. A poet? Markham's head buzzed. *No, a general. Took Britain.* He heard the commander say in a flat, almost unaccented voice, "He looks new to me. He may know Guevara from his lifetime."

"That right?" the guard asked, jabbing his boot into Markham's ribs. "You recognize Guevara if you see him?"

"Uh, yeah. He died several decades ago, but I saw the pictures, sure."

"Was it him, then?" Hadrian spat out impatiently. The horses pounded the sand and whinnied at the sharp, imperious note in his voice.

"I . . . I guess it might've been." Markham couldn't rummage through his memory and be sure, but that seemed to be the answer these bastards wanted. Maybe it would get rid of them.

"Anyone with him?"

"Not that I saw." Markham looked into Hadrian's face. A

beak nose, sensuous full lips, a mouth accustomed to asking questions, not answering them. Intelligent green eyes set beneath bushy black brows that arched with nervous energy.

"How long ago?"

"Ten minutes, maybe."

"His horse, was it lathered?"

"Yeah."

Hadrian jerked a thumb at a man beside him who was burdened with a large backpack. "Get on that field telephone! Call ahead to Nuevo."

The man's mouth puckered with concern. "Well, I'll try, but these bumps, this equipment wasn't meant to take that sort of pounding, y'know, Commander. I—"

"Do it!" Hadrian muttered to himself, "Miserable cur."

Markham whispered to the nearest guard, "What's the nearest town that way?"

"Nuevo," the guard said. "Guevara's got support there. Me, I think we oughta burn the whole thing. Torch every shack."

The signals man fruitlessly turned the crank on his backpack. It made a *rrrrrttt* sound but nothing more. Hadrian fumed, slammed his palm against the side of his chariot, and finally barked, "Enough! We'll catch him ourselves. Come!"

The guards barely made their leaps into their chariots. The whole lot clattered off in a furious pounding of hooves and excited shouts. Markham got to his feet. *Hadrian.* He wished he had his *Britannica* handy. No, not a poet.

Markham trudged into Nuevo without thinking what to expect. In a realm where anything, presumably, could happen, he still was not prepared for the tanned and sandy chaos sprawled beneath the unwavering skyglow, unrelieved by slant of shadow or hope of waxing light. Roofs of hammered tin, steaming sewage in old creeks, shanties of warped wood and flapping canvas, lice on the bare necks of infested chickens, gnarled figures cooked on cracked palm fronds held over snapping open fires, scaly old men with twisted yellow faces, children hunched in ditches gnawing at dead animals, smelly old women caked with dirt.

Nuevo was a harbor, the water black and greasy. Wooden-hulled scows bobbed in oily swells, thumping against creosoted pilings of pine docks. Scum had left its tracery along the quay-side of square granite blocks that looked scarred and worn and ancient.

It could all be a hundred thousand years old, he realized. *Stonemasons from Ur, cavemen able to fashion bark canoes, an Australopithecus who could chip flint and stack stone—they all could've had a hand in this place. Hell,* we're *having a hand.* Any of the walnut-skinned dwarfs laboriously stacking mud bricks could be older than Gilgamesh, wiser than Homer.

Nobody paid the slightest attention to Markham. He passed along the mud-colored walls of a long, official-looking building. Some guards at the entrance wore the same olive fatigues as Hadrian's men, though with rakish tan campaign hats worn at a tilt. They stood at parade rest, swarthy hands cupping what looked like Springfields or some other World War I vintage rifle.

Markham strolled casually by, guessing that to turn back would invite attention. He passed by some high windows framed with chipped brown wood. He only glanced upward at them, but in that moment a hand clasped the wood from inside and strained, turning white in someone's attempt to pull himself up. A sharp, surprised cry. The hand slipped, vanished. A thud as a body hit the floor inside.

He hurried on.

At the corner was a small, dusty lot. Three crosses of chunky oak stood there, apparently permanent, canted at angles. On each someone was crucified, head down.

Wasn't that some ancient way to do it, particularly for bad crimes? Markham's scholarly interest stirred and he slowed to stare. Bloated purple heads, engorged tongues lolling from warped yawns. One was a woman, breasts bared. A pine stake had been driven through her vagina and protruded from her mouth. The men—

He gagged and turned away before he could fully see all the effects. Yet passersby scarcely glanced toward the grotesque figures, contorted with unspeakable—but for Markham not now unimaginable—agonies.

Awful, but not final, he reminded himself. *Poor bastards are probably reentering this charnel house right now.*

The point of executing anybody that way, obviously, was the pain. The experience of the past few—days? hours?—had ground that into his bones. In Hell you always came back, like a ball batted around on a rubber band by a malicious giant. But the *pain*—he shuddered at the memories that came crowding in. How could anybody overcome the automatic human terror of death, coupled with the unbearable, ravaging way Hell apparently contrived it?

Is this it? I'm to be killed, then let recover, only to die again? Forever? And why? *What did I do to be sent here?*

He lurched against a stucco wall, weak with fevered confusion. For the first time he could remember, he felt stirrings of hunger. *So the appetites still exist here*, he thought groggily. *And the means to satisfy them, too, apparently.* He had seen babies eagerly crunch beetles in tiny teeth, old women licking toasted black beans from rusty plates.

He wobbled into the middle of a muddy street. There were few signs anywhere. He had already asked the way of dozens of people, but none ever replied. There was little talk in the streets, no overheard conversations. *What was it Sartre said? Hell is other people? Well, that's proved wrong. Or maybe it's worse to be ignored.*

Between slumping two-story apartment houses stood a large white building in the classic Spanish style, red tile roof and big, wide windows with shutters. Above the broad entrance, swooping black calligraphy announced FLORIDITA. Markham, his suit grimy and wrinkled, went in.

He swayed at the entrance of the ample room. A high vaulted arch gave an airy generosity to the warming mixture of brown wood tables, muted red upholstery, and lush hangings of trailing vines. Nobody at the tables looked up.

At least the bartender has to talk to you, Markham thought sourly.

The bartender's fixed smile was like the rictus of a man who has died of a broken back. "A . . . beer." Markham lowered himself onto a stool, feeling every joint and muscle protest.

The bartender nodded and drew a pale amber glass. The man kept up the frozen smile as he placed the fat glass before Markham and then glanced significantly at the cracked wooden bar surface. Markham was suddenly conscious that he had no money. Somehow, it had not seemed important.

"Pedrico, put this *padrone* on my tab," a gravel voice said next to Markham's elbow. He turned. A deep-chested man in a woodsman's shirt and baggy drawstring pants held out a hand. "You just come through?"

"Yes. Several times."

"Sit over here." The man grinned, a sudden white crescent against a tan almost mahogany-deep. His face was furrowed as though a thunderstorm had cut ruts in a soft mound of dark clay. Gray stubble began at his chin and thickened as it ran along the jawline into thick, bushy hair. He led Markham to a corner table.

"Thanks. You're just about the only person who'll even notice I exist."

The old man sat down with a grunt and knocked back half of a frosted drink he carried. "They spotted you right away."

"As what?"

"New. Full of questions."

"So?"

"Ever have to explain the completely mysterious?"

"Ah."

"And do it again and again? Gets boring."

"I'm not expecting a Welcome Wagon or anything, just—"

"You got the woman."

"What? Well, yes . . . *that* was the welcome?"

The old man chuckled. "In a way."

"She threw me out the elevator door, but before that she . . . offered herself."

"No self there to offer."

"Her body."

"Won't do you much good. She gives it away and it's worth what you pay for it."

"That bad?"

"She's got rid of the clap, I heard."

"A demon with a disease?"

"They're all diseased."

"I hardly touched her."

The man's face crinkled as he chuckled darkly. "You're lucky the Agedness wasn't coming on her. There's fungus, brown stuff like shit with roots. Lives in her armpits. Comes out about once a month, grows down the arms. She returns to her true state then, and looks it."

"True?"

"Her real age. One, two hundred thousand years."

"She . . . ages . . . that much?"

"Guy in here a while back, he was ramming it to her when that came on. He's not going to forget that right away."

"How could he bring himself to . . . ?"

"Don't be so picky. This guy, he'd been fighting in Afghanistan. Thought he was in the Moslem heaven at first. Figured the Welcome Woman was a houri."

"Even so—"

"Man was horny. Not that she's any good for that."

"Why not?"

"You'll never get your rocks off with her. Impossible."

"But *why?*"

The old man grinned. "Them's the rules."

"Says who?"

"The Boss."

"Who is . . ."

"Right. Satan. Stay away from him."

Markham paused, took a long drink. The beer was thin and frothy and without any taste. Somehow it seemed like beer when you held it in your mouth, but as soon as you swallowed, it was like lifeless, tepid water. This old man wasn't going to lay out a little lecture, but he did have information. Markham decided to get as many facts as possible and reason from there. "So you can't come with the Welcome Woman?"

"Nope. You want a better time, try Angelique. She's the whore over by the window."

Markham covertly studied the slim woman with smoky skin who was chattering amiably to a tight-faced man across the bar. "She . . ."

"There's a special rate if you take a room, too."

"Ah, well . . ."

"Otherwise it's standing up in the alley out back."

"No, I meant . . ." It was ridiculous to be embarrassed, but he was.

"Oh, you won't come with her, either—but she's good at the early stuff."

"Well, how—"

"You don't." The man's face collapsed into a swarm of wrinkles. "Or at least I don't."

Markham finished his beer silently. "I like the way this stuff tastes," the man said gruffly, holding up his empty glass. "Fresh green lime juice. Pedrico uses that coconut water that is still so much more full-bodied and takes the Gordon's gin just right. Bitters to give it color. A hell of a good drink."

The bartender brought fresh ones. "Greg's my name," Markham toasted.

"I'm Hem. Try this."

After the description, Markham had expected something good or at least different. But the cold fluid from Hem's glass, while it felt good when it first came into his mouth with a chilling rush, soon tasted like the same days-old water that had been left somewhere too long. "Ah, yes," he managed to say.

Hem gave him a narrow, silent look, and then drank half the glass himself with gusto, smacking his lips afterward. "Yeah, that's the stuff."

"Have . . . have you tried to figure out what's going on?"

The condescending expression on Hem's face was softened by a warmth in the eyes, as if the old man were looking back on some memory. "That's not the point."

"What is?"

"To bear up under it."

"Under what?"

"Whatever they throw at you."

"How?"

"Gracefully."

"No, I mean, how do they do it?"

"Not the point at all," Hem persisted, and drank more, throwing his head back with relish and seeming to go into a momentary swoon as the frothy tan drops overflowed and trickled into his beard, clinging as glimmering amber dabs.

"Look, you have to start by figuring out how things work. That's my training. I was—am—a physicist."

Hem laughed. "We don't get a lot of them here."

"But you get some?"

"They pass through."

"Going where?"

"Mostly they end up in the Guard. Or else working for Hadrian's gang."

Markham rubbed his face where the heelprint of a boot still left its bruise. "Why?"

Hem peered moodily into his drink. "Keep the whole business running."

"How?"

Hem's jaw tightened and his mouth compressed as sudden life flared in him. "Boy like you ought to learn, it's not *how* that matters here. It's *why.*"

Irritated, Markham countered, "O.K., have it your way. What's this place mean, then?"

Hem leaned close to Markham's face, a cold, hard smile playing on his lips as he shaped the words very carefully, as though he had done this to newcomers countless times before. *"Nada. Nada. Nada. Nada."*

"What?"

"One single thing. *Nada.*"

"Nothing?"

Ponderously, Hem held up a thumb and forefinger forming

an *O*. "And if you want, you can have two things. *Un doble remordimiento.*"

Markham looked puzzled. Was Hem getting drunk, or was the man's personality slowly emerging from behind a protective shield?

"Two remorses," Hem said. "First, remorse for what you did. Second, for what you didn't."

Markham decided to humor him, like any drunk you meet in a bar. Though Hem did not appear to be drunk, really, only pivoting with Keplerian inevitability about some inner axis concealed from outsiders.

"O.K., what're *you* sorry for?"

Abruptly, Hem sat up straight, stopped clutching at the stem of the high glass. "The sky. I never looked at the sky enough when I had the chance. Like the way the blue was as hard and cold as good Arab steel. The solid blue and the big white clouds sailing in it. On a good day the sea was like that, good and hard and true."

Markham saw abruptly who this man was.

"I . . ."

"There are a lot of suicides here," Hem said slowly.

And Markham remembered. The shotgun placed carefully against the forehead, a cold winter day in Ketcham, Idaho, sometime in the early sixties.

"There are lots of girls from Spain," Hem said dreamily. "Plenty. Ones who got crossed in love or whose fiancés did not keep their promises and did the things to them anyway and then went off without marrying. They poured alcohol on themselves and set fire in the classic Spanish way."

Markham saw that it would be easier, and maybe better, too, if he made no sign of knowing. Maybe Hemingway would understand.

"You may enjoy these ladies. They come to town every now and then."

"They don't live here?"

"No, they're in the convents."

"Convents? *Here?*"

"They figure that's a way out."

"Is it?"

A bearish, sad-faced shrug.

"How . . . can anybody . . . get out?"

"Can't."

"But . . . we're still *people*. And this is like Brazil or some-place, not Hell at all."

"Ever been to Brazil?"

"Uh, no."

"Hell's more like Cuba, really. Even got Guevara."

"I heard."

A prick of alertness in the gray eyes. "Where?"

"On the road. A bunch in fatigues asked about him."

"How many?"

"Half a dozen or so. Guy named Hadrian in charge."

Hem relaxed. "So it worked."

"What?"

"Guevara's trying to draw Hadrian down this way."

"Why?"

"Hadrian's the—" Hem puffed up his chest and boomed out—"*Supremo Commandante!* Defender of the Antifaith. Ceaseless fighter against the Dissidents. Mean and faggoty and all-round asshole."

"He was in a hurry."

"Old Hadrian, either chasing D's or chasing ass—literally, in his case."

"What's there to dissent about?"

Hem blinked. "Why, getting out."

"How?"

"Nobody knows."

"Has anyone ever gotten out?"

Hem smiled evilly. "Nope."

"Then how the hell—"

"Look, Satan's got cops and the Fallen Angels and the rest. Guevara figures, knock them over and we can run things our-selves."

"And escape from Hell?"

"That's what he figures."

"What are the chances of that?"

Hem grinned. *"Nada."*

"Then why's Guevara trying?"

"Our *nada* who art in *nada, nada* be thy name."

"Look, Guevara hasn't been here more than a few decades. I remember he died in the sixties, the same as . . ."

Only a quick pained flicker passed over Hem's face, like a storm cloud that moved on and wasn't going to drop any rain this time. "Go on."

"So have the Dissidents been operating only that long?"

"No. Hell, I heard Socrates led them when he first came."

"They've been going thousands of years?"

"Sure. Maybe hundreds of thousands."

"Without success?"

This time Hem laughed. "No, this is really the other place." A sudden belch erupted from Hem and he belly-laughed again. "Hey. *Un poco pescado? Puerco frito?*" he called to the bartender. "Any cold meats?"

The bartender scuttled over with a plate of twisted brown things. Markham suddenly felt hungry and ate one. It was tasteless but seemed to fill his need.

"So it's hopeless?"

"I don't know."

"Can't you find out?"

"How, Mr. Professor?" Hem leaned toward him, lips smacking with the grizzled meat. "Look it up in the library?"

"You guessed that I'm—?"

"Sure. I always had the angle on you guys."

"I'm not a literary critic."

"Thank God."

"Nothing happens if you say that?"

Hem's eyes widened. "Say what?"

"God."

"Nope. You can swear all you like."

"You call on Him, He doesn't answer?"

"Maybe there isn't any."

"But if there's a Hell, there's—"

"Our *nada*, who art in *nada*."

Markham jumped to his feet. "Dammit! I'm trying to find out—"

"Shut it! Just shut it!" Hem lumbered to his feet and bunched a hairy fist under Markham's nose. "You want to argue, you argue with this."

Markham was speechless. In his confusion a small part of him kept on observing and remarking. *A classic macho confrontation with the all-time macho figure, and it just comes over as a dumb drunken quarrel.*

"Look, I . . . isn't there something I can *do?*"

Hem breathed heavily for a moment, staring at Markham with gray eyes that seemed to peer through him, toward a distant something. The man looked tired and out of condition. Against the sullen glow from a big side window, his gray hair formed a silvery nimbus about his skull.

"Yeah, maybe. Depends on what you want to find out."

"I'd like someone to talk to who has, well, really thought about this."

Hem smiled without humor. "You mean, thought the way *you* think?"

"I suppose so."

"Some professor?"

"No . . . a scientist. That's what I am." He paused, quelled a rush of emotions with a sip of the beer. "Was."

"There's some physicist Hadrian's got up at Kilimanjaro."

"Who?"

"Does it matter?"

"I need someone who knows modern physics, has kept up with quantum mechanics and—"

"No libraries here."

"If he simply questioned scientists who came through, he could keep current."

"I don't think many do show up."

Markham wanted to scream, *Then why am I here?* but he knew that would make Hem mad again to no point.

"Bohr? Einstein? Coleman?"

"Never saw them. I don't hang around much with—"

"Oppenheimer?"

Hem chuckled. "Yeah. He's here."

"Why?" Markham's voice sharpened. "The bomb?"

"People don't come in with tags on 'em."

"How about Feynman? Bethe? Fermi? Teller?"

Hem shook his head. "I don't keep track. Just know this English guy's supposed to be good at a lot of stuff. Hadrian uses him for advice."

"How do I find him?"

"He's under lock and key near Kilimanjaro."

"The mountain's really here?"

To Markham's surprise, Hem looked down at the rough wood tabletop, fingered a dab of meat. "I . . . call it that."

"Where is it?"

"About twenty miles north."

"How can I get there?"

"Not easy. Have to work around some of Guevara's plans. We must find out when he'll create a certain diversion I know is coming up. Otherwise it's too dangerous."

"Why?"

"Kilimanjaro's dead in the middle of the war zone."

5.

A mud-brown village looked across a broad river at the foothills of the big mountain. In the bed of the clear water, there were pebbles and boulders and fish swimming among them. Troops went by the last house, and Markham stood in the doorway and watched them march toward the rolling thunder up in the hills.

Troops of all times. Detachments of vested longbowmen, thick quivers of arrows slanted across their backs. A squad of swarthy, dwarfish swordsmen, beetle eyebrows bunched in concentration. Lines of singing, scimitar-wielding, red-robed women. Haughty grinning grenadiers. Long columns of ruddy Roman shields-and-lances, stepping smartly in the churning dust, clanking and shouting and sporting gaudy yellow ribbons atop beaten iron helmets. Yet among them all were other weapons—flintlock rifles, oiled Springfields, bluntsnouted heavy pistols, sleek crossbows, chunky black grenades, even a stubby iron cannon lumbering forward on wooden wheels behind a sweaty team of Chinese women. Muslims in filmy shirts and leggings plodded remorselessly, swords dangling at leather belts. A brown-skinned officer in blue and gray dashed among the columns, shouting.

The woman who kept the place said the men had been going by like that all day. Their dust powdered the shimmery green leaves of the spindly trees beside the road. They came from all times and kept steadily on, most without looking to the side or talking, just the glazed eyes staring narrowly and keeping to the road.

"What's the officer saying?" Markham asked.

Hem chewed meditatively on a toothpick. "Greek."

"You understand it?"

"No. It's ancient Greek, not modern. Everybody spoke that until about a thousand years ago, somebody told me. A lot of the fighters still do. They don't see any point in learning English, which is what most people switched to."

The dust prickled the inside of Markham's nose and he sneezed loudly. "Where are they going?"

"Up to one of the formations."

"To fight whom?"

"Whoever's there."

Hem's eyes looked out from deep hollows, never leaving the ragged parade and the endlessly billowing dust. "The Moslems think if they can just defeat enough infidels, they'll be released to the cool garden oasis where houris wait and water runs and there are dates and grapes for all. The Christians believe they have to prove themselves against the heathen. Those dwarfs who went by think they're in some sort of battle for possession of heaven. The Egyptians believe they're going to rescue the pharaoh."

"They must have caught on by now that those stories are bullshit."

Hem laughed sourly. "Are they?"

"Of course. This isn't *any* traditional Hell."

"Most others think this is a test, a trial—not Hell at all. They'll tell you straight. What they've got to do is show their stuff."

"Why?"

"They want to do as well as the Greeks at Marathon. Or as well as the Yanks at Shiloh. That's the code they knew and died by, and that's what they'll stick with."

"And hope it saves them?"

Hem turned and peered at Markham in the dim bleached light. "What're *you* doing?"

"I'm trying to find out how . . . oh."

Hem slapped the doorframe with an abstract, pensive glee, grinning, and the old woman who served watery, tepid drinks looked up, hoping for more business. The troops didn't stop often, they were too remorseless. But others did, spectators like Markham and Hem.

"Y'know, I ran into General Cambronne along here once. He was leading a regiment of French regulars, some of them in the Old Guard Cambronne had commanded at Waterloo. I asked him about that story, the one about what he said when the Brits called on him to give up."

"Oh. 'The Old Guard dies but never surrenders,' right?"

"So say the books. Cambronne told me all he said was, 'Merde!' When I was in Paris in the twenties, proper people when they did not wish to pronounce it said 'the word of Cambronne.' It means 'shit', of course, shit of purest ray serene. All the truth of the things is in that one word, not in the big phrases people make up afterward."

"Then *why* are these—"

"It's the only action that means anything, can't you see that? They've got no God anymore, but there's still some chance that if they prove themselves, they can get out. The religious Johnnies think that, sure. But the rest of 'em—what was it that Patton said? Something about war being the greatest sport. Well, they're sporting men."

"And if they die?"

Hem waited a long time, staring out at the restless eternal columns. "You've been through that already."

"So they keep coming back?"

"Yeah. It's all they know."

"They like it?"

"Look at them. You think they do?"

Markham studied the faces—drawn and whitened, lined and grimed, mouths twisted and obsessed, eyes advancing with fiery mad zeal.

He hadn't read any Hemingway in decades, didn't remember much except the way the prose turned a spotlight on one luminous point after another, bringing small things fugitive and insubstantial in their own right into sharp focus like an Impressionist painting: daubs of light hanging in the vacant, airless space of your mind. A pressing sense of hazard, peril, danger oozed through that crisp frozen canvas, constant rehearsal of the final and perhaps only real battle. Hem's carefully chipped sentences had embodied a universe that was not man's alone, perhaps not man's at all, fragile and precarious and yet, when you paid exact attention to it, absolutely solid. Unalloyed. Irreducible.

To all that, Hem's response had been a stoic sense of personal integrity, expressed through a cold, proud know-how, detached. He had studied life as if he were watching a painting in the Louvre, trying to enter into it by applying a consistent, systematic method to everything he described.

But now they were all beyond that sharp, clear world, well past the looming test of death.

"Let's go," Markham said, shuddering.

"The guide's coming along now."

Hem had paid for a man who knew the way around the main battle zones, to the camp where Hadrian kept his supply depots and administrative offices. There the trading and supplying and manufacture for the incessant war went on. There, Hem said, was the English physicist.

The guide was short, black, with wary eyes. He took his money up front and spoke little. The coins Hem gave the man were octagonal beaten copper. A crude grinning face marked both sides, struck off-center.

As the guide counted the coins, a sudden rattling of gunfire came down the road. Markham saw lines of men wavering at the nearest hilltop. Then some antlike figures turned and ran down the hill and others came after them. Thin cries rose. An artillery shell burst on the hilltop and bodies flew about the sudden ball of smoke, turning lazily in the air before bouncing down among the rocks.

"Outflanked them," Hem said.

"Why doesn't everybody use guns, at least? Those lancers, they're falling like wheat."

"Guns take factories, people who know how to mine, make machines—a lot. Most people here never saw a gun in their . . . first lives. They prefer to fight with what they know."

The lines broke and men scattered everywhere. They tried to reach the road, but their enemy poured forward, the swordsmen coming ahead and chopping them down from behind as they ran. Markham could hear screams, shouts. The columns on the road milled, surprised, and did not form up.

"Shouldn't we . . ."

"Yes. Let's go around this."

They moved quickly to the right, behind a long, straggly line of Arab archers. The guide said they would get clear easily. Markham kept up his loping run and after a few minutes saw that the man was right. The engagement swirled in confusion on the hillside, a knot of smoke and rushing figures.

They cut down a narrow draw and scrambled across a stream,

leaping among a jumble of rocks and logs. Halfway across, Markham felt something soft beneath his feet and saw that they were running across a jam of bodies that had drifted downstream and fetched up among the debris of combat. The bodies were so plentiful that they stacked three deep against the rocks. *So you don't just vanish when you die,* he thought.

They reached a stand of fragrant eucalyptus. He said, "The victors in this battle—does anything happen to them?"

Hem said, "Nah. They go on to the next battle tomorrow."

"So even if you win the rat race, you're still a rat."

Hem shrugged. "These fought even when they thought they had only one life. Why shouldn't they fight now?"

"Why don't you?"

"I'm no rat."

Something fat and leathery flapped overhead, wheeled, and dove toward the distant clamor. Great wings supported what looked to be a swelling black intestine. "Satan," Hem said. "That's the form he prefers when he's feeding."

"On what?"

"Soldiers he feels aren't eager enough for the battle."

Markham watched the huge thing descend upon a luckless band atop a far hill. Satan picked up a struggling figure, bit off a piece and—apparently finding it not to his taste—flung it aside.

Hem ignored this and peered at clouds scudding toward the snubby, snow-crested mountain he called Kilimanjaro. "Looks good for the next few hours. Storm moving in."

6.

Three hours later, according to his Seiko, Markham lay in the gloom beneath rolling skies and appreciated the shelter of the storm. Rain-soaked, muddy, sore from falls and sudden wild dashes to escape artillery bursts, he peered ahead. A drop traced itself down his brow, hung on his nose. Insects buzzed and stung at the nape of his neck. Things rustled in the weeds. Markham tensed and knew there was nothing he could do. Earlier he had seen an emaciated brown man get bitten by something long and yellowish, an incredible slick, shiny snake with a lashing tail. The man had rolled and kicked and died with an awful rattling cough, even before the snake could uncoil and glide into the bushes.

Artillery muttered over the horizon. Clouds boiled in, bringing sounds of clanging steel and distant anguished cries. Markham turned his head slowly as Hem had said, using peripheral vision. Nothing.

"Move on up," Hem whispered.

Markham wriggled on, mud's liquid fingers tugging. Their guide had abandoned them a hundred meters behind, pointing in the gloom toward the jumbled buildings of Hadrian's Office of Military Supply.

They had reached the right place at what Hem's informant said was the right time. Che Guevara planned to capture Hadrian somewhere a few kilometers away in some complicated maneuver. That would provide distraction and allow Markham and Hem to slip in this way. The attempt should have started half an hour before—though what anyone meant by time here Markham had not discovered, since there was no daily cycle to give it meaning or measurement.

"Sounds like some rifle fire over that way," Hem said.

Quick snapping sounds, then nothing. "It's probably had time to draw away most of the guards."

"Let's go, then," Markham whispered.

He and Hem slipped from shadow to shadow. The unmoving glow above could not penetrate the hovering rain clouds. "You hear anything?" Hem asked.

Markham listened. Then he did. A scrabbling of nails on a rocky outcrop, a dark mass oozing out of shadow coming fast—a dog?—and before he could think, it hit him. He rolled, then felt a wet, hot mouth, and then sharp teeth coming together on his fingers. He bit his lips to stop from screaming. The thing grunted with eager hunger. Something broke in his hand.

He rolled the thing against the ground, slamming it hard,

and managed to twist the head away with his left hand. A corrosive reek of musk and acid filled his nose. Its mouth free, the thing said clearly, "You. Die. Now."

Markham grabbed at matted, bristly hair and wrenched the thing away, keeping the mouth back with a punch to the throat. He felt a dull impact transmitted through the bulk of it and saw Hem stab down again, then again. The weight came on Markham fully, and he realized the thing he held was a large, misshapen dogman, four sinewy legs tapering into sharp claws, head narrowing to a snout and slack, drooling mouth. He pushed it away with disgust.

"One of Hadrian's breeding programs," Hem said thoughtfully, wiping his blade on the dog-man's coat.

"Good God."

"I should've mentioned them. A good sign though."

"Why? If there are more of these—"

"Means Hadrian's pulled his men off this post right now. He must be using them for personal guards, worried about Guevara."

"So?"

"Means we'll have less to go through."

He was right. They crawled another hundred meters and this time were ready when a black shape came lumbering at them. Hem caught it in the throat with a single quick jab. Markham had his knife out—bought from the guide—but wondered if he could use it properly. They duck-walked toward the first low wooden frame building when a voice called from startlingly nearby, "Jumbar! here, ole fella! Jumbar boy!"

Ole Jumbar isn't in the watchdog business anymore, Markham thought with satisfaction. He lay down to let the man pass.

A crunch of boots on gravel that seemed only inches away. Markham saw a moving patch against the sky. The knife was firm in his hand. He leaped up, lunging—and grabbed the man around the throat, silencing him. He dropped the knife and twisted the man down into the mud. Hem came swarming over them, swearing in a quick, angry whisper.

"No!" Markham cried, but he felt Hem's arm come down and plunge a blade to the hilt in the man's chest. The body jerked, coughed, rattled—and went limp.

"Why in hell didn't you cut his throat?" Hem whispered.

"I . . . I thought . . . I could keep him quiet."

"And if he got his mouth free? Want to bring everybody?"

Markham still felt all the prohibitions against killing, though he didn't want to say that. Hem seemed to understand, but said nothing. He motioned and they trotted toward a squat wooden frame building, one of the few whose windows spilled warm yellow light onto the muddy field.

Markham inched open an unlocked door and looked inside. A lone man hunched over a table, scribbling. Markham slipped inside.

The man looked up. His mouth formed a startled pouch below darting, intelligent eyes. The face held a look of concentrated energy, yet the man said nothing as Markham approached, whispering, "Just keep quiet."

"In faith, you much surprised me."

"I'm looking for a scientist," Markham said as Hem slipped into the room. "An English—"

"I be the only such abouts."

"I've just . . . arrived here."

"Come ye in."

The man appeared about forty, dressed in green fatigues. His skin was bone white, as though he never went out, and his long face had a look of pensive, dreamy power. Markham approached the table and glanced at the familiar sight of pages covered with equations. "I labor most times to set right Hadrian's turgid shops and yards, to manufacture the implements of retribution for use against the armies of darkness engendering. These restful hours I pursue mine own works."

"You're a physicist?"

"Aye, much as these rogue Moors and heathen let me be."

"Your name?"

"Isaac. Isaac Newton, late—very late—of Cambridge and London."

Good grief. "I . . . sir, I have come to you for help. You are widely regarded as the greatest intellect of all time."

"Stuff and drivel." Newton threw down his quill, spattering pages with ink. "Many pass through with such words slithering from their rubied lips, but I think it is one more Mephistophelian ruse."

"No, honestly, you are. You started modern science. You've heard of Einstein? He—"

"I've met a conjuration of that name."

"You know of his, ah, advancements beyond your work?"

Newton sniffed. "I heard of melting clocks and sliding sticks."

"It's more than that, I assure you. But my real question is, sir"—Markham gestured wildly, his head aswarm with questions—"what *is* this place?"

Newton looked sternly at him, ignoring Hem. "All mankind is of one author, and is one volume. When one man dies, no chapter is torn from that great book, but translated into a better language."

"Uh, what?"

"This is but another edition. A fresh tongue. A proving ground, God wot."

"To prove . . . what?"

"The Lord's eternal lesson. We are cast here amongst shameless Papist logicians, slimy Portugals, wily wenches fit solely for rutting, blackamoor armies, dark dread powers—all to find our own writ way."

"To . . . What?"

"The Lord's great mercy."

"But we're in *Hell.*"

Newton frowned. "So it would seem to the unattended eye. I assure you though, fresh traveler full of gapes—this is no damnation. Such destiny would make the reason reel."

"What is it then?"

"A fool's test."

"And if we pass?"

"Heaven then, for the quick-eyed."

"And the rest?"

"More dour fretting. Here we feel the sharp bite of guilt, for life brief and nought done."

"You're . . . sure?"

"As sure as I fix on the rheumy ancientry. Bookish learning, the pen's fair incessant wallow—that be our exit for this nightless inspection."

"Then we can find a way out?"

"With proper twist to the ken, aye."

"Using science?" Markham gestured toward the mounds of sheets that sprawled across the ample pine table. An oil lamp cast sharp shadows across endless hen-scratch lines.

"Oh, nay. Nor vain tattle, waffling poesy, or any other airy art."

Markham shook his head. "But science is the only way I ever knew to understand the world."

Newton gave him a warm, broad smile, yet the eyes remained intent, unyielding. "So thought I, long ago. But a man might as well study rubor, calor, tumor, and cholor—they are equal afflictions. Science sleeps here."

Markham glanced to the side, saw that Hem was leaning against the door, grinning slyly. "What changed your mind?"

"The Eye," Newton said softly, a bony white finger spiking upward.

"You mean . . . the sun?"

"Ha! 'Tis no sun. It never moves."

"We could be locked to it by tides, like the moon."

" 'Tis an eye that watches all below."

"*Whose* eye?"

"Satan lives among us here, bleak-spirited and vexed, powerful and lightning-swift. It be not he above."

"So?"

"The *Lord* witnesses. The Lord judges. His single all-seeing eye, cloud-shrouded ever. And it falls to us to riddle our way into his good light."

"Riddle?"

"To fathom heavens that the mere present man's eye cannot glimpse."

"Look, you just *said* nobody sees the Eye through the clouds. So what heavens are there to, uh, fathom?"

"The astrological pattern, fat with truths."

Dizzy, Markham leaned on the table, disturbing a sheet. Newton leaped up, snatching at it. "No! You'll not see the traceries!"

Markham had glanced at a sheet, and saw that elaborate signs and emblems of the zodiac covered them. He remembered that Newton, though the greatest of scientists, had in fact devoted most of his career to theology and alchemy. The man's mind had been broad and not always able to discern what was science and what was sheer humbug. He had also been deeply suspicious of others stealing his work. That led to a nervous breakdown. Abandoning his Cambridge chair, he had become Warden of the Royal Mint, a scourge of counterfeiters. That surprising administrative ability, combined with sharp intelligence, was undoubtedly why Hadrian had used him here.

Newton rushed around the table, spitting oaths. "I knew you when you appeared! Last time it was offers of gold, of ambergris and musk, of unicorns' horns, was it not? I see you, Quathan the Unrepentant. Begone!"

"No, you don't understand. I'm a scientist, a natural philosopher like yourself."

"Necromancer at best, deceiver!"

"I studied your laws in school! I, I—"

"Such laws as were, rule not here. Aristotle's rude rub holds in the flattened land. Things left alone do not glide serene—they stop, velocity eaten by friction's waste. For such are we—waste."

"But you founded true astronomy. You could apply your laws here, or something like them. By careful observation . . ." Markham's voice trailed off. "You've already tried, haven't you?"

"Only astrology functions here. Reading signs, divining portents—that is the true learning."

"You can make real, rational predictions that way?"

Newton's face twisted into a congested mask. "Newcomer, on Earth you and I knew that Reason led to understanding, but Death ruled. Here Death can merely return you to Hell. Otherwise it is powerless. If there is a divine transition from this place, it must come from Reason—but not the narrow notions of mechanistic science."

"But that's all we have!"

"So?" Newton's eyes became crafty. "Yet I know what your scientism did after my departure."

"We advanced, built on your foundations—"

"And rid yourselves of God. Swept Him from the world's stage. Ordained that the equations ruled, that the mere will of man or God was as nothing compared to them."

"Well . . ." Markham began uncomfortably.

"Having displaced human will from the natural world, Doctor Scientist, now explain *this* place." Newton swept an arm in an all-encompassing circle.

"Well, what can we study, how—"

"We must rely not on forces and fluxions, but upon the innate sympathies and antipathies of occult knowing."

Markham could not help himself. He had had a lifetime of dealing with cranks at cocktail parties, with otherwise reasonable people who believed in fortune-telling or ancient astronauts or dead superstitions. "That stuff is nonsense."

"Is it! Well!" Newton's eyes now blazed and jerked with fevered energy. His bony fingers clamped the table, long arms braced to defend the field of scribbled scraps. "You'll not learn how I read the heavens through blankets of sulphurous cloud— not until I have finished my researches! Tell the Devil *that*, if you dare."

Markham sighed. "I'm not from the Devil. I don't give a damn—literally—about your astrological garbage."

"Then get thee hence on any account, conjuration! What a sorry thing you be."

With that, Newton abruptly began to mutter to himself and

stir the sargasso of papers. Markham could hear: ". . . if only I'd not . . . the Trinity, had I but believed truly in Father, Son, and Holy Ghost . . . or not castigated so Flamsteed for that data . . . or Leibniz over discovery of that trifle, the calculus . . . this is the third temptation of a week, by my troth . . ."

Markham followed Hem's beckoning hand at the door. "We better go before the next round for that guard," Hem said. "Somebody'll notice."

Out, into muggy air beneath a cold gray mass of mottled clouds that hugged the hillsides.

As he stumbled down a steep slope, letting the bushes scratch him, Markham knew there was a kernel of truth in what Newton said, an idea . . . It slipped away.

Clearly any mechanistic physics was inadequate to deal with a place where ancient evils reigned. Somehow this filled him with joy, though he could not say why. If he got a moment to think . . .

"Patrol over there. This way!" Hem whispered. They bent and crawled through scraping manzanita.

Hem, Newton, Hadrian . . . what are the odds on meeting them? Maybe Hell has most of the famous . . . a place for unique, consuming sins . . . but then why me? I was nobody special. Some good physics, minor transgressions, nothing lurid. Why me?

They worked their way down an arroyo and into a dried creek bed. The going was easier, and Markham felt good to be trotting doggedly away from the confusions that Newton had planted in his mind. It was a *stage*, where dead players trod . . .

They passed through low scrub trees, and up ahead there was only gloom. They ran for ten minutes. Markham panted, trying to keep up. Hem was older but had a solid, steady pace and puffed easily.

"Alto!"

The shout from the trees made Hem duck and roll away, into the bushes. An arrow whistled by. Markham froze, then dove for cover—only to find two big men with gleaming shortswords blocking his way.

Hem got no further. Quickly a squad prodded them into a clearing nearby and a scowling man came striding over, whispering, "Who this?"

Hem said, "We're just passing through."

"You are from Hadrian?"

"No, we're leaving the battle."

The man laughed. "Cowards? You run?"

"Let's say we bore easily," Markham said.

"I say you are Hadrian men."

The accent, the flinty eyes, scruffy beard—Markham saw suddenly that this was Guevara. *Hell is for the famous. Maybe that's the ultimate sin, after all. But there were plenty of spear carriers—literally—here. So maybe they were famous ten thousand years ago. But then, why me?*

Hem said casually, "I drank with you once, remember?"

Guevara peered through the dusty light. "Ah, yes. The writer. Two Americans we have here, where they should be not."

Hem said contemptuously, "Hell is free. Perfectly free."

"Not for all," Guevara said. He snapped his fingers and a short fat man came hurrying over. Markham could see there were about twenty men with weapons forming lines in the gloom. A short distance away, three held a man captive, hands tied. Markham recognized Hadrian's long, fleshy nose. The face was withdrawn, somber. Blood dripped slowly from his nose and spattered a luxuriant white tunic.

"Tickle them," Guevara said.

The fat man in filthy fatigues took out a knife and without hesitation casually jabbed Markham in the ribs.

Guevara asked, "Where? You from where?"

Markham kicked him in the balls. Someone grabbed Markham from behind and pulled his arm up so that it twisted in the socket. Markham shifted right and Hem came down on the man's back, and then there was the fat man's face in front of him

and he punched at it. The fat man stabbed with the knife but
missed, and then they were all rolling hard on the ground, the
dust filling Markham's nostrils.

Someone kicked him in the side, and then he was on his feet
again, hands pinned behind him. Guevara stepped near, smiling.
"You are confessing your opposition to the revolution."

"What revolution?"

"Against all. You are newcomer? *Sí.* You would join, then?
To revolt! To fight our way through Hadrian and the devils and
all."

"Then where'll you go?"

Guevara gestured expansively. "Beyond."

"You know a way out?"

"We will find one."

"You're condemned to perpetual revolution?"

Guevara's mouth tightened. "You try to be funny."

Markham felt heady from the curious elation that had been
slowly gathering in him since he had left Newton. In his life on
Earth, he would have been cautious of a man like Guevara, but
now he saw this man as negligible, the macho posturings a mere
show.

"Not as funny as all this empty ritual."

"You are a friend of Hemingway?"

"Sure."

Guevara smirked at Hem. "You escaped Cuba before we had
chance to slit throat."

Hem smiled coldly and said nothing.

Guevara looked at both men, calculating. "This time I make
no mistake. I not trust you."

"Trust us with what? Just let us go, dammit."

"When the rescue party following Hadrian fans out, they
question you, find which way we go."

A sinking cold feeling ran up Markham, and he tensed painfully, fighting the old fear. "Take us with you, then."

Guevara shook his head dismissively. He waved a hand and
said to the short fat man, "Do these."

Guevara said it with such obvious ease that Markham knew he had given the order before on this mission, would give it again with equal unconcern.

From Markham's experience, he could see Guevara's logic. Though the dead returned to Hell, they reappeared elsewhere, and later—well after this skirmish would be over. A simple way to get rid of troublesome types.

The short man was quick and came in with the knife low, tilted up, eyes fixed and feet shifting lightly in the dust. Markham strained against the hands holding his arms behind him. The fat man plunged the knife into his belly, and for an instant he felt the impact but nothing more. Then the slow, cold ache of it came into him, and he convulsed with fear, and then the hands were no longer holding him and he ran straight at the fat man. His fist lashed out and caught the man solidly on the cheek. The face fell away and he was running hard, shouts all around him, the pain now a low, slumbering ache and his bunched muscles feeling good to be used and to breathe deeply and run.

Someone chopped at him with a sword, but he ducked and lurched to the side, feeling light on his feet and quick. The faces swept past in a liquid way as if underwater, and he heard feet pounding behind him. When he came to a narrow lane free of brush, he looked back expecting to see Guevara's men pursuing, but it was Hem, doggedly loping behind.

He went that way for a while. It felt good, and there might be Guevara's murderers behind him, and anyway, he could not feel the pain this way. It sat there, a glowing, smoldering ember waiting to burst into fire, but he could keep it that way if he didn't stop.

But then a fire grew in his lungs and his heart racketed in his chest and he slowed.

Hem was far behind. Maybe Hem had called to him, but it would not come clear and solid in his mind. He remembered a movie he had seen, *Barry Lyndon,* and how at the end, in a final freeze-frame of a crippled and sour man getting into a carriage, some cold, modern typeface said: *Whatever you may think of these people, they are all equal now.*

But it wasn't true. Nobody was equal here, they were all following their own trajectories, shaped by their obsessions.

Somehow that seemed to matter, and as he ran on and felt the wetness running down his legs, he knew finally what Newton meant.

Markham came to some rocky ground and scrambled over some boulders. He could not see well, there were purple specks swarming in his eyes, so in a way he was not surprised when his foot slipped from the blood and he felt the boulder give way. It lurched aside, teetered—and was gone, thumping below.

He clutched for something, anything—caught a shrub—lost it—raked fingers across a smooth rock face—clasped at a dusty ledge—thrashed madly—and was gone—falling straight down, tumbling. He caught a glimpse of a narrow box canyon, the ground swelling up so fast he could not cry out—

He woke sometime later.

This time they would not let him die so quickly. He tried his legs and saw the left shinbone jutting out, a white blade like a knife thrust clean through him. The left arm, too, was turned wrong and he could not move it.

The pain did not seem to matter so much this time. It was just another thing that got in the way of thinking.

Hem came out of the shrouded dusky radiance and said, "Damn fool. I told you not to run when you're wounded."

"You're just pissed 'cause I beat you."

He had meant at running, but Hem took it differently. The big, rough man looked at Markham's wounds and nodded. Markham studied Hem's face and knew that whatever happened, Hem would not die, could not die. That thing had been denied Hem and would be forever. The thing he had prepared for in life, he could not have here.

Hem squatted down and said, "That bunch wouldn't have followed us, anyway. They've got to make tracks themselves."

"Ye . . . yeah."

"Let me see."

"I'm all right."

"The hell you are."

"*Oh.*"

"Pretty bad?"

"I'm getting better at it."

"Breathe deeply. It helps."

He did, and then a slow, seeping weakness came up from the gut and he felt it in his chest and in his arms.

"They got you, too." He pointed at Hem's shirt where a red splotch grew.

"Little bastard slipped it into my ribs as I went past him."

"They used the old falling number again."

"It work?"

"No. I'm not scared of it. They're running out of ideas."

"They've got plenty."

The clouds above were thinning but not breaking up. He saw as he moved to ease the low ache in his gut that more light poured through the clouds from the Eye or the star or whatever it was, but the foggy bank would not break and let him see what lay above them. He would never get to stare directly into the Eye.

He was far away now, even though he could feel the gritty, hard sand he lay on, and there were no problems at all. It was going to be bad this time, and he knew that, but it did not matter now. He had the fear of death in him that the devils had used and he knew that fear would not go away, but he had learned how to risk death now and know what the risk was worth. He had learned something from Newton, even if he did not fully comprehend all of it. He had beaten *them*, whoever or whatever ran this place, just by facing the thing he feared.

Hem was saying something, but he could not hear very well now for the ringing.

Church bells? Sure, church bells in Hell.

It was just the endless chiming of shock and blood loss in his ears, he was sure of that, his reductionist self hovering there ready with an easy explanation. Always ready.

He felt damp air and tasted it, and it came into him.

The thought that had been trying to get through finally did then, and Markham nodded to himself with professorial pride, glad to finally see.

They are all equal now. And equally important.

The swarm of tics and traits that was each human personality, that came out of swimming mystery and persisted . . .

"It's not over," he said.

. . . science had brushed that aside, enshrined instead the mindless physical world as the provider of order . . .

Hem laughed. "It sure isn't," he said gently.

. . . what was important was not some nebulous Word Mind or Spirit of the Universe that was a hollow echo of the old dead God . . . not some flaccid compromise substitute, some abstract idea served up by embarrassed modern theologians . . .

"Y'know, when I come back . . ."

"I'll save a beer for you."

". . . I think I'll take up hang gliding."

No—it was *you* and all your fragile vexing memories and hates, loves and dreads that mattered.

"Screw science," Markham said. "I like this better."

Dimly he saw, too, that because a choice of actions still persisted, Hell could not be final. His mathematician's habits immediately gave him a vision of an infinite series of airless alabaster hyperspaces, each folded one into another, and the raw white Ping-Pong ball of Self bouncing among them all . . .

He relaxed completely on the pine-scented sand and prepared to let himself be carried off in the jaws of jackals, off to greater adventures and places unknown in the bowels of the Great Beast.

RHYSLING POETRY AWARD WINNERS

Susan Palwick
Andrew Joron

Although there is no Nebula Award for poetry, the situation is more than remedied by the Science Fiction Poetry Association's Rhysling Award for long and short poems. The award is named after the blind poet of the spaceways who appears in "The Green Hills of Earth," a story written by Nebula Grand Master Robert A. Heinlein and published in 1947. It has become traditional to publish the Rhysling winners in the annual Nebula anthology.

Susan Palwick, winner in the short-poem category, has published both fiction and poetry in *Isaac Asimov's Science Fiction Magazine* and in *Amazing Stories*. A graduate both of Princeton University, where she won the American Academy of Poets Poetry Prize, and of Clarion West, she serves on the editorial board of *The Little Magazine*.

Andrew Joron, winner in the long-poem category, is now a three-time recipient of the Rhysling Award. His poems and essays have been published in numerous magazines, including *Isaac Asimov's Science Fiction Magazine, Amazing Stories, New Worlds, Portland Review*, and *Foundation*. He is the editor of *Velocities: A Magazine of Speculative Poetry* and the *Velocities Chapbook Series*. About *Force Fields*, a recent collection of Joron's poetry, Brian Aldiss writes: "Joron's economical line strikes a true nerve of feeling, light on the eye and ear, but heavy with meaning."

Joron studied the history of science at the University of California at Berkeley and makes his home in that community. He sees the recent growing emergence of SF poetry as a vital trend:

"The American poet Hart Crane once suggested an analogy between chemistry and writing. All writing that lacks the poetic

is as distant from reality as the formula used to describe a chemi-
cal reaction; whereas poetic writing is the chemical reaction it-
self. By this analogy, SF poetry would be a reaction akin to
superfluid helium 3, a substance recently discovered that, at close
to absolute zero, obeys none of the classical laws governing liq-
uids in motion—in much the same way that a real SF poetry
would obey none of the standard laws of story-telling prose.''

Susan Palwick
The Neighbor's Wife

It sprouts wings every few weeks
but as yet has flown no further
than the woodpile in the yard
where we found it six months ago.

Colin Wilcox thought it was his wife
returned as an angel. It still wore
its headset then, lying trapped
in a crushed metal basket; Colin freed it,

muttering something about harps and haloes,
and the rest of us stayed quiet. Colin carried it
into the house and for three weeks nursed it
in his bed, on the side unwarmed since Marella,

the old Marella, had her heart attack.
When it could walk on six legs Colin taught
it to fry bacon, weed the garden, milk
the goats, which cower at its touch.

"Reminding her what she forgot in Heaven,"
he tells us, but she has not remembered speech,

this new Marella who is purple and croaks
like bullfrogs on the hottest summer nights,

who surely came from somewhere, if not from God.
Lately it uses those stubby wings to carry
the heaviest logs from the woodpile. For Colin's sake
no one has tried to frighten it away.

Andrew Joron
Shipwrecked on Destiny Five

Final communiqué: long wanderings
     near the edge
Of the so-called "fractured" terrain
Where night is always falling

The largest of three suns
     is tidally distorted
     perpetually
Smeared above the south horizon
     while the smallest
When eclipsed, burns a hole
Right through that giant's helium husk

None of us has spoken
     much this morning
Since we sighted the Carven Cliffs
     spectro-
Analyzed from orbit: walls of unnatural smoothness
     reflective as water
But splashed at intervals
By a dark symbology

We buried Johnson there
Another case of petrifaction
—why
Should they all freeze
In that characteristic attitude
	lacking instruments
It's sometimes difficult to tell
Death from life
	there are nine of us left

Other phenomena, so far
Unreported: surely no miracles
Only a few
Sensory tricks—auguries in clear weather

	the floating columns
Of indeterminate size
& substance—still pacing us in our travels
Like spirit-stanchions, an all-surveying
Ennead
	the guardians
Of an abandoned world?—or the roving
Geometric shadows of our minds

An ocean clotted with pink algae
	—their floral
Cycles of tiny outgassing
Fill the air
With the clamor of a million violins

	weedy tissues
Woven into rocks—that seem to pulsate
Altering their hue
With the pattern of our voices

Mists of metallic particles
	gathering in shapes

That tease and respond to the artistry of our
  despair

The whistling body of the atmosphere
Lowers upon us like a mountain
The very pores of skyflesh
    appearing
In skeins and sinews of the airflow
Opening like graves of light around our heads

The chromium bones of
    our landing craft become
A lost language of shiny objects
    —the sacred gears
Of a god machine

& we must tread among these
    warped totems
A crew of empty spacesuits
Mantled in corrosive
    & caressing spume
Remote-controlled
By a host of artificial memories
    motiveless, we must continue
Searching
For some piece of fallen science

    ground down
To our knees by the heavy gravity
Until we assume
    our final
    & somehow mystical
Postures
    forming a tradition
Of abstract sculpture
Scattered along a scarlet beach

SCIENCE FICTION MOVIES OF 1986

Bill Warren

It's important to observe what happens in visual SF. This one aspect of the field reaches the widest audience and most distorts SF's possibilities. SF filmmakers can't help but work against a background of SF in print, however unconsciously, and they have the double problem of being true to the demands of good filmmaking and the demands of good SF. The demands of good filmmaking are often better met than those of good SF. Yet filmmakers should have no more of a problem fulfilling these dual demands than do writers fulfilling the dual demands of good SF and good fiction.

In the absence of a Dramatic Nebula Award, Bill Warren has kept an eye on SF film in these volumes. He is the author of the witty and comprehensive two-volume *Keep Watching the Skies!*, a survey of American SF films from 1950 to 1962. An occasional story by him appears in *Amazing Stories* and *Worlds of Fantasy*. He has worked as a film researcher, comic-book scriptwriter, and film reviewer. About his survey for this year he writes:

"What follows is an examination, film by film, of the SF movies released in the United States in 1986. I have tried to include a few made-for-TV movies, as well as the majority of those titles released directly to videocassette, an increasingly large percentage of all films. This is not analytical; this is reportage. I am greatly indebted to Bill Thomas for his assistance in preparing this annual report, as I am in all matters of this nature. He's a good friend and a dedicated researcher, and I could not do without him."

Nineteen eighty-six seems to be a trough year for science fiction movies: fewer had big budgets than in recent years, and more were derivative of earlier films. But any year including a film likely to be regarded as one of the classics of the genre is important.

When I was a kid growing up in the 1950s, obsessed with science fiction in and out of movies, I passionately wished for the millennium to come when Hollywood would make big-budget science fiction movies, with real stars and real directors. Then, I was sure, they would discover written science fiction and all my favorite stories would be filmed. How could they *not* be, after all? There was so much cinematic stuff just hanging around there: Lewis Padgett, Robert A. Heinlein, Asimov, Anderson—you have your own list.

Well, friends, the millennium has done arrived; here we are surrounded by people making science fiction movies. Almost every studio has at least one out each year, and they often make mints.

Now here's another phenomenon: *Stand by Me, The Color of Money, About Last Night, Children of a Lesser God, Crimes of the Heart*—all these profitable 1986 films were adaptations. Granted, the biggest money-makers were "original" screenplays, but there are always adaptations, and the number of original screenplays that were *flops* is much larger than the number of failures that were adaptations.

So where are the SF adaptations? One industry insider says they are so scant partly because the money people, those who finance the pictures, are far more stupid than you can possibly imagine: they know *nothing* about films, *nothing* about books, *nothing* about *anything* except making money. Furthermore, middle-level executives, those who actually decide what to make, are terrified of losing their jobs and so want to make only movies that are smash hits. But originality worries them; they feel they *must* make movies like previous hits. (Note how often the word *derivative* occurs in the following article.) And most written SF is not much like previous movies. Even if an adaptation was incredibly profitable, it wouldn't lead to more adaptations—but to imitations.

The message from almost everyone in movies who can put

together a sentence and has read something more fictional than a contract is this: just be glad movies aren't any worse than they are. The potential for sheer rottenness is higher than in your most pessimistic nightmares. Yes, *The Clan of the Cave Bear* is pretty bad, and *Maximum Overdrive* stinks like two-week-old roadkill—but at least 1986 gave us *The Fly*.

It's terrific, a creepy, funny, revolting, touching shocker like no other film ever made. Cronenberg is an artist of the ghastly, a sardonic wit with a mission. As in other Cronenberg films, in *The Fly*, scientist Seth Brundle (Jeff Goldblum in one of the great SF performances) is meddling with the flesh. Here, as in the 1958 film and George Langelaan's original story, it's via matter transmission. Brundle is a reclusive, asocial, brilliant guy who becomes involved with science journalist Veronica Quaife (Geena Davis), annoying her former lover, Stathis Borans (John Getz), editor of her magazine. Fearing that Veronica has gone back to Stathis and hoping to prove himself to her, Seth transmits himself, overlooking a fly that has entered the transmission booth, and comes out of the booth apparently perfectly normal. But eventually body parts start dropping off, and Seth undergoes a metamorphosis.

Cronenberg knows computers are stupid, that they know only what we tell them. And the computer operating Seth's teleporter, having no other options, has gene-spliced Seth and the fly. Seth is slowly and hideously turning into an amalgam of human being and fly. Chris Walas, who designed and created the fly-thing, has done impressive work.

But *The Fly* is not about the ghastly sights we see; it is about the people to whom these horrible things happen. It is partly a love story, partly a serious drama; it's also surprisingly funny throughout. A monster making bitter jokes about its condition is something new and something wonderful. The screenplay is credited to Charles Edward Pogue and Cronenberg, but though Pogue's story was retained, the director rewrote all the dialog and created new characters. Even more than his previous films, this establishes David Cronenberg as a top-rank director.

Some commentators have felt that Seth's metamorphosis is

an allegory for debilitating diseases, like AIDS; Cronenberg himself feels that, if anything, it's a metaphor for aging. The persistence of love in the face of increasing horror brings a powerful emotion to the film. This is more than a horror movie; it's an authentic tragedy. *The Fly* is one of the best science fiction films I have ever seen.

The other best SF movie of the year is *Star Trek IV: The Voyage Home.* The plotline is, to say the least, contrived, but it's smoothly told with familiar, friendly actors happily playing roles they've shaped to themselves for twenty years. Of the four Star Trek movies, this one comes closest to capturing the best of the old TV series, even though it is probably the cheapest.

You probably know the story: Kirk, Spock, and their pals go back in time to 1986 and get a couple of humpback whales and a cetacean biologist. The business about the whales is a heartfelt but never heavy-handed Message, like those the TV series fed its audiences. Leonard Nimoy, who directed this far better than he did the previous outing, wrote the story with producer Harve Bennett, and the script is by Bennett, Steve Meerson, Peter Krikes, and Nicholas Meyer. *Star Trek IV* is of a piece, with some imaginative ideas, a warm heart, and plenty of funny lines for almost everyone. The crew of the Enterprise are back, just as the Trekkeroonios—and, obviously, much of the movie-going audience—wanted them to be. Supposedly, William Shatner will direct number five, if it is made.

Star Trek IV, to the surprise of everyone, outgrossed *Aliens*, which developed a strong reputation even before it was released. Critically, it was overrated, and is neither as good nor as original as *Alien.* In terms of plot, *Aliens* isn't even a science fiction movie. The same story, with the same characters and most of the same action, could have been set in any time period; it could be the cavalry rescuing a kid from Indians, British lancers rescuing a kid from Fuzzy-Wuzzies, cavemen rescuing a kid from nasty apes. It breaks no new ground as science fiction or as an adventure.

But *Aliens* was the best action picture of the year, a sizzling, scary rollercoaster of a movie. Written and directed by James Cameron of *The Terminator* (and cowriter of *Rambo*), the movie moves fast and looks great. (Designs are by Ron Cobb of *Alien* and Syd Mead of *Blade Runner*.) It has problems: I didn't like Cameron jettisoning Dan O'Bannon's carefully developed alien biology. Cameron is clearly in love with weaponry, but why are all these futuristic characters using *current* state-of-the-art guns and ammo? And the climax, involving an air lock, is scientifically outrageous.

The last half of the film is an almost continuous onslaught of action, with crashing space helicopters, face-grabbers running wild, attempted murder, guns going off everywhere, aliens dropping from the ceiling, and only four hours to get off the planet before everything goes blooey. Yet Cameron manages to squeeze in some characterization, by using stereotyped characters but good actors, the classic, Howard Hawks–John Ford way of dealing with stereotypes. And Sigourney Weaver makes a terrific hero.

A British TV movie turned up on videotape, but the central character had already become familiar to Americans, so much so that in late March 1987, a six-episode tryout series based on him began on ABC-TV. The eponymous hero turned up in commercials for Coke, on magazine covers, and in jokes. This was Max Headroom, a (supposedly) computer-generated talking head— wise-cracking and ad-exec sharp, vaguely New Wave but crossing age boundaries. Even those most in love with Max remain unaware that he's actor Matt Frewer in latex hair and bright blue contact lenses. His image has been manipulated with video technology, but he is in no way computer *generated*: if you like Max, it's because of Frewer and his writers. I hope Frewer is getting ridiculously rich.

The flashy, funny *Max Headroom* is one of the best SF movies of 1986, full of smirky wit and crackerjack ideas. Since Max himself is so stuffed with pop-culture crap, it's only fitting that his story is highly derivative: it's as if the worlds of *Blade Runner* and *Brazil* were scrunched together with a story line written by Monty Python's crew. Set "twenty minutes into the future," *Max Headroom* posits a world run by greedy television executives—even bums in the streets have several color sets each—but saved from oblivion by crusading TV reporter Edison Carter (also Frewer, a real find). The forces of Evilness try to kill snoopy Carter, who's on the verge of finding out that compressed TV commercials detonate habitual viewers. Though Carter is only wounded, his psyche is imperfectly copied into a computer, resulting in the living cockeyed doppelganger, Max Headroom. The movie was directed by Rocky Morton and Annabel Jankel, written by Steve Roberts (from an idea by George Stone, Morton, and Jankel), designed by Maurice Cain, and photographed by Phil Meheux, all of whom do sharp, stylish turns.

Television does not thrive on self-reflexive satire, except when aimed (like *SCTV*) at a young audience. Max is more dangerous than previous TV satirists—he doesn't make fun of old shows, but of the very concept of television. Kids both drink it in and scoff at it, and being a mocking TV image, Max is perfect for this audience—time alone will have to reveal if others will get the jokes. (They didn't. The renewed U.S. series was quickly canceled.)

In the created-to-formula *Short Circuit*, the robot hero Number Five is so endearing that he wipes the human characters right off the screen, which doesn't take much doing; all the characters are standard clichés. Fortunately, however, Number Five is the star of this highly predictable but reasonably entertaining movie, thanks to Syd Mead, who designed the robot, Eric Allard, who made it work in the movie, and Tim Blaney, who provides the voice for the robot.

The story doesn't bear close examination as science fiction. Five super-soldier robots are being put away after a successful demonstration, when Number Five is hit by lightning, a gimmick that went out with Boris Karloff. The robot, now fully aware and an individual (i.e., "alive"), rolls off to see the world. It is to the credit of director John Badham *(WarGames)* that the film works as well as it does. It loses many points on originality—

being a virtual reply of *E.T.*, it has none—but gains on scenery, pace, a sense of good fun, and the charming Number Five himself. Some people who love SF films squirm at this one, but their kids probably adored it.

Some movies lurk around odd TV channels late at night, waiting for people to discover and flip over them. One of the most famous—or notorious—was the two-day wonder *Little Shop of Horrors*, written by Charles B. Griffith and directed by Roger Corman. Howard Ashman, who liked the old film, wrote the off-Broadway musical of the same title. The musical was filmed by director Frank Oz, working from a script by Ashman himself. *Little Shop of Horrors* is a fast-paced, hilarious, and immensely imaginative delight, one of the best Hollywood films of 1986.

Nerdy Seymour Krelborn (Rick Moranis), a clerk in Gravis Mushnik's Skid Row flower shop, finds and raises little plant Audrey II. He names the plant after squeaky Audrey (Ellen Greene), who also works in the shop. There's a love triangle, a plot by the talking plant (just arrived from outer space) to conquer the world, and several lively musical numbers. The plant is awesome. With the rich, funny voice of Levi Stubbs (of the Four Tops) and the incredible work of plant designer & creator Lyle Conway, Audrey II is one of the best on-the-set effects ever done. With moist, expressive lips, a tilt of the "head," and endlessly curling tendrils (constantly making their *own* jokes), Audrey II is almost beyond description.

Frank Oz is probably best known for two of his alter egos, Miss Piggy and Yoda: he is one of the Muppeteers. In *Little Shop*, Oz moves decisively away from the Muppets and into an additional career on his own. Alas, the film was not the financial success it deserved to be but will find its audience in time.

A film probably destined never to find its audience is the remake of *Invaders from Mars*. There *is* an audience for it, however: those who recognize its careful balance between parody and melodrama. The script of Tobe Hooper's remake of William Cameron Menzies's original, credited to Dan O'Bannon and Don Jakoby, is a clever blend of spoof and science fiction thrills. It seemed likely to me that kids under twelve would take it straight while older viewers would have a good time laughing with the film.

I was wrong. The film was a certifiable flop, returning less than $2 million on its large investment. Partly this was due to the failure of the distributor (Cannon) to promote the picture properly, to advise audiences that it was largely a romp. But it is also due to Tobe Hooper's persistence in misunderstanding that most people simply don't share his sense of humor. It's patently obvious—to me—that the laughs in *Invaders from Mars* are supposed to be there and that the weirdly funny edge improves and sharpens as the film proceeds and the pace picks up. But I am in a minority on this regarding *Invaders from Mars* 1986.

Another catastrophe, financially and critically, was Lucasfilm's *Howard the Duck.* Some critics blasted the harmless movie as being violently untrue to its source, a briefly popular Marvel Comics character of the 1970s. But the film has all the virtues and all the defects of the comics, especially when Steve Gerber, Howard's creator, was still writing them.

But even if the film had been brilliantly made—and it wasn't—it has at its very core a problem that simply cannot be overcome: Howard is played by a midget (or a series of them) in an inexpressive, unconvincing duck suit and never looks like anything else. Furthermore, the script by director Willard Huyck and his wife Gloria Katz just isn't sharp and witty enough. And Huyck is a lame director. He's an old pal of George Lucas—they wrote *American Graffiti* together—who, as executive producer, did this movie a disservice in hiring friends. The highlights of the movie are Jeffrey Jones and the superior animation effects from Industrial Light & Magic.

Howard the Duck is pretty limp between the highlights; ultimately, the film has no point—and no apparent audience. The relatively few who remember the comic, entirely a cult phenomenon, were turned off by advance publicity. No wonder the film was a flop.

I am usually sorry when a film is a failure; I know almost every movie is made by hardworking, talented people who are doing their best to create something worth seeing. (Maybe I shouldn't be a reviewer.) But every now and then a film comes along that I find so loathsome it fills me with evil glee when it bombs. Such a movie was *King Kong Lives.*

Actually, he dies, but that wouldn't make much of a title. Although I certainly didn't like it, I was not appalled by the Dino de Laurentiis 1976 remake of the 1933 masterpiece. But a sequel was clearly uncalled for: the '76 *King Kong* was not especially popular and has mostly been forgotten except for being Jessica Lange's first film. De Laurentiis seems to have done this sequel mostly to use up studio space in Wilmington, North Carolina.

Kong survived his fall off the World Trade Center but is in a coma, so an artificial heart is installed in his body. Meanwhile, an explorer in Borneo—a Borneo including jaguars, Indians, and macaws—happens upon a *female* giant ape with big, pendulous breasts. Naturally, she's Lady Kong. Naturally, she's brought back to the States, and naturally King Kong breaks out to be with her. After further dust-raising activity, Kong wipes out the army, while the army wipes out Kong, and Kong sees his son born before croaking. There wasn't a moist eye in the house.

It's flat, styleless, uninvolving; the "cute" script by Ron Shusett and Steven Pressfield is insolent and arrogant. Director John Guillermin's approach is commonplace: the film lacks even the weak spectacle of the first Dino Kong, also directed by Guillermin. There's one, maybe two good scenes when Kong attacks the army at the end, but it's too little, too late.

Sean Connery's charm couldn't save *Highlander.* Connery, a talented, charismatic actor and a genuine movie star—ask me sometime about a screening he attended—seems to choose precisely the wrong material these days. As Joe Dante suggested, maybe he has Bela Lugosi's agent: there must be some explanation for Connery pounding his career flat with awful material like this.

It's unclear as to whether this overly stylish movie is SF or fantasy; whatever its genre, it is very silly. It involves immortals who kill one another. Immortal, you say, and they kill one another? Why are these guys—and only men can be immortal—blessed with eternal life? "Why does the sun come up?" shrugs Connery. The immortals eventually have to fight, beheading one another, until only one is left; that immortal will receive The Gift. Why do they kill each other? Why does Connery help freshly minted immortal Christopher Lambert, the highlander of the title? Why *does* the sun come up, Sean?

The movie is very long on style, with gorgeous landscapes, sets, and costumes; flashy special effects; and a portentous mood, but it is short on logic and interest. It is also cursed with a standard but god-awful rock sound track. At the end, the hero defeats the bad guy; demons or something pick him up but then let him go. Now he is no longer immortal, and he has The Gift: he knows what people are thinking all over the world. So what?

Highlander may eventually be best known for the scene in which a French actor, playing an eighteenth-century Scotsman, explains haggis to Sean Connery, a Scotsman playing an Egyptian disguised as a Spaniard. It was written, badly, by Gregory Widen and directed, flashily, by Russell Mulcahy.

Twentieth Century-Fox, which released *Highlander*, displayed an admirable but largely misplaced faith in genre films during 1986; they were most of the studio's output. Perhaps the success of *Aliens* and *The Fly*, both commercially planned but made by strong directors with clear intentions, will keep them from backing such a weak product as *SpaceCamp* in the future. However, they probably ascribed the low returns on this film ($5 million on a $20 million budget) to the *Challenger* disaster and the public's lack of interest in space travel. They might even be right.

But *SpaceCamp* gives you exactly the story line you expect with no surprises whatsoever. Some kids at a representation of the real Space Camp are accidentally launched in a shuttle and must figure out how to get back. The story wrote itself, and feels like it. There's a painfully cute and preposterous robot existing only to get everyone into orbit. *SpaceCamp* is a cynical product designed solely for consumer consumption.

Fox also tried with *The Manhattan Project.* Perhaps the financial failure of this one ($2 million return on an $18 million budget) was due to its peculiarly misleading title. To those who had no idea what the Manhattan Project was—and this was the target audience—the title was singularly uninteresting. It's a fast-paced and often funny thriller about bright teenager Paul Stephens (Christopher Collet) who steals some plutonium from John Lithgow's lab and builds his own nuclear device. The film was obviously modeled on *WarGames* and has a confused, disturbing viewpoint.

Director Marshall Brickman, who cowrote with Thomas Baum, was hoping to make the audience realize the real problems involved in living in a world perpetually on the brink of nuclear destruction. Brickman achieves this goal in Lithgow's character, who finally realizes that his research, always more like a game to him, is actually designed for death. The teenager is the focus, and he seems amoral. Although *The Manhattan Project* is entertaining and suspenseful, it unintentionally makes a joke of nuclear fears; this is wrong.

In 1985, audiences were both delighted and appalled by director Stuart Gordon's debut film, *H. P. Lovecraft's Re-Animator.* His next Lovecraft film, *From Beyond,* was again full-throttle horror, fancier but not as odd as *Re-Animator.* It tends to take itself too seriously in some sections and introduces too many ghoulish elements. Dennis Paoli's script really does use Lovecraft's story of the same title as a jumping-off place, but where *From Beyond* jumps to might have made old Howard Phillips faint. His unnamed horrors come rocketing into our dimension, changing shape like mad, chuckling over the terror felt by mere human beings, torn between the desire to devour and ravish Barbara Crampton, who appears dressed in dominatrix duds for much of the climax. The later stretches of the gory, gooey, sardonic movie are unnecessary in terms of plot line and are too conventionally modern-day horror stuff.

The movie overall is still intended for adults, however, not just the glop-and-gore crowd. Stuart Gordon's talent is evident and he's wildly imaginative; his dry humor leavens the grue. There's no point in questioning his taste or what he might accomplish if he used his powers for "good" instead of "evil." He really is an artist, and artists must do what they are driven to.

Then we have Stephen King's directorial debut, *Maximum Overdrive*. In interviews, the cheerful King announced that this movie was aimed at his readers. He must have a dismayingly low opinion of the people who buy his books, because *Maximum Overdrive* is crude, clumsy, and trite.

Machinery begins turning on humanity, all kinds of machines: street rollers, motorcycles, toy cars, carving knives, automatic teller machines. But the bad guys are mostly trucks, who pen up a boring group in a small diner in the south. The characters are broad and uninteresting, so it's difficult to care about their fates. King goes for cheap jokes and for the gruesome: the film had to be cut several times to avoid an X rating for violence. His direction is unimaginative and limp, lacking the vitality that low-budget schlock often has; timing is off in scene after scene; things don't reach a climax—they simply go on until they stop. This is an aberration those who appreciate his novels will forgive, but the movie is likely to haunt King for years. The elusive shards of promise aren't enough to make him in demand as a director.

The year also brought with it, mostly on videocassette, the usual quota of post-apocalypse movies. The bleak, post-nuclear disaster storylines are so standard that it's unusual when a film is set in the future and is *not* based on this idea. Even those films that don't deal with the aftermath of a nuclear war are usually set in a time when some *other* kind of disaster has befallen the world. And as usual, most of these films are notably unsuccessful, although two of them give glimmerings of hope that there may be traces of life in this subgenre.

By far the best was the Italian-U.S. coproduction, *Endgame*. The script is by Alex Carver, and the film was directed by Steven

Benson (these may be pseudonyms for Italians). *Endgame* is far from being a good movie, but it is an interesting one. Carver has a slightly different idea of a future society; most people live in cities, where disfigured mutants waylay and devour hapless passersby. The population not affected by radiation is addicted to "Endgame," a televised murder game like those appearing in other SF stories, including Robert Sheckley's *The Prize of Peril* and Stephen King's Bachman novel *The Running Man.* The best Endgame player is recruited by telepathic mutants to get them out of the city so that they can join a colony some distance away. The hero enlists the aid of other tough guys, and, followed by the military (out to exterminate all mutants) and a rival Endgame player, they cross a dangerous terrain populated by enclaves of violent people: blind religious fanatics who see through the eyes of a telepath, road-warrior types holed up in a strangely plush building, and "inverts"—mutants who are reverting to apes, fish, and other "primitive" forms.

Endgame features better acting, use of color, and style than you'd expect. It sustains itself surprisingly well from beginning to end, pulls no rabbits out of hats, and remains true to conceptions of characters. Though it's too episodic and derivative, for those interested in this kind of stuff, it's worth taking a look at.

Writer-director Franky Schaeffer claims *Wired to Kill* is "an allegory, a twentieth-century version of Homer's *Odyssey*—it's as simple as that." Yeah, sure, Franky. And *Death Wish* is the *Iliad.* Weirdly, the film was financed by a Christian organization. The story is set near the end of this century, after economics have basically run down and a plague has devastated the world. Although it takes a printed legend at the first to give us the background, Schaeffer's future world seems consistent, well thought out, and far more plausible than most in this genre. It's too bad that Schaeffer, a promising newcomer, had to drape this believable future fabric over a standardized, predictable revenge plot. It's the same old vigilante territory that has been wearily plowed by cheapo filmmakers since *Death Wish.*

Radioactive Dreams should be avoided—or doesn't the title

suggest that already? Written and directed by Albert Pyun with a lot of heavy style and complete incoherence, the film sat on the shelf for two years before being tossed out the door of a studio. It played only a few days and was a financial disaster.

Two young men calling themselves Philip (John Stockwell) and Marlowe (Michael Dudikoff) leave the bunker where their fathers abandoned them just after the big nuclear war of 1996. They soon come into possession of the key that can launch the one remaining nuclear missile, and everyone is out to get it from them. The last third of the film is baffling and impenetrable, stuffed with references to hard-boiled detective novels and authors, but this has nothing to do with the story line. What all this was supposed to mean is a mystery, known only to Pyun.

Mel Brooks's production company is daring, thanks to Brooks himself; he backed *The Elephant Man* and *The Fly*, among others. But Brooks also put his weight behind the awful *Solarbabies*. This post-holocaust future involves a roller-skating, game-playing team calling themselves Solarbabies (why solar? why babies?), one of a larger group in an orphanage run by Charles Durning out in a desert. They find a glowing sphere, apparently an alien, called Bodhi (the Buddhist term for enlightenment), which changes hands a bunch of times. The evil Energy Protectorate, represented by a hammy Richard Jordan, has captured all the water and wants Bodhi, too.

The film, written by Walon Green and Douglas Anthony Metrov, is achingly pretentious and predictable. Its dazzling absurdity would have made it one of the great, silly camp classics if it weren't so boring. Director Alan Johnson can't generate any interest; the film seems to have been intended for humorless, twelve-year-old philosophy students with a bent for athletics.

Unquestionably the freakiest and no doubt the worst of 1986's post-apocalypse movies was *Roller Blade*. It was written by Donald G. Jackson and Randall Frakes; Jackson also produced, photographed, and directed the film, so he's responsible for this astonishing farrago. In The City of Los Angeles during the Second Dark Age, Mother Speed, now confined to a wheelchair, leads a group of red-clad, roller-skating nuns in defending Goodness and Truth as The Holy (sometimes Cosmic) Order of Roller Blade. They all have Sacred Knives, which they whip through the air like samurai swords before applying the broad edge to wounds; a Happy Face appears, and the wounds are healed.

Despite some dubbed gags, added after the film was completed, *Roller Blade* is not intended to be a comedy, even though the head villain is literally a hand puppet. *Roller Blade* is one of the silliest movies ever made, but it's cheap, poorly made, and boring. I hope I have not made it sound appealing.

The other post-apocalypse films I somehow managed to miss: Cannon barely released *America 3000*, a spoofy epic written and directed by David Engelbach. Shot in Israel, it tells of a world ruled by warrior women nine hundred years after a nuclear war. *Variety* called it "silly . . . suited to homevideo use" and added that it "never becomes more than an imitation of numerous [other] pics." The Italian movie variously called *The Final Executioner* and *The Last Warrior* was written by Roberto Leoni and directed by Romolo Guerrieri; the only actor in it known to Americans was Woody Strode. In a future world, the rich upper classes hunt the radiation-damaged lower classes; after eighty million are killed, they start hunting healthy folks. So a computer genius and an ex-cop (Strode) team up to attack the rich folks and stop them from doing all this. "Subpar," said *Variety*'s "Lor." The U.S.-made *Land of Doom* scarcely sounds better. Director Peter Maris worked from Craig Rand's screenplay on this low-budget imitation of the Mad Max films. In this particular war-devastated future, a warrior woman and a man try to organize wandering bands to rebuild the world, but they are opposed by the villain. "Lor" felt the movie was "uneventful" and "of little interest to exploitation film fans."

I don't regret missing these derivative movies, but *Population: One* sounds much more interesting. Directed and written by Renée Daalder, this U.S.-Dutch coproduction is set after a nuclear holocaust in which, supposedly, Tomata DuPlenty (as himself) is the only survivor, using video screens to examine the history of the U.S. and the love of this country for destruction. Michael Dare in the *L.A. Weekly* said, "It's terrifying and indulgent, but if you don't mind getting clobbered, it's worth the trip [although] almost too strong to take in one setting." Among those appearing in this rarely screened movie are Sheela Edwards, Jane Gaskill, Gorilla Rose, Tommy Gear, Cherie Penguin, Penelope Houston, K.K., and Vampira.

From Australia came one of the few movies of 1986 set in the future that wasn't specifically a post-holocaust adventure. *Dead-End Drive-In* is full of action and sex, but with a focused viewpoint and a sense of style and wit. Brian Trenchard-Smith directed Peter Smalley's script, adapted from a story by Peter Carey, author of *Bliss*, another 1986 Aussie film well received in the United States.

When troublesome kids visit a drive-in to watch action pictures, police sabotage their cars, trapping them at the theater—in the morning, they're simply not allowed to leave. The leading character is Jimmy, also known as "Crabs" (Ned Manning), not really a criminal, just a wild kid. Crabs hates the situation the adults have set up, but his girlfriend (Natalie McCurry) and everyone else at the drive-in are content, as the government provides food, drugs, and entertainment. The only problem is that all these non-whites are now being bused in by the government. . . .

The drive-in is clearly a microcosm of Australia or any other society whose members become complacent. It's a cry for individuality and more freedom of choice, even if that choice is, as with Crabs at the end, merely to drive down long, empty streets. Ironically, the satiric intent of the film probably went by the youths who saw it, and the adults who might have appreciated it were probably turned off by the movie's kid-thriller aspects.

The Italian *Hands of Steel* was set in 1997 but is apparently not post-holocaust. Evil industrialist John Saxon, too good an actor to waste in these things, has a man turned into a cyborg to kill an ecologist, but the cyborg finds love and arm wrestling in Arizona, so Saxon tries to kill him with a laser cannon. Genre specialist Sergio Martino directed.

Set in the *past* rather than the future, *The Clan of the Cave Bear* took forever to get made. The final script was credited to John Sayles, but it's not likely that he wrote it. Director Michael Chapman was stuck with an impossible task: to create a believable prehistoric world. The previous films with such a setting that have worked can be counted on the noses of one face: *Quest for Fire.* Daryl Hannah made a gorgeous Cro-Magnon and comes away unscathed as an actress, but "The Flintstones" hover just beyond view, chortling and cavorting, and *The Clan of the Cave Bear* is absurd.

One SF movie with a very restricted venue was *Captain Eo,* produced by Disney with Lucasfilm and directed by Francis Coppola, starring Michael Jackson. The seventeen-minute short is shown exclusively in its own, specially built theaters at Disneyland and Disney World, in 70mm and 3-D, and cost over a million dollars a minute. It is only a pretty good rock video with excellent photography and good, if familiar, special effects. Some of the 3-D effects are outstanding; in fact, the first shot is the single best 3-D effect I have ever seen. Everyone has gone all out to make this a spectacle—everyone but the writers, if there were any. *Captain Eo* simply is not worth the $20 million it cost—but then again, you don't have to pay extra to see it.

Among the other films, mostly derivative and low-budget, were some interesting attempts. Undoubtedly the weirdest and, in its schlocky way, most original was *The Toxic Avenger.* This Troma production was a cult hit in New York but didn't catch on elsewhere. No wonder; it was made for, to say the least, specialized tastes. Writer Joe Ritter and codirectors Michael Herz and Samuel Weil (Lloyd Kaufman) have made the first gruesomely violent superhero monster comedy. A terminally dorky mop boy at a health club in Tromaville, New Jersey, Toxic Waste Capital of the World, plunges into a barrel of bright green radioactive waste and mutates into—ta dahh—The Toxic Avenger, a muscular monster with a face like a fist. He gallumphs around Tromaville, graphically slaughtering street punks and holdup men.

Reaction was incredibly divided: some reviewers found its gross-out anarchy liberating, while others were repelled by the violence and crudity. I thought it cheesy, brassy, and bloody. Its virtues, though real, are scant, and unless you have a taste for the surreally grotesque and a large tolerance for cheap production values, you can avoid *The Toxic Avenger* and probably lead a full, rewarding life.

When *The Terminator* made a mint, other titles ending in *-ator* were rushed to an eager public. The funniest such title was *Eliminators*, sounding more like laxatives than a daring group of heroes. *Eliminators* features a cyborg with detachable tank treads, robots (called droids), cavemen, a mad scientist out to conquer the world, ray guns, karate, cannibalism, and time travel. It's brash and amusing, very much aware of itself, entertaining, though dopey, throughout—and it improves as it goes. Andrew Prine, Denise Crosby, and Patrick Reynolds are all better than the material, deriving from a wide range of sources, largely Marvel Comics. It's a perfect time-waster if viewed in the right frame of mind. From Empire Pictures, determined to produce endless miles of science fiction movies.

Among the other Empire efforts for 1986 were several that sat on the shelf awhile. The best of these was *Zone Troopers*, a mildly gripping tale of World War II soldiers encountering friendly aliens. It's weakly made but has an oddly interesting plot, with some good acting and nice photography by Mac Ahlberg that takes no advantage of the real Italian locations. It's onesy-twosy-threesy filmmaking but competent on that level. It was written by Danny Bilson and Paul De Meo, and directed by Bilson.

Incompetent on any level, unfortunately, was the cofeature with *Zone Troopers*, Empire's *Terrorvision*. Written and directed by Ted Nicolaou, the movie is a thick-eared spoof of family life. An alien pet, the Hungrybeast, has mutated into a monster that eats anything; it's sucked in through the fancy TV set Daddy has been working on and begins eating the family. There's an effort to make the film seem cartoony, with broad acting and vividly colored sets, but Nicolaou's pacing is leaden; the movie seems to go on forever.

Somewhat better but still of little interest was Empire's *Ghost Warrior*, made in 1983 and originally titled *Swordkill*. J. Larry Carroll directed from Tim Curnen's script, derivative of *Iceman*. Here the frozen survivor is a samurai warrior (Hiroshi Fujioka) who fell into an icy lake in 1552. He's thawed out in present-day Los Angeles and wanders around town slicing up bad guys and being befriended by a cantankerous old black man, played by Charles Lampkin. The major virtues of the film are Lampkin, Fujioka's glowering presence, and Mac Ahlberg's efficient, attractive photography. *Ghost Warrior* is silly and superficial, but it does have some entertainment value.

Critters is a brash imitation of *Gremlins* but has virtues of its own. Director Stephen Herek, working from a script written by himself and Dominic Muir, doesn't try effects the budget can't handle and keeps all aspirations within reasonable limits.

A group of small, vicious aliens (called "krites") escape from a penal colony and arrive on Earth, menacing Farmer Brown (Billy Green Bush) and his family; Mom is Dee Wallace Stone, who was the mommy in *E.T.* Two bounty hunters with malleable faces show up and devastate the nearby town in their search for the krites, finally eliminating those bedeviling the Browns. As a comedy, the film is weak—the jokes are ineptly scripted and timed—but the acting is good throughout. It's a workmanlike, efficient film. (Critters II arrived in 1988.)

Another alien-invasion film, which received few bookings, was *Night of the Creeps*, written and directed by Fred Dekker, a first-time director. In the common let's-be-cute style today, there are characters named after current horror movie directors: Cameron, Landis, Raimi, Cronenberg, Hooper, and Romero. The cast includes Jason Lively, Steve Marshall, Jill Whitlow, and Tom Atkins, who got most of the praise; Dick Miller also appears. It opens with scenes set in the 1950s; swift black alien slugs enter brains and lay eggs; during incubation, people act like zombies; then heads explode when the eggs hatch; and the slugs slither off in search of other victims. Nina Darnton in the *New York Times* said that "the film shows a fair ability to create suspense, build tension, and achieve respectable performances," but like *Variety*'s "Lor," she found it "derivative" of many another thriller. It's annoyingly smirky and artificial, a sophomoric movie all round.

From Disney came the unassuming *Flight of the Navigator.* Randal Kleiser directed from a script by Douglas Day Stewart and Michael Burton, who adapted a story by Mark Baker. In Florida, twelve-year-old David Freeman (Joey Cramer) goes for a walk in the woods one night and gets knocked out. He awakes eight years later, unchanged and with no memory of the intervening time. We eventually learn an alien craft took him to its home planet for examination, then returned him to Earth. It *could* go back in time, it says, but that's unsettling to human beings.

The visual effects by Peter Donen are outstanding. The voice of the craft was originally to have been done by Tony Urbano, a puppeteer who manipulates the seeing-eye extension of the ship that chats with the boy; he also did some thoroughly awful alien puppets that keep the boy company in the ship. But the voice was ultimately done by—it says in the credits—Paul Mall, concealing Paul Reubens, better known as Pee Wee Herman.

Flight of the Navigator is a pleasant, trivial little picture; gentle and lacking in all violence, it's a bit dull. The dangers are not physical at all, but emotional. There are too many gimmicks in the film and not enough story, and it contradicts itself several times. But during a period when virtually all genre films are aimed squarely at teenagers, it's nice to see one having the entire family in mind. Too bad it didn't do well financially.

Director Wes Craven has occasionally made effective shockers, but *Deadly Friend* isn't one of them. It's a flat, silly, and pointless movie about a boy, his robot, and the girl next door.

There's no adolescent romance, though; the girl (Kristy Swanson) really is just a friend. A nasty old lady in the neighborhood blows up the kid's robot, and the girl's drunken father accidentally injures her, leaving her in a brain-dead condition. So the boy sticks the robot's main memory bank into the girl's head and, bingo, she's alive again. Acting kind of strange, though, and with these loud blue circles around her eyes so you can tell she's dead, or the robot, or something. She kills a few people.

Deadly Friend is ponderous, predictable, and badly written (by Bruce Joel Rubin). Some of the performances are okay, and there's a moment or two here and there, but the film is basically a TV movie with some snatches of gore. The ending is gross and insulting.

Chopping Mall, originally released as *Killbots,* did only fair business under either title. It's Jim Wynorski's second outing as a director, working from a script he cowrote with Steve Mitchell. It's a moderately slick action piece, a slasher movie with robots set in a shopping mall closed for the night. Teenagers hang around to have some fun and are pursued and killed by guardian robots sent haywire by lightning. The humor in the film is thick-eared, with clumsy references to other films and guest appearances by Paul Bartel, Mary Woronov, Dick Miller, Mel Welles, Gerrit Graham, and Bob Greenberg. The cast includes Kelli Maroney and Barbara Crampton, who've been similarly menaced in better films. Although it's not remotely a good movie, *Chopping Mall* is brash enough to get by for undemanding viewers.

New World briefly released a double bill of low-budget and derivative films in 1986; the more interesting of the two was *The Aurora Encounter.* Narrated throughout by Charley Hankins (scene-stealing Jack Elam), the story is set in Aurora, Texas, during President McKinley's term of office and announces itself as the true story of the encounter between homespun Texans and a winsome alien in a flying saucer. The complicated plot involves children, Indian burial mounds, a sentient alien crystal, a crusading newspaperwoman, a touch of romance, a checker game the silent alien cheats at to win, and a Texas Ranger sent by the governor (played by Spanky McFarland!), who guns down the harmless alien visitor.

The movie resembles various allegedly-true regional pieces but also draws vampirically on Spielberg for ambience and style, most obviously on *E.T.* The photography is occasionally very good; director Jim McCullough, Sr., working from the script by Jim McCullough, Jr., chooses odd things to show and odd angles to show them, but they aren't good. It's a trite, obvious film, though an idea here and there has some value. The alien is played by a little boy suffering from "progeria"—premature, accelerated aging.

The cofeature was the far less professional *Star Crystal.* Writer-director Lance Lindsay tells a confusing and poorly structured tale. After an odd crystal is found on Mars (played as usual by California's Red Rock Canyon), it pops open and the crew of a ship all die. While it's aboard a space station, apparently in orbit somewhere beyond Jupiter, something similar happens and the station blows up. The growing wormlike thing from the crystal is now aboard a fleeing shuttlecraft, and *Alien* is reenacted aboard the absurdly designed ship. But lo and behold, at the climax the alien, now like a snail without a shell, yet oddly convincing, learns to be benign by reading the Bible and apologizes to the survivors for the previous deaths. The alien sets free the two survivors and continues on its way.

Star Crystal is notable in being the first movie in which you can tell who is going to be killed by their footgear. The producers apparently could spring for only one pair of John Byrne–style oversized boots; whenever the characters, who otherwise wear sneakers, are suddenly seen at a low angle with their feet in these big boots, you know the alien is going to get them.

The movie creaks with blunderous technical botches, but even sound technical advice could not have helped this lame, derivative, and smarmy *Star Crystal.*

Another New World release going swiftly to video after only limited theatrical release was *Eat and Run,* a comedy about a people eater from space. It was written by Stan and Christopher

Hart, and Christopher directed. An alien eats an Italian in New Jersey, giving him a taste for Italian food, ha ha ha. The ending, says "Lor" in *Variety*, is "ridiculously unsatisfying. . . . Pic is deadly dull, hammering its gag firmly into the ground via repetition."

The Class of Nuke 'Em High came from the same company and from some of the same filmmakers as *The Toxic Avenger.* Kids at a high school are exposed to marijuana made radioactive by nuclear waste. Some monsters result, one when the heroine gives birth to a little critter that finally turns into a big one. Honor students turn punk, and there's lots of the usual Troma ultra-violence. David Edelstein in *The Village Voice* said it has a terrific premise—shameless, outrageous—but has no story, no characters, and does have "bad taste with no good wit. [It] makes sex and violence seem boring." *Class of Nuke 'Em High* was written by Richard W. Haines, Lloyd Kaufman, Mark Rudinsky, and Stuart Strutin and directed by Haines and Kaufman (again as "Samuel Weil").

In *Nightmare Weekend*, a British film only *distributed* by Troma, teenagers are subjected to experiments by a mad scientist, who turns them into "neuropaths." The scant reviews were all unfavorable.

Another comedy getting virtually no theatrical *or* video release was the Spanish-Swiss coproduction shown here as *Star Knight.* Set in medieval times, it tells of a friendly, mute, humanoid alien named Ix who lands in the middle of an ongoing feud between an alchemist (Klaus Kinski) and a corrupt priest (Fernando Rey). Harvey Keitel plays a moronic knight who's shot into space in the alien's ship, along with the priest, while the alien gets the girl.

Produced and directed by Fernando Colomo from a script by Andreu Martin, Miguel Angel Nieto, and Colomo, *Star Knight* is apparently moving slowly around the country. *Variety*'s "Besa" said, "Although by international standards, the special effects, sets, and occasional swordplay are far from spectacular, director Fernando Colomo fills in the shortcomings by winning humor and amusing performances by his cast. [It's] an innocuous, occasionally droll fable, but one that never packs a punch."

As usual, several toy-oriented animated films based on TV shows were released in 1986. The two that were science fiction came from almost identical toy sets: the Gobots and the Transformers, toys that change from robots into trucks, guns, planes, what have you. *Gobots: Battle of the Rock Lords* was, according to reports, the lesser of the two films, but not by much. Expressing the opinion of the majority of the reviewers, Tom Matthews in *Boxoffice* said it is "a dismal excuse for pint-sized entertainment [and] a confusing mish-mash of lifeless cartoon clichés." The only aspect of any interest was that several known actors provided some of the voices; they included Margot Kidder, Roddy McDowall, Michael Nouri, and Telly Savalas. But even this was not original, as it has become a standard practice in this subsubgenre. But why? Adults are not likely to see the film just because Margot Kidder provided a voice, and kids couldn't care less.

The Transformers, with its very similar toys, also had a similar script, by Ron Friedman, and used even more known actors. Among those participating were Eric Idle, Judd Nelson, Leonard Nimoy, Robert Stack, Lionel Stander, Roger C. Carmel, Scatman Crothers, and Orson Welles, who, as an evil planet, had his last professional acting role. Most reviewers felt that even the intended kiddie audience would find the film uninteresting, and indeed it was counted as a financial failure, grossing $2.6 million—but it's not likely to have cost much more.

Choke Canyon, written by a whole raft of contributors and directed by Chuck Bail, was an international coproduction. Stephen Collins, experimenting with turning sound waves into energy, wants to test his device in Choke Canyon while Halley's Comet passes by and runs afoul of a bad guy dumping nuclear waste in the canyon. At the climax, according to the *New York Times*, "the comet's gravity produces such stresses that the rock walls bulge like globs of hot caramel." Reviewers generally enjoyed the fast-paced action and stunt flying scenes but found the story too preposterous to take seriously. Collins is amusing.

Sky Bandits had an odd premise—a pair of western outlaws become daring pilots during World War I—but it was also tepid and poorly developed. The science fiction element was quite large—a 2,500-foot German zeppelin—but it made a late and unspectacular appearance. There's some fun to be had in the attack on the zeppelin by a squadron of pieced-together planes, but director Zoran Persic is unable to generate any consistent sense of fun. *Sky Bandits* has a great title and some wonderful air-wonder-stories pulp ideas but lacks any spark or zest.

There were quite a few SF movies made for television in 1986. Some were unsuccessful pilots, but fortunately I missed most of them. *Condor, The Fifth Missile, The Flight of Dragons, The Great Heep, The Last Electric Knight, Northstar, The Rise and Rise of Daniel Rocket, Under Siege, Who Is Julia?*, and *Young Again* gave me little reason to want to watch them. Of the TV movies I did see, none were as good as the average theatrical film of the year—and it was a low-average year.

The Annihilator was a dismal failed pilot about the only man on Earth who knows that alien robots in the shape of humanoid lizards have infiltrated human society on all levels. It might have had value as a campy, unintentional comedy, but except for Geoffrey Lewis's funny portrayal of a malfunctioning alien robot and a scene in which Lisa Blount thrashes hero Mark Lindsay Chapman with an arm she's ripped off herself, laughs were few and far between. It was billed (and titled) as an imitation of *The Terminator* but is actually an imitation of *V*—not quite what the world is waiting for.

Assassin was another of the many recent films featuring robots undetectable from human beings, bopping around in today's world. The movie, an actual imitation of *The Terminator*, pits tough Robert Conrad against a robot programmed to kill. The smiling android-robot is even an expert lover, and his partner never notices his movements are a bit mechanical. (Thank you, Jean-Claude Forest.) It's predictable throughout, below average for a TV movie.

Shown late in the year, *Outlaws* was just another pilot—this one temporarily successful. In 1899, marshal Rod Taylor corners an amiable group of owlhoots he used to pal around with. Lightning strikes them and they wake up in present-day Texas, where they become private detectives with six-shooters—all the SF there is in this silly waste of time. The resulting series gave employment to solid character performers but failed to give any interest or fun to viewers, and was soon canceled.

The Disney Sunday TV Movie was also used as an out-of-town tryout for pilots disguised as TV movies. One, *The Last Electric Knight*, actually made it as a short-lived series; others did not. *I-Man* was a Spielbergian travesty in which gas from an alien planet's atmosphere makes Scott Bakula indestructible; his son, played by Joey Cramer, soon follows, as (in the last scene) does their dog. It was slow, obvious, trite, and uninteresting. Another Disney TV movie, *Hero in the Family*, was even worse. The hot-dog astronaut father (Cliff De Young) of our teenage hero (Christopher Collet) gets his mind switched with that of a chimpanzee, and no one notices. The science and plot developments indicate this was not made for children, but for someone even younger, perhaps fetuses. However, Cliff De Young does a great impersonation of a chimp.

The British miniseries *Edge of Darkness* was outstanding on all levels, even to its uncompromisingly bleak and pessimistic ending. The tale of illicit production of nuclear missiles was a knee-knocker from beginning to end and should be watched if at all possible.

Videocassettes are an increasingly important market, turning some flops into successes. An increasing number of films are released directly to this market, even if intended to be theatrical releases. *Making Contact* had a high budget but only the foggiest ideas of what the story was about. A West German film shot in English under the title *Joey*, it slavishly copies *everything* from Steven Spielberg films but his virtues.

The screenplay by Roland Emmerich (who directed), Hans J. Haller, and Thomas Lechner wildly mixes fantasy, occult, and science fiction ideas, resulting in a mess puzzling to behold. Little Joey's father has died, and he talks to him on a toy phone (from *Poltergeist*); the toys in Joey's room come to life (from *Close Encounters*) and later fly around (*Poltergeist* again); he is having trouble at school with other kids (from *E.T.*) and has become telepathic, thanks to contact with his father. A living ventriloquist's dummy resembling the Count from "Sesame Street" is evil. When Joey's new friends try to help him in the house of the dead ventriloquist, they are menaced by Darth Vader and a carnivorous hamburger. At the end, Joey dies but comes back to life.

There are still *Jaws* imitations swimming around, surfacing briefly before diving back into the hidden shoals of out-of-print videocassettes. The oddest was no doubt *The Sea Serpent*, apparently the last film of Ray Milland. Timothy Bottoms is a wildly unlikely Spanish fisherman. He has seen a genuine sea serpent, roused by an atomic bomb, devour his crew, but no one except Ray Milland and Taryn Power believe him. The boring, aimless film—from Spain—has several exuberant scenes of the comically unconvincing, gaping serpent encircling and demolishing, at one point, a lighthouse (Ray Bradbury, are you listening?) and, at another point, a railway trestle. The serpent gets away at the end. The many boring dialog scenes are easily dodged by the fast-forward button on the VCR.

Monster Shark, also known as *Devil Fish*, an Italian-French film from 1984, was directed by Lamberto Bava, son of the famed Mario. This time the menace is a prehistoric shark with octopoidal tendencies. It menaces Florida until brought to bay, so to speak, by Michael Sopkiw. Even "Lor" found it awful.

Originally called *Frankenstein 1988*, *The Vindicator* sat on the shelf awhile. Director Jean-Claude Lord and writers Edith Rey and David Preston show damned little originality in this tale of a scientist murdered by his bosses and converted into a controllable cyborg—until he goes haywire. At the climax, the bad guy has somehow turned *himself* into a cyborg, too, but the intended clash of the titans doesn't come off. The only virtues are David McIllwraith as the cyborg and Pam Grier as a hired killer. Also, the makeup by the Winston labs, although unveiled in a notably badly handled unmasking scene, is truly ghastly.

Another film that awaited release for several years was *What Waits Below* (née *Secret of the Phantom Caverns*). Christy Marx and Robert Vincent O'Neil's script is unventuresome and uninteresting, though not badly crafted. In Central America, a cavern is discovered to be populated by albino troglodytes, descendants of Lemurians; they capture a group of people from the surface. Director Don Sharp has done much better in the past and presumably will again in the future.

If you call your movie *Bloodsuckers from Outer Space*, you've got to do one of two things: deliver the goods or deliver a comedy. In it, Pat Paulsen finally makes it to the Oval Office. The film, in which some kind of plague from space turns bucolic Texans into vampiric ghouls, starts straight and sort of backs into the comedy. Writer-director Glen Coburn does have a few funny lines here and there, but the material is so shoddy and the budget so low that his efforts get lost in the crud.

Another regional film (Seattle, this time) that got videocassette distribution was the dopily titled *Revenge of the Teenage Vixens from Outer Space*. The title is neither funny nor evocative enough, serving only as a warning to avoid the film. Jeff Farrell directed and cowrote with Michelle Lichter; between them, they did most of the other jobs on the film, as well. A boy discovers that his mother was an alien, and some teenage aliens from her home planet show up in Seattle about the same time. They are here for sex and sometimes turn their targets into big tomatoes, carrots, or other vegetables. *Variety*'s "Lor" found it "more childish than titillating" but "an okay video timekiller."

Breeders was made for cassette sales and rentals directly. It has a cheap, repellent premise: a monster from outer space rapes virgins, later summoning them as zombies to splash around in what looks like a vat of semen. It was directed and written by Tim Kincaid, who shows some promise as a writer of dialog and characterization, but the movie is so poorly structured and so cheesily sensationalistic that it's undoubtedly going to be ignored by anyone who might do something for his career.

As if she weren't getting enough work otherwise, the awesomely ambitious Sybil Danning coproduced *Panther Squad,* a Belgian-French coproduction, to star herself. In the near future, the successor to the UN (its initials are NOON) launches the Space Jeep, a new shuttle-type craft, but evil environmentalists (!) destroy it and kidnap the astronaut (a woman). Enter Sybil and her Panther Squad of macho women, who eventually set things right. "Lor" thought it was "dumb."

Director Ulli Lommel showed some promise in his European films, but all of his American movies have been pretty rotten. He wrote *Strangers in Paradise* with his wife Suzanna Love; Lommel stars as the hero and as Hitler. A stage mentalist in 1939 Berlin is frozen and thawed out in 1983 (when the film was shot) by a madman who wants him to brainwash California teenagers out of liking rock and roll. The unavoidable "Lor" called it a "misfire."

This was the year in SF films, 1986. As said much earlier, no trends can be spotted at all, although that might indicate something itself. Because of *Platoon,* we'll see lots more movies about the Vietnamese war and more recruiting-poster trivialities like *Top Gun* (plus, I suspect, at least one SF movie imitation of that smash hit). But with science fiction movies spread all over the grossing charts, the only prediction that can be made for sure is that there will be more science fiction movies in 1987. They are here to stay—for the time being.

APPENDIXES

ABOUT THE NEBULA AWARD

The Nebula Awards are voted on, and presented, by active members of the Science Fiction Writers of America. Founded in 1965 by Damon Knight, the organization's first president, the SFWA began with a charter membership of seventy-eight writers; it now has over eight hundred members, among them most of the leading writers of science fiction.

Lloyd Biggle, Jr., the SFWA's first secretary-treasurer, originally proposed in 1965 that the organization publish an annual anthology of the best stories of the year. This notion, according to Damon Knight in his introduction to *Nebula Award Stories: 1965* (Doubleday, 1966), "rapidly grew into an annual ballot of SFWA's members to choose the best stories, and an annual Awards Banquet." The trophy was designed by Judith Ann Lawrence from a sketch made by Kate Wilhelm; it is a block of lucite in which are embedded a spiral nebula made of metallic glitter and a specimen of rock crystal. The trophies are handmade, and no two are exactly alike.

Since 1965, the Nebula Awards have been given each year for the best novel, novella, novelette, and short story published during the preceding year. An anthology including the winning pieces of short fiction and several runners-up is also published every year. The Nebula Awards Banquet, which takes place each spring, is held in alternate years in New York City and on the West Coast. The banquets are attended by many leading writers and editors and are preceded by meetings and panel discussions. In 1986 the nominated works included books and stories by both established writers and promising newcomers.

The Grand Master Nebula Award is given to a living author for a lifetime's achievement. This award is given no more than six times in a decade. In accordance with the SFWA bylaws passed in 1979, a nomination for the Grand Master Nebula Award is made by the SFWA president, who, traditionally, consults with past presidents and the board of directors in making the choice. The nomination is then submitted to the officers for a vote and approved by a consensus of the majority.

The Grand Masters, and the years in which they won, are Robert A. Heinlein (1974), Jack Williamson (1975), Clifford D. Simak (1976), L. Sprague de Camp (1978), Fritz Leiber (1981), Andre Norton (1983), Arthur C. Clarke (1985), and Isaac Asimov (1986).

PAST NEBULA AWARD WINNERS

1965

Best Novel: *Dune* by Frank Herbert
Best Novella: "The Saliva Tree" by Brian W. Aldiss
         "He Who Shapes" by Roger Zelazny (tie)
Best Novelette: "The Doors of His Face, the Lamps of His Mouth" by Roger Zelazny
Best Short Story: " 'Repent, Harlequin!' Said the Ticktockman" by Harlan Ellison

1966

Best Novel: *Flowers for Algernon* by Daniel Keyes
         Babel-17 by Samuel R. Delany (tie)
Best Novella: "The Last Castle" by Jack Vance
Best Novelette: "Call Him Lord" by Gordon R. Dickson
Best Short Story: "The Secret Place" by Richard McKenna

1967

Best Novel: *The Einstein Intersection* by Samuel R. Delany
Best Novella: "Behold the Man" by Michael Moorcock
Best Novelette: "Gonna Roll the Bones" by Fritz Leiber
Best Short Story: "Aye, and Gomorrah" by Samuel R. Delany

1968

Best Novel: *Rite of Passage* by Alexei Panshin
Best Novella: "Dragonrider" by Anne McCaffrey
Best Novelette: "Mother to the World" by Richard Wilson
Best Short Story: "The Planners" by Kate Wilhelm

1969

Best Novel: *The Left Hand of Darkness* by Ursula K. Le Guin

Best Novella: "A Boy and His Dog" by Harlan Ellison
Best Novelette: "Time Considered as a Helix of Semi-Precious
Stones" by Samuel R. Delany
Best Short Story: "Passengers" by Robert Silverberg

1970

Best Novel: *Ringworld* by Larry Niven
Best Novella: "Ill-Met in Lankhmar" by Fritz Leiber
Best Novelette: "Slow Sculpture" by Theodore Sturgeon
Best Short Story: No Award

1971

Best Novel: *A Time of Changes* by Robert Silverberg
Best Novella: "The Missing Man" by Katherine MacLean
Best Novelette: "The Queen of Air and Darkness" by Poul An-
derson
Best Short Story: "Good News from the Vatican" by Robert Sil-
verberg

1972

Best Novel: *The Gods Themselves* by Isaac Asimov
Best Novella: "A Meeting with Medusa" by Arthur C. Clarke
Best Novelette: "Goat Song" by Poul Anderson
Best Short Story: "When It Changed" by Joanna Russ

1973

Best Novel: *Rendezvous with Rama* by Arthur C. Clarke
Best Novella: "The Death of Doctor Island" by Gene Wolfe
Best Novelette: "Of Mist, and Grass and Sand" by Vonda N.
   McIntyre
Best Short Story: "Love Is the Plan, the Plan Is Death" by James
   Tiptree, Jr.
Best Dramatic Presentation: *Soylent Green*

1974

Best Novel: *The Dispossessed* by Ursula K. Le Guin
Best Novella: "Born with the Dead" by Robert Silverberg
Best Novelette: "If the Stars Are Gods" by Gordon Eklund and
   Gregory Benford
Best Short Story: "The Day Before the Revolution" by Ursula
   K. Le Guin
Best Dramatic Presentation: *Sleeper*
Grand Master: Robert A. Heinlein

1975

Best Novel: *The Forever War* by Joe Haldeman
Best Novella: "Home Is the Hangman" by Roger Zelazny
Best Novelette: "San Diego Lightfoot Sue" by Tom Reamy
Best Short Story: "Catch That Zeppelin!" by Fritz Leiber
Best Dramatic Presentation: *Young Frankenstein*
Grand Master: Jack Williamson

1976

Best Novel: *Man Plus* by Frederik Pohl
Best Novella: "Houston, Houston, Do You Read?" by James
   Tiptree, Jr.
Best Novelette: "The Bicentennial Man" by Isaac Asimov
Best Short Story: "A Crowd of Shadows" by Charles L. Grant
Grand Master: Clifford D. Simak

1977

Best Novel: *Gateway* by Frederik Pohl
Best Novella: "Stardance" by Spider and Jeanne Robinson
Best Novelette: "The Screwfly Solution" by Raccoona Sheldon

Best Short Story: "Jeffty Is Five" by Harlan Ellison
Special Award: *Star Wars*

1978

Best Novel: *Dreamsnake* by Vonda N. McIntyre
Best Novella: "The Persistence of Vision" by John Varley
Best Novelette: "A Glow of Candles, a Unicorn's Eye" by
                 Charles L. Grant
Best Short Story: "Stone" by Edward Bryant
Grand Master: L. Sprague de Camp

1979

Best Novel: *The Fountains of Paradise* by Arthur C. Clarke
Best Novella: "Enemy Mine" by Barry Longyear
Best Novelette: "Sandkings" by George R. R. Martin
Best Short Story: "giANTS" by Edward Bryant

1980

Best Novel: *Timescape* by Gregory Benford
Best Novella: "The Unicorn Tapestry" by Suzy McKee Charnas

Best Novelette: "The Ugly Chickens" by Howard Waldrop
Best Short Story: "Grotto of the Dancing Deer" by Clifford D.
                  Simak

1981

Best Novel: *The Claw of the Conciliator* by Gene Wolfe
Best Novella: "The Saturn Game" by Poul Anderson

Best Novelette: "The Quickening" by Michael Bishop
Best Short Story: "The Bone Flute" by Lisa Tuttle*
Grand Master: Fritz Leiber

1982

Best Novel: *No Enemy But Time* by Michael Bishop
Best Novella: "Another Orphan" by John Kessel
Best Novelette: "Fire Watch" by Connie Willis
Best Short Story: "A Letter from the Clearys" by Connie Willis

1983

Best Novel: *Startide Rising* by David Brin
Best Novella: "Hardfought" by Greg Bear
Best Novelette: "Blood Music" by Greg Bear
Best Short Story: "The Peacemaker" by Gardner Dozois
Grand Master: Andre Norton

1984

Best Novel: *Neuromancer* by William Gibson
Best Novella: "PRESS ENTER ■" by John Varley
Best Novelette: "Bloodchild" by Octavia E. Butler
Best Short Story: "Morning Child" by Gardner Dozois

1985

Best Novel: *Ender's Game* by Orson Scott Card
Best Novella: "Sailing to Byzantium" by Robert Silverberg
Best Novelette: "Portraits of His Children" by George R. R.
              Martin
Best Short Story: "Out of All Them Bright Stars" by Nancy
              Kress
Grand Master: Arthur C. Clarke

*This Nebula Award was declined by the author.